A History
of the
End of the World

A History
of the
End of the World

*How the Most Controversial Book
in the Bible Changed the Course of
Western Civilization*

Jonathan Kirsch

HarperSanFrancisco
A Division of HarperCollins*Publishers*

Designed by Joseph Rutt

ISBN-13: 978-0-7394-8131-8

For Ann, Jennifer, Adam, and Remy (Holzer) Kirsch,
Paul and Caroline Kirsch,
Marya (Kirsch) and Ron Shiflett,
and
Lillian Heller Conrad
"... inscribe us in the Book of Life ..."

Contents

Itself a cabalistic book, the night was crowded with sacred names and symbols—mystery upon mystery. The stars looked like letters of the alphabet, vowel points, notes of music. The world was a parchment scrawled with words and song. He was surrounded by powers, some good, some evil, some cruel, some merciful, but each with its own nature and its own task to perform.

ISAAC BASHEVIS SINGER,
The Slave

One

Something Rich and Strange

Revelation has as many mysteries as it does words.
JEROME

I know the ending," goes the slogan on a license-plate frame that can be spotted here and there on the streets and highways of America. "God wins."

It's a credo that pious Jews, Christians, and Muslims hold in common, although they might quibble on exactly what is meant by the word "God." But the plainspoken slogan conceals a profound and enduring mystery: human beings of all faiths, in all times and all places, have wondered when and how the world will come to an end. Nowadays, of course, the very same questions are being asked (and answered) by scientists rather than theologians. For the Christian true believer, however, "the ending" refers to a scenario that is described in horrific and heart-shaking detail in the single scariest book in all of scripture, the book of Revelation.

The beginning of the end, according to Revelation, will be augured by mysterious signs and wonders—a black sun and a blood-red moon, the stars falling to earth, persecutors and false prophets, plague and pestilence and famine. Then the satanic arch-villain who has come to be called the Antichrist will rise to absolute power on earth. After seven years of oppression and persecution under the Antichrist, Jesus Christ will descend from heaven in the guise of a warrior-king, lead a celestial army of resurrected saints and martyrs to victory over the demonic hordes at the Battle of Armageddon, drape Satan in chains and confine him in a bottomless pit, and reign over an earthly kingdom for one thousand years.

At the end of the millennium, Satan will break out of his bonds, and Jesus Christ will be compelled to fight a second and final battle. At last, the dead will be resurrected, the living and dead alike will be judged, and the earth as we know it will be destroyed once and for all. The end of the world, according to Revelation, will be followed by the creation of "a new heaven and a new earth," a celestial paradise where the Christian saints and martyrs will spend eternity in perfect bliss. Everyone else will sizzle forever along with Satan in a lake of fire and brimstone.

That's the pitch line for the book of Revelation, so to speak, but the text itself is something even richer and stranger.* The nightmarish landscape conjured up by its author is stalked by God and the Devil, the Lamb and the Beast, a lascivious whore and a woman in labor, angels and demons in the countless thousands, and a bestiary of monsters so grotesque and so implausible that they would not seem out of place in a comic book or a horror flick. At certain moments, in fact, the book of Revelation resembles nothing so much as an ancient prototype of the psychological thriller and the monster movie, and its imagery seems to fire the same synapses in the human brain.

Nowadays, Revelation finds its most ardent readers in Christian fundamentalist circles, but even someone who has never opened the very last book of the New Testament is likely to find the plot and characters to be hauntingly familiar. The idea that the world will end (and soon)—and the phantasmagoria of words, numbers, colors, images, and incidents in which the end-times are described in the book of Revelation—are deeply woven into the fabric of Western civilization, both in high culture and in pop culture, starting in distant biblical antiquity and continuing into our own age. The Battle of Armageddon, the Four Horsemen of the Apocalypse, the Seventh Seal, the Great Whore of Babylon, and, more obliquely, the Antichrist, the Grim Reaper, and the Grapes of Wrath have migrated from the pages of Revelation to some of our most exalted works of literature, art, and music as well as the sports pages, the movie screen, and the paperback best seller.

Above all, the book of Revelation has always been used as a kind of code-

---

* For the convenience of the reader, the text of the book of Revelation in English translation as it appears in the King James Version is reproduced in its entirety in the Appendix, along with headings that identify key characters, events, and themes.

book to discover the hidden meanings behind the great events and personages of history—war and revolution, kings and conquerors, pandemic and natural disaster. And the words and phrases of Revelation, its stock figures and scenes, have been recycled and repurposed by artists and poets, preachers and propagandists—all in service of some religious or political or cultural agenda. The conquest of Jerusalem by medieval crusaders, the Bonfire of the Vanities in Florence during the Renaissance, the naming of the newly discovered Americas as the New World, and the thousand-year Reich promised by Adolf Hitler are all examples of the unlikely and unsettling ways that the book of Revelation has resonated through history. Even today, end-of-the-world fears and fantasies are peddled by Hollywood moviemakers and best-selling novelists, hard-preaching televangelists and presidential hopefuls.

Still, the book of Revelation is regarded by secular readers—and even by progressive Christians of various denominations—as a biblical oddity at best and, at worst, a kind of petri dish for the breeding of dangerous religious eccentricity. Most Jewish readers have never bothered to crack open a copy of the Christian scriptures, and when they do, they are deeply offended to find that Jews are described in Revelation as members of "the synagogue of Satan."[1] Indeed, the fact is that Revelation has *always* been regarded with a certain skepticism—as "a curiosity that accidentally and embarrassingly belongs to the New Testament"—even within pious Christian circles, and even in antiquity.[2] So the ironic and disdainful treatment of Revelation in Ingmar Bergman's *The Seventh Seal,* a darkly postmodern motion picture that questions whether God exists at all, is not wholly anachronistic.

"Death is behind your back. His scythe flashes above your heads. Which of you will he strike first?" cries an overwrought preacher of the High Middle Ages as he wanders through a plague-ridden countryside in the company of flagellants and penitents. "You are all doomed, do you hear? Doomed! Doomed! Doomed!" And a battle-scarred squire, newly returned from the Crusades and wholly disillusioned with both God and humankind, retorts: "Do they really expect modern people to take that drivel seriously?"[3]

Whether we approach the book of Revelation as drivel or divine mystery, however, the fact remains that Revelation is still embraced with credulity and deadly seriousness by a great many men and women in the modern world, and not only by the kind of true believers who announce their deepest convictions on their bumpers. Indeed, the readers of Revelation in modern America include a few men who have possessed the god-like power to incinerate the world with the launch codes of the American nuclear arsenal.

Like the popes and kings of the Middle Ages who consulted with apocalyptic seers for advice on statecraft, more than one recent American president was raised in a faith that instructs him to read and heed the book of Revelation as God's master plan for human history. And so, if the book of Revelation is still embraced by men with the power to destroy the world, we urgently need to know what is written there, how it came to be written in the first place, and how it has been used and abused throughout the history of a world that refuses to end.

Revelation has been described as "future history."[4] Looking forward from his vantage point in distant antiquity, its author confidently and colorfully describes "things which must shortly come to pass."[5] But none of his prophecies have yet been fulfilled, at least not in any plain or literal way. That's why readers in every age have tried to explain away the failed prophecies of Revelation by arguing that its visions must be understood as a symbolic depiction of events that will take place long after its disappointed author died a natural death. And yet, significantly, every new generation urgently believes that its own times will be the end-times.

Thus, for example, when Hal Lindsey ponders one of the fearful but baffling passages of Revelation in his best-selling *The Late Great Planet Earth*—"I saw the horses in a vision, and the heads of the horses were as the heads of lions; and out of their mouths issued fire and smoke and brimstone"—he concludes that the author of Revelation has glimpsed "some kind of mobile ballistic missile launcher" that will be deployed in a future (and final) thermonuclear war. Ironically, such pious readings are based on the assumption that the author of Revelation and his original audience could not and did not grasp the real meaning of the phenomena that are depicted in the biblical text.[6]

But even if Revelation is manifestly a work of failed prophecy, it has come to play a unique and ubiquitous role in the world in which we live today. Indeed, Revelation has always served as a lens through which the recorded history of Western civilization can be seen in fresh and illuminating ways. Across the twenty centuries that have passed since it was first composed—and, above all, at every point where contesting ideas of culture and politics have come into conflict—Revelation is always present, sometimes in plain sight and sometimes just beneath the surface.

The book of Revelation (or the Apocalypse, as the last book of the New Testament is also known) has been variously identified as the revealed word of God, the masterwork of a gifted if also calculating human author, or the ravings of a deluded religious crank—and some readers are capable of holding the thought that it is all three things at once.

For the true believer, of course, the book of Revelation is "the only biblical book authored by Christ," as one pious commentator puts it, since its author claims to be reporting only what was revealed to him from on high.[7] Other readers of Revelation, however, are willing to allow that human intelligence—and human artifice—are at work: "[I]t is the one great poem which the first Christian age produced."[8] And a few otherwise admiring critics find themselves compelled to characterize Revelation as "apocalyptic pornography," "an insane rhapsody," "the creative imagination of a schizophrenic," or, as Thomas Jefferson memorably put it, "merely the ravings of a maniac."[9]

The text of the book of Revelation was probably first spoken aloud nearly two thousand years ago by a charismatic if also overwrought preacher who wandered from town to town in Asia Minor and delivered his dire warnings about the end of the world to a few small clutches of early Christians who consented to listen. "Blessed is he who reads aloud the words of the prophecy, and blessed are those who hear," the author declares, "for the time is near."[10] That is why Bible scholars often refer to the men and women for whom Revelation was originally intended as "hearers," a phrase that reminds us that Revelation was almost surely a sermon before it was a text and explains why the power of its language and imagery can be appreciated only "when the text is read aloud as the author intended it to be."[11]

Ironically, the author of Revelation was almost certainly a Jew by birth and upbringing, perhaps a war refugee from Judea who had witnessed the destruction of the Temple of Yahweh at Jerusalem by the Roman army of occupation and seethed with contempt and loathing for the conquerors of the Jewish homeland. To be sure, the author was one of those Jews who regarded Jesus of Nazareth as the long-promised and long-delayed

Messiah. Yet Revelation remains so deeply rooted in Jewish history, politics, and theology that it has been called "a Jewish document with a slight Christian touch-up."[12] Indeed, Revelation can be described as kind of midrash on the prophetic texts of the Hebrew Bible, and its author has been described as a "Christian rabbi."[13]

Once fixed on parchment or papyrus toward the end of the first century, the book of Revelation was regarded with alarm and suspicion by some of the more cautious church authorities. They were offended by the scenes of blood-shaking violence and lurid sexual promiscuity that are described so memorably in its pages. They were put off by the very idea of the thousand-year reign of King Jesus over an earthly realm, which struck them as a purely Jewish notion of what the messianic kingdom would be like. And they were equally troubled by what is *not* mentioned: none of the familiar scenes of the life and death of Jesus of Nazareth, and none of his sublime moral teachings, are to be found in Revelation.

Most alarming of all, then as now, is the unsettling spectacle of an otherwise ordinary human being who claims to have heard the voice of God. "I was in the Spirit on the Lord's day, and heard behind me a great voice," writes the author of Revelation, "saying, What thou seest, write in a book, and send it unto the seven churches which are in Asia."[14] Inspired by the example of Revelation, men and women with lesser rhetorical gifts but even more febrile imaginations have heard voices from on high—and more than a few have ended up hanging from a gallows or burned at the stake. Freelance prophecy, the authorities feared, could lead only to theological error, social and political chaos, or even worse—a fear that turned out to be thoroughly justified, and never more so than in our own world.

Indeed, Revelation can be literally crazy-making. For anyone who reads the book of Revelation from beginning to end, the experience resembles a fever-dream or a nightmare: strange figures and objects appear and disappear and reappear, and the author himself flashes back and forth in time and place, sometimes finding himself in heaven and sometimes on earth, sometimes in the here and now and sometimes in the end-times, sometimes watching from afar and sometimes caught up in the events he describes. The author refers to the same characters by different names and titles, and he describes the same incidents from different vantage points. All the while, the characters and incidents, the words and phrases, even the letters and numbers of Revelation seem to shimmer with symbolic meanings that always float just out of reach.

The sheer weirdness of Revelation has always been vexing to sober and sensible readers, starting in biblical antiquity and continuing without interruption into our own times. The early church fathers debated among themselves whether Revelation belonged in the Bible at all. Martin Luther was tempted to leave it out of his German translation of the Bible because, as he put it, "Christ is not taught or known in it."[15] More recently, George Bernard Shaw dismissed Revelation in its entirety as "a curious record of the visions of a drug addict,"[16] and C. G. Jung deemed the visions of Revelation to be unworthy of serious study "because no one believes in them and the whole subject is felt to be an embarrassing one."[17] Even otherwise pious religious scholars have always been openly skeptical about what an earnest seeker can hope to achieve by parsing out the text.

"Revelation either finds a man mad," quipped one exegete, "or leaves him so."[18]

Revelation is so shackled by its own riddles and ciphers and symbols that the text must be decrypted rather than merely read. "[E]ither it has been abandoned by the readers of the Bible as being almost completely unintelligible," observes a twentieth-century Bible scholar, "or it has become the happy hunting ground of religious eccentrics."[19] One medieval theologian, for example, was moved to scribble out more than one thousand pages of exegesis in an effort to explain his own understanding of Revelation, which itself consists of only twelve thousand words or so in the English translation of the King James Version. Still, the cast and plot of Revelation—the raw material out of which the author composes one of the great and enduring works of the human imagination—can be summed up with far fewer words.

Ω

The book of Revelation consists of a series of prophecies about the future, most of them eerie and scary. To be sure, the author opens with a few words of grudging praise or, more often, bitter denunciation for his fellow Christians, most of whom he finds to be complacent, gullible, self-indulgent, and woefully lacking in zeal. "Because you are lukewarm," he tells the church at Laodicea, attributing his admonition to God himself, "I will vomit you out of my mouth."[20] Now and then, he embellishes the text with a few pious beatitudes that are intended to authenticate his visions: "And behold, I am coming soon. Blessed is he who keeps the words of the prophecy of this book."[21]

Mostly, however, the author of Revelation devotes himself to an account of the disturbing sights that he has seen during a vision that came to him on the island of Patmos off the west coast of Asia. The author has achieved a trancelike state of mystical ecstasy in which he sees, among a great many other and even odder things, a scroll on which is written God's secret plan for the end of the world. The scroll has been closed with seven seals, presumably of wax or clay, and all seven seals must be broken before the scroll can be opened and read.

Here begins the single most insistent motif of Revelation—the author's almost obsessive use of the number seven. He sees not only seven seals but also seven angels, seven bowls, seven candlesticks, seven churches, seven crowns, seven eyes, seven heads, seven horns, seven kings, seven lamps, seven mountains, seven plagues, seven spirits, seven stars, seven thunders, and seven trumpets. The story of Revelation, such as it is, focuses on what will happen in heaven and on earth when, after the ever-mounting terror of the last days finally reaches a climax, the seventh trumpet is sounded, the seventh bowl of God's wrath is poured out, and the Lamb of God breaks the seventh seal.

The celestial figure who reveals the divine plan for the end of the world is variously called "one like unto the Son of Man," "the Son of God," "the Spirit," and "the Lamb"—all of which are terms borrowed from Jewish messianic tradition. The author also coins an elegant and enduring phrase that appears nowhere else in Christian scripture: "I am Alpha and Omega, the beginning and the ending."[22] Only rarely does he invoke the unambiguous name and title of "Jesus Christ," and he prefers to conceal the identity of his celestial source in puzzles and riddles: "I am He who lives, and was dead, and behold, I am alive forevermore," says the nameless visitor by way of self-introduction, "and I have the keys of Hades and of Death."[23]

Then, too, the deity who stalks the pages of Revelation is a shape-shifter. At the outset, he is a celestial king dressed in a golden robe, with hair "as white as snow," eyes "like a flame of fire," holding seven stars in his right hand, "and out of His mouth went a sharp two-edged sword."[24] Later, the author beholds the odd and eerie figure of a lamb, looking "as though it had been slain," and yet standing upright, with "seven horns and seven eyes."[25]

At the climax of Revelation, the author sees a divine warrior mounted on a white horse, crowned with "many diadems" and wearing a bloodstained robe. Here, too, the author engages in conjuration of the now-you-see-it, now-you-don't variety: "He has a name inscribed which no one knows but himself," the author writes—and then, a moment later, he reveals: "On his robe and on his thigh he has a name inscribed, King of kings and Lord of lords."[26]

The most memorable characters in the cast of Revelation, however, are the bad guys. The arch-villain is "a great red dragon, having seven heads and ten horns, and seven crowns upon his heads," who is later revealed to be "that ancient serpent who is called the Devil and Satan, the deceiver of the whole world."[27] The earthly agents of the Devil are two "beasts," one with seven heads and ten horns who emerges from the sea, and the other with two horns and a voice "like a dragon," who emerges from the land.[28] And there are cameo appearances by false prophets and prophetesses, corrupt and decadent kings in great profusion, and various other malefactors, both human and demonic.

The single most provocative character in Revelation, for example, is the Great Whore of Babylon. She is depicted as a sexual monster with whom "the kings of the earth have committed fornication," and her lovers are so numerous and far-flung that "the inhabitants of the earth have been made drunk with the wine of her fornication." The woman is drunk, too, but her intoxicant is "the blood of the saints and the blood of the martyrs of Jesus." She is "arrayed in purple and scarlet" and "bedecked with gold and jewels and pearls," and she carries a golden cup in her hand as she rides on the back of the scarlet-colored beast with seven heads and ten horns. And, in a startlingly explicit image, the author points out that the cup itself is "full of abominations and impurities of her fornication."[29]

Just as the Lamb is the counterpart of the Dragon, the counterpart of the Great Whore is the celestial figure of "a woman clothed with the sun, and the moon under her feet, and upon her head a crown of twelve stars." At the very moment when the woman goes into labor, the red dragon sets upon her, waiting to devour her newborn baby. When she gives birth to "a man child, who was to rule all nations with a rod of iron," the newborn is snatched up to God's heavenly throne, and the woman is given "the two wings of a great eagle, that she might fly into the wilderness," where she will be nourished and sheltered from the predatory dragon. Meanwhile, a battle is fought in heaven between Satan and the archangel Michael, each one at the head of an army of angels. Satan is defeated and cast out of heaven, but he descends safely to earth and sets out to establish a kingdom over humankind.[30]

Indeed, the only way for God to defeat the Devil and his servitors, according to the author, is to destroy the world and start all over again with "a new heaven and a new earth." But the end-times are wired to a slow-burning fuse. First, the Christian true believers must endure a period of oppression and persecution—the so-called Tribulation—at the hands of Satan's deputies, including the "beast" who is nowadays better known as the Antichrist, although the latter term itself does not appear in the text of Revelation. The beginning of the end will be signaled by signs and wonders: earthquakes and floods, comets and eclipses, famine and plague and pestilence, and a series of mighty battles in heaven and on earth.

The afflictions of the end-times are described in some of the most memorable passages in the Bible. For example, the famous Four Horsemen of the Apocalypse, each rider mounted on a horse of a different color, "kill with the sword, with hunger, with death, and by the beasts of the earth." What we might understand as natural disasters are described in fanciful language: "The sun became black as sackcloth, and the full moon became like blood, and the stars of the sky fell to earth." And the author conjures up monsters like nothing in nature. When he describes a flight of locusts, for example, they are insects with the face of a man, the long hair of a woman, the body of a warhorse, the teeth of a lion, and the stinging tail of a scorpion.[31]

"And in those days men will seek death and will not find it," writes the author of Revelation in one almost poignant passage. "They will long to die, and death will fly from them."[32]

After seven years of suffering under the Beast, Jesus Christ will descend to earth as a mounted warrior-king at the head of an army of angels and resurrected saints and martyrs, and a decisive battle will be fought at a place called Armageddon. The author of Revelation delights in describing the revenge that the Lamb of God will take on those who once tormented his faithful worshippers. "Come, gather for the great supper of God," an angel will cry to the birds of prey, "to eat the flesh of kings, the flesh of captains, the flesh of mighty men, the flesh of horses and their riders, and the flesh of all men, both free and slave, both small and great."[33]

Satan will be bound in chains and confined in a bottomless pit, and the survivors of the Tribulation will live in an earthly kingdom under the authority of King Jesus and his resurrected saints and martyrs for exactly one thousand years. But the end-times are not quite over yet. Satan will break his fetters, and Jesus Christ will be forced to go to war yet again against his archenemy and the far-flung nations that are the Devil's human allies, now called "Gog and Magog." Only then will Satan and his minions be cast once and for all into "the lake of fire and brimstone," where they will be "tormented day and night for ever and ever."[34]

Now, at last, our benighted world—"the first earth"—will be brought to an end. Everyone who has ever lived will be resurrected, and living and dead alike will be judged and rewarded or punished as God sees fit. And the litmus test for salvation is true belief: "Those who keep the commandments of God and the faith of Jesus" will be permitted to spend eternity in perfect bliss in the new heaven. Everyone else—men, women, and children—will be cast into the lake of fire and brimstone, "which is the second death," along with the Devil and "the cowardly, the faithless, the polluted, murderers, fornicators, sorcerers, idolaters, and all liars."[35]

Revelation, quite in contrast to the Gospels, is notoriously lacking in loving-kindness. Rather, it is a punishing text, full of rage and resentment, almost toxic in its longing for bloody revenge against one's enemies. Only rarely does the author allow his readers to glimpse a kinder and gentler realm, and when he does, he explains that it will arrive only after the earth as we know it, strewn with corpses and flooded "as high as a horse's bridle" with blood, is finally destroyed. And only "the ones who come out of the great tribulation," the ones who have "washed their robes and made them white in the blood of the Lamb," will be granted admission to a celestial paradise.[36]

"He will wipe away every tear from their eyes, and death shall be no more," writes the author in a rare and almost grudging moment of tenderness and compassion. "[N]either shall there be mourning nor crying nor pain any more, for the former things have passed away."[37]

For all of its Sturm und Drang, then, the book of Revelation offers a happy ending, at least for "them which are saved."[38] Everyone on earth in the end-times is destined to suffer horribly at the hands of the Antichrist—and most of them will die just as horribly—but a select few will be resurrected, judged, and granted eternal life in the world to come. The yearning to be counted among the saved, and the loathing of everyone who is *not* saved, turns out to be one of the great engines of history.

No better example can be found than the ancient but enduring practice of linking the Antichrist to a living historical figure. The "beast" of Revelation has been a man of all seasons: Muhammad was seen as the Antichrist in the early Middle Ages, Saladin at the time of the Crusades, the Grand Sultan of the Ottoman Turks when they threatened the gates of Vienna, Napoleon in the aftermath of the French Revolution. Martin Luther denounced the pope (or, more precisely, the papacy) as the Antichrist, and the pope returned the favor. Each generation churns up its own candidates: Lenin and Stalin, Hitler and Mussolini, Roosevelt and Kennedy, Moshe Dayan and Anwar el-Sadat have all been proposed at various times as the human manifestation of the Beast.

Speculation on the identity of the Antichrist, in fact, can be seen as a kind of Rorschach test for the anxieties of any given age. Henry Kissinger, for example, came under suspicion when he was shuttling between Washington, Moscow, and Beijing in the 1970s, and the Ayatollah Khomeini was first nominated only after Americans were taken hostage in Tehran during the aftermath of the Islamic Revolution in Iran in 1979. Only a few years ago, Saddam Hussein was seen as a promising contender; significantly, the best-selling Left Behind series identifies Baghdad as the seat of its fictional Antichrist. Nowadays, of course, Osama bin Laden seems to have taken Saddam's place as the satanic adversary whose coming is predicted in Revelation.

A closely related enterprise is the effort to crack the code that the author of Revelation planted so intriguingly in his text—the identity of the "beast" whose name is symbolized by the number 666. As we shall see, there *is* a convincing answer to the question: 666 is an alphanumeric code that can be translated into the Greek, Latin, or Hebrew name of the human being whom the author of Revelation regards as a tool of Satan. But that hasn't stopped the biblical code-breakers, amateurs and professionals alike, from wringing new and ever more exotic meanings out of the same blood-curdling number.

The imagery of Revelation, as we shall see, meant something quite specific—and quite different—to its author and his first readers and hearers.

But the fact that we are able to understand what the "number of the beast" and the Great Whore of Babylon actually meant to a Christian visionary of Jewish birth in Asia Minor in the first century has never deterred subsequent generations from finding entirely different meanings for themselves. That's the strange and powerful magic of Revelation: each new generation of readers is convinced that God planted a secret meaning in the text that was meant only and especially for them. And, remarkably, the failure of each previous generation to crack the Revelation code only encourages the next generation to try harder.

Ω

As a work of prophecy, of course, Revelation is wholly and self-evidently wrong. "How long, O Lord, holy and true, until you judge and avenge our blood on those who dwell on the earth?" demands the biblical author, quoting the souls of the dead martyrs, and he answers his own question by attributing an unambiguous promise to Jesus Christ: "Behold, I am coming soon."[39] Those words were first reduced to writing nearly two thousand years ago, but the readers of Revelation are still waiting for the day of revenge that is predicted with such clarity and confidence in the ancient text.

The author of Revelation is not the only figure in Christian scriptures whose prediction of the end-times was mistaken. Jesus, according to some awkward sayings attributed to him in the Gospels, assures his followers that at least some of them will see the end of the world with their own eyes. The apostle Paul, in turn, offered the same assurance to *his* generation of Christians. Both Jesus and Paul were gone by the time the author of Revelation set down his vision of "things which must shortly come to pass."[40] All of them turned out to be dead wrong, and the world is still here.

The utter, obvious, and persistent failure of the world to "end on time," as one contemporary Bible scholar wryly puts it, has compelled Christianity to reconsider how life ought to be lived in the here and now, no less in late antiquity than today.[41] Once a Christian emperor seated himself on the imperial throne of pagan Rome in the early fourth century, all the bitter rhetoric of Revelation, so clearly aimed at the power and glory of the Roman Empire, was suddenly an embarrassment that needed to be explained away. By late antiquity, Revelation suddenly seemed less relevant than, say, the Gospel of Mark: "But when you hear of wars and rumors of war, do not be troubled," Jesus is shown to sensibly caution his followers, "for such things must happen, but the end is not yet."[42]

Still, more than a few readers of Revelation in every age, including our own, have thrilled at the idea that the end is near. Indeed, they are perfectly willing to overlook the plain fact that the world has not ended as predicted, and they persist in poring over the text of Revelation in a fresh attempt to figure out the precise date when it will. They have always been wrong, too, of course, but nothing has discouraged the so-called date setters who study the text, crunch the numbers, and come up with dates when the world *must* end. Not a single century has passed since the ink dried on the first copy of Revelation without some new prediction of the precise date when its prophecies will finally come to pass.

Ω

Above all else, the author of Revelation is a good hater, and he embraces the simple principle that anyone who is not with him is against him. He rails against his rival preachers, condemning them as fornicators and false prophets. He heaps abuse on those of his fellow Christians whom he regards as insufficiently zealous for the Lamb of God. He offers the ultimate insult to Jews who do not embrace Jesus as the Messiah by insisting that Christians are the only authentic Jews. He reserves special contempt for anyone who indulges in carnal pleasure and, especially, the getting of goods. And, in a gesture of rhetorical overkill that is the hallmark of Revelation, he condemns his adversaries as not merely wrong, not merely sinful or criminal, but wholly corrupted by "the deep things of Satan."[43]

The black-or-white morality of Revelation—everyone and everything in the world is either all good or all bad—is artfully expressed in the author's insistent pairing of opposites. The Great Whore is the evil twin of "the woman clothed with the sun," the Beast is a vile parody of the Lamb of God, and the destruction of Babylon, Mother of Harlots, is followed by the creation of the New Jerusalem, a construction of crystal and precious stone that floats down from heaven. Here we find a particularly heartless theology of exclusion: the saints and martyrs will be granted eternal life, as the author of Revelation sees it, and the rest of humanity will burn in hell. Indeed, the book of Revelation fairly sizzles with the deferred pleasure of revenge.

Thus the author of Revelation, like Jesus as depicted in the Gospels, is a radical remaker of Judaism—but each moves in the opposite direction from the other. "Thou shalt love thy neighbor," commands God in the Hebrew Bible (and not only one's neighbor but even "the stranger that sojourneth with you"). Jesus cites the traditional Jewish commandment and then intensifies it: "But I say to you, Love your enemies and pray for those who persecute you."[44] By contrast, the author of Revelation unambiguously promises his readers and hearers that God will avenge himself on their enemies and persecutors in a spasm of divine violence that can only be described as a holocaust.

"The second half of the Apocalypse is flamboyant hate and simple lust ... for the end of the world," writes novelist D. H. Lawrence, who was so appalled by what he found in Revelation that he was moved to write a commentary of his own. By his lights, the author of Revelation had devised "a grandiose scheme for wiping out and annihilating everybody who wasn't of the elect [and] of climbing up himself right on to the throne of God."[45]

Thus, for example, the final destruction of "Babylon the Great, Mother of Harlots and Abominations of the Earth"—the author's symbol for pagan Rome in particular and all human sinfulness in general—betrays the lust for revenge that Lawrence discerns in the text. "Therefore shall her plagues come in one day, death, and mourning, and famine, and she shall be utterly burned with fire," writes the author of Revelation, displaying not a hint of Christian charity but plenty of smug satisfaction at the scourging of his enemies. "Rejoice over her, thou heaven, and ye holy apostles and prophets, for God hath avenged you on her."[46] At the climax of his vision of the end of the world, the author of Revelation is seized with the uncompromising (and unseemly) desire to watch his enemies suffer and die.

"Do unto her as she has done to your people," he implores the sword-wielding Lamb of God. "She brewed a cup of terror for others, so give her twice as much as she gave out. She has lived in luxury and pleasure, so match it now with torments and sorrow."[47]

Ω

The conventional apology for such rhetorical excess is that Revelation consists of morale-boosting propaganda by and for the victims of oppression and persecution—"the messages addressed by ancient apocalyptic seers to those engulfed by suffering and overwhelmed by dread."[48] That is why, for example, one modern theologian insists that Martin Luther King Jr.'s

Letter from a Birmingham Jail, a stirring manifesto of the American civil rights movement, reflects "experiences and hopes similar to the theology of Revelation."[49] More recently, however, some courageous scholars have suggested that the author of Revelation was probably not himself at risk of torture and death at the time and in the place where he lived and worked. Indeed, as it turns out, the rhetoric of Revelation is no less compelling to those who imagine themselves to be persecuted than it is to those who actually are persecuted.

"When thinking of the torments which will be the lot of Christians at the time of Anti-Christ," mused Thérèse of Lisieux, a nun in nineteenth-century France, shortly before her death from illness at the age of twenty-four, "I feel my heart leap with joy and I would that these torments be reserved for me."[50]

But it is also true that Revelation, now and then, moves some of its more excitable readers to act out their own fantasies of revenge and martyrdom. "Assurance that the end is nigh," observes one contemporary scholar, "often brings with it profoundly dangerous baggage."[51] A young man named Vernon Howell, for example, joined an apocalyptic sect called the Branch Davidians, dubbed himself "David Koresh" in a coded reference to two messianic figures of the Hebrew Bible, and led his followers into martyrdom in a standoff with federal law-enforcement agents, all because he was convinced that God had revealed to him that the battle of Armageddon was destined to start in Waco, Texas. Koresh, too, is an unremarkable example of a very old phenomenon, and we shall see how the apocalyptic idea has worked on unstable minds over the last twenty centuries.

Some of the recent readings of Revelation would be laughable if they were not so creepy. Contemporary traffickers in end-of-the-world prophecy have resorted to the ancient biblical text to find explanations for various phenomena of our anxiety-ridden age, both real and imagined, including alien abduction, UFOs, nuclear proliferation, the Kennedy assassination, the sexual revolution, the digital revolution, the AIDS epidemic, and much else besides—"an example of Americans' insatiable appetite for the unusual, spectacular and exotic," as one scholar proposes.[52] And Revelation, which imagines the existence of a vast conspiracy of princes, powers, and principalities in service to Satan, feeds even the most outlandish paranoid fantasies about the hidden workings of the world in which we live.

Above all, Revelation is now—and has always been—a potent rhetorical weapon in a certain kind of culture war, a war of contesting values and aspirations, that has been waged throughout human history. The author of Revelation, as we shall see, condemns any Christian who partakes of the pleasures and rewards of classical civilization at the peak of its enduring achievements in art, letters, and philosophy. When Savonarola called upon his parishioners to cast their paintings and pretty things on the Bonfire of the Vanities—and to thereby turn Florence into the "New Jerusalem" that is promised in Revelation—he was fighting a culture war against what he called paganism and we call the Renaissance. And modern readers of Revelation who inject the Bible into the rancorous public debate over the role of religion in American democracy are fighting the same war all over again.

"It's not a shooting war, but it is a war," declared one recent appointee to a federal judgeship, a religious fundamentalist whose nomination sparked a crisis in Congress. "These are perilous times for people of faith, not in the sense that we are going to lose our lives, but in the sense that it will cost you something if you are a person of faith who stands up for what you believe in and say those things out loud."[53]

So the book of Revelation cannot be dismissed as a biblical oddity that belongs only to professional theologians, media-savvy preachers, and a few religious crackpots. The fact is that Revelation has come to be regarded by certain men and women in positions of power and influence as a source of inspiration, if not a divine handbook, for the conduct of war, diplomacy, and statecraft in the real world. When Ronald Reagan moved into a house whose street number was 666, he insisted on changing the address to a less satanic number, and he readily interpreted an otherwise unremarkable coup in Libya as the fulfillment of biblical prophecy:

"That's a sign that the day of Armageddon isn't far off," he declared. "Everything's falling into place. It can't be long now."[54]

Such beliefs are especially alarming in a man with the power to inflict a nuclear Armageddon on the enemy he dubbed "the evil empire," yet another oblique reference to the book of Revelation. Yet Reagan is hardly the only American politician to hold such beliefs. All occupants of the White House since Reagan—and many of their most trusted counselors and confidantes—have declared themselves to be "born again," a phrase that identifies them with a strain of religious fundamentalism that assumes the accuracy and inevitability of biblical prophecy, including the end-time prophecies of Revelation. Such literalism in the reading of the Bible was regarded as a problem by the earliest Christian authorities in late antiquity, and it is no less problematic in the culture war that is being fought in American today.

Indeed, as we shall shortly see, Revelation has served as a "language arsenal" in a great many of the social, cultural, and political conflicts in Western history.[55] Again and again, Revelation has stirred some dangerous men and women to act out their own private apocalypses. Above all, the moral calculus of Revelation—the demonization of one's enemies, the sanctification of revenge taking, and the notion that history must end in catastrophe—can be detected in some of the worst atrocities and excesses of every age, including our own.

For all of these reasons, the rest of us ignore the book of Revelation only at our impoverishment and, more to the point, at our own peril.

Two

Spooky Knowledge and Last Things

What, will the line stretch out to the crack of doom?
WILLIAM SHAKESPEARE, *Macbeth*

A pocalypse" is derived from the Greek word that means "unveiling," and "Revelation" is its Latin equivalent. Both words suggest the disclosure of something that has been kept secret. Both carry the sense that the secret being revealed is not merely arcane but also deeply mysterious and perhaps even dangerous—"spooky knowledge," as pop philosopher Alan Watts laughingly puts it.[1] And nothing else in the scriptures of Judaism *or* Christianity is quite so spooky as the book of Revelation.

Yet, as it turns out, Revelation is hardly unique among the writings in which men and women have set down their spiritual imaginings. Seers, shamans, and self-appointed prophets, in every age and all over the world, have claimed to hear voices and see visions, sometimes with divine assistance, sometimes by means of mystical incantations or magical potions, and sometimes using only their own powerful insight. The oracle at ancient Delphi, who may have begun to babble her words of prophecy after inhaling hallucinogenic vapors rising from a fissure beneath her hillside shrine, has something in common with the contemporary computer scientist who used a microprocessor to decipher what he dubbed the "Bible Code."

The original author of Revelation, as we shall see, stands squarely in the same tradition. He was surely a gifted poet and a powerful preacher, and some of his readers may be willing to regard him as an authentic visionary who heard voices and saw sights from on high. But the book of Revelation did not spring from his forehead as something fresh and fully formed. A kind of theological and scriptural DNA can be extracted from the text of Revelation, and its bloodlines can be traced back to far older and even stranger texts that were regarded as sacred long before the author of Revelation was inspired to speak out loud about his visions of the end of the world.

The author, for example, was hardly the first human being who claimed to see mystical visions, nor was he the first whose claims were greeted with skepticism by the guardians of religious law and order. Organized religion has always been troubled by any mere mortal—and especially any mortal who has not been duly ordained as a rabbi, priest, imam, or minister— who insists that he or she has come into contact with God. The Hebrew Bible includes a passage that rules out any direct encounter between a human being and the deity: "Man shall not see me, and live," decrees God in the book of Exodus.[2] Now and then, God may choose to communicate with a human being, of course, but only in oblique ways: "If there be a prophet among you, I, the Lord, do make myself known to him in a vision, I do speak with him in a dream."[3] Even then, some divine mysteries are deemed to be wholly unfit for human consumption: "The secret things," warns Moses in the book of Deuteronomy, "belong unto the Lord our God."[4]

The same strict rule is carried forward into Christian scripture, a fact that prompted some early Christian authorities to declare the book of Revelation to be unworthy of admission into the New Testament. "I will come to visions and revelations of the Lord," allows Paul—but not until God is good and ready to grant them. "For now," he goes on, "we see through a glass darkly."[5] And, to illustrate the point, he tells a tantalizing tale about a man he once knew who was carried all the way up to "the third heaven," where he "heard unspeakable words"—is Paul speaking coyly of his own ecstatic visions?—but he refuses to repeat what was heard in heaven because "it is not lawful for a man to utter."[6]

So the perils of prophecy have always been obvious to guardians of orthodoxy, starting in biblical antiquity and never more so than today. David Koresh and the Branch Davidians, Jim Jones and the Peoples Temple, Osama bin Laden and al Qaeda, and miscellaneous other religious zealots, less celebrated but no less dangerous, are only the most recent examples of what can happen when a human being with delusions of grandeur, paranoid tendencies, an overheated imagination, and a certain dark charisma convinces himself and his dutiful followers that he is on a mission from God. Indeed, we will encounter many such men and women in these pages, all of whom were agitated and provoked by what they read in the book of Revelation. More than a few of them ended their days on the torturer's rack or the executioner's block.

Not every self-appointed seer ends in death and disgrace. A few men and women throughout history have come to be revered as authentic prophets. Moses, Paul, and Muhammad are accepted and celebrated as makers (or remakers) of the three great faiths of the West, but the roster also includes more recent religious innovators such as Joseph Smith (1805–1844), the founder of Mormonism, and Mary Baker Eddy (1821–1910), the creator of Christian Science. To this day, the president of the Church of Latter-Day Saints bears the title Prophet, Seer and Revelator.

Somewhere between these two realms—the prophets whom we are taught to take seriously, and the prophets whom we are inclined to regard as dangerous lunatics—lays a kind of no-man's-land of religious imagination and speculation. Here we find a colorful assortment of eccentrics and ecstatics who asked their contemporaries to believe that the secret things of God had been revealed to them after all. Among them is the author of Revelation, and we will see that his visions are deeply rooted in the soil of that spooky landscape.

To understand Revelation at all, in fact, we have to explore the far older and even odder writings that shaped the imagination of its author. He apparently knew and loved many of the earlier apocalyptic writings, and he borrowed freely from them. Some of the most puzzling and perplexing passages of Revelation, in fact, snap into sharp focus when they are viewed through the lens of the apocalyptic tradition. The biblical book that is sometimes known as "*The* Apocalypse," as we shall see, is only one of many apocalypses.

"Apocalypse" is one of the various titles that appear on ancient manuscripts of the last book of the New Testament, but the same word is also used by scholars to identify *any* text in which the author describes the secret knowledge that has been revealed to a human being by a supernatural figure of some kind. The book of Revelation, then, is *an* apocalypse, but it is hardly the first or only one; a whole library of apocalypses, some composed long before Revelation and some long after, has accumulated over the centuries. A Jewish source from the first century, for example, apparently knew of some *seventy* apocalypses that were already on offer at the moment in history when Revelation first appeared.

All but two of the apocalypses that have survived from antiquity were wholly excluded from the Bible as it is known and used in both Jewish and Christian tradition. The only exceptions are the book of Daniel in the Hebrew Bible, and the book of Revelation in the New Testament. Indeed, the extrabiblical Jewish apocalypses were shunned by the rabbis of late antiquity who were the custodians of Jewish texts. Ironically, weird but illuminating Jewish writings such as *The Book of Watchers* and *The Animal Apocalypse* survive only because they were preserved and studied by ancient Christian scholars and theologians.

Some of the strangest apocalyptic texts, in fact, were lost to both Christians and Jews until they were rediscovered and retrieved in the twentieth century. Apocalypses were found among the Dead Sea Scrolls at a site called Khirbet Qumran in the Judean desert, for example, and the buried archive of Gnostic texts at Nag Hammadi on the banks of the Nile River in Egypt. Many of the earliest apocalyptic writings came to be included in a collection of ancient texts known to scholars as Pseudepigrapha—that is, "false writings," a term that refers to the fact that they are often ascribed to biblical figures who manifestly did not write them.

Strictly speaking, an apocalypse might reveal all kinds of "secret things," including mysteries and marvels that have nothing to do with the end of the world. Typically, the author of an apocalypse will start by describing a visitation by God or an angel or some other heavenly creature. The visitor from on high might conduct the author on a "guided tour" of the heavens, or grant the author a vision of Jerusalem as it will appear in the far-distant future, or show the author some "cosmological wonder" like the "storehouse of winds" or the "cornerstone of the earth."[7] Sometimes the spectral visitor will allow the author to glimpse a parallel universe that is ordinarily hidden from the eyes of ordinary human beings. And sometimes the visitor will reveal the inner meaning of God's secret master plan for humankind, including the significance of events that have already happened and events that are yet to come—that is, both "past history" and "future history."[8]

But the key concern in most (if not all) apocalyptic writings is the "eschaton" or end-times—that is, how and when the world will end. And curiosity about the end-times is an outgrowth of one of the great theological innovations of Judaism. The pagan civilizations of antiquity, according to a certain conventional wisdom, saw the world as an endless cycle of birth, death, and rebirth—"the eternal return of the same," according to Friedrich Nietzsche's memorable phrase.[9] But the authors of the Hebrew Bible embraced the revolutionary new idea that the God of Israel is a deity who works his will through human history—and history, like any well-crafted story, has a beginning, a middle, and an end.

"An apocalypse only makes sense," explains contemporary historian Rennie B. Schoepflin, "in a universe ruled by a God of history."[10]

The end-times as they are imagined in both Jewish and Christian apocalyptic tradition have certain features in common—an ordeal of human suffering at the hands of a satanic oppressor, the arrival of a divine savior or redeemer, a final battle between the forces of good and evil, a resurrection of the dead, a day of judgment, and, finally, the advent of a new and eternal era of divine perfection, sometimes right here on earth and sometimes in a heavenly realm. All of these story lines figure prominently in the book of Revelation, of course, but they are also found in far older texts that were already being read long before the Christian era.

In fact, the apocalyptic tradition dates back at least several centuries before Revelation was set down in writing, and—as it turns out—the idea was not confined to the Judeo-Christian world. Contrary to Nietzsche's assertion, speculation about the fate of the world in the far-distant future can be found in the pagan writings of Mesopotamia, Egypt, Greece, and Rome. For example, the Sibylline Oracles—the enigmatic utterings of women who were believed to possess the divine gift of prophecy—were routinely consulted throughout the classical pagan world to predict the fate of both human beings and empires. The practice was so unsettling to Augustus, the first Roman emperor, that he ordered the confiscation and incineration of two thousand copies of the Sibylline Oracles—an example of how dangerous the pursuit of "future history" could be.[11]

Some scholars argue that the apocalyptic tradition can be linked to far older and even more exotic sources. Many of the end-of-the-world auguries that appear in the Bible—"the signs and tribulations of the end, the struggle of God and his Messiah against evil, [and] the figure of Satan and his demons"[12]—can be traced all the way back to the Zoroastrian writings of Persia, the earliest of which may be several hundred years older than any of the Jewish or Christian texts. For that reason, the birthplace of the apocalyptic idea, and much else that we find in the so-called Judeo-Christian tradition, may have been ancient Persia rather than the Holy Land.

The first apocalyptic authors, then, may have been familiar with "proto-apocalypses" that originated outside the land of Israel and served as "models and sources" for the apocalyptic tradition whose highest expression is the book of Revelation.[13] And it is tantalizing to speculate on exactly how the eerie and exotic visions of Egyptian priests, Persian magi, and Greek sibyls may have insinuated themselves into the heart and soul of the Jewish and Christian scriptures. Still, the "models and sources" that inspired the book of Revelation are much closer at hand: they are to be found in the biblical writings of ancient Judaism that the author of Revelation knew, loved, and copied.

$$\Omega$$

Some of the most familiar figures and scenes in the book of Revelation, in fact, can be traced back to specific passages of the Hebrew Bible—Satan, the demonic armies of Gog and Magog, the Day of Judgment, the end of the world, and much else besides. When we read what is plainly written in the source texts, however, it is clear that the author of Revelation did not feel obliged to remain faithful to what he regarded as Holy Writ. Rather, he felt at liberty to embroider upon or wholly reinvent what he found in the pages of the Bible, and he borrowed ideas and images from far stranger sources, or, perhaps even more likely, he did both at once.

Satan, for example, is given only a cameo role in the Hebrew Bible, and he is never depicted as the arch-demon that the author of Revelation imagines him to be. When he is mentioned at all, Satan is merely an "accuser" or "adversary"—the literal meaning of the Hebrew word—and *not* the diabolical counterpart of God. Indeed, when the word is first used in the Hebrew Bible, it is applied to King David by a Philistine king to mark David as an enemy on the battlefield.[14] Even when used to identify a celestial figure, Satan is "not a proper name, but merely a title defining the function of a member of God's heavenly court," explains H. H. Rowley, an influential Baptist scholar and theologian of the early twentieth century. "He was a sort of Public Prosecutor at the bar of divine justice."[15]

The most prominent mention of Satan in the Hebrew Bible is found in the book of Job, where he is shown to be a divine counselor who slyly suggests that Job may be less truly pious than God believes him to be. Once his curiosity is piqued by Satan's remark, God empowers Satan to test Job's faith by afflicting him with various woes, starting with those famous boils and ending with the death of Job's beloved wife and children: "Behold, he is in your hands," says God to Satan, "only spare his life."[16] So the only power that Satan enjoys in the Hebrew Bible is the power that God grants him to test Job's faith, and the whole affair is a kind of laboratory experiment in the limits of human endurance under torture.

Similarly, Gog and Magog are described in Revelation as nations who put their armies under Satan's command in the final battle at the end of the world. But when they are first mentioned by the prophet Ezekiel in the Hebrew Bible, Gog is a monarch, Magog is the country over which he reigns, and Satan is not mentioned at all. To be sure, Ezekiel predicts a battle between Israel and "Gog of the land of Magog," but it is *not* a cataclysmic clash of arms that brings the world to doomsday.[17] Rather, God himself invites King Gog to invade the land of Israel so that the God of Israel can "manifest My greatness and My holiness" by granting the Israelites a glorious victory.[18] And, in fact, when the army of Gog is destroyed and the battlefield is cleansed of corpses, the Israelites will once again "dwell in their land secure and untroubled."[19] Like the incident with Job, the whole bloody affair has been contrived by God himself to make a point: "They will know that I the Lord am their God when, having exiled them among the nations, I gather them back into their land."[20]

Even when one of the Hebrew prophets *seems* to predict the end of the world, using words and phrases that will be familiar to readers of Revelation, he is actually describing something very different from what we find in Christian scripture. "The hour of doom has come," vows God in the book of Amos. "I will make the sun set at noon, I will darken the earth on a sunny day."[21] But the prophet Amos, quite unlike the author of Revelation, does *not* predict that God will destroy the earth and replace it with a celestial paradise in the clouds. Rather, as Amos sees it, God will spare the Israelites who have remained faithful to the divine law, and he will grant them nothing more exalted than a good life in the here and now.

They shall rebuild ruined cities and inhabit them;
They shall plant vineyards and drink their wine;
They shall till gardens and eat their fruit.

And I will plant them upon their soil,
Nevermore to be uprooted
From the soil I have given them.[22]

To be sure, some of the Hebrew prophets were capable of weird and wild-eyed visions of the kind that we find in Revelation and other apocalyptic writings. Ezekiel, like the author of Revelation, claims to have beheld grotesque monsters and bizarre phenomena that exist nowhere in the natural world. Among the sights that Ezekiel sees, for example, are four creatures with the torso of a human being, a single calf's hoof, four wings with a human hand beneath the feathers, and a head with four faces—a human face in front, an eagle's face in the back, and the faces of a lion and an ox on the sides.[23] And he describes how these creatures move on fiery "wheels," a contrivance that convinced some of Ezekiel's later readers that what he had actually seen were UFOs: "And when the living creatures were lifted up from the earth," writes Ezekiel, "the wheels were lifted up."[24]

So there is a kind of genetic linkage between the classical prophets of the Hebrew Bible and the authors of the apocalyptic writings: "Apocalyptic," as H. H. Rowley puts it, "is the child of prophecy."[25] But the biblical prophecies differ in significant ways from the ones we find in the apocalyptic writings. Unlike the writers of the apocalyptic tradition, who delight in "guided tours" of the seven heavens, the biblical prophets always remain right here on earth. "No Hebrew prophet, not even Isaiah and Ezekiel, had gone up to heaven," explains historian Bernard McGinn, a prominent figure in the study of Christian mysticism and apocalypticism in the Middle Ages.* "God had always condescended to come down to earth."[26] And, significantly, when the Jewish prophets look into the future to determine the fate of humankind, they imagine not a heavenly paradise but an earthly one.

The Jewish notion of an earthly kingdom under a God-sent king, as we shall see, shows up in the book of Revelation in the vision of the thousand-year reign of Jesus Christ that will follow the battle of Armageddon. Indeed, that's one clue to the Jewish origins of its author and first readers,

---

* "Apocalypticism" is a term used by scholars to identify various ideas and texts, including the book of Revelation, that focus on beliefs about how the world will end. For a brief discussion of apocalypticism and other specialized terms used throughout this book, see the Glossary on page 317.

and that's one of the reasons why Revelation was such a hard sell when the early Christians were deciding which writings belonged in the Bible. But that's hardly the only or even the most crucial difference between the classical prophets of the Bible and the apocalyptic authors. The single greatest theological innovation in the apocalyptic tradition was a new and revolutionary answer to an old and enduring question: Why do bad things happen to good people?

The author of Revelation, of course, sets up "that old serpent, called the Devil and Satan," as the source of all evil in the world.[27] By contrast, as we have seen, the Hebrew prophets do not seem to know or care much about Satan, and they embrace the simple if also harsh idea that everything, good *or* bad, begins and ends with God. If the armies of Gog invade the land of Israel, for example, it is because God sent them to do so—and if the Israelites defeat the invader, it is because God grants them victory in battle. And if the Chosen People forfeit the favor of God, they have only themselves to blame.

The moral equation is plainly written in the Bible. God, we are told in the Torah, offers the children of Israel a "covenant"—that is, a contract, and a simple one at that. If the Israelites obey the laws that God is shown to reveal to Moses on Sinai, God will bestow blessings upon them, and if they disobey those laws, God will afflict them with curses. Thus, according to the core theology of the Bible, God is the sole author of history and the sole arbiter of what happens to humankind. And so, if God is sufficiently provoked by the stubbornness and sinfulness of the Chosen People to make them suffer famine or pestilence, conquest or exile, it means only that they are getting what they bargained for and what they deserve.

Some of the most heart-shaking and stomach-turning passages of the Bible, in fact, are the ones in which Moses provides a catalog of the curses that God will bring down on the children of Israel "if you are not careful to do all the words of this law which are written in this book, that you may fear this glorious and awful name, the Lord your God." So ghastly is the parade of horribles, warns Moses in the book of Deuteronomy, that "you will be driven mad by the sights you see."[28]

God will afflict the Chosen People with "extraordinary plagues, strange and lasting," starting with "hemorrhoids, boil-scars, and itch," escalating to "madness, blindness, and dismay," and ending with the emblematic curse of the Jewish people—conquest and dispersion, exile and enslavement. "The Lord will bring a nation against you from afar," vows Moses, "a nation whose language you do not understand, a ruthless nation that will show the old no regard and the young no mercy."[29]

Remarkably, the innocent will suffer along with the guilty—men, women, children, and babies alike—and all because God himself wills it. "You shall betroth a wife, and another man shall lie with her," rants Moses. "Your sons and your daughters shall be given to another people and it shall not be in the power of your hand to stop it."[30] And, besieged in their cities by the conquering armies, the children of Israel will be reduced to cannibalism. Perhaps the most horrific scene in all of the Bible is the one in which a "dainty and tender" young mother hides the afterbirth of her newborn infant—and the baby itself—from her husband and other children: "She shall eat them secretly," says Moses, "because of utter want, in the desperate straits to which your enemy shall reduce you."[31]

So the Hebrew prophets find fault only with the Israelites. They do not mention Satan at all, and they do not blame the unhappy fate of the Israelites on the various pagan kings who are shown in the Bible to invade and conquer the land of Israel. Indeed, according to the logic of the biblical prophets, as we have seen, the foreign oppressors are sent *by* God, and the Israelites suffer precisely the fate that God promises them in Deuteronomy. The point is plainly made by the prophet Jeremiah by way of explanation of the Babylonian conquest and exile in 586 B.C.E.*: "And when your people say, 'Why has the Lord our God done all these things to us?,' you shall say to them: 'As you have forsaken me and served foreign gods in your land, so you shall serve strangers in a land that is not yours.'"[32]

God, too, decides when to remove the curses that he has called down on his own people, according to the biblical prophets. When the Babylonians were later defeated by the rival empire of the Persians, the exiled Jews were allowed to return to their homeland in Judea and rebuild the Temple in Jerusalem. That is why the emperor of Persia, Cyrus, is hailed in the Bible

---

* The abbreviation B.C.E. (Before the Common Era) is the equivalent of B.C. (Before Christ), and C.E. (Common Era) is the equivalent of A.D. (*Anno Domini,* or "In the Year of Our Lord"). The abbreviations B.C.E. and C.E. are used by scholars to avoid the theological implications of B.C. and A.D., and I have used them here for the same reason.

as a savior of the Jewish people, and that's why God is given all the credit for sending him to their rescue: "Thus says the Lord to Cyrus, His anointed one, whose right hand He has grasped," writes the prophet Isaiah in one poignant passage. "'For the sake of Israel, I call you by name, though you have not known Me.'"[33]

The phrase "anointed one," of course, is a literal translation of the original Hebrew word that comes down to us in English as "messiah." And so the biblical author makes it clear that even a pagan may serve as a messiah if the God of Israel wills it. The name of Cyrus, the pagan messiah from ancient Persia, is rendered in biblical Hebrew as "Koresh," and it is a name that we will encounter again in the long and exceedingly strange history of Revelation. Indeed, the fact that the name "Koresh" first appears in the Bible and then figures in the headlines of the late twentieth century shows the remarkable staying power of the messianic idea.

But the simple idea that God alone is the source of both good and evil began to lose its appeal at a moment when the biblical texts were still being composed and the Bible as we know it did not yet exist. On precisely this point, as we shall see, the earliest apocalyptic writers in Jewish tradition came up with one of their most startling and enduring innovations—the notion that Satan, and not God, is to be blamed for the bad things that happen. Some pious and prideful Jewish men and women simply refused to believe that God would afflict *them* merely because some of their fellow Jews were less than pious, and they began to look for someone else to blame—a supernatural arch-villain who was God's adversary and enemy.

The idea that God is forced to struggle against an Anti-God would have struck the classical prophets of the Hebrew Bible as alien, baffling, and even heretical. But the idea captured the hearts and minds of Jewish men and women who suffered conquest and exile, occupation and oppression, estrangement and disempowerment, all at the hands of pagan kings and armies whom the God of Israel seemed unwilling or unable to defeat. So a few daring innovators set out to work a theological revolution by raising the biblical Satan from divine counselor and public prosecutor to the new and elevated role of master conspirator and maker of war on God himself. Here begins the apocalyptic tradition that will figure so prominently in Christian theology, and nowhere more prominently than in the pages of Revelation.

Ω

By an old tradition in rabbinical Judaism, the end of the Babylonian Exile in 538 B.C.E. also marks the end of prophecy. God was willing to speak in dreams and visions to a few exceptional men and women who lived in the distant past, the rabbis conceded, but they found it harder to believe that human beings in the here and now had been granted the same divine gift. While the ancient rabbis were willing to imagine the coming of a savior who would bring an era of peace and security to the Jewish people, they were less credulous about men and women who offered their own prophecies and revelations about the end of the world. And, for that reason, most of the apocalyptic writings of the late biblical era were not only excluded from the Hebrew Bible itself, they were wholly written out of Jewish tradition.

"The day the Temple was destroyed, prophecy was taken from prophets," says the Talmud, "and given to fools and children."[34]

But, tragically, the Jewish experience of conquest did not come to an end. After a few centuries of relative peace and security as a provincial backwater of the Persian empire, Judea was invaded yet again by the armies of a conqueror from a far-off country whose language the Jewish people did not speak. His name was Alexander, and among his celebrated accomplishments was the spread of the classical pagan civilization that we call Hellenism. For the Jewish fundamentalists in ancient Judea, the arrival of Greek art, letters, manners, philosophy, and religion was as threatening as the arrival of any pagan army.

Notably, the very first apocalypses were written in direct response to the danger posed by Hellenism, a danger that manifested itself sometimes in occupation and oppression by a foreign army, but far more often as a kind of seduction by a foreign culture that was rich, worldly, sophisticated, and pleasure seeking. And so, by a strange irony, Alexander the Great, too, can be regarded as one of the fathers of the apocalyptic tradition that will ultimately produce, several centuries later, the book of Revelation.

Alexander himself was dead by 323 B.C.E., only thirty-three years old and already weeping for want of new worlds to conquer, but he left behind an empire that now included the land of the Jews. And in Judea, as elsewhere throughout the ancient world, the local gentry were eager to embrace the alluring new ways of their latest overlords. So it was that the Jewish aristocracy and intelligentsia began to speak and write in Greek. The earliest translation of the Bible into a language other than Hebrew, for example, is the Greek version called the Septuagint. But, significantly, the aping of Greek ways by Jewish men and women went far beyond the otherwise pious study of scripture in translation.

"They frequented the theatres and sports meetings, held drinking bouts, and generally adopted the Greek manner of gay living," writes Simon Dubnow, the twentieth-century scholar who revolutionized the study of Jewish history before his death during the Holocaust.[35] They sent their sons to gymnasia, a form of schooling borrowed from the Greeks. They consorted with female dancers and singers, "the attractive vice which the Judaeans learned from the Greeks," according to Heinrich Graetz, the pioneering Jewish historian of the nineteenth century.[36] They even participated in the athletic competitions that were the centerpiece of Greek culture. And, because the athletes in the Greek games competed in the nude, some assimilated Jews sought to conceal the fact that they had been circumcised by a primitive version of plastic surgery, "submit[ting] to painful operations in order to remove the sign of the covenant," as Graetz puts it, "and thus avoid the ridicule of the Greeks on the occasion of the Olympic Games."[37]

So powerful was the allure of Hellenism that it worked its seductive magic even on the priests who served in the Temple of Yahweh at Jerusalem. At one point, for example, the two rivals for the high priesthood were Jewish men known as Jason and Menelaus; their names can be found nowhere in the Torah, of course, but they feature prominently in its pagan equivalent, the sacred myths of ancient Greece and Rome. And when Jason was elevated to the post of high priest, he found it appropriate to establish a palaestra—a public facility for the training of young men in the art of wrestling and other Greek sports—in the very heart of Jerusalem, the holiest place in all of Jewish tradition. To the horror and outrage of pious Jews, even the priests charged with the sacred duty of conducting daily sacrifices to Yahweh "neglected their duties to join the games."[38]

All of these practices were deeply offensive to the strict fundamentalists of Judaism, a faction that has come to be known as the Hasidim ("Pious Ones"). They detested the hedonistic ways of Hellenism, including the promiscuous display of the naked human body and the idle distractions of the theater and the stadium. They condemned their fellow Jews who embraced the Greek way of life as "violators of the Law" and vilified them as "evildoers against the Covenant."³⁹ The bitter struggle between the assimilationists and the fundamentalists of ancient Judea has been called "a 'Kulturkampf' between Judaism and Hellenism."⁴⁰

"Kulturkampf," of course, is a term commonly used nowadays in its rough English translation—"culture war"—to refer to any struggle between two warring value systems and ways of life.⁴¹ Just as the "pro-life" and "pro-choice" movements confront each other across the front lines of the culture war in the modern world, the pious Jews of antiquity who insisted on circumcision as a sacred rite confronted the assimilated Jews who chose to forgo the old ways. And so, as we shall come to see, "culture war" is equally useful in describing what was really at stake in the apocalyptic tradition and, especially, the book of Revelation.

But the tensions in the Jewish world of the second century B.C.E. were not merely the result of a clash between assimilationists and fundamentalists. The pagan king who ruled over Judea, as the ancient chroniclers described him, was a monster whose excesses eventually sparked a war of national liberation under the leadership of a man called Judah Maccabee, "Judah the Hammer." Here, for the first time in recorded history, we are able to glimpse the remarkable power of the apocalyptic idea to move otherwise ordinary men and women to offer their lives, sometimes as soldiers and sometimes as martyrs, in the name of God.

O n the death of Alexander the Great, his vast empire was divided up among his generals. The land of Judea, a small but strategically significant province that served as a land bridge between Europe, Asia, and Africa, passed under the control of the Syrian dynasty founded by one of Alexander's generals, a man called Seleucus. Starting in 175 B.C.E., the reigning king of the Seleucid dynasty was a particularly vile and hateful man called Antiochus IV. By an accident of history, as we shall shortly see, he will figure crucially in the book of Daniel, the only apocalypse in the Hebrew Bible and a text that served as one of the "models and sources" for the book of Revelation.

One of the glories of Hellenism was its open-mindedness toward religious beliefs and practices, a core value that characterized the world of classical paganism. But Antiochus IV was an aberration among the monarchs of the Greco-Roman world, an arbitrary and impulsive autocrat who sought to suppress the unruly Jewish fundamentalists in Judea by force of arms. He called himself Antiochus Epiphanes ("Antiochus the Manifestation of God"), but his excesses against the Jewish people were so much at odds with the tolerance that Hellenism displayed toward the religions of conquered people that he earned himself the moniker Antiochus Epimanes—Antiochus the Madman.

Antiochus was troubled by the unsettled state of affairs in Judea for mostly geopolitical reasons. The culture war among Jewish factions was approaching a state of civil war, and the Jewish fundamentalists were seeking to ally themselves with a rival pagan monarch, the pharaoh of Egypt, the descendant of yet another general who had served Alexander. When Antiochus finally marched into Judea on his way to Egypt in 168 B.C.E., his strategic objective was to secure his southern flank in Judea before making war on the meddlesome pharaoh. But he resolved to restore law and order in Judea by rooting out the practice of Judaism through a series of hateful and humiliating decrees.

Under Antiochus, the fundamental rites of Judaism—circumcision, the observance of the Sabbath, and the dietary laws of kashrut—were criminalized. The worship of the God of Israel was forbidden, and an image of Zeus, the high god of the Greek pantheon, was installed in the inner sanctum of the Temple of Yahweh at Jerusalem. Thus, we are told, a pig was offered as a sacrifice on the altar of Yahweh, the high priest was ordered to eat its flesh, and its offal was poured over the scrolls of the Torah. All over the land of Judea, anyone who refused to turn over the Torah for public burning was subject to arrest, torture, and execution by the death squads of the Syrian king.

"They were whipped with rods and their bodies were torn to pieces," reports Josephus, the Jewish general-turned-historian who eventually put himself in service to the Roman Empire in the first century of the Common Era, "and they were crucified while they were still alive and breathed."[42]

Such atrocities sparked the Maccabean Revolt, an uprising against Syrian occupation and oppression led by the celebrated Judah Maccabee. Under Judah's command, the Jewish resistance fought on two fronts, one a war of national liberation against the Syrian army, and the other a struggle against the assimilated Jews whom they regarded as both apostates and collaborators. Among the exploits of the Maccabees, for example, was the forcible circumcision of Jewish males, infant or adult, who had neglected the ancient rite that symbolized the covenant with the God of Israel. The armies of Antiochus were finally defeated in 164 B.C.E., and the Maccabees established the first independent Jewish state since the last Jewish king had been sent into captivity in Babylon.

Along with acts of martyrdom and feats of arms, the Jewish people of the second century B.C.E. offered another kind of resistance to the foreign army of occupation and their native collaborators. A few charismatic and visionary authors began to tell tales that were intended to strengthen the resolve of the "Pious Ones" who refused to compromise their true belief. They draped the stories in veils of mystery, and they conjured up strange visions, some terrible and some tantalizing. And they spiced the stories they told with a longing for—and a sure promise of—a day of bloody revenge against their enemies.

The texts that were composed during the days of the Maccabean Revolt "are born out of a sense that the world is out of joint," according to historian John J. Collins, one of the leading scholars in the modern study of apocalypticism, and they were "written to exhort and console."[43] Indeed, the tales of revenge and redemption in the end-times can be seen as a tool of propaganda in both a shooting war and a culture war. And, as we shall see, they were the earliest stirrings of the apocalyptic tradition in Judaism and Christianity that would one day result in the writing of Revelation.

Ω

One repository of the early apocalyptic tradition is the book of Daniel. The texts that are collected and preserved in Daniel are set in Babylon in the early sixth century B.C.E., some four centuries before the Maccabean Revolt. The monarch who is depicted in Daniel is Nebuchadnezzar, the Babylonian emperor who conquered Judah, destroyed the Temple at Jerusalem, and carried the Jewish royals, priests, and gentry into exile. But scholars agree that the various stories in the book of Daniel were actually composed and compiled in the second century B.C.E., and Nebuchadnezzar would have been recognized by the original readers of the book of Daniel as a stand-in for Antiochus the Madman.

"If the author wished to hearten the faithful in the time of affliction and persecution, what better medium could he have chosen?" writes H. H. Rowley.[44]

"They were entertainment, as well as charged with a message, and so they could easily be remembered and passed from mouth to mouth."[45]

Indeed, a certain fairytale quality suffuses the book of Daniel. Among the exiles in the court of Nebuchadnezzar, we are told, are young Jewish men of noble blood, "fair to look on, and skillful in all wisdom," and Daniel is the fairest and wisest of them all.[46] When the pagan king threatens to put Daniel to death unless he reveals the meaning of a dream so mysterious that it has baffled all the royal astrologers, enchanters, and magicians, Daniel prays to the God of Israel for a revelation. God grants Daniel's prayer and discloses the meaning of the dream.

"Blessed be the name of God, for wisdom and might are his," says a thankful Daniel. "He revealeth the deep and secret things, he knoweth what is in the darkness."[47]

The "secret things" that God reveals to Daniel are quite at odds with what the other biblical authors say about the fate of the Chosen People. Elsewhere in the Bible, as we have seen, God himself is identified as the one who sends Nebuchadnezzar and other foreign invaders to afflict the children of Israel, and all because of their own apostasy and harlotry. Here and now a new idea enters the Bible: the Jewish people are afflicted not by God on high but by evildoers on earth, and God will one day rescue them from their oppressors by sending a savior to defeat the enemy and establish an eternal kingdom of divine peace and perfection for the pious Jews who remain faithful to the Torah.

"Then the holy ones of the Most High will receive the kingdom," Daniel is told by a heavenly emissary, "and possess the kingdom forever—forever and ever."[48]

The idea is memorably expressed the "night visions" that Daniel describes. Four nightmarish beasts, "dreadful and terrible," crawl out of the sea and range over the earth, devouring all in their path. God, depicted here as the "Ancient of Days," a white-haired king on his celestial throne, attended by angelic minions numbering a "thousand thousands," bestirs himself to defeat the last and most dreadful of the beasts, a monster with ten horns, iron teeth, and brass claws: "And as I looked," affirms Daniel, "the beast was slain, and its body destroyed and given over to be burned with fire." At last, a celestial savior—"one like unto a son of man"—is sent to earth on a cloud. "And there was given him dominion, and glory, and a kingdom," writes Daniel, "an everlasting dominion, which shall not pass away."[49]

All of these motifs—God enthroned in heaven, the angels who serve him, and the self-evidently symbolic monsters who stalk the earth—will be reworked and repurposed in the book of Revelation. The book of Daniel is perhaps the single most important of the various "models and sources" that the author of Revelation seems to have invoked in his own writings. And that's exactly why we must try to understand the methods and meanings of the book of Daniel before we can hope to solve the even deeper mysteries of Revelation.

Ω

The key to Daniel—and *all* of the apocalyptic writings, including the book of Revelation—is found in the simple fact that its night visions are *not* to be taken literally. Indeed, Daniel himself says so.

"The vision of my mind alarmed me," he writes. "I approached one of the attendants and asked him the true meaning of all this."[50] And the angelic "attendant" patiently explains that the beasts are, in fact, purely symbolic. "This is what he said," explains Daniel. "These great beasts, four in number, mean four kingdoms will arise out of the earth."[51] The fourth kingdom, symbolized in the vision by a beast with ten horns, will endure through the reign of ten powerful kings, but it will finally be destroyed. "And the kingdom and the dominion shall be given to the people of the saints of the Most High"—that is, the Jewish people, or, at least, the "holy ones" among them who have remained faithful to the Covenant.[52]

Once we are given permission to read the book of Daniel as a symbolic rather than literal account of history—and, in fact, we are instructed to do so by the author himself—new and illuminating meanings emerge from the otherwise mysterious text. Indeed, the book of Daniel speaks directly to the experience of the Jewish people who were confronting both the excesses of Antiochus the Madman and the seductions of Hellenism at the time when the book was first written and first read—the very men and women whom the author seeks to "exhort and console." To put it bluntly, the book of Daniel, like much else in the Bible, is propaganda, not prophecy.

Thus, for example, Daniel refuses to eat the rich food and fine wine offered by the court chamberlain of the pagan emperor, and contents himself with a daily ration of beans and water—an example of right conduct for Jews who were being invited (or compelled) to break the laws of kashrut. When Nebuchadnezzar decrees that a golden idol be erected and worshipped, the readers of Daniel were meant to think of Antiochus, who defiled the Holy of Holies in the Temple at Jerusalem by installing an idol of Zeus. And when Daniel's three companions—Meshach, Shadrach, and Abednego—choose death by fire rather than bow down to the idol, they are spared from suffering by a guardian angel who joins them in the furnace, a consoling thought to any Jewish man or woman facing the tortures that are described by Josephus or the author of the book of Maccabees.

"Lo, I see four men, walking in the midst of the fire, and they have no hurt," declares the pagan monarch, who is scared out of his wits by what he beholds, "and the appearance of the fourth is like a son of the gods."[53]

Above all, Daniel holds out the promise that the Jewish people will be relieved of *all* suffering because history itself, as we know it, will come to an end. "Now I am come to make thee understand what shall befall thy people in the end of days," says one of the heavenly messengers who grant Daniel a series of revelations. A cunning and deceitful king "shall stand up against the prince of peace," says one messenger, "but he shall be broken," although the instrument of his defeat shall be "no human hand." After a final period of tribulation—"a time of trouble such as there never was"—the archangel Michael will descend from heaven to make war on the last of the evil kings, "and at that time, thy people shall be delivered."[54]

Thus does Daniel put a new spin on the old theology of the Hebrew Bible. Daniel's night visitors readily concede that God afflicts the Jewish people for their faithlessness, just as Moses had warned, but they also promise that one day God will "make reconciliation" and "bring in everlasting righteousness."[55] As if to make amends for the fact the God does nothing to prevent various oppressors from torturing and murdering their Jewish subjects, the angels hold out the prospect of a day of resurrection when the dead will be judged, and rewarded or punished appropriately.

"Many of them that sleep in the dust of the earth shall awake, some to everlasting life and some to shame and everlasting contempt," the angels promise. And, when the end of the world finally comes, it is not merely a good life on earth that awaits the worthy souls but an eternal life in heaven: "Those who are wise," the visitors assure Daniel and his readers, "shall shine like the stars for ever and ever.[56]

The newfangled ideas in the book of Daniel were meant to soothe the sufferings of Jewish men and women who lived during the Maccabean

Revolt or, at least, the most pious among them. But the scenes of resurrection, judgment, and eternal life would have been as unfamiliar and off-putting to the classical biblical prophets as the notion that God and Satan are at war for the hearts and minds of the Chosen People. Nor did these ideas come to play a commanding role in Jewish tradition, which continued to focus on the intimate relationship between the God of Israel and the Chosen People in the here and now rather than the hereafter.

But when the author of Revelation unpacked the theological baggage of the book of Daniel during the first century of the Common Era, he found fresh and powerful ways to address the sufferings of a new generation of pious men and women. They were no less estranged from the high culture of classical paganism than the victims of Antiochus had been, and they felt themselves no less at risk of persecution and death. And the first readers and hearers of Revelation responded to the new way of reading the Hebrew Bible. If the apocalyptic tradition is the "child of prophecy," the apocalyptic tradition itself is "the mother of Christianity."[57]

$$\Omega$$

Nor are the ideas of resurrection and judgment the only theological innovations that we find in the book of Daniel. Other biblical authors, for example, describe angels as not much more than celestial errand boys; indeed, "messenger" is the literal meaning of the Hebrew word (*malak*) that came to be rendered in English as "angel." The author of Daniel, by contrast, appears to borrow the idea of an elaborate hierarchy of angels directly from the Persian tradition of angelology: "Thousands upon thousands served Him," says Daniel of the heavenly court of the Ancient of Days. "Myriads upon myriads attended him."[58] And he is the first biblical author to refer to the archangels Gabriel and Michael, who will play such a prominent role in the book of Revelation and other apocalyptic writings.[59]

Daniel is also the first biblical author to use the phrase "son of man" in the paradoxical sense that will be familiar to readers of the Christian scriptures; when Daniel refers to someone as "the son of man," the prophet means to say that he is *not* the offspring of ordinary human beings. Elsewhere in the Hebrew Bible, however, the phrase is given its natural meaning; the book of Job, for example, uses "son of man" in making the point that God is incomparably greater than any mere mortal: "How much less [is] man, a worm; the son of man, a maggot."[60] For Daniel, by contrast, the "son of man" is exalted, eternal, and all-powerful: "I saw in the night visions, and, behold, one like the son of man came with the clouds, and came to the Ancient of Days, and there was given him dominion, and glory, and a kingdom, that all the peoples, nations, and languages should serve him, an everlasting dominion which shall not pass away."[61]

The book of Daniel also offers the first example in the Bible of the kind of number crunching that came to be such an obsessive practice among readers of Revelation. Daniel begins with an apparently straightforward passage from the book of Jeremiah in which the prophet predicts that the Babylonian Exile will last exactly seventy years: "After seventy years are accomplished for Babylon," God tells Jeremiah, "I will remember you, causing you to return to this place."[62] But the angel Gabriel explains to Daniel that the old prophet actually meant to say seventy *weeks* of years— that is, seventy times seven, or a total of 490 years. And, what's more, Jeremiah meant to predict not merely the end of the exile in Babylon but the end of all earthly evil and the advent of a celestial paradise: "Seventy weeks of years are decreed," reveals the archangel, "to put an end to sin, and to bring in everlasting righteousness."[63]

In fact, Daniel is told *exactly* when the sinful world will be destroyed, although the angel provides two different calculations of the end-times. Daniel is granted a vision in which it is revealed that the end will come either 1,290 or 1,335 days after "the abomination of desolation is set up."[64] The angel does not explain what is meant by "the abomination of desolation," but scholars suggest that the phrase refers to the statue of Zeus that Antiochus installed in the Temple at Jerusalem. Perhaps the author of Daniel was thinking only of the period of time that passed between the erection of the idol and the rededication of the Temple after the offending image had been removed—an event that is celebrated in the Jewish festival of Chanukah. And the fact that *two* periods of time are specified may mean that the date predicted by the first author passed uneventfully and so a scribe who came along later felt obliged to insert a second and longer period into the text.

Of course, the second date was wrong, too, at least if it was intended to mark the end of the world. But such quibbles have never mattered much to Bible readers who are searching for secret meanings in the text, then or now. After all, if biblical prophecy is "a coded message to be deciphered by the inspired interpreter," as John J. Collins puts it, then it is up to the discerning reader to break the code and reveal the hidden message. And, as we shall see, men and women have been inspired to invest endless energy and enterprise in doing so ever since.[65]

"As a prediction of the end, it was a failure," writes H. H. Rowley, "but as a powerful spiritual force it was a great success."[66]

For all of these reasons, the book of Daniel is the font of apocalyptic speculation, and its words and phrases have been mined for revelatory meanings over the last two thousand years. The Western apocalyptic tradition in its entirety has been characterized as "footnotes to the apocalyptic visions of Daniel."[67] And the so-called Little Apocalypse of the Gospels—the passages in Matthew, Mark, and Luke where Jesus describes how the world will end—has been called "a very early Christian midrash, or expansion, on the Danielic account of last events."[68]

The best measure of Daniel's stature and influence in the apocalyptic tradition is found in the book of Revelation, whose author draws from the book of Daniel more often than from any other scriptural text, Jewish or Christian. But the book of Daniel is hardly the only or even the oldest apocalypse of the ancient Jewish world. In fact, the author of Daniel may have been inspired by still older texts, and not only by the prophetic writings that are readily found in the Bible. Once we follow the author of Revelation down the rabbit hole of the apocalyptic tradition, we find ourselves in a place where the sights are curiouser and curiouser.

The starting point of the apocalyptic tradition in Judaism may well be found in a strange and unsettling collection of ancient texts called the First Book of Enoch, the oldest of which predate the book of Daniel by a half century or so.[69] All of the writings are attributed to the biblical figure of Enoch, but they were composed by various flesh-and-blood authors over a period of several centuries. Here we find "the kernel in which the essence of apocalypticism is contained," according to Italian scholar Paolo Sacchi, a specialist in apocalyptic studies, "and from which the whole tradition grows."[70]

Enoch, the father of Methuselah, figures prominently in both the apocalyptic and mystical traditions because of the mysterious circumstances of his passing as reported in a single line of text in Genesis: "And Enoch walked with God, and he was not, for God took him."[71] By an ancient and enduring tradition, the passage is understood to mean that Enoch is spared an ordinary death and is, instead, elevated to heaven while still alive. And so he came to be used as a stock character by various apocalyptic authors who imagined what "secret things" are revealed to him in the celestial realm.

The First Book of Enoch, for example, picks up and elaborates upon a lively tale about a band of randy and rebellious angels that is only briefly mentioned in the book of Genesis. The biblical account describes how the so-called sons of God (*b'nai elohim*) descend to earth in pursuit of "daughters of men" whom they have spied from heaven and thus sire a race of giants.[72] *The Book of Watchers* goes on to reveal that the fallen angels are, in fact, the minions of the Devil and "the cause of all the evil upon the earth."[73]

Significantly, the author of *The Book of Watchers* uses the term "watcher" to identify the celestial figures who are elsewhere called angels, a turn of phrase that also appears in the book of Daniel: "I saw in visions of my head upon my bed," writes Daniel, "and, behold, a watcher and a holy one came down from heaven."[74] Here is yet another point of linkage between Daniel and the other writings in the apocalyptic tradition: nowhere else in the Hebrew Bible is an angel called a "watcher." And here, too, the author chooses language that is eerie and even scary: the watchers are spies and provocateurs rather than guardians.

The watchers are guilty of more than crimes of passion, or so Enoch discovers. They also reveal "heavenly secrets" to the human race, including "charms and spells" for working feats of magic, "the art of making up the eyes and of beautifying the eyelids" for purposes of seduction, and the craft of fashioning "swords and daggers and shields and breastplates" for use in making war. God sends the archangel Raphael to bind the chief of the defiant angels, a demonic figure here called Azazel, and cast him into a pit in the desert until "the great day of judgment" when "he may be hurled into the fire."[75] But the damage is already done.

"The world was changed," goes one passage in *The Book of Watchers* that must have resonated with the life experience of its first readers, the "Pious Ones" who were fighting a culture war against Hellenism. "And there was great impiety, and much fornication, and they went astray, and all their ways became corrupt."[76]

Another tale in the first book of Enoch, *The Animal Apocalypse*, surely resonated in a very different but equally powerful way with the same readership. All of the figures in the tale are depicted as animals: Adam, for example, appears in the guise of a white bull, and the rebellious angels sire not human offspring but elephants, camels, and asses. At the climax of *The Animal Apocalypse,* the evildoers on earth are vanquished by an army of "small lambs" who grow horns—the leader of the flock is the lamb with the biggest horn—and they go into battle with a sword bestowed upon them by "the Lord of the sheep."[77] The elaborate and highly fanciful allegory would have been clear to readers in Judea in the second century before the Common Era: "The lamb with the big horn is clearly Judas Maccabee," explains John J. Collins, "and the context is the Maccabean revolt."[78]

The Book of the Watchers and *The Animal Apocalypse* are only two of the texts that have been gathered together in the first book of Enoch. Other apocalyptic writings in the same collection include *The Astronomical Book, The Book of Dreams,* and *The Apocalypse of Weeks,* all equally exotic to any reader whose experience of Judaism is based on the Torah and the Talmud. Two additional collections, known as second and third books of Enoch, also contain apocalyptic writings, and so do many of the other works that are characterized as Pseudepigrapha—the Apocalypse of Abraham, the Testament of the Patriarchs, the Book of Jubilees, and the Third Sibylline Oracles, among many others.

All of these apocalyptic texts, as we have already noted, were wholly excluded from the Hebrew Bible itself. In fact, they represent the imaginings and yearnings of men and women who placed themselves at the outer fringes of the Jewish community and sometimes, as in the case of the community at Qumran, far beyond it. And yet these texts are the place where some of the most familiar figures in both Judaism and Christianity were first fleshed out, including the divine redeemer known as the Messiah and the divine adversary known as Satan. Indeed, the apocalyptic texts were the alchemist's crucible in which the raw materials extracted from the Bible were refined and recoined into something shiny and new.

Ω

The biblical version of the Messiah, for example, is hardly the exalted figure that he would become in the apocalyptic traditions of both Judaism and Christianity. His title is derived from the Hebrew word *mashiach,* which literally means "anointed one"—that is, someone over whose head oil has been poured in a ritual of sanctification that was used to initiate a man into the priesthood or to crown a king. For the authors of the Hebrew Bible, a "messiah" is nothing more than a human being who holds some high office or who has been charged with some special duty.

Thus, for example, Aaron, the first high priest of Israel, is anointed, and so are the first two kings of Israel, Saul and David. But, according to the Bible, a man need not be a king or a high priest, or even a worshipper of the God of Israel, to merit the lofty title of "anointed one." As we have seen, the Bible also refers to the pagan emperor of Persia as an "anointed one"—a messiah—simply because he succeeded in defeating the rival pagan empire of Babylon and thus restored the exiled Jewish people to their homeland. For that reason, if the author of Revelation had confined himself to the Hebrew Bible, he would never have given us the exalted figure of the Messiah who is celebrated so magnificently in Handel's oratorio.

Indeed, the more familiar notion of the Messiah as a celestial savior is given its first and fullest expression only in the apocalyptic writings, where it also comes to be fused with the divine redeemer who is known, rather paradoxically, as "Son of Man." For Daniel, the "one like a son of man" and the "one anointed" are apparently two different figures; the first is a celestial figure who is granted an eternal kingdom by God, but the second is a mortal prince who shall "be cut off, and be no more."[79] By contrast, *The Apocalypse of Weeks,* one of the writings in the first book of Enoch, describes the Son of Man as precisely the kind of judge, redeemer, and savior who came to be identified in both Jewish and Christian tradition as *the* Messiah:

"And [the people of God] had great joy because the name of that Son of Man had been revealed to them," goes a passage in the first book of Enoch. "And he sat on the throne of his glory, and the whole judgment was given to the Son of Man, and he will cause the sinners to pass away and be destroyed from the face of the earth. And from then on there will be nothing corruptible."[80]

Even after "Messiah" took on its meaning as a God-sent savior, the varieties of Judaism as practiced in the ancient world did not agree on who the Messiah would be or exactly what he would do. Some apocalyptic sources envision *two* Messiahs, one from the tribe of Judah and another from the tribe of Levi, one a king and the other a priest. Nor could they agree on how long the earthly reign of the Messiah would last. One of the Dead Sea Scrolls, for example, envisions the messianic era as nothing more than a forty-year war against the Roman occupiers of Judea, and an apocalyptic text called *4 Ezra* puts the reign of the Messiah at four hundred years, after which the whole world would come to an end.

Satan, too, as we have seen, is relegated to the role of divine prosecutor in the Hebrew Bible, and he is elevated to the rank of Prince of Darkness only in the apocalyptic writings. Indeed, Satan is imagined to be the demonic counterpart to God, a powerful and willful figure whom the Messiah would fight and defeat in the end-times. The satanic archvillain is known by many names in the apocalyptic texts—Asmodeus, Azazel, Mastema, Belial (or sometimes Beliar), and many more besides—but all of them came to be understood as one and the same as the malefactor whom the author of Revelation later calls "that old serpent, called the Devil and Satan."

So the colorful cast of characters that will later show up in the pages of Revelation is neither wholly invented by its author nor wholly faithful to the biblical texts that he knew so well. Rather, they were all stock figures in the apocalyptic subculture of ancient Judaism. And they were not meant merely to amuse or thrill or frighten the readers and hearers of the oldest apocalyptic texts. Rather, as we have seen, the characters in the apocalyptic drama were meant to inspire ordinary men and women to serve as good soldiers, both in the culture war against classical paganism and in the war of national liberation that was fought against the pagan invaders of the ancient Jewish homeland. For pious Jews and patriotic Jews alike, then, the apocalyptic writings of antiquity were the literature of resistance—but it was resistance of a very different kind than the first readers of Revelation were encouraged to offer to their Roman persecutors.

Ω

Josephus shows us that the Jewish people adopted a variety of tactics in responding to the temptations of Hellenism and the threats of Roman imperialism. Some Jews, like Josephus himself, made a profitable peace with Rome. Other Jews, like the Zealots, took up arms against Rome in the name of God and country. And a few Jews, whom Josephus calls the "Essenes," retreated into the wilderness to await the end of the world, when the armies of God would go to war against the armies of Satan.

Some scholars identify the Essenes with the "apocalyptic community" at Qumran, the site where the Dead Sea Scrolls were discovered. Their urgent expectations are set down in the so-called *War Scroll,* which envisions a final battle between the "sons of light" and the "sons of darkness," captained on one side by the archangel Michael and on the other side by the demonic figure known as Belial.[81] Here is yet another example of how the raw material of the Bible was mined by the apocalyptic authors for new and revolutionary meanings—"Belial" appears nowhere in the Bible itself except as an abstract noun "whose meaning is probably 'worthlessness,'" but he is conjured up in the apocalyptic tradition as "the supreme adversary of God."[82]

Still, we simply do not know whether the authors of Daniel, the first book of Enoch, and the Dead Sea Scrolls were members of the same movement in early Judaism—or whether they were worthy of being called a "movement" at all. Scholars can only speculate whether the "Pious Ones" (*hasidim*) who are mentioned in the Book of Maccabees, the "Wise" (*maskilim*) who are mentioned in Daniel, and the Essenes who are mentioned by Josephus are different names for the same people. Thus, for example, the Dead Sea Scrolls were once confidently ascribed to the Essenes, but more careful scholars refer only to "the Qumran sect" and wonder out loud if and how they were linked to the other apocalyptic communities of ancient Judaism.[83]

What they have in common, however, is clear. All of these men and women felt estranged from—and, in a real sense, betrayed by—the world in which they found themselves. Even when they were not prevented from practicing the pure and rigorous strain of Judaism that they embraced, they felt insulted and injured when their fellow Jews failed to do the same. And so, when they contemplated a Jewish king who took the name of a pagan conqueror, or a Jewish high priest who schooled youngsters in how to compete naked in Greek athletic games, or any number of Jewish parents who neglected to circumcise their sons, their true belief instructed them that they were beholding yet another manifestation of what the Bible condemns as "the abomination of desolation."

For such men and women, then, the apocalyptic idea was both a balm and a liquor. Today you are oppressed and persecuted, they are told by the apocalyptic texts, but tomorrow your oppression and persecution will end because the whole world will end. And, what's more, they are encouraged to look forward not only to relief from suffering—a messianic hero and his army of holy warriors who will defeat the demonic arch-villain and his army of evildoers—but also revenge against those who made them suffer in the first place. Thus, the end of the world is the occasion for a resurrection of the dead, the Day of Judgment, and the meting out of punishments and rewards.

Above all, the apocalyptic tradition was addressed to an audience of men and women who regarded themselves as outsiders and victims even if they were not actually suffering oppression or persecution at any given time and place. Apocalyptic writings reflect "the experience of alienation [in] times of crisis," according to a certain conventional wisdom in scholarship, but John J. Collins reminds us that "alienation, and crises, may be of many kinds," including "culture shock," "social powerlessness," and "national trauma."[84] By the first century of the Common Era, all three kinds of crisis were afflicting the Jewish world where the apocalypses were being written and read, including those Jewish men and women who would soon begin to call themselves Christians.

Ω

The culture war that began during the Maccabean Revolt never really abated. The last Jewish king to carry the blood of the Maccabees in his veins, Alexander Jannaeus (103–76 B.C.E.), was an enthusiastic Hellenist who became the target of rioting by the religious fundamentalists in Judea, and he turned his army on the most pious of his own Jewish subjects in a campaign that lasted six years and cost fifty thousand lives. On his death, the various rivals for kingship courted the favor of the Roman Empire, the latest superpower of the pagan world. But Rome resolved to bring law and order to Judea once and for all, and a Roman legion marched into Jerusalem in 63 B.C.E. Thus did the stars come into alignment for the unlikely chain of events that would result in nothing less revolutionary than the reinvention of Judaism and the invention of Christianity.

At first, Rome was content to administer the Jewish homeland through a series of puppet rulers, the most famous of whom was Herod, a man of Arab blood whose family had been forcibly converted to Judaism under the Maccabees. Herod was a good Hellenist who remodeled the Temple of Yahweh at Jerusalem in the classical style of Greco-Roman architecture and decorated the towns and cities of Judea with stadiums and gymnasia. But when Herod died—and Judea once again fell into chaos—a Roman general marched into Jerusalem, and Judea came under the direct rule of imperial Rome as a newly established province.

As during the Maccabean Revolt, the Jews who resented the invasion of a foreign army and the Jews who resented the invasion of a foreign way of life tended to overlap. The Jewish resistance was dismissed by the Roman authorities as "bandits" and "brigands," but they called themselves "Zealots," thus invoking the heroic example of the biblical heroes who were "zealous for the Law and the Covenant." Again like the Maccabees, they took up arms against both the army of the occupation and the assimilated Jews who collaborated with the Romans. The Sicarii ("dagger-men"), for example, were urban terrorists who targeted Jewish collaborators for assassination in public places. And the apocalyptic ideas and images that were first written down during the Maccabean Revolt found a new readership in the latest generation of Jewish freedom fighters.

Perhaps the most potent (and poignant) of these apocalyptic ideals was the longing for a Messiah, the liberator who would be sent by the God of Israel to defeat the forces of evil and bring peace, security, and sovereignty to the Jewish people. Josephus may have been mindful of the passage in the book of Daniel where "one like the son of man" is granted "dominion, and glory, and a kingdom" when he describes the power of the apocalyptic idea during the Jewish resistance against Rome.[85] "What more than all else incited them to the war," writes the ancient Jewish historian, "was an ambiguous oracle, likewise found in their sacred scriptures, to the effect that at that time one from their country would be become ruler of the world."[86]

Josephus, writing from the perspective of a collaborator with the Romans, was contemptuous and dismissive of the ideals that motivated the Jewish partisans. "Deceivers and impostors" is how Josephus describes the self-styled prophets "who, under the pretense of divine inspiration fostering revolutionary changes, persuaded the multitude to act like madmen."[87] He derisively notes that one such prophet, known only as "the Egyptian," persuaded his followers—"about 30,000 dupes," as Josephus puts it—that he could and would cause the walls of Jerusalem to collapse upon his command.[88] But, almost inadvertently, Josephus also allows us to see exactly how powerful and provocative these ideas could be.

To rally the defenders of Jerusalem during the final battle of the Jewish War in 70 C.E., for example, the leaders of the Zealots and the other factions resorted to the same rhetoric that had worked so well during the Maccabean Revolt. "A number of hireling prophets had been put up in recent days by the party chiefs to deceive the people by exhorting them to await help from God," writes Josephus, "and so reduce the number of deserters and buoy up with hope those who were above fear and anxiety." When the Roman soldiers set fire to the colonnade of the Temple where some six thousand men, women, and children were sheltering, the most ardent among them chose to martyr themselves: "Some flung themselves out of the flames to their death, others perished in the blaze; of that vast number there escaped not one."[89]

The Jewish War ended in the utter defeat of the armed resistance against Rome. Yet again, the Temple was destroyed, and yet again the Jewish people were sent into exile. Over the next century or so, new Jewish free-dom fighters—and new claimants to the crown of the Messiah—struggled against the Roman occupation, but none of them were victorious. The last major war of national liberation against Rome was fought under the lead-ership of a heroic guerilla commander named Simon Bar Kochba, who was hailed as "King Messiah" by Rabbi Akiva, one of the most revered of the ancient rabbinical scholars. But Bar Kochba, too, was defeated by the Romans. His torture and death in 135 c.e. was proof to his Jewish follow-ers that he could not be the Messiah after all: "It will only be demonstrated by success," explained one medieval rabbi, "and this is the truth."[90] And so the messianic idea in ancient Judaism began to turn from an urgent expec-tation into an attenuated and fatalistic longing.

"Grass will grow in your jawbones, Akiva ben Yosef," one pragmatic rabbi is quoted in the Talmud as saying to Rabbi Akiva, "and the Messiah will not have appeared."[91]

Not all of the self-styled messiahs of the early years of the Common Era, however, can be so easily written off. Among the most charismatic and visionary figures of the apocalyptic tradition in Judaism was one whose mission and message were destined to change the history of the world. He, too, allowed his followers to believe that he was the Messiah, and he prom-ised them that the prophecies of Daniel would soon be fulfilled.

His name was Yeshua bar Yosef but he is known to the world as Jesus.

The historical Jesus, in fact, "is best understood as a first-century Jewish apocalypticist," according to contemporary Bible scholar Bart D. Ehrman. An "apocalypticist," as the term is used by scholars, means someone who embraces most or all of the strange new ideas that we find in the book of Daniel and the apocalyptic writings that did not make it into the Bible: "Jesus thought that the history of the world would come to a screeching halt, that God would intervene in the affairs of this planet, overthrow the forces of evil in a cosmic act of judgment, and establish his own utopian Kingdom here on earth," writes Ehrman in *Jesus: Apocalyptic Prophet of the New Millennium*. "And this was going to happen with Jesus' own generation."[92]

The idea that Jesus embraced the same urgent and dire expectations that we find in the first book of Enoch, Daniel, and Revelation has always been unsettling to some Christians. Indeed, most contemporary Bible scholars are more comfortable in regarding Jesus as a kind and gentle moral teacher who taught his followers how to lead decent lives here on earth rather than one of those prophets of doom who are depicted in *New Yorker* cartoons with a signboard that declares: "The End Is Near!" When cutting-edge Bible critics argue that we ought to understand Jesus as a crypto-communist, a proto-feminist, or a gay activist, they are seeking to paint over the portrait of Jesus that we actually find in the New Testament.

A plain reading of the Gospels, however, is the best evidence that Jesus believed and taught that the world was coming an imminent end. "Truly, I say to you," says Jesus in the Gospel of Mark, "there are some standing here who will not taste death before they see that the kingdom of God has come with power."[93] Taken literally, the passage openly and confidently predicts that the events described in the apocalyptic writings will take place within the lifetimes of his contemporaries. The same notion is found in the letters of Paul, which are among the earliest of all Christian texts and the ones whose flesh-and-blood author is most confidently identified by scholars.

"For the Lord himself will descend from heaven with a cry of command, with the archangel's call, and with the sound of the trumpet of God," writes Paul in the First Letter to the Thessalonians. "And the dead in Christ will rise first; then we who are alive, who are left, shall be caught up together with them in the clouds to meet the Lord in the air; and so we shall always be with the Lord."[94]

Indeed, the suggestion that Jesus was a believer in the apocalyptic idea is obliquely confirmed in the historical record. By a tradition common to both Judaism and Christianity, for example, it was held that the Messiah would be a direct descendant of King David—"a shoot out of the stock of Jesse," according to a potent phrase from the prophecies of Isaiah.[95] The Romans, mindful of the tradition, regarded the mere claim of Davidic blood as a claim to Jewish kingship. In fact, the Tenth Legion of the Roman army of occupation in Judea remained under standing orders from four successive emperors "to hunt out and execute any Jew who claimed to be a descendant of King David."[96]

And so, when Paul declares that Jesus "was made of the seed of David, according to the flesh,"[97] and when Matthew reports that the Romans crucified Jesus because he claimed to be "King of the Jews"[98]—a political rather than a religious offense under Roman law—their accounts are wholly consistent with what we know from sources outside the Bible about the messianic beliefs of the ancient Jewish world. And when Jesus and his disciples are shown to use the resonant words and phrases that appear in the prophetic and apocalyptic texts, they are speaking a coded language that their Jewish followers would have clearly understood.

The debate over whether Jesus is properly regarded as an apocalyptic prophet began in earnest in the opening years of the twentieth century with the writings of Albert Schweitzer, who may be better remembered today for his medical missionary work in Africa or even his expertise in the music of Bach than for his pioneering research into the life of the historical Jesus. But the earliest stirrings of the same argument go back to the very beginnings of Christianity. Nor was it merely a dispute over some abstract point of theology. The fact that the world did not end when Jesus promised it would meant that "the Church, of necessity, had to come to terms with its own foundational prophecy," according to contemporary Bible scholar Paula Fredriksen.[99]

At the very moment when the first Christians were struggling with the failure of the world to "end on time," as Fredriksen puts it, the church was suddenly confronted with a new and startling document in which all of these tensions and contradictions were writ large. Its author boldly claims to have been granted a vision by Jesus himself. His vision is populated with characters that come directly out of the pages of the Hebrew Bible and the Jewish apocalyptic texts. He portrays Jesus as a messianic warrior-king reigning over an earthly realm. And, like Jesus and Paul, he insists that the end of the world is nigh: "Surely, I come quickly," says Jesus at the very end of the author's vision.[100]

That highly provocative and problematic document, of course, is the book of Revelation.

Three

The History of a Delusion

And I went unto the angel, and said unto him, Give me the little book.
And he said unto me, Take it, and eat it up; and it shall make thy belly
bitter, but it shall be in thy mouth sweet as honey.
REVELATION 10:9

By a long and cherished tradition in Christianity, the author of the
book of Revelation has been identified as John, son of Zebedee, the
presumed author of the Fourth Gospel and, by yet another tradition,
the so-called beloved disciple of Jesus. "The Apocalypse of the Apostle
John the Evangelist" is one of several titles that appear on various ancient
manuscripts of Revelation. Although the question of who actually wrote
Revelation has been a matter of hot controversy since the book first began
to circulate in the earliest Christian communities of the Roman empire,
some otherwise secular scholars still piously refer to the author of Revelation as "Saint John."

As it turns out, we can discern a great deal more about the author of Revelation than most other biblical authors, Jewish or Christian. We know that
he regarded himself as a special favorite of God—and, at the same time, a
victim of persecution by a few of his fellow Christians and the whole of the
pagan world in which he lived. He probably worked as a kind of freelance
prophet, wandering from town to town throughout Asia Minor, delivering
his strange visions and strict admonitions to whomever would gather and listen, and relying on their hospitality to fill his belly and to provide a place to
lay his head at night. And he plainly nursed a bitter grudge against a couple
of rival preachers whom he regarded as so unforgivably lax in their Christian

beliefs and practices that he condemned them not only for spiritual error but also for acts of apostasy and even harlotry.

Remarkably, we can come up with an even more detailed and nuanced profile of the man who wrote Revelation. He was probably born in Judea, and he may have been an eyewitness to one of the great and terrible moments in ancient history—the defeat of the Jewish partisans known as the Zealots by a Roman army in 70 C.E., the destruction of the Temple at Jerusalem, and the dispersion of the Jewish people. His native tongue was probably Aramaic, a Semitic language that replaced Hebrew as the lingua franca in the Jewish homeland in antiquity, and he never really mastered Greek, the international language of civilized men and women in the classical pagan world. And, perhaps most remarkable of all, he was almost surely a Jew by birth, upbringing, and education, a fact that casts an unaccustomed and ironic light on a text that has been embraced by the most zealous of Christians over the last two thousand years.

For many readers of Revelation, as we shall come to see, such biographical details are awkward, embarrassing, and wholly beside the point. The author's Jewish roots—and the linkages to Jewish texts and traditions that abound in the text of Revelation—are at odds with the crucial role the book has come to play in Christian fundamentalism. And, by the deepest of ironies, a great many readers over the ages have succeeded in convincing themselves that the author of Revelation was a benighted soul who failed to grasp the actual meanings of the visions that he beheld and described so vividly.

To the author himself, for example, the "beast" whose name is symbolized by the number 666 was almost surely a flesh-and-blood Roman emperor who lived and died in the first century of the Common Era— but generation upon generation of subsequent readers of Revelation insist that he was simply and flatly wrong. How else to explain the fact that the "beast" identified by the alphanumeric code 666 has been seen as one or another figure in a whole rogue's gallery of malefactors, ranging from Muhammad in the Middle Ages to Napoleon in the nineteenth century to Mussolini in the twentieth century, and countless others in between?

Yet Revelation is not quite as mysterious as it seems. Scholarship, both ancient and modern, allows us to catch a glimpse of the man who composed the strange text, the world in which he lived and worked, the passions that burned so hotly in his heart and mind, and the true beliefs that he meant to instill in his first readers and hearers. Above all, it is possible to penetrate the enigmatic text and extract the coded meanings that are so deeply enciphered in the book of Revelation.

As we move forward in history, we will see that Revelation has been reread and reinterpreted in startling and even shocking ways over the centuries, and never more so than in our own times. If the author of Revelation had been granted an accurate vision of the distant future, surely he would have been appalled not only by the plain fact that the end of the world was *not* near but also by what would become of his "little book" in the hands of popes and kings, grand inquisitors and church reformers, messianic pretenders and self-appointed prophets—or, for that matter, best-selling novelists like the authors of the Left Behind series, televangelists like Pat Robertson and Jerry Falwell, or a president like Ronald Reagan.

To measure how far the book of Revelation has strayed from its original uses and meanings—and to appreciate how the text has been reinterpreted and misinterpreted over the last twenty centuries—we need a benchmark: Who actually composed the book of Revelation? Where did he come from, and where did he wander? What did he know, and what did he believe? And what did he hope to achieve by setting down the extraordinary visions that we find in the "little book" that he left behind?

One of the identifying characteristics of an apocalypse is what scholars call "pseudonymity." That is, most apocalyptic texts are written by flesh-and-blood authors who conceal their own identities behind the names of revered biblical figures. Thus, for example, the "false writings" of the Pseudepigrapha include works ranging from *The Apocalypse of Adam* to *The Apocalypse of the Virgin Mary*, none of which were actually written by their named authors. From its first appearance, in fact, Revelation has been regarded with skepticism by some readers who have dared to wonder out loud whether it was really written by St. John the Evangelist.

Of course, the same question can be asked about all but a few books of the Bible, including both its Jewish and Christian versions. Some Bible readers, for example, are still shocked to learn that scholars no longer believe that Moses wrote the Five Books of Moses, as the first five books of the Hebrew Bible are known in Jewish usage, or that any of the Gospels were written by the apostles whose names appear in their titles. Indeed, the bulk of the Jewish scriptures and a good deal of the Christian scriptures can be regarded as "false writings" in the sense that they were not actually written by the authors who are credited in their titles.

Exactly how the books of the Bible came to be written and named has always been the subject of much argument and speculation. One theory, for example, is that the author was followed around by a dutiful secretary who took notes and then polished up what the great man said, or that the author actually sat down and dictated to the secretary. That's exactly how the book of Jeremiah supposedly came into existence according to an explanation that we find in the Hebrew Bible itself: "Then Jeremiah called Baruch the son of Neriah, and Baruch wrote from the mouth of Jeremiah all the words of the Lord, which He had spoken unto him, upon a roll of a book."[1]

Another theory holds that all but a few books of the Bible are composed of writings from several different sources, all of which were collected and compiled at some point in history by one or more editors or "redactors." The raw material consists of myths, legends, folktales, poems, prayers, and songs—the so-called oral tradition—but also chronicles, genealogies, law codes, and works of biography and autobiography. But the received text of the Bible is the work product of the editors who stitched them together and polished them up. A variant of the same theory is that some or all of these redactions were actually composed by several individuals, or even several generations, all working together in what scholars loosely call a "school" or a "circle" or a "tradition."

Of course, a few scholars are still willing to argue that some biblical writings were authored by a single gifted human being, man or woman, who put pen to paper (or, perhaps more accurately, a goose quill to a sheet of papyrus) and composed an immortal work of literature in exactly the same manner as Dante or Shakespeare, Mark Twain or Isaac Bashevis Singer. The biblical life story of David as we find it in the book of Samuel may be the work of a writer of genius known in biblical scholarship as the Court Historian, or so it has been suggested, and many of the most beloved and compelling stories in the book of Genesis may have been written by an even more accomplished author known as "J." And, famously, it has been suggested that J was a woman, first by Richard Elliott Friedman in *Who Wrote the Bible?* and later by Harold Bloom and David Rosenberg in *The Book of J.*

All of these theories of biblical authorship have been applied to the book of Revelation, and with some very curious results. Some scholars, for example, argue that Revelation as we know it is actually the work of "a Johanine circle, school or community."[2] Others see Revelation as a composite of several different and unrelated texts, each one written in a different time and place by a different author—or by various "schools"—and all of them cobbled together at some later date by a pious editor who struggled to impose some kind of order on the chaos of words and images.

But, thrillingly, most modern scholars agree that the book of Revelation is the work of a single author who was a mystic and a visionary, a charismatic preacher and a poet of unexcelled and enduring genius. Whether Revelation is read as Holy Writ or a work of literature, one of the great enterprises of biblical scholarship has been the effort to extract the biography of its author from the text itself and the traditions that have grown up around it. As we begin to glimpse the details of his life and work, however obliquely and speculatively, we will be able to read the book of Revelation in new and illuminating ways.

Ω

Not unlike the book of Jeremiah, Revelation opens with a straightforward claim of divine authorship with the assistance of a few celestial go-betweens and a human secretary. The text passes from God to Jesus to an angel and finally to a human being whose name is given as John: "The revelation of Jesus Christ, which God gave him to show to his servants what must soon take place," according to the opening lines of text, "and he made it known by sending his angel to his servant John."[3] On the strength of these assertions, pious Christians have embraced the book of Revelation as "the only biblical book authored by Christ."[4]

The claim of divine authorship is not so clear in the rest of the text itself. Revelation is written in the first person, but more than one narrator is speaking to us. Sometimes the voice we hear belongs to the human author who calls himself John, and sometimes John is merely quoting the various celestial figures whom he encounters—God, Jesus, and a series of angelic emissaries. Still, John clearly presents himself as the human being whose visions are recorded in the text, and he is commonly credited as its author. But we are still left with a nagging question: Is he the apostle whose name is given in the New Testament as John, son of Zebedee?

By way of self-introduction, John describes himself to the seven church-es in Asia Minor for which the book of Revelation was originally intended: "I, John, your brother and comrade in tribulation and patient endurance in Jesus."[5] The fact that the author of Revelation calls himself "John," how-ever, hardly means that he is the same John who is mentioned in the Gos-pels. The Hebrew name "Yohanan" and its Greek equivalent, "Ioannes," both of which are rendered in English translation as "John," had been in common usage among both Jews and Christians long before the Gos-pels *or* Revelation were first composed. Indeed, the New Testament itself knows of several men called John, including not only the apostle John but also John the Baptist, a wandering preacher who is among the first to pro-claim Jesus to be the Messiah.

The tradition that the apostle John wrote the book of Revelation began with its first appearance among the Christian communities of the Roman Empire. Irenaeus (ca. 120–ca. 200), an influential Christian bishop in what is now the city of Lyons in southern France, reports that Revelation "was seen not very long ago, almost in our generation, at the close of the reign of Domitian"—that is, no later than 96 C.E.[6] And Irenaeus is the very first commentator to attribute the authorship of Revelation to "John, the dis-ciple of the Lord," a belief that was affirmed by several other early church fathers, including Justin Martyr and Origen. But a more cautious bishop, Dionysius of Alexandria (ca. 200–ca. 265), while conceding that Revela-tion is a work "of which many good Christians have a very high opinion," was the first to insist that Revelation and the Fourth Gospel "could not have been written by the same person."[7]

Dionysius, like countless other Bible critics to come, was alert to the obvious and disturbing contrasts between the Fourth Gospel and Reve-lation, including the marked differences in the fundamental theological stance of each work: the Gospel embraces what theologians call a "pres-ent" eschatology, while Revelation knows only a "futuristic" one.[8] Accord-ing to certain passages in the Gospel of John, for example, Christians need not wait until the end-times to enjoy the blessing of eternal life; rather, they are saved in the here and now: "Whoever lives and believes in me shall never die," says Jesus. "He who hears my word and believes him who sent me has eternal life."[9] By contrast, Revelation insists that salvation must await the end of the world—the Tribulation, the Resurrection, and the Day of Judgment—at some unknown moment in the future when "the trumpet call is sounded by the seventh angel" and "the mystery of God is fulfilled."[10]

Perhaps even more provocative, at least to expert readers of ancient Greek, are the differences in language and literary style between the Gospel of John and the book of Revelation. When scholars compare the words and phrases of Revelation and the Fourth Gospel in order to calculate the number of Greek terms that are used in both texts but nowhere else in the New Testament, they find only eight words in common.[11] An even more unsettling difference between the two texts is found in each author's command of the common (or "Koine") Greek in which the Christian scriptures are written. The Greek used in the Gospel is "correct and elegant," while the Greek used in Revelation is "inaccurate and even barbarous," according to Adela Yarbro Collins, a leading expert on the book of Revelation (and the spouse of John J. Collins, a fellow specialist in apocalyptic studies).[12]

Nowhere in Revelation, in fact, does the author claim to be the apostle John, nor does he refer to any experiences that might place him among the apostles during the lifetime of Jesus. Indeed, he appears to be uninterested in—and perhaps even unaware of—the life story of Jesus as it is described in such evocative detail in the Gospels. At one point in Revelation, he makes a passing reference to the twelve apostles in the third person, which strongly suggests that he was not claiming to be one of them. And when he mentions the apostles at all, it is only in his celebrated vision of the New Jerusalem that will descend from heaven after the end of the world: "And the wall of the city had twelve foundations," he writes, "and on them the twelve names of the twelve apostles of the Lamb."[13]

Pious theologians and secular scholars alike have proposed some highly imaginative scenarios to explain how the same author might have written both Revelation and the Fourth Gospel. Perhaps, they suggest, the apostle John wrote Revelation when he was younger and wilder and only newly arrived in the Greek-speaking provinces of the Roman Empire—and he wrote the Gospel when he was older and wiser, and only after he had acquired a mastery of Greek over long years of practice. Or perhaps he dictated the text of each book to a different secretary or translator, one far more skilled than the other—and, if so, the Gospel is the work of the more accomplished secretary, while Revelation suffered at the hands of the incompetent one.

Yet another explanation is that the apostle died before finishing one or both of the books. According to one ancient tradition, John was martyred for his faith sometime before 70 C.E., which is earlier than the dates assigned to the Fourth Gospel *or* Revelation by contemporary scholars. Perhaps, then, one or both of the books were completed after John's death by two separate redactors, each with a different understanding of his theology and an unequal mastery of Greek. One modern Bible scholar strikes an even more provocative stance when he imagines that the text of Revelation fell into the hands of a posthumous ghostwriter who was not merely inept but intent on ruining the work of St. John the Evangelist—"an archheretic who betrays a depth of stupidity all but incomprehensible, and only matched by his ignorance."[14]

Dionysius himself read the two books with pious but discerning eyes and was forced to conclude that Revelation was written by "another John"—that is, someone named John but not St. John the Evangelist.[15] Modern scholars share the same conviction. Bart Ehrman, for example, points out that the apostle John is described in the Gospels as illiterate, and thus could not plausibly have written *any* of the biblical works that are attributed to him.[16] And the question of authorship is still being debated by scholars and theologians: "No subject of Biblical studies has provoked such elaborate and prolonged discussion," complains one scholar, "and no discussion has been so bewildering, disappointing and unprofitable."[17]

Indeed, readers of Revelation across the ages have never been able to resist asking the most daring and tantalizing question of all: If the author was not St. John the Evangelist, then who was the *other* John, the man who really wrote the book of Revelation?

Ω

One early and intriguing candidate for the authorship of Revelation, for example, is an otherwise obscure elder (or "presbyter") of the early Christian church whose name was also John. He is first mentioned in the work of Papias, a bishop of the second century who is the earliest known commentator on the book of Revelation. The original writings of Papias are lost, but he is cited and quoted by other ancient sources who knew his work. According to a passage in the influential church history composed by Eusebius in the fourth century, for example, Papias was in the habit of seeking out elderly Christians of his acquaintance, the presbyter John among them, in an earnest effort to learn about the life of Jesus from eye-witnesses to the events that are described in the Gospels.

"I do not regard that which comes from books," insists Papias in an intriguing aside, "as so valuable for myself as that which comes from a living and abiding voice."[18]

Significantly, Papias was the bishop of Hierapolis, which was located in the vicinity of Laodicea, one of the cities in Asia Minor to whose churches the author of Revelation addresses himself. Since Papias was already at work on his commentaries in the first decades of the second century, it is plausible that his sources might have included an aging eyewitness who had known the historical Jesus or, at least, a living apostle. So Papias's passing reference to the presbyter John was enough to catch the eye of Eusebius, an early and authoritative chronicler of the Christian church. "Eusebius concludes that if John the son of Zebedee did not see the Revelation," explains Adela Yarbro Collins, "then John the presbyter probably did."[19]

An entirely different John, and a much more famous one, has been proposed as the author of Revelation by Catholic scholar J. Massyngberde Ford, author of an idiosyncratic translation of Revelation that appears in the Anchor Bible series. Ford argues that the original author of Revelation is neither the apostle John nor the presbyter John but rather a third man—John the Baptist, the fiery Jewish prophet who is mentioned in the Gospels as well as the writings of the ancient Jewish historian Josephus. According the Gospels, John the Baptist was beheaded before the crucifixion, a fact that may explain why the author of Revelation seems to know so little about the biblical life story of Jesus of Nazareth.

Ford suggests that Revelation includes "additions" that were written into text by Jewish followers of John the Baptist "who may or may not have converted to Christianity." But she also points out that, when all the apocalyptic passages in the New Testament are compared, "Revelation is the only one in which Jesus is *not* the central figure."[20] For that reason, she concludes that the core of the book of Revelation is "an essentially Jewish apocalypse" that was only later repurposed for a Christian readership and then, even later, admitted into the Christian canon.[21] Far from being a book written *by* Jesus Christ, the core text of Revelation may not have been originally written by a Christian at all.

Indeed, the author of Revelation seems far more familiar with the Hebrew Bible—and perhaps even such obscure apocalyptic writings as the book of

Enoch—than with the Christian texts that came to be collected in the New Testament.[22] Some 518 allusions to passages of the Hebrew Bible can be found in the book of Revelation, but only fourteen references to "Jesus" or "Jesus Christ," most of which appear in the portions that she characterizes as "Christian additions."[23] Even Austin Farrer, a gifted and revered Bible critic of the mid–twentieth century who piously assumes that the author of Revelation is John the Evangelist, readily concedes that he is working with ancient Jewish sources and refers to him as "the Christian rabbi."[24]

Notably, Revelation is largely free of the anti-Jewish rhetoric that can be found in certain passages of the Gospels, and John proudly characterizes himself and his followers as authentic Jews. Above all, the author is plainly intrigued by such purely Jewish themes as the Temple and the Ark of the Covenant.[25] By contrast, Ford finds "practically no unambiguous references to the earthly life of Jesus," and no interest at all in such basic Christian rituals and doctrines as baptism, communion, or the Trinity.[26] For these reasons, she searches for the original author of Revelation among the Jews of first-century Judea who did not live to see the crucifixion of Jesus or the birth of Christianity. "The candidate who seems most suitable," she insists, "is John the Baptist."[27]

Like Jesus, John the Baptist is depicted in the New Testament as an apocalyptic prophet. But the Baptist offers a far gloomier vision of the end-times than anything attributed to Jesus in the Gospels: "His message is radically different from that of Jesus," Ford writes. "John's is one of wrath and doom rather than salvation."[28] And it is the fierce and frightening rhetoric of John the Baptist, rather than the kinder and gentler teachings of Jesus, that is echoed in the pages of Revelation. "Repent, for the kingdom of heaven is at hand," John the Baptist is depicted as saying in Matthew. "I baptize you with water for repentance, but he who is coming after me is mightier than I, whose sandals I am not worthy to carry; he will baptize you with the Holy Spirit and with fire. His winnowing fork is in his hand, and he will clear his threshing floor and gather his wheat into the granary, but the chaff he will burn with unquenchable fire."[29]

None of the theorists, ancient or modern, have managed to convince a majority of modern Bible scholars that the man who calls himself John in the book of Revelation is John the Evangelist, John the Baptist, *or* the presbyter John. "Sound judgment leads to the conclusion," urges Adela Yarbro Collins, "that it was written by a man named John who is otherwise unknown to us."[30] Yet, as we shall see, the identity of the author of Revelation is one mystery that *can* be solved. And the telling details of his life offer a key to decoding the secret meanings that he wrote into the remarkable text of Revelation.

Ω

A close reading of Revelation, in fact, reveals a great deal more about its author than we know about the writers of most other biblical texts. Let's begin with the simple fact that his Greek is flawed by "gross errors in grammar and syntax," a fact that has prompted some scholars to conclude that John was a Jewish man born in Judea, where he grew up speaking Aramaic and acquired a lifelong hatred for the Roman army of occupation under which he lived.[31] The evidence for such telling biographical details, which help to explain some of the most baffling mysteries of Revelation, is subtle and speculative, but also intriguing and illuminating.

John, for example, seems to avoid using syntax that is unique to Greek and prefers to use phrasings that have a counterpart in Hebrew or Aramaic.[32] And the precise wording of his allusions to the Jewish scriptures suggests that he knew the original Hebrew text of the Bible—or perhaps one of the ancient Aramaic translations—rather than the Septuagint, the Greek translation of the Bible that was used by Jews in the Diaspora and by the authors of other books of the New Testament.[33] Such habits of language would have been characteristic of someone who was born and raised in Judea, studied the Jewish scripture in original Hebrew or an Aramaic translation, and emigrated to the Greek-speaking provincial towns of Asia Minor only late in life.

"He writes as one who had spent many reflective years in the synagogue before his conversion," proposes Austin Farrer in *A Rebirth of Images,* his masterwork on the book of Revelation. "So, if we put together his Jewish and his Christian periods, we may be wise to suppose that he is over fifty years old when we first hear of him."[34]

Then, too, the book of Revelation betrays a hatred for the Roman empire of the kind that we might expect to find in someone whose birthplace was the Roman province of Judea. Rome, as we have seen, occupied the Jewish homeland throughout the first century, fought a long and bloody war to suppress the Jewish resistance movement, and finally destroyed the Temple of Yahweh in Jerusalem in 70 C.E., thus putting an end to the ancient rituals of Judaism as they are described in the Hebrew Bible. The slaughter of the Jewish population, including the mass crucifixion of surviving defenders of Jerusalem, is characterized as "the Roman Shoah" by Jack Miles, an acclaimed Bible critic and Pulitzer Prize–winning biographer of God, in *Christ: A Crisis in the Life of God*.[35] Perhaps John saw such atrocities with his own eyes, and when he fled Judea to nearby Asia Minor as a war refugee, he carried a burning desire for revenge against Rome.

Some of the most lurid and disturbing imagery in the book of Revelation, in fact, amounts to an unsubtle attack on Roman imperialism. John, for example, conjures up the famous vision of "the great whore with whom the kings of the earth have committed fornication," a woman "arrayed in purple and scarlet, and decked with gold and precious stones and pearls, having a golden cup in her hand full of abominations and filthiness of her fornication."[36] John sees the great whore riding on a scarlet beast with seven heads, and an angel explains to him that "the seven heads are seven mountains on which the woman is seated."[37] As his first readers and hearers would have understood without further explanation, Rome was commonly known in the arts and letters of the classical pagan world as "the city of seven hills."[38] When they cracked the code of Revelation, they saw the Beast as the Roman conqueror of the Jewish homeland.

The poor Greek in which Revelation is written—"John's language," declares one scholar, "is a ghetto language"—may reveal more about John's white-hot hatred for the Hellenistic civilization of ancient Rome than it does about his deficiencies in language and learning.[39] Indeed, Adela Yarbro Collins suggests that John was perfectly capable of writing in proper Greek but chose to intentionally "Semiticize" his work as "a kind of protest against the higher form of Hellenistic culture" and "an act of cultural pride of a Jewish Semite."[40] To help the modern reader understand the significance of his choice of language, she likens it to the use of "Black English" as a badge of honor: "It is analogous to the refusal of some American blacks to 'talk right.'"[41]

Here is the first, but hardly the last, example of why the author of Revelation can be seen as a propagandist on the front lines of a culture war. Like all apocalyptic authors since Daniel, the writer of Revelation sets himself against the alluring ways of Greco-Roman civilization as practiced in his own lifetime by the subjects of a superpower that he so memorably dubbed "the mother of harlots and abominations of the earth."[42] He regarded anyone, Christian or Jew, who collaborated with Roman authority, enjoyed the pleasures of Roman arts and letters, or earned a living in commerce with the Romans as a traitor to the one true God. Indeed, as we shall see, even the simple act of taking a Roman coin in hand was the moral equivalent of apostasy in John's eyes—an uncompromising stance that would endear him to the activists and ardent true believers in every generation that followed, including our own.

Ω

Once John left the war-torn and bloodstained Jewish homeland, or so we might speculate, he made his way to the Roman province known as "Asia"—that is, an area of Asia Minor that is largely contained in what is now modern Turkey. From the vantage of the imperial capital at Rome, the province of Asia was only a backwater, full of unsophisticated and untutored yokels, but the cities that John visited were lively places where the local gentry aspired to make themselves over in the image of Roman civilization. And John, as we shall see, was as deeply troubled by the Roman way of life as he was by Roman imperialism or the religious practices of classical paganism.

John himself tells the reader that he was on "the isle that is called Patmos" when he was granted the strange and shattering visions that are described in the book of Revelation. Patmos is one of the so-called Dodecanese, a cluster of twelve Greek islands in the Aegean Sea, located along the southwestern coast of Asia Minor. Only eleven square miles in area, Patmos is a harsh and hilly volcanic island rising to about a thousand feet. And so it was proposed in the fourth century by Victorinus, author of the earliest commentary on Revelation to survive intact, that John had been sentenced to a term of hard labor on Patmos—"condemned to the mines by Caesar Domitian"—and released on the death of the emperor who sent him there. Like so much else in Revelation, the grain of speculation grew by accretion over the centuries: Austin Farrer, writing in the aftermath of World War II, provocatively refers to John's place of confinement as "the concentration-camp at Patmos."[43]

John himself is not entirely clear on the question of how or why he came to Patmos. Some translations suggest that he was on Patmos "*for* the word of God and the testimony of Jesus Christ"—that is, for the purpose of preaching the Gospel to any Jews or pagans who might be willing to listen. Other translations, however, render the same passage to suggest that he had been exiled to Patmos "*on account of* the word of God and the testimony of Jesus Christ"—that is, as punishment for his missionary work, which is the meaning favored by modern scholars.[44] Indeed, the New Living Translation, the work of contemporary evangelical scholars, takes the liberty of adding an explanatory phrase that appears nowhere in the original Greek text of the New Testament: "I was exiled to the island of Patmos for preaching the word of God and speaking about Jesus."[45]

No ancient source other than Revelation itself suggests that the Romans used Patmos as a place of exile, although political prisoners were apparently banished to other nearby islands in the Dodecanese. Then, too, Adela Yarbro Collins wonders out loud whether *any* Christians would have been granted the relatively benign punishment of exile: "The odd thing about this hypothesis," she asserts, "is that most condemned early Christians were executed, not deported."[46] Still, it is hardly plausible that John would have gone to Patmos merely to preach the Gospel, given the scanty number of souls that would have been available in such a small and remote island. John looked for—and found—a much more promising place to deliver his startling message about the end of the world.

Ω

John makes it clear that his missionary work was conducted not on the barren island of Patmos but in the bustling commercial centers of Asia Minor. The opening chapters of Revelation consist of a series of messages addressed by John to the Christian churches of seven cities in western Asia Minor—Ephesus, Smyrna, Pergamum, Thyatira, Sardis, Philadelphia, and Laodicea. These messages, or "letters" as they are often called, are the best evidence that John had spent enough time on the ground in these cities to gain an intimate knowledge of the politics and personalities of each place. Indeed, one of the keys to understanding the anger and resentment in the book of Revelation is the prickly relationship between John and the preachers, congregants, gentry, and provincial authorities, all of whom were far more comfortable than John himself with the good life that was available to the citizens of the Roman Empire, whether they were pagan, Christian, or Jewish.

Ephesus, for example, was a mercantile center that hummed with civic pride and ambition. The city lay at the mouth of a major river and at the junction of three busy roads, and thus it served as a hub for all of western Asia Minor. Designated as a "free" city by Rome, Ephesus was governed by an assembly of its own citizens—an *ekklesia,* the same Greek word that is used to identify a church—and never suffered the indignity of occupation by the Roman army. Still, it was one of the so-called assize towns where the Roman governor routinely stopped to hear and decide important legal cases, a fact that only added to its stature among the provincial towns and cities of the far-flung Roman Empire. For all of these reasons, Ephesus was "a city where men might look on the pageant and panorama of Greco-Roman life at its most brilliant."[47]

Ephesus was also the site of the so-called Artemesium, a temple dedicated to the goddess of chastity and childbirth (as well as fauna, flora, and the hunt) who was known to the Greeks as Artemis and to the Romans as Diana. First erected by the famously rich King Croesus, the temple had been rebuilt several times over the centuries. The Artemesium as it existed during the lifetime of John—fashioned of marble and rare woods, adorned with gold and jewels, and featuring a statue of the goddess rendered in ebony and precious metals—was regarded as one of the seven wonders of the ancient world.

But for a true believer like John, the statue would have been properly called an idol, and the whole spectacle was yet another example of what the Bible condemns as an abomination. "We think of Diana as the loveliest of the goddesses," writes one exegete of the mid–twentieth century, reminding us of how *all* pagan art was regarded by the first Christians. "But the image was a black, squat, repulsive figure, covered with many breasts—a strange, unlovely, uncouth figure."[48] Perhaps it was the figure of Diana, or some other exotic work of pagan statuary on which his eye might have fallen, that John has in mind when he conjures up the Mother of Harlots, "decked with gold and precious stones, having a golden cup in her hand full of abominations and filthiness of her fornication."[49]

A far less extravagant practice of paganism, however, was even more provocative to a strict monotheist like John. By the first century, a fashionable new cult had come to Rome from the Asiatic provinces, and patriotic Roman citizens began imagining the Roman emperor to be the symbol of the spirit (or *genius*) of the Roman Empire. For that reason, they saw praying for his well-being as a way of praying for the welfare of the empire. Here, too, was an opportunity for a provincial town to enhance its celebrity and stature; an official sanction from Rome to raise a temple in honor of the emperor might be likened to the bestowal of an NFL franchise. In 26 C.E., for example, Sardis was among ten cities in competition for the privilege—and Smyrna was the ultimate winner. In fact, Ephesus, Pergamum, and Thyatira, along with Sardis and Smyrna, were all centers of the so-called emperor cult.

The veneration of the emperor, as we shall shortly see, was hardly the occasion for the heathenish excess that paganism was advertised to be in Jewish and Christian propaganda; nothing more was required of the worshipper than to spill a few drops of wine and cast a pinch of incense on the coals of a brazier placed before an image of the imperial *genius*. But John would have regarded the newfangled practice as even more offensive than the worship of the old gods and goddesses. When John conjures up the seat of Satan in his letter to the church in Pergamum— "where Satan's throne is"—he may have been thinking of the temple that was erected there in 29 B.C.E. in honor of "divine Augustus and the goddess Roma."[50] As a man raised and tutored in traditional Judaism, he would have found any gesture of worship toward a mere human being enough to put him in mind of another emperor who demanded worship—Antiochus the Madman—and thus to provoke his rage against the reigning Roman emperor.

The seven cities that John visited, however, were more notable for their political and cultural ambitions—and their mercantile accomplishments—than for their practices of pagan worship. Smyrna, for example, was an important seaport and a center of the wine trade, and its rich merchants supported a library, a stadium, and the largest public theater in Asia Minor. Pergamum, too, boasted of its library, and the name of the city is the root of the English word "parchment," which was supposedly invented there. Ephesus hosted the gladiatorial games that provided a spectacular if also bloody form of popular entertainment. And, significantly, Thyatira quartered a great many of the guilds that figured so crucially in trade and commerce in the ancient world—the artisans and craftsmen, merchants and traders who were the makers and sellers of the beautiful and useful things that the Roman population found pleasurable or practical or both.

Nothing in the picture of the seven cities that is preserved outside the pages of Revelation suggests that they were "seats of Satan." Rather, they appear to be places where ordinary men and women—Christians, Jews, and pagans alike—could and did lead prosperous, safe, pleasurable, and

decent lives. But the picture is distorted when viewed through the eyes
of true belief. For the author of Revelation, the unremarkable compromises that a man or woman might be willing to make in order to live the
good life in a cosmopolitan city were just as sinful as the veneration of the
Roman emperor or the offering of prayer to the many-breasted Diana.
To him, as to religious fundamentalists in every age, from the Maccabees
of the late biblical era to the strict and self-denying Jews, Christians, and
Muslims in the modern world, the seeking and getting of the good things
in life was something demonic.

Ω

Indeed, what really troubles John is the fact that the seven cities offered so
many opportunities for Christians to embrace the Roman ways of life and
rewarded them so richly for doing so. And nothing is more contemptible
in his eyes than the simple and unremarkable act of buying and selling. Of
all the satanic excesses that John condemns with such fury and disgust, he
seems to regard commerce as the cardinal sin.

Perhaps the best evidence is found in the punishments that John envisions for the enemies of God in the end-times. John begins by introducing
his readers and hearers to the "beast" who symbolizes Rome as the earthly
agent of Satan. Anyone who "worships the beast and its image," he insists,
will be identifiable by "a mark on his forehead or on his hand"—a symbol,
as we shall see, that can be best explained as a reference to the most fundamental tool of commerce, the coin of the realm. And then he warns that a
special punishment is reserved for anyone who is so marked.[51]

"He shall drink the wine of God's wrath, poured unmixed into the cup
of his anger, and he shall be tormented with fire and sulphur in the presence of holy angels and the presence of the Lamb," says one of the angels
who appear in John's visions. "And the smoke of their torment goes up for
ever and ever; and they have no rest, no day or night, these worshippers of
the beast and its image, and whoever receives the mark of its name."[52]

Indeed, the very first sinners to be punished in the end-times will be
those who bear the mark of the Beast. Seven angels will pour out seven
vials containing "the wrath of God"—and the first vial poured by the first
angel will cause "foul and evil sores" to come upon those "who bore the
mark of the beast and worshiped its image."[53] And, at the end of the long
ordeal that is described in such harrowing detail in Revelation, all of those

who bear the mark of the Beast will be "cast alive in a lake of fire burning with brimstone."[54]

The mark of the Beast is apparently a name, presumably the name of a Roman emperor, or perhaps the numerical equivalent of the letters in his name. Elsewhere in Revelation, as we shall shortly see, John famously reduces the name of the Beast to the number 666, a kind of alphanumeric code that is possible only in languages (including both Hebrew and Greek) in which letters also serve as numbers. Here, too, is evidence of his Jewish roots: the extraction of mystical meanings from the biblical text by calculating and manipulating the numerical values of letters, a practice known as *gematria,* was favored by Jewish mystics. And John gives us an important and illuminating clue to what he has in mind about the thoroughly mundane function of "the mark of the beast":

"[The beast] causes all, both small and great, both rich and poor, both free and slave, to be marked on the right hand or the head," explains John, "*so that no one can buy or sell unless he has the mark,* that is, the name of the beast or the number of its name."[55]

Buying and selling, as we have seen, were among the principal occupations of the seven cities where John preached, a source of wealth and the pleasurable things that wealth can bring. Wealth, of course, is measured in money. And the money in circulation throughout the Roman Empire was prominently marked with the name and image of the Roman emperor in whose reign it was minted. Some coinage, in fact, plainly identified the emperor with the Latin word *divus* or the Greek word *theos,* both of which mean "god."[56] Significantly, the Greek word in Revelation that is translated as "mark" is also "a technical term for the imperial stamp on commercial documents and for the royal impression on Roman coins."[57] When a coin crosses the palm of a Christian, John seems to say, he or she is marked by the Beast.

John is seldom content with using a word or a phrase to express just one thing, and the mark of the Beast fairly shimmers with deeper meanings. The Greek word for "mark," for example, is also used to refer to the brand that was burned into the flesh of cattle to identify their owner. A few ancient sources suggest that slaves and soldiers were similarly branded (or tattooed) as a deterrent to escape or desertion. One source insists that prostitutes, too, were branded with the mark of the man who owned or employed them. And the third book of Maccabees recalls one hateful

Egyptian pharaoh of the Hellenistic era who orders a few of his Jewish subjects to be branded with the figure of an ivy leaf, the mark of the god Dionysius.[58]

Another ancient practice that might explain John's curious reference is the mark that was applied to the forehead, neck, or hand of someone who had been granted membership in a craft or trade guild or initiated into the cult of a pagan deity. Since the guilds invoked the patronage of a god or goddess, membership in a guild and initiation into a cult may have been one and the same thing. And the marking of guild and cult members is explained as a conscious imitation of the branding of slaves: the initiate acknowledges his or her bondage to the deity "by indentures not written on pieces of parchment," as first-century Jewish philosopher Philo puts it, "but, as is the custom of slaves, branded on their bodies with a red-hot iron."[59]

Still, the root meaning of "the mark of the beast" may be best understood as the names, numbers, and symbols that appeared on Roman coinage. For John, coinage is the ultimate and ubiquitous symbol of imperial authority graven in gold and silver—and a symbol, too, of the comforts and luxuries that some Christians buy at the price of their souls when they make the compromises that he so hotly condemns. To a culture warrior like John, a coin fashioned of gold or silver and bearing the profile of the emperor is an example of exactly what the God of Israel condemns in the Ten Commandments. Indeed, John's fear and loathing of Roman coinage is yet another clue to his Jewish identity and yet another example of the Jewish values that suffuse the book of Revelation.

The idea that handling a Roman coin is an act of idolatry would have been an article of faith for a pious Jew from Judea. At the Temple of Yahweh in Jerusalem, for example, men and women on pilgrimage to the Jewish homeland from far-distant communities did not bring along the animals they would offer for sacrifice on the altar of God. Rather, they purchased what livestock they needed on arrival in Jerusalem. And, lest the pilgrims pollute the Temple by using coinage bearing the name and profile of some pagan emperor or some pagan deity, money changers were available along the approaches to the Temple to exchange pagan coins for temple currency on which no offensive names or figures were permitted to appear.

The money changers and the sellers of sacrificial animals who plied their trade at the Temple in Jerusalem are memorably featured in the Gospels, of course, but only in a tale that profoundly misrepresents why they were there in the first place. "And [Jesus] entered the temple and began to drive out those who sold and those who bought in the temple" goes the account in Mark, "and he overturned the tables of the money-changers, and the seats of those who sold pigeons."[60] Jesus condemns the money changers and the sellers of sacrificial animals for turning the Temple into a "den of thieves"—but the fact is that they were providing a service that *prevented* the Temple from being tainted by commerce with coinage bearing "the mark of the beast."[61]

The Gospel story is not mentioned at all in Revelation, whose author would have surely understood the pious function of the money changers. For him, the only coinage that a true believer must refuse to handle is the kind that bears the names and images of the Roman emperor and his divine patrons and patronesses—that is, money inscribed with the mark of the Beast. But John's contempt for money and his contempt for commerce are, so to speak, two sides of the same coin. When he describes the final destruction of "Babylon"—a code name for imperial Rome, not only in Revelation but also in other ancient apocalyptic writings such as the Sibylline Oracles and the Apocalypse of Baruch—John reserves some of his most wrought prose, and a certain bitter sarcasm, too, for those who profit from the buying and selling of luxuries.

"And the merchants of the earth weep and mourn for her, since no one buys their cargo anymore," writes John in his vision of the final destruction of Rome.[62] And he proceeds to provide a catalog of their wares in such sumptuous detail that it betrays both a certain envy as well as contempt: "Cargo of gold, silver, jewels and pearls, fine linen, purple, silk and scarlet, all kinds of scented wood, all articles of ivory, all articles of costly wood, bronze, iron and marble, cinnamon, spice, incense, myrrh, frankincense, wine, oil, fine flour and wheat, cattle and sheep, horses and chariots, and slaves, that is, human souls."[63]

Elsewhere in Revelation, John imagines that sinners will sizzle in a lake of fire for all eternity, a lake that "burneth with sulphur and brimstone."[64] Here, however, he contents himself with visions of merchants and shipmasters who suffer only from broken hearts at the loss of a lively trade in luxury goods as they witness the destruction of Babylon.

"The merchants of these wares, who gained wealth from her, will stand far off, in fear of her torment, weeping and mourning aloud," writes John. "And all shipmasters and seafaring men, sailors and all whose trade is on the sea, stood far off and cried out as they saw the smoke of her burning, 'What city was like the great city?' And they threw dust on their heads, as they wept and mourned, crying out, 'Alas, alas, for the great city where all who had ships at sea grew rich by her wealth! In one hour she has been laid waste.' And a craftsman of any craft shall be found in thee no more, and the sound of the millstone shall be heard in thee no more."[65]

If John is seeking to scare his readers and hearers into shunning their pagan friends, neighbors, and kinfolk, the demonization of Roman coinage—and the condemnation of the "cargo" that it could buy—was a clever psychological tool. After all, Christian true believers could congratulate themselves on their own poverty, whether self-imposed or not, by reminding themselves that participating in pagan commerce was equivalent to bargaining with the Devil. They are encouraged by the book of Revelation to console themselves with dreams of the day when God will punish the collaborators who took the Devil's coin. And revenge, as we shall see, is among the core values of Revelation.

John's condemnation of coinage and cargo is also consistent with what we can discern about his own way of life. Nothing in Revelation states or implies that John himself practices a trade or engages in buying and selling, or even that he holds a clerical rank in any of the seven churches that he addresses. Rather, he appears to follow the example of Jeremiah and John the Baptist; he is purely a prophet, wholly self-announced and bearing no ordination or official title. Nor does he seem to have a home in any of the seven cities. John apparently wanders from town to town, relying on the people he meets to offer him a bite to eat and a place to bed down. In that sense, he would have lived and worked in conscious imitation of Jesus and the disciples as they are described in the Gospel of Matthew.

"Take no gold, nor silver, nor copper, no bag for your journey, nor two tunics, nor sandals, nor a staff," Jesus is shown to instruct the twelve disciples. "And whatever town or village you enter, find out who is worthy in it, and stay with him until you depart."[66]

John's life as an itinerant preacher would have been an advertisement for the ideas that he embraces with such fervor in the pages of Revelation— "an enactment of the ascetic values of homelessness, lack of family ties, and the rejection of wealth and possessions," as one scholar has explained.[67]

These are the same values that are expressed in the strict rules that governed the members of an apocalyptic community like the one at Qumran near the Dead Sea, and in the pronouncements of the apocalyptic prophet whose name was Jesus: "Foxes have holes, and birds of the air have nests," says Jesus, "but the Son of man has nowhere to lay his head."[68]

Some scholars speculate that John renounced a life of wealth and privilege in order to take up his calling as a prophet. The argument is highly speculative but intriguing. Since banishment was a penalty reserved for aristocrats under Roman law, they imagine, John himself must have been a member of the Jewish priestly caste and a man of high rank in the Jewish homeland. One ancient source, a bishop of Ephesus called Polycrates, seems to affirm as early as the late second century that John was an ordained priest rather than a self-appointed preacher. Based on such meager evidence, one scholar proposes that John was banished to Patmos directly from a life of comfort in Jerusalem, Alexandria, or perhaps even the imperial capital of Rome.[69] But the text of Revelation suggests that John, like Jesus himself, was a man of humble origins who never aspired to rank or riches and, in fact, detested those who did.

A wandering preacher and missionary like John would have been a familiar figure among the Christian communities of the seven cities. The Didache, a Christian manual of religious instruction from roughly the same era—and a work with its own apocalyptic passages—calls on all good Christians "to share their firstfruits, money, and clothes with any true prophet who wishes to settle among them."[70] And the Didache confirms that prophets—or at least the authentic prophets who speak "in the spirit"—deserved to be taken seriously.[71] Long after the Jewish rabbinical tradition had declared the age of prophecy to be over, the Christian churches of the Roman Empire were still prepared to welcome any man (or woman) who claimed and appeared to be a "true prophet."

In fact, John was forced to contend with more than one rival among the self-styled prophets of Asia Minor, including a man and a woman whose competition he regards as so dangerous that it inspired some of the most vicious verbal abuse in a book that is full of rage. We do not know their real names, but he dubs one "Jezebel" and the other "Balaam," borrowing the names of a couple of notorious malefactors from the Hebrew Bible. And he condemns both of his rivals with the single most serious charge that he could have laid against them, the sin of false prophecy.

John's obsession with false prophets, as it turns out, anticipates one of the besetting problems with the book of Revelation, then and now. By the time John appeared in Asia Minor, Jewish tradition was already deeply skeptical of self-announced seers and messianic pretenders. The infant church, too, would soon come to distrust men and women like John who insisted that they were messengers of God. Indeed, John's own prophetic credentials would be challenged before the book of Revelation was finally admitted into the Christian scriptures. And, as we have seen in our own lifetimes, readers of Revelation who regard themselves as prophets can be dangerous and even deadly. Yet, ironically, the fear of false prophets is writ large in Revelation itself.

Ω

The letters to the seven churches that open the book of Revelation include a general warning against false prophets—"those who call themselves apostles but are not"—and a series of messages to various churches about specific men and women whom John accuses of the same sin.[72] Thus, John passes along the praise of the "Son of God" for the church at Ephesus for recognizing and rejecting the apostates whom he calls "Nicolaitans": "Thou hatest the deeds of the Nicolaitans, which I also hate."[73] But he censures the members of the church at Pergamum for their laxity toward the false prophet he calls Balaam. And he condemns the church at Thyatira for embracing the seductive prophetess he calls Jezebel.

"I know your works, your love and faith and service and patient endurance," writes John to the church at Thyatira, passing along a message from the Son of God. "But I have this against you, that you tolerate the woman Jezebel, who calls herself a prophetess and is teaching and beguiling my servants to practice immorality."[74]

As elsewhere in Revelation, John draws on Jewish scriptures in denouncing his rivals. Balaam is the pagan enchanter who is sent by the king of Moab to pronounce a curse on the invading Israelites, according a memorable tale in the book of Numbers, and ends up being scolded for his dimwittedness by his own ass. The humble creature plainly sees an angel of the Lord barring their path with a drawn sword, but the benighted Balaam does not.[75]

And Jezebel is the apostate wife of the Israelite king called Ahab. She seduces her husband into worshipping pagan gods and goddesses, contrives to murder the prophets of Yahweh, and is condemned in the Second Book of Kings for her many "harlotries" and "witchcrafts."[76] Once again, John is assuming that his hearers and readers would recognize and understand these associations, a fact that suggests they were fellow Jews who had only recently come to embrace Jesus as the Messiah.

Some measure of professional jealousy might have been in play here. John, after all, would have been forced to compete with other wandering prophets for the attention and, crucially, the generosity of the Christian communities where they all trolled for followers and benefactors. But he also appears to hold a principled objection to his rivals: they are apparently encouraging Christians to go along and get along with the pagan authorities of the cities where they live and work. Exactly here we find the front line in the culture war that John is fighting in the pages of Revelation. For a man like John, a Christian who compromises is a Christian who sins.

To understand the compromise that a Christian in Pergamum or Thyatira might be willing to make, we need to recall what a convert to Christianity was expected to do—and to refrain from doing. At a crucial moment in the early history of Christianity, the first Christians decided to abandon the bulk of Jewish law, including the ritual of circumcision, the dietary laws of kashrut, and the strict observance of the Sabbath, all of which were hindrances to the conversion of pagans to the new faith. But they retained a few taboos: a pagan convert to Christianity could forgo the painful ordeal of adult circumcision, but he (or she) had to "abstain from the pollution of idols and from unchastity and from what is strangled and from blood"— that is, they must refrain from dining on meat that had been sacrificed to a pagan god or goddess.[77]

Even these minimal rules, however, meant that a Christian man or woman would be cut off from the ordinary pastimes and transactions of daily life in a Roman town—or so a strict and uncompromising Christian like the author of Revelation would have insisted. The craft and trade guilds opened their meetings with a few words of prayer to one or another god or goddess from the pantheon of classical paganism. The imperial coinage carried the faces and figures of the Roman emperor and the Roman gods. Even a casual meal taken with friends or family who were still pagans would be likely to include a course prepared with meat that had been "sacrificed" to the gods, for the simple reason that animal offerings and butchering for human consumption were virtually one and the same thing in the ancient world. And so a good Christian, lest he or she be sullied with the sins of idolatry, ought to shun the pagan coinage, the pagan guilds, *and* the table fellowship of their pagan friends and relations.

Not a few Christians were apparently willing to compromise on some or all of these points. Like the Jews who adopted Greek ways of life during the Maccabean Revolt, at least some Christians in the cities of Asia Minor apparently did the same. Thus, the Christian communities where John preached included Christians who joined the pagan guilds, bought and sold merchandise with the imperial coinage, and sat down to dinner with friends and relations who were not Christians. And some of their pastors, including the ones John calls Jezebel and Balaam, apparently blessed the compromise. For some Christians and their clergy, the compromise was a way of sparing themselves from persecution and, at the same time, availing themselves of the profits that were available for those who engaged in the crafts or in commerce.

But for the author of Revelation—as for Daniel and other apocalyptic writers before him and various true believers who came after him— even the slightest compromise with true belief is condemned as a crime against God. John values rigor and purity of belief above all else, and he makes no meaningful distinction between handling a Roman coin and engaging in Satan worship. Indeed, he finds halfhearted Christians to be literally stomach turning, and he imputes the same revulsion to God himself: "Because you say, 'I am rich, have become wealthy, and have need of nothing,'" God is made to announce in the book of Revelation, "so then, because you are lukewarm, and neither cold nor hot, I will vomit you out of my mouth.'"[78]

Lack of zeal, in other words, literally makes John (or, more precisely, God himself) sick to his stomach. But an even more exacting standard is applied to his fellow preachers: if they fail to meet his exacting standards of piety and true belief, they are no better than harlots and witches. And that's what has always made the moral logic of Revelation so appealing to men and women in every age who, like John, who regard the slightest misstep as a plunge into hell.

Ω

John, always given to rhetorical excess, does not restrict himself to quibbling with Christians who do not bother to ask their hosts exactly how the meat on the table came to be slaughtered. To be sure, he accuses both Balaam and Jezebel of teaching faithful Christians "to eat things sacrificed unto idols." But he goes on to denounce them for "seducing" Christians "to commit fornication," the emblematic moral crime that so obsessed the classical prophets of the Hebrew Bible.[79] Indeed, both John and his Jewish role models regarded apostasy and sexual promiscuity as interchangeable sins.

The Greek word that is customarily translated as "fornication" (*porneusai*) carries the sense of "playing the harlot,"[80] but it is unlikely that Jezebel and her followers engaged in literal acts of prostitution or even sexual promiscuity. Rather, fornication is probably best understood as a code word used by biblical authors to describe what scholars call "syncretism"—that is, the mixing and matching of various religious beliefs and practices that was so common in classical paganism. John, in fact, may have used the word "fornication" to refer to nothing more scandalous than the making of marriages between couples who would be forbidden to marry under Jewish law but not Roman law.

But the words and phrases selected by John are intended to suggest that Jezebel herself and her Christian followers were, quite literally, willful and defiant sexual outlaws who insisted on engaging in their carnal adventures even after they had been warned of the consequences. Indeed, the text of Revelation suggests (even if it does not describe) scenes of ritual harlotry, orgiastic sex, and the careless spawning of bastard children, all of which have prompted some scholarly readers to regard Revelation as a work of "apocalyptic pornography."[81]

"And I gave her time to repent of her sexual immorality, and she did not repent," says the Son of God in condemning Jezebel. "Behold, I cast her into a sickbed, and those who commit adultery with her I will throw into great tribulation, unless they repent of her doings, and I will strike her children dead."[82]

The same double-edged meanings may be buried in John's condemnation of "the doctrine of the Nicolaitans, which thing I hate" and other Christians who embrace what he darkly refers to as "the deep things of Satan."[83] Although the Nicolaitans are wholly unknown outside the pages of Revelation, the early church fathers suggested that they were a band of heretics led by Nicolas, a wholly obscure figure who is mentioned briefly in Acts.[84] Some scholars are willing to entertain the notion that John is referring to "a Christian libertine group" whose teachings included not only sorcery and other satanic practices but also "sexual license" as a tool of spiritual enlightenment.[85] The Nicolaitans supposedly taught that "the really wise and mature Christian must know life at its worst as well as at its best," according to Scottish biblical scholar and broadcaster William Barclay, and so "it was right and necessary to commit the grossest and the most depraved sins in order to experience what they were like."[86]

But it is also possible (and even more likely) that the Nicolaitans, like Jezebel and Balaam, were easygoing and open-minded Christians who were willing to make the compromises that allowed them to participate fully in the "social, commercial, and political life" of the pagan communities in which they lived. The hateful and inflammatory labels that John slaps on his theological enemies may be no more than "code names" that he uses to identify Christian pastors and preachers who "allowed eating food sacrificed to the idols and accepted compromise with the emperor cult."[87] If so, their worst offense—and perhaps their only offense—was placing themselves on the wrong side of what John regarded as the no-man's-land of a culture war.

Ω

John reveals nothing about the more intimate aspects of his life, and we simply do not know whether he has a wife and children or, for that matter, any family at all. But he allows us to see that he is plainly put off by human sexuality, and when he mentions sex at all, he cannot seem to conceive of a sexual encounter between a man and a woman as something other than fornication. Indeed, John makes it clear in the book of Revelation that he regards *all* sexual conduct—even sex within marriage—as a kind of defilement.

For example, John predicts that 144,000 souls will be taken up to some celestial counterpart of Mount Zion, where they will be granted the privilege of following the Lamb "wherever he goes."[88] They are "redeemed from mankind as first fruits for God and the Lamb,"[89] a phrase that harks back to the ritual of animal sacrifice at the Temple in Jerusalem and suggests that they are martyrs who made the ultimate sacrifice to God. To distinguish the "first fruits" from the rest of humanity, they will be "sealed upon their foreheads" with the name of God and the name of the Lamb.[90] And John carefully notes that they are also distinguishable for a less obvious reason: all of them are lifelong celibates.

"These are the ones who were not defiled with women," writes John, "for they are virgins."[91]

A certain discomfort with sexuality of all kinds, even within marriage, can be found throughout the apocalyptic tradition. *The Book of Watchers,* for example, blames the existence of evil in the world on the fact that angels descended from heaven and "corrupted themselves" by engaging in sexual intercourse with women "in all their uncleanness."[92] Josephus reports that at least one order of Essenes shunned marriage and childbearing, and archaeologists suggest that the apocalyptic community at Qumran was largely, if not entirely, celibate. And the idea of sex as a defilement is deeply rooted in certain passages of the Hebrew Bible, where sexual conduct between any man and woman renders both of them ritually impure: "If a man lies with a woman and has an emission of semen," goes a passage in Leviticus, "both of them shall bathe themselves in water, and be unclean until the evening."[93]

The same fussy attitude toward sex can be found in both Jewish *and* pagan tradition. A priest or a soldier need not be celibate, but he must refrain from sexual intercourse in advance of certain activities, including both the performing of rituals and the fighting of battles. The requirement of sexual abstinence before battle is one that the Maccabees embraced in their own war against assimilation and occupation, but a pious pagan soldier might do the same. John, too, appears to believe that Christian soldiers must prepare themselves for the final battle between God and Satan by avoiding all defiling conduct, including sex. But John's stance toward sex, as toward everything else, is absolute and uincompromising.

Here is a clear example of John's distinctive approach to the moral instruction of the Hebrew Bible. He seizes upon a biblical commandment, and then he proceeds to radicalize it. Sex is a "removable defilement" under biblical law—one who has been defiled by engaging in sex need only immerse oneself in a ritual bath to purify oneself—but John seems to argue that *any* sexual encounter between men and women ought to be avoided.[94] Since he is convinced that the end-times are approaching but he does not know exactly when they will arrive, John seems to recommend that men and women alike ought to stop sleeping with each other once and for all so they will be ritually pure when the end comes, whether that happens tomorrow or at some unknowable moment in the future.

So John sees sex as something dirty and defiling under *all* circumstances. The only truly exalted human beings in Revelation are virgins and martyrs, and all his enemies are whores and whoremongers. And he is both distrustful and disdainful of women in general: the only mortal woman whom John mentions by name, the rival prophet whom he calls Jezebel, is condemned as a seducer and a fornicator. All of the passages of Revelation that touch on encounters between men and women betray a deeply conflicted attitude toward sexuality, according to Adela Yarbro Collins, "involving perhaps hatred and fear of both women and one's own body."[95]

Other readers of Revelation suspect that John may protest too much when it comes to the condemnation of sex. D. H. Lawrence, far better known for erotic novels like *Lady Chatterley's Lover* than for his biblical exegesis, points out that the greatest fornicator in all of Revelation, the Whore of Babylon, is a titillating figure, and perhaps intentionally so. "How they *envy* Babylon her splendour, envy, envy!" rails Lawrence in his own commentary on the book of Revelation. "The harlot sits magnificently with her golden cup of wine of sensual pleasure in her hand. How the apocalyptists would have loved to drink out of her cup! And since they couldn't how they loved smashing it!"[96]

Indeed, John betrays something dark and disturbing in his own sexual imagination at precisely the moment when he conjures up the famous seductress, richly draped in silk and jewels, and casts his mind's eye on what she carries in her hand—"a golden cup full of the impurities of her fornication."[97] In a book full of revelations great and small, it is highly revealing passage. When John invites us to imagine exactly what "abominations" and "impurities" are sloshing around in that golden cup, the man who wrote the book of Revelation is telling us everything we need to know about his own tortured attitude toward human sexuality.

John is plainly obsessed with purity in all things, including not only abstract notions of theology but also such thoroughly human concerns as sex, food, and money. And his obsessive personality may help us understand why the book of Revelation has always exerted such a powerful influence on readers with similar traits, ranging from religious zealots to the clinically insane. Indeed, as we shall see, John provides a proof text for code breakers and conspiracy theorists who, like John himself, are prone to see the Devil in the unlikeliest of guises.

Among the mysteries that John scatters through the text of Revelation, none has borne such strange fruit as "the number of the beast"—that is, the alphanumeric code that is meant to symbolize the name of the Roman emperor under whom John is living and working, the emperor whose name is chiseled on stone altars in the seven cities and stamped on coins of gold and silver that circulate throughout the empire. "Here is wisdom," writes John in what may be the single most obsessively pondered passage in the whole of Revelation. "Let him that hath understanding count the number of the beast: for it is the number of a man; and his number is six hundred threescore and six."[98]

One approach to penetrating the secret of the number 666 focuses on the contrast between the symbolic meaning of sixes and sevens in the book of Revelation. John, as we have seen, was obsessed with the number seven, a symbol of divine perfection that derives from the fact that God is shown in Genesis to complete the creation of the world in exactly seven days. If seven symbolizes divine perfection, as Bible commentators have long suggested, then six symbolizes human (rather than satanic) imperfection—and 666 "is the number of a man," as John plainly states.

But the number 666 also means something else and something quite specific to the author of Revelation. John, as we have noted, is engaging in the ancient practice of numerology—that is, the extraction of supposedly secret meanings from the arrangement and manipulation of numbers, a commonplace in biblical and mystical writings. Here, John is suggesting that the number 666 is a cipher that contains the name of the human being whom he denounces as the "beast": 666 is, quite literally, "the number of his name." And John suggests that at least some of his readers and hearers have already cracked the code: "Let him that hath understanding count the number of the beast."[99]

In ancient Hebrew, Greek, and Latin, the letters of the alphabet were also given numerical values, and thus the letters could be used in the way that we use Arabic numerals today. The most familiar example—and the only one still common in the Western world today—is the use of Roman numerals to indicate a date; for example, this book was first published in 2006—that is, MMVI. To give a simple example of the alphanumeric code that the author of Revelation is using, suppose that "A" can also be used to indicate "1," "B" to indicate "2," "C" to indicate "3," and so on. Thus, the common English word "cab" could be encoded in the number "6," which is the total of the numerical value of each of its letters.

So when John refers to the "number of the beast," he means the numerical value of the letters of a name as it is written in Greek, Latin, or Hebrew. The name, it is commonly assumed, belongs to a Roman emperor. The traditional solution to the puzzle that John has planted in Revelation is that 666 is the numerical value of the letters that spell out the name of the first Roman emperor to persecute the Christians, Caesar Nero (37 C.E.–68 C.E.). But, as we have noted, the earliest commentators on Revelation insist that the text first appeared during the reign of Domitian (51 C.E.–96 C.E.) in the last decade of the first century, nearly thirty years after Nero had taken his own life. For that reason, most scholars agree that any reference to Nero in the number of the Beast is a backward glance into recent history rather than a prophecy of things to come.

No single line of text in Revelation, however, has prompted more conjecture and dissension than "the name of the beast." Some early manuscripts of Revelation give the number of the Beast as 616 rather than 666, for example, and a few scholars propose that 616 encodes the name of Gaius or Caligula rather than Nero. Then, too, the numerical value of a word depends on the vagaries of its spelling, and the various imperial names and titles are formulated and spelled differently in Greek, Latin, and Hebrew. Thus, for example, the numerical value of Nero's name and title in Hebrew can be either 616 or 666, depending on how they are spelled, and that may explain why both numbers appear in the ancient manuscripts of Revelation.

John himself vastly complicates the problem by introducing an eerie but deeply enigmatic prophecy about the Beast that begins with the Great Whore of Babylon riding around on a red beast with "seven heads and ten horns."[100] Like the Hebrew prophets who were his role models, John is quick to assure his readers that the whore, the beast, the heads, and the horns are all purely allegorical: "Why marvel?" says his angelic guide. "I will tell you the mystery of the woman, and of the beast with seven heads and ten horns that carries her." The seven heads, for example, are revealed to symbolize "seven kings, five of whom have fallen, one is, the other has not yet come, and when he comes he must remain only a little while."[101]

The enterprise of identifying the seven Roman emperors who are symbolized by the seven heads is yet another cottage industry among the interpreters of Revelation, both amateur and professional, ancient and modern. Some start counting with Julius Caesar, and others with Augustus; some count all the early Roman emperors, both famous and obscure, while others find themselves forced to pick and choose among them in order to come up with Nero as the emperor who "is." The emperor-counting game, however, turns out be a dead end when it comes to fixing the identity of the emperor whose number is 666.

Indeed, even when John promises to solve the mysteries in Revelation, he cannot seem to resist the impulse to make them even more mysterious. Moments after the angel begins to explain the symbolism of the seven heads, for example, he offers yet another mind-bending riddle: "The beast you saw," says the angel, "was, and is not, and is to ascend from the bottomless pit."[102] Some scholars suggest that John is now thinking of the ancient Roman tradition that the slain Nero would one day rise from the dead and return to the throne. Nero *redivivus,* they propose, is "the beast that was, and is not, and yet is," the arch-villain in whose reign the world will finally come to an end.[103]

Some expert readers of Revelation, fatigued and frustrated by the effort to crack all the codes and solve all the riddles, dismiss the whole enterprise as nothing more than "arid conjecture."[104] The reality is that we do not and cannot know exactly which Roman emperor John has in mind when he speaks of "the beast." As far as John is concerned, however, it hardly matters. If John makes one thing clear in Revelation, it is that he regards *all* of the Roman emperors—and each one of his many enemies, regardless of rank or citizenship—as equally worthy of fear and loathing.

Ω

John conveys the impression that Christians in the seven cities face a terrible choice. They are at risk of forfeiting heaven if they yield to the temptations of Roman paganism, and they are at risk of forfeiting their lives if they remain strictly faithful to Christian beliefs and practices. Indeed, the book of Revelation encourages us to imagine its first readers and hearers as a community of imminent martyrs, each in peril of betrayal, arrest, torture, and execution by Roman authority, and each one willing to face death at the hands of the satanic deputy who sits on the imperial throne of Rome rather than engage in an single act of idolatry.

"Fear none of those things which thou shalt suffer," writes John, passing along the word of God. "Behold, the devil shall cast some of you into prison, that ye may be tried; and ye shall have tribulation ten days: be thou faithful unto death, and I will give thee a crown of life."[105]

The point is made in several of the stranger visions that John describes in Revelation. Among the diabolical creatures that he beholds, for example, are those two "beasts," one rising out of the sea and the other rising out of the land. The first beast is given the power "to make war on the saints,"[106] by which John means the faithful Christians, and the second beast is empowered "to cause those who would not worship the image of the beast to be slain."[107] Later, when the Lamb opens the fifth seal of the scroll on which the fate of the world is written, John sees an eerie sight "under the altar" in the celestial temple: "the souls of them that were slain for the word of God"—that is, the Christians who were martyred by the Roman authorities.[108]

Yet, among all the Christians in all of the seven cities of Asia, John identifies only a single flesh-and-blood victim who has apparently been put to death for refusing to submit to the demands of Roman law. "You did not deny my faith," he writes to the church at Pergamum, quoting the Son of God, "even in the days of Antipas, my witness, my faithful one, who was killed among you, where Satan dwells."[109] The word that is used to identify the unfortunate Antipas—"witness"—appears in the original Greek text of Revelation as "martys," the root of the familiar English word *martyr*.[110] Antipas, as it turns out, is the one and only martyr in all of Revelation whom we know by name.

The fate of the lone martyr is consistent with what we know about the historical setting of Revelation. Pergamum was, in fact, one of the towns where the Roman governor stopped to hear cases and hand out judgments, and it may have served as his official place of residence toward the end of the first century. And it is true that the death penalty was inflicted on some Christians who took the counsel of preachers and prophets like John and refused to make any gesture of compliance with Roman authority. Indeed, precisely such a scene is described by Pliny the Younger, who was called upon to examine and judge a few suspects who had been denounced as Christians by an informer when he served as governor of Bithynia and Pontus in the early second century.

"The method I have observed towards those who have been denounced to me as Christians is this: I interrogated them whether they were

Christians," writes Pliny to the emperor Trajan. "Those who denied they were or had ever been Christians, who repeated after me an invocation to the Gods, and offered adoration with wine and frankincense to your image, which I had ordered to be brought for that purpose, together with those of the Gods, and who finally cursed Christ—none of which acts it is said, those who are really Christians can be forced into performing—these I thought it proper to discharge; if they confessed it, I repeated the question twice again, adding the threat of capital punishment; if they still persevered, I ordered them to be executed."[111]

"Emperor worship," as Pliny allows us to see, amounted to nothing more elaborate than spilling some wine, a so-called libation offering, and casting a pinch of incense on the altar fire before an image of the emperor. The ritual was seen less as an affirmation of religious faith than a gesture of civic virtue not unlike the recital of the Pledge of Allegiance in contemporary American classrooms. But the ritual also served as a kind of loyalty test: if a symbolic offering to the emperor was meant to ensure the safety and security of the empire, then any citizen who refused to make the gesture was suspected of disloyalty if not outright treason. And so the crime that a martyr committed in the eyes of Roman law, like the offense for which Jesus of Nazareth was condemned to death, can be understood as a purely political one.

Pliny also makes it clear that only the most zealous Christians were made to suffer the death penalty. Someone who confessed to being a Christian was made to repeat the confession three times—and they were pointedly reminded of the penalty for sticking to their story, an interrogation technique that apparently prompted a great many of the accused to withdraw their confessions of faith. "Others who were named by that informer at first confessed themselves Christians and then denied it," writes Pliny, referring to the informant who had laid secret charges against the Christians under interrogation. "They all worshipped your statue and the images of the Gods and cursed Christ."[112]

So it is plausible that Antipas suffered the same fate that Pliny describes. Perhaps he was denounced to the authorities, interrogated by a magistrate, and executed on the order of the Roman governor, just as John seems to suggest. But all the other Christians whose deaths are contemplated in the book of Revelation—the souls whom John glimpses "beneath the altar," and the 144,000 male virgins whom we are invited to regard as sacrificial offerings to God—appear only in John's visions of the end-times.

Is it possible, then, that John himself knew only a single Christian martyr?

Ω

John insists that Christians must endure a long and bitter ordeal—the Tribulation, as it has come to be called—before they are finally admitted into "a new heaven and a new earth."[113] And modern scholars agree that Revelation and the whole apocalyptic tradition are best understood as a way of coping with oppression and persecution by imagining a better world to come: "The theology of the Apocalypse is formulated in the face of persecution, banishment, jail and execution," according to Elizabeth Schüssler Fiorenza, a feminist Bible scholar and advocate of "liberation theology" who is also a leading Catholic commentator on the book of Revelation.[114] If Revelation makes sense at all, it does so only as a verbal balm for the bodies and souls of suffering saints.

"One thing of which we may be certain is that the Apocalypse, unless the product of a perfervid and psychotic imagination," writes New Testament scholar J. A. T. Robinson, echoing a certain conventional wisdom, "was written out of an intense experience of the Christian suffering at the hands of the imperial authorities, represented by the 'beast' of Babylon."[115]

Yet it is *not* a settled fact that the first readers and hearers of Revelation were themselves the victims of imprisonment, torture, and death. John himself appears to live in a pagan world in which it was all too easy for a Christian to make his or her peace with Roman authority. Indeed, John would have been far happier if it had been otherwise; clearly, he prefers dead martyrs to faithless Christians who are willing to compromise with Roman authority in order to live the good life. Only in John's visions of the end-times, and *not* in the historical record, do we find the worst excesses of Roman persecution. Or, to put it rather more charitably, the book of Revelation "expresses the author's *expectation* of persecution," as Adela Yarbro Collins explains, rather than his *experience* of persecution.[116]

A Christian tradition dating back to the fifth century counts ten periods of persecutions by pagan Rome, starting with Nero, "the archetypal persecutor," in the first century and ending with the Great Persecution of Diocletian in the fourth century.[117] To judge from the martyrologies that were composed in the Middle Ages, throwing a Christian to the lions was the kindest and gentlest of the atrocities. And yet, by 1776, Edward Gibbon was already expressing a new frankness on the subject of Christian martyrdom: he counts only two thousand or so victims during the so-called Great Persecution; he insists that many of the martyrs actively and eagerly sought the opportunity to die for their faith; and he questions whether their deaths were, in fact, the occasion for the scenes of Grand Guignol that we find in the martyrologies.

"It would have been an easy task to collect a long series of horrid and disgustful pictures, and fill many pages with racks and scourges, with iron hooks, and red-hot beds, and with all the variety of tortures which fire and steel, savage beasts and more savage executioners, could inflict on the human body," writes Gibbon in *The Decline and Fall of the Roman Empire*. "But I cannot determine what I ought to transcribe till I am satisfied how much I ought to believe."[118]

Modern scholars find themselves forced to concede that the persecution of Christians, especially at the time and place of the writing of Revelation, was not nearly as gruesome or as widespread as John suggests. Nero may have been the "beast" of Revelation, but the arrest and punishment of Christians during his reign took place "only in Rome and on a single occasion," according to George Eldon Ladd, a leading Protestant theologian and commentator on Revelation.[119] What's more, they were arrested and punished on trumped-up charges of arson rather than any specific religious offense. That is why Adela Yarbro Collins calls the episode a "police action" rather than a persecution.[120]

During the lifetime of John, and for a couple of centuries afterward, the punishment of Christians by Roman authority remained "local in character or relatively mild in execution." Domitian, another favorite candidate for the Beast whose number is 666, may have confined his own persecution of Christians, such as it was, to "a few families in Rome."[121] And even then, most of the Christians who fell afoul of Roman authority may have been those true believers who actively sought martyrdom. Indeed, as John himself seems to suggest, it was all too easy for a compliant Christian to escape punishment of any kind by compromising with pagan authority and casting a pinch of incense on the altar fire.

Thus, the book of Revelation must be understood as the work of a man who may not have been persecuted at all but who surely "seems to *feel* that he is a victim of injustice,"[122] according to Adela Yarbro Collins. Nor does

John regard the Roman authorities as his only or even his worst enemy. He is equally aggrieved by those of his fellow Christians whom he condemns as insufficiently pure and zealous. He is enraged, too, by the Jews who refuse to embrace Jesus of Nazareth as the promised Messiah despite the urgings of preachers like himself. And it is John's habit of mind to characterize *all* of his adversaries, real or imagined, not merely as mortal enemies but as agents of the Devil—a rhetorical ploy that may be his single most enduring gift to posterity.

Ω

Of course, John was not the first or only apocalyptic prophet to see the world in which he lives—and all of human history—as a battleground in the war between God and the Devil, a theological notion known as "dualism." The idea may have seeped into Jewish tradition from the theology of ancient Persia, and it was very much on Daniel's mind when he beheld the horrors of occupation and oppression under the Syrian king a couple of centuries before John was born. Still, John is forced to offer his own answer to the question that asks itself: What is the proper stance of a faithful believer who is forced to live in a satanic kingdom?

One answer is to pick up the sword and fight. The Maccabees and the Zealots, for example, were willing to risk death in combat against their pagan foes and preferred to take their own lives rather than surrender when defeated in battle. Another answer is to remove oneself from the temptations and afflictions of the pagan world and to live in apart in the purity and isolation of the wilderness. The Essenes, for example, sought refuge in utopian communities like the one at Qumran in the Judean desert. But there was a third answer, and that's the one that John chooses—to do nothing at all except watch and wait until the end-times, when God will destroy the world as we know it, raise the "saints" from among the living and the dead, and reward them with "a new heaven and a new earth."

The same range of choices can be discerned in earlier apocalyptic writings. Both the book of Daniel and portions of the book of Enoch, for example, were written during the period of the Maccabean Revolt, but each one takes a very different stance toward the evils of paganism. *The Dream Visions of Enoch,* one of the apocalyptic works collected in the book of Enoch, seems to endorse the armed struggle of the Maccabees when it depicts the transformation of a lamb, meek and feeble, into a mighty horned ram, "an image for great military leaders and for a warrior-messiah."[123] By contrast, the "wise ones" in Daniel are willing to wait patiently and passively for the archangel Michael to come to their rescue in the end-times, even if it means martyrdom in the here and now.

"They can lose their lives in this world," explains John J. Collins, "because they are promised a greater glory in the next."[124]

Daniel, rather than Enoch, is John's greatest influence. For all of the Sturm und Drang of Revelation, John is what scholars call a "quietist"; that is, he teaches his readers and hearers to do nothing about the evil that surrounds them except to keep the faith and keep quiet. To be sure, he envisions a bloody battle between the army of God and the army of Satan—"the battle of that great day of God Almighty"—but it will be a "war in heaven." At the end of the world, when Rome is finally destroyed, it will be by God's hand alone: "Rejoice over her, O heaven, and you holy apostles and prophets, for God has avenged you on her!"[125]

John, like other apocalyptic writers, seizes upon the lamb as the symbol of the Messiah. Remarkably, a helpless creature that serves as a sacrificial offering in the earthly temple at Jerusalem is transformed in the book of Revelation into a warrior-king in the heavenly Jerusalem. The Roman emperors who serve the Beast "shall make war with the Lamb, and the Lamb shall overcome them," he writes, "for he is Lord of lords, and King of kings." The Lamb is armed with an arsenal of celestial weaponry, including "a sharp two-edged sword," and John promises that the King of Kings will one day bring them to bear in a holy war against the Devil and his minions among whom faithful Christians, John among them, are now forced to live.[126]

John, however, does not counsel his readers and hearers to pick up the sword themselves. For the pious and faithful Christians here on earth, John recommends patience and passivity even if it means imprisonment, torture, and death. Indeed, he predicts that Rome will drink itself into a stupor on "the blood of prophets and saints," but he is instructed (and he instructs his readers and hearers) that a martyr's death is something earnestly to be wished for: "Then I heard a voice from heaven saying to me, Write: 'Blessed are the dead who die in the Lord from now on.'"[127]

Revelation is, among other things, a revenge fantasy. But it is the fantasy of someone who imagines himself to be utterly powerless. John is full of sputtering rage against Rome, but he is reduced to nursing his grudge until the great day when God deigns to descend from heaven and put an end to his enemies. "He has judged the great harlot who has corrupted the earth with her fornication," John writes of the end-times, "and he has avenged on her the blood of his servants."[128] The end-times may be near, as John repeatedly assures his readers, but they are not yet. And in the meantime, he urges his fellow Christians to sit and wait.

"If any one has an ear, let him hear," writes John. "Here is a call for the endurance and faith of the saints."[129]

Here, too, is a piece of plain advice that was overlooked by some of the most famous (or notorious) readers of Revelation. Now and then, as we shall see, Revelation has roused more than a few men and women to regard themselves as avenging angels rather than suffering saints, a roster that ranges from Savonarola in the fifteenth century to David Koresh in the late twentieth century. To his credit, John demands no such thing of his readers and hearers, and surely he would have been amazed and aghast at what some of them insisted on making of his work. But, then, the greatest failure of prophecy in the book of Revelation—aside from the fact that the world did not end as predicted—is the fact that the "Christian rabbi" did not suspect how the meanings and uses of his "little book" were destined to change as the text passed out of the seven cities of Asia Minor into the rest of the Roman Empire and, thereafter, into world history.

John, as we have seen, was almost certainly born and raised as a Jew, and he seems to be addressing an audience for whom the Jewish scriptures are familiar and compelling. Within the 404 verses that make up the book of Revelation, by one scholar's count, more than five hundred allusions to the Hebrew Bible can be discerned. Revelation is virtually a catalog of Jewish themes and traditions, ranging from the Twelve Tribes to the Temple of Yahweh. And yet, ironically, the best evidence of John's Jewish identity is buried away inside the single most hateful line of text in Revelation, where John implies that he is more authentically Jewish than his adversaries in the Jewish community.

"Behold," writes John, attributing his words to Jesus Christ, "I will make those of the synagogue of Satan who say that they are Jews and are not come and bow down before your feet and learn that I have loved you."[130]

Even John's near-obsessive use of the number seven can be read as an allusion to Jewish scripture. God's primal act of creation as depicted in Genesis is completed in seven days—"And on the seventh day God ended his work which he had made"[131]—and thus seven becomes the symbol of divine wholeness in Jewish tradition. When John refers to signs and symbols in groups of seven—seven angels, seven seals, seven trumpets, seven thunders, and so on—he means to suggest that God's will is at work in both the creation and destruction of the world.

"And the angel whom I saw lifted up his hand to heaven," writes John of the seventh angel who appears after the seventh thunder, "and swore by him who lives for ever and ever, who created heaven and what is in it, the earth and what is in it, and the sea and what is in it, that there should be time no longer."[132]

Other scenes in Revelation are hot-wired to specific passages of the Hebrew Bible. John, for example, knows the passage in Ezekiel in which God hands the prophet a book of "lamentations and moaning and woe" and then issues a strange command: "Son of man, eat this scroll and go speak unto the house of Israel."[133] And John claims precisely the same experience for himself: God sends a scroll (or a "little book," according to the King James Version) by means of an angelic messenger, and John, too, is ordered to "take it and eat it up." Here John is incorporating the Jewish scriptures into his own writing in the most literal possible way: "And I took the little book from the hand of the angel and ate it," reports John. "And I was told, 'You must again prophesy about many peoples and nations and tongues and kings.'"[134]

The pointed reference to "peoples and nations and tongues" allows us to understand the hatred and resentment that wells up in John and spills over into the book of Revelation. "John makes a plea to Jews ... who 'own' the tradition to accept him and his vision," according to Elizabeth Schüssler Fiorenza, but his preachments are rejected by the Jewish men and women in his audience. If the house of Israel refuses to recognize Jesus of Nazareth as the Messiah, John resolves to address himself to other peoples and nations and tongues. But he cannot overlook the insult that has been offered by the Jews who remained faithful to their own traditions, and so he returns the insult by consigning them all to the "synagogue of Satan."[135] And so, ironically, what is arguably the single most anti-Semitic line of text in all of Christian scripture can also be understood, almost poignantly, as the outcry of a Jew who has been spurned by his fellow Jews.

Ω

While John delights in alluding to and borrowing from the Hebrew Bible, he does *not* quote its text verbatim. Rather, he uses Jewish scripture as a "language arsenal," according to Elizabeth Schüssler Fiorenza, and he picks and chooses the ideas, images, and incidents that suit his own rhetorical purpose.[136] Perhaps he did not have a copy of the Bible at hand as he spoke and wrote, or perhaps he simply did not care to cut and paste from the ancient texts: "The prophetic spirit creates," explains one Bible scholar, "it does not quote in order to teach or argue."[137]

Nor does John confine himself to strictly Jewish sources. He may denounce Greco-Roman civilization in all of its richness and splendor as the work of the Devil, but he appears to know and borrow freely from pagan iconography. Seven is a sacred number in Jewish tradition, to be sure, but it was also significant in the astrological beliefs and practices of classical paganism, which knew only seven heavenly bodies. Twelve is the number of the tribes of Israel, but it is also the number of signs in the zodiac. Astrology, in fact, is condemned in the Bible as one of the great besetting sins of paganism—"offerings to the sun and moon and constellations, all the host of heaven"[138]—and yet John may have invoked precisely these images and associations in the text of Revelation.

Among the most sublime and exalted scenes in Revelation, for example, is the "great portent" that will appear in heaven to mark the beginning of the end-times: "[a] woman clothed with the sun, with the moon under her feet, and on her head a crown of twelve stars." The woman, pregnant and already in labor, is stalked by "a great red dragon," which waits to devour the newborn child as soon as she gives birth. But the archangel Michael—a figure who first appears in the book of the Daniel, John's single favorite source in the Hebrew Bible—makes war on the red dragon, who is here and now revealed to be Eve's original tempter, "that old serpent, called the Devil and Satan."[139]

Conventional readings of Revelation see the woman as the Virgin Mary and the newborn infant as Jesus, "a man child who was to rule all nations with a rod of iron" and who "was caught up unto God, and to his throne."[140] But it is also possible to discern less orthodox origins and meanings. "St. John's mind sets to work on the lines of a very old mythic pattern," writes Austin Farrer, who suggests that John borrowed the figure of the woman from pagan astrology—"the Lady of the Zodiac" who is "crowned with the twelve constellations."[141] Other scholars see the goddess Artemis, who was worshipped in such splendor in the Artemesium at Ephesus, or the goddess Roma, the "queen of heaven" whose divine child the Roman emperor was imagined to be and whose attributes are found on imperial Roman coinage from the first century.[142]

Indeed, precisely the same figure is found in sacred myths all over the ancient world—"a high goddess with astral attributes: the sun is her garment, the moon her footstool, the stars her crown."[143] Even the dire predicament of a laboring woman beset by a ravening monster is a familiar motif in pagan iconography. The Egyptian goddess Isis, for example, struggles to save her son from attacks by snakes and scorpions, and the Greek goddess Leto is menaced by a python when she is pregnant with Apollo. "In each of these myths the dragon seeks the child, not yet born, in order to devour or kill him," explains Elizabeth Schüssler Fiorenza. "The woman, still pregnant, is pursued for the child she carries. She gives birth with the dragon only moments way, and the male child she has just delivered is caught up to the Heavens, safe from the dragon's reach."[144]

Above all, the "war in heaven" between the archangel Michael and the red dragon—the eschatological high point of Revelation—is strongly reminiscent of the so-called combat myth that can be found in stories of creation in pagan texts from all over the ancient Near East. Indeed, the notion of a primal struggle between a high god and a primal beast—that is, a symbolic account of the struggle between order and chaos, creation and destruction—can be discerned within the Hebrew Bible itself, where Isaiah (among other biblical authors) refers to the defeat of Leviathan, "the twisting serpent and the dragon of the sea," by a sword-wielding Yahweh.[145] The combat myth of pagan tradition can be glimpsed only through the cracks of the biblical text, but it is the centerpiece of the book of Revelation.

Some scholars insist that such pagan associations are mostly in the mind of the beholder. And, in any event, none of the pagan subtext that might be teased out of the book of Revelation need be seen as evidence of hypocrisy on John's part. Rather, it is a sign of John's savvy that his "language arsenal" is not confined to Jewish sources. "John co-ops this imperial propaganda," proposes Adela Yarbro Collins, "to claim that the true golden age will come with the messianic reign of Christ."[146]

After all, once he resolved to look beyond the Jewish community in search of readers and hearers, John apparently realized that he needed to use scenes and stories that would be meaningful to pagans who were strangers to the Jewish scriptures. John's preachments would transcend both the Jewish and pagan sources that seem to have inspired him, and the words and images of Revelation came to be imprinted, deeply and inerad-icably, on the Western imagination, ranging from the church paintings of medieval Europe to the music videos in heavy rotation on MTV. John, of course, fully expected that his words of prophecy—and the world itself—would last "but a short time," and yet the sheer staying power of Revelation turns out to be John's greatest achievement.[147]

A few pious readers of Revelation imagine that John travels to the remote and barren island of Patmos on a kind of vision quest—he seeks a revelation and, like others who have done the same over the centuries and millennia, finds what he is looking for. Although there is nothing in the text to justify such speculation, the idea links John to the long line of mystics and ecstatics who come before him and long after him. Like the oracle of Apollo at Delphi, Moses on Mount Sinai, and Muhammad in the hill caves around Mecca, John finds the wilderness to be a good place to get a glimpse of the divine.

John himself describes his visionary experience on Patmos in way that is surely meant to remind his readers of the classical prophets of the Hebrew Bible. Like Ezekiel, Jeremiah, and Daniel, among his other role models, John is favored with a series of revelations by a "God in heaven who revealeth secrets," as Daniel puts it.[148] And, like other prophets who struggle to use mere words to convey something ineffable, John describes his experience as both exalting and shattering, sublime and horrific.

"I was in the Spirit on the Lord's day," he writes, "and heard behind me a great voice, as of a trumpet."[149] When he turns around to see who is speaking, John beholds the first of the many strange sights that fill the pages of Revelation: "One like unto the Son of Man," a robed and girded figure whose face is "like the sun shining in full strength" and whose eyes are "as a flame of fire," with a "sharp two-edged sword" projecting from his mouth and "seven stars in his right hand." And John is literally staggered by what he sees: "When I saw him, I fell at his feet as though dead," he explains, "but he laid his right hand upon me, saying, 'Fear not, I am the first and the last.'"[150]

Significantly, John is specifically charged by his celestial visitor with the task of writing down and publishing his revelations. "Write the things which thou hast seen, and the things which are, and the things which shall be hereafter," says the Son of Man. "Write what you see in a book, and send it to the seven churches."[151] Here, too, John places himself squarely in perhaps the single most crucial tradition in monotheism—the making of books. Then as now, human beings are more likely to believe what is written than what is said aloud, and John pronounces a curse on anyone who might be inclined to tamper with his text. And John makes it clear that the divine secrets revealed to him by God are meant to be secrets no longer: Revelation is intended for the ages and for the whole world.

"Do not seal up the words of the prophecy of this book, for the time is near," says the last of the angelic messengers to John at the very end of Revelation. "And if anyone takes away from the words of the book of this prophecy, God will take away his share in the tree of life and in the holy city, which are described in this book."[152]

$$\Omega$$

John's writings were to be preserved, passed along, and read with ever-greater ardor and imagination over the centuries to come, and he continues to serve as a shining role model for generation upon generation of visionaries. A couple of examples of the influence he wields on the religious imagination, one dating back to the Middle Ages and another of more recent vintage, allow us to glimpse the workings of the visionary mind, including his own, with far greater clarity than he records in his own writings.

Hildegard of Bingen (1098–1179) was first blessed with visions—or, perhaps more accurately, afflicted by them—at the tender age of five. By the time she was eight years old, her mother and father felt compelled to deliver young Hildegard into the custody of the abbess of a monastery in Germany where she spent the rest of her life—an indication of what it must have been like for parents who were raising a juvenile mystic. Hildegard echoes the words and phrases that she read in the book of Revelation when she describes how she is "taken up in spirit" and hears voices "like thunder,"[153] and she gives us an illuminating account of an experience that John himself may have shared.

"Heaven was opened and a fiery light of exceeding brilliance came and permeated my whole brain, and inflamed my whole heart and my whole breast," writes Hildegard in her masterwork, *Scivias,* "and immediately I knew the meaning of the expositions of the Psalter, the Gospel and the other catholic volumes of both the Old and New Testament."[154]

Some of Hildegard's visions are populated with creatures who seem to have crawled out from the pages of Revelation. While at prayer in church, for example, she sees the spectral figure of a woman in front of the altar— and, as she watches in horror, she realizes that the woman is ready to give birth. But, unlike the laboring woman in Revelation—the woman clothed with the sun whose child is the Messiah—the one in Hildegard's vision delivers herself of a monstrous beast: "From the navel to the groin she had various scaly spots," writes Hildegard. "In her vagina there appeared a monstrous and totally black head with fiery eyes, ears like the ears of a donkey, nostrils and mouth like those of a lion, gnashing with vast open mouth and sharpening its horrible iron teeth in a horrid manner."[155]

Not every reader of Revelation is attracted to the moments of terror and horror in John's text. Twentieth-century poet and novelist Robert Graves, for example, was more intrigued by what he calls "St. John's cryptogram"—that is, the meaning of 666, the number of the Beast—and he describes the experience in *The White Goddess* as an exercise in both ecstatic vision and number-crunching. Graves renders 666 in Roman numerals as D.C.L.X.V.I., and, like Hildegard, he imagines that a secret has been suddenly revealed to him. He sees the letters as an acronym for a Latin phrase that he translates as "Domitian Caesar basely killed the Envoys of Christ."[156] We might wish that John had described his own revelations as clearly as Graves does, and we might speculate that he experienced them in much the same way.

"I saw in a sort of vision the Roman numerals flash across the wall of the room I was in," writes Graves in *The White Goddess.* "I had been aware that the *Apocalypse* was referred by most Biblical scholars to the reign of Nero, not to that of Domitian. And yet my eye read '*Domitianus.*'"[157]

Between Hildegard and Graves, we are given two very different but equally enlightening ways of understanding the visionary experience that came to be preserved in the book of Revelation. Hildegard, like John, reports what might described in the language of psychopathology as a series of auditory and visual hallucinations, and, again like John, she claims to have been given the divine power to see the secret meanings of the known world that are denied to others. That's what prompts Adela Yarbro Collins to point out "a certain analogy between the creative imagination of the schizophrenic and the vision of the Apocalypse."[158]

Graves, too, claims that a flash of insight can reveal secret meanings that are hidden from everyone else. But when he refers to 666 as "St. John's cryptogram," he is crediting John, rather than God, for putting the secret meanings in the text in the first place. That's quite another way of understanding the author of Revelation: John can also be seen as a compulsive game player who delights in ornamenting his text with riddles and puzzles, signs and symbols that are meant to engage and tantalize his readers and hearers. Indeed, John repeatedly uses a kind of trademark phrase—"He that hath an ear, let him hear"—as if to say that we must penetrate his own wordplay and mind games in order to "get it."[159]

Still, there is nothing cynical or calculating in John's visions. He is clearly a driven man, wholly consumed with the fires of his own true belief and wholly persuaded that God has charged him with the task of spreading the word to the whole world. The point is made in the musings of perhaps the greatest apocalyptic preacher in history after John himself, the Dominican friar who set Florence afire in the fifteenth century, Girolamo Savonarola. Not coincidentally, Savonarola's text of choice was Revelation, and his sermons must have resembled the ones that John himself delivered in the cities of Asia.

"I have sometimes thought, as I came down from the pulpit, that it would be better if I talked no more and preached no more about these things—better to give up and leave it all to God," mused the fiery monk in the last sermon he delivered before his own martyrdom. "But whenever. I went up into the pulpit again, I was unable to contain myself. To speak the Lord's words has been for me a burning fire within my bones and my heart. It was unbearable. I could not but speak. I was on fire. I was alight with the spirit of the Lord."[160]

We do not know when or how John himself died. But we know that some of his most ardent readers, including both Savonarola and David Koresh, were literally consumed by the flames that they sparked with their own sermons on the Apocalypse. Their endings remind us that the book of Revelation is not—and was never intended to be—a safe and soothing book. Rather, John sought to set the souls of his readers and hearers on fire, and in that effort he was wholly successful.

Ω

John may have been convinced that he was hearing the voice of God, but the sheer virtuosity on display in the book of Revelation marks it as work of human contrivance—"an act of creative imagination," as Adela Yarbro Collins puts it, "which, like that of the schizophrenic, withdraws from real experience in the everyday world."[161] He is an astute propagandist who expertly stokes the hopes and terrors of his readers and hearers, an accomplished showman who delights in confounding and amazing his audience. But surely John believes that he is speaking the truth, as God gave him the light to see the truth, when he reveals what he calls "things which must shortly come to pass."[162]

John does not seek to win praise as a great author, nor can the book of Revelation be safely contained and dismissed as a work of literature. Rather, he clearly means to win converts for Christianity, and he wants his message, so fierce and so dire, to reach the whole world. And, significantly, he does not intend his message to endure for the ages for the simple reason that he is convinced—and wants to convince his audience—that the end of the world is nigh: "Behold, I come quickly," John hears Jesus Christ say in his vision. "Blessed is he that keepeth the sayings of the prophecy of this book.[163]

Surely the greatest of all the ironies in John's life and work is the simple and unavoidable fact that the things he predicts in the book of Revelation did *not* come to pass quickly or, for that matter, at all. John himself would have been shocked and heartbroken to know that we are all still here to read what he wrote two thousand years ago. That is why the book of Revelation and the apocalyptic tradition in Judaism and Christianity have been called, aptly if also poignantly, "the history of a delusion."[164] To put it another way, Revelation is the history of the end of the world and, as we shall see for ourselves, the history of a world that refused to end.

Four

The Apocalyptic Invasion

I don't know what is happening in other parts of the world,
but in this country where we live the world no longer announces
its end but demonstrates it.
POPE GREGORY THE GREAT (540–604)

When Jerome set himself to the task of translating the Bible into Latin in the fourth century, he was forced to confront all the bafflements and contradictions of the book of Revelation. The tale that John tells, as we have seen, is hard to follow and even harder to understand. The names, colors, numbers, and images that John conjures up are freighted with secret meanings, but exactly what they are supposed to signify is mostly a matter of speculation. At certain moments, John salts his text with what can only be described as brainteasers. Now and then, John explains a few of the symbols and solves a few of the riddles, but even when he does, the answers only raise more questions: "Revelation," concluded the frustrated Jerome, "has as many mysteries as it does words."[1]

Some of the most famous mysteries, like the identity of the Roman emperor whose name is enciphered as the satanic number 666, are hidden in plain sight in the text. Other mysteries are to be found in questions that seem to ask themselves: John insists that the world will end soon, but he never reveals exactly when. And some mysteries are woven deeply and intricately into the theological fabric of the text itself. Where in the book of Revelation, for example, is the kind and gentle teacher whom Jesus is depicted to be in some of most exalted passages of the Gospels? "Love your enemies," says Jesus in the Gospel of Matthew, "bless them that curse you, do good to them that hate you, and pray for them which spitefully use you, and persecute you."[2] By contrast, the author of Revelation knows only a violent and vengeful Jesus, "clad in a robe dipped in blood," armed with a two-edged sword, mounted on a warhorse, and commanding the "armies of heaven" in a war of extermination against his enemies.[3]

"From his mouth issues a sharp sword with which to smite the nations, and he will rule them with a rod of iron," writes John, who seems to delight in describing the carnage that the celestial warrior-king will leave behind on the battlefield after the war between God and Satan. "Come, gather for the great supper of God," calls an angel to the vultures in mid-flight, "to eat the flesh of kings, the flesh of captains, the flesh of mighty men, the flesh of horses and their riders, and the flesh of all men, both free and slave, both small and great."[4]

Perhaps the single greatest contrast between the rival theologies of Revelation and the Gospels is found in the passages where the end-times are described. According to the vision of judgment day in a passage of the Little Apocalypse as it appears in Matthew, Jesus will welcome into the heavenly kingdom all those who gave food to the hungry and drink to the thirsty, clothed the naked and sheltered the homeless, and visited the sick and the imprisoned. "Verily I say unto you," announces Jesus in what is arguably the single most sublime and yet revolutionary line of text in all of the Christian scriptures, "inasmuch as ye have done it unto one of the least of these my brethren, ye have done it unto me."[5]

John, however, has nothing quite so encouraging or elevating to say to good-hearted men and women who hope to achieve salvation through acts of kindness and compassion here on earth. According to Revelation, the first souls to be saved—or "sealed," as John puts it—will be the 144,000 men whose only apparent merit is that they "have not defiled themselves with women."[6] At the time of the first resurrection and judgment, only the saints and martyrs—those who refused to worship the "beast" or receive his mark on their hands and foreheads, and those who were beheaded for professing their belief in Christ—will be raised from the dead to reign alongside Jesus during the millennium that he will spend as king on earth.

Then, after Satan is released from the bottomless pit and defeated once and for all, the rest of the dead will be resurrected and judged "by what they had done."[7] John does not specify what kind of conduct in life will bring salvation after death, but the strong implication throughout the book of Revelation is that faith counts more than good works, and only the "saints" will be spared from eternal punishment. Everyone else—including not only "murderers, fornicators, sorcerers and idolators" but also "the cowardly, the faithless, and the polluted"—will spend all of eternity in "the lake that burns with fire and brimstone, which is the second death."[8]

Readers of the Christian scriptures, ancient and modern, have been troubled by the contrast between these two ways of imagining the end of the world. One modern scholar, for example, characterizes Revelation as "sub-Christian" precisely because John is so obsessed with vengeance-taking and so little concerned with the acts of care and mercy that Jesus advocates in the Gospels.[9] The Christian case against Revelation is memorably summed up by Martin Luther at a point in his life when he was not yet fully convinced that Revelation belonged in the Bible at all.

"My spirit cannot accommodate itself to this book," Luther writes in the preface to a German edition of the Bible that he published in 1522. "There is one sufficient reason for the small esteem in which I hold it—that Christ is neither taught in it nor recognized."[10]

Luther, as we shall see, was hardly the first or only Bible reader to view the book of Revelation with alarm and concern. At its first appearance, Revelation was nearly excluded from the Christian scriptures, and its strange and punishing text has always puzzled, agitated, threatened, and offended many Christians who were prepared to accept Revelation as Holy Writ. But it also true that Revelation ultimately seized and held the Christian imagination—and, in some ways, the Western imagination—over the next fifteen centuries. John's little book, sweet in the mouth but bitter in the belly, may have turned out be a failure as a work of prophecy, but it remained the equivalent of a best seller in the Middle Ages and long after.

R evelation has always been regarded by some Christian authorities as a dangerous book. Just as John seems to have intended, the text is capable of stirring up powerful emotions in its readers and hearers. Revelation is, by turns, a revenge fantasy, a parade of horribles, and something of a freak show. And the potent and intoxicating text sends some readers into their own fits of mystical ecstasy in which divine voices are heard and miraculous sights are seen. Nowadays, of course, we may be tempted to regard such phenomena as manifestations of mental illness, but the clergy of the infant Christian church were equally skeptical of ordinary men and women who claimed to be visionaries.

The earliest recorded example of religious excess inspired by the book Revelation dates back to the middle of the second century, a half century or so after the text first appeared in the Christian world. Revelation was the favorite biblical text of a man called Montanus, who appeared around 156 in the region of Asia Minor known as Phrygia, not far from the seven churches to which John addresses his letters, and announced himself to be a prophet in his own right. Among his coterie were Maximilla and Prisca, two charismatic young women who—like Montanus himself—were able to put themselves into ecstatic trance states at will and claimed to receive their own revelations directly from God, a phenomenon that came to be known as "New Prophecy."

Like other freelance prophets who came before and after them, the Montanists were regarded as intolerably high-spirited by the clerical authorities who preferred to confine prophecy to the approved biblical texts. After all, if any man or woman was at liberty to advertise himself or herself as a prophet, the imaginations of otherwise good Christians might be set afire with odd, dangerous, and uncontrollable visions. For that reason, the church condemned the Montanists as heretics, but Montanus and his pair of prophetesses persisted in their self-appointed mission. Indeed, they insisted that the church need not be worried about a flurry of false prophets precisely because their own prophecies of the end-times were about to be fulfilled once and for all.

"After me there will be no more prophecy," declared Maximilla, "but the End."[11]

Inspired by the visions in Revelation, the Montanists convinced themselves—and sought to convince everyone else—that the end was near. They taught that good Christians should abandon the ordinary pastimes of life and prepare to meet their maker. Thus, for example, they discouraged the remarriage of widows and widowers and the bearing of children by married couples: "The biblical command, 'increase and multiply,' is annulled by the fact that we are living in the last age."[12] And, significantly, they refused to regard the fantastic imagery of Revelation as a set of signs and symbols to be mined for hidden meanings. Rather, like countless other mystics and visionaries down through the centuries and millennia, they insisted on reading the text of Revelation as absolute and literal truth.

John, for example, describes in Revelation how he is transported "in the Spirit" to a mountaintop where an angel has promised to show him "the Bride, the wife of the Lamb." What he sees, however, is the city of Jerusalem "coming down out of heaven," radiant with the glory of God, its foundations fashioned out of precious stones in every color, its walls of jasper and pearl, its streets and buildings of pure gold.[13] John himself seems to concede that the Bride of the Lamb is merely a symbol for the celestial Jerusalem, and he suggests that the heavenly city is something that will be seen only by the resurrected saints and martyrs, and only after the world has finally been destroyed.

The Montanists, however, lived in urgent anticipation that they would soon behold the New Jerusalem in the here and now, a miraculous construction of gold and gemstone descending through the clouds and landing on the solid ground. They ignored the passages in Revelation where John's announces that the text must be read "spiritually"—that is, as a set of allegories and symbols.[14] Rather, they were convinced that the heavenly city would come to rest in the vicinity of a town called Pepuza, a place not far from the seven cities whose churches are addressed in Revelation and conveniently located in the region of Phrygia where the Montanists originated. Like so many other readers and hearers of Revelation, starting in antiquity and continuing into our own age, they cherished the notion that John was prophesying the plain truth of things that must shortly and literally come to pass.

$$\Omega$$

Anxious and gullible Christians in the backwater of Asia Minor were not the only ones to fall under the spell of Montanus and his prophetesses. The most famous convert to Montanism was Tertullian (ca. 160–ca. 220), a fiery theologian of the early church in Carthage, who was convinced that he, too, would see the same remarkable sights with his own eyes. Tertullian writes credulously of reports from soldiers stationed in the Roman province of Palestine who claimed to have seen the spires and towers of a city hovering above the horizon at dawn—surely an early sighting of the celestial Jerusalem! And Tertullian's anticipation of the final day of judgment betrays the same longing for revenge that is so prominently featured in the book of Revelation.

"How vast a spectacle then will burst upon the eye!" enthuses Tertullian, who predicts that the Roman governors who persecuted the Christians will suffer "in fires fiercer than those with which, in the days of their pride, they raged against the followers of Christ."[15]

Nor were the Montanists the only self-styled prophets who stoked the anxiety and anticipation of the Christian populace. A prophetess at work elsewhere in Asia Minor in the second century, for example, urged the men and women of Cappadocia to abandon their homes and make their way en masse to Jerusalem to greet Jesus Christ at the Second Coming. And a visionary named Judah, following the example of Revelation by reinterpreting the book of Daniel for himself, assured his fellow Christians in Alexandria that the Antichrist was at hand—a claim that, according to revered church historian Eusebius (263–339), was taken seriously only because a wave of persecution had "unsettled the popular mind."[16]

Then, too, Prisca and Maximilla were not the first or only women in early Christianity who believed themselves to be filled with the prophetic spirit. Indeed, the prophetess whom John calls "Jezebel" was an even earlier example of the same phenomenon. But the church authorities, like the author of Revelation himself, were especially prone to dismiss as a false prophet any self-styled seer who happened to be of the wrong gender. Against every effort of the organized church to suppress these visionary women, however, they have not been wholly erased from history, and we will meet them again and again in these pages. "What we hear of them, we hear from their sworn enemies," feminist Bible scholar Mary T. Malone points out. "We hear enough, however, to be assured that many women, in many different parts of Christianity, still sought access to teaching, preaching and priestly roles."[17]

Paradoxically, the fact that Montanus and other doomsayers were demonstrably wrong in their predictions did not really seem to matter to the true believers among their followers—another phenomenon that we will encounter repeatedly in the history of the end of the world. Indeed, the failure of the New Jerusalem to descend at Pepuza only gave the Montanists "a new life and form," according to one Catholic historian, "as a kind of Christianity of the elite, whom no other authority guided in their new life but the Holy Spirit working directly upon them."[18] After all, if John had been singled out by God to receive the remarkable visions that are recorded in Revelation, the same divine gift might be bestowed on others who came after him—and perhaps they would succeed where he had apparently failed in discerning the divine master plan for the end of the world.

And so, precisely because some church authorities feared what might boil up out of the overstimulated imaginations of the readers and hearers of Revelation, the adversaries of New Prophecy sought to discredit the book of Revelation itself. They argued that it was not actually the work of St. John the Evangelist; rather, they attributed its authorship to a man called Cerinthus, who had been declared a heretic and a sexual outlaw because he supposedly envisioned Christ's thousand-year reign on earth as an opportunity for the "saints" to indulge themselves in "unlimited gluttony and lechery at banquets, drinking-bouts, and wedding feasts."[19] By denying that Revelation is a work of Holy Writ, the enemies of Montanus sought to strike an oblique blow at the charismatic but uncredentialed prophet, his little coven of amateur prophetesses, and all of their ardent followers.

But something more than the antics and excesses of Montanus and Cerinthus were at stake in the campaign against the canonization of the book of Revelation. Freelance prophets, male or female, were regarded by the high clergy as a grave threat to theological law and order. Since Revelation, then as now, seems to be the "text of choice" for visionaries and ecstatics—and, indeed, since it seems to sanction their febrile dreams and bizarre visions—the text itself is often considered suspect.[20] For some of the sterner Christian authorities, then, cutting Revelation out of the Bible was like cutting out a dangerous cancer.

Ω

Revelation posed another awkward problem for the early Christian church as it struggled to find a way to survive in pagan Rome. The Roman emperors in Revelation are likened to demonic beasts who have seated themselves on the throne of the Devil. The richness and splendor of the Hellenistic way of life are denounced as "abominations and impurities."[21] Any Christian who makes his or her peace with the status quo of imperial Rome is condemned for trafficking in "the deep things of Satan."[22] Precisely because John is an uncompromising culture warrior whose sworn enemy is Roman civilization itself, his writings were an embarrassment to any Christian who sought to win friends and influence people in the Roman Empire.

Elsewhere in the New Testament, in fact, the authors are much more accommodating toward Rome. An unmistakable "spin" in the Gospel account of the arrest, trial, and execution of Jesus, for example, shifts the blame from the Roman authorities in occupied Judea to the Jewish priests of the Temple at Jerusalem. Jesus himself is shown to utter the words that can be understood as an instruction to submit to Roman authority: "Render therefore to Caesar the things that are Caesar's, and to God the things that are God's."[23] Significantly, Jesus illustrates the point by holding up a Roman coin that bears the name and portrait of a pagan emperor—the "mark of the beast," as John sees it. And while the famous saying of Jesus can be understood in more than one way, the apostle Paul unambiguously endorses making peace with Rome: "Let every soul be subject to the governing authorities," writes Paul. "For there is no authority except from God, and the authorities that exist are appointed by God."[24]

As long as the Christians faced—or feared—persecution by the Roman authorities, of course, the book of Revelation offered consolation for their present sufferings, real or imagined, and the promise of a bloody revenge in the end-times. But the contempt for imperial Rome that suffuses the book of Revelation was rendered suddenly and wholly obsolete when Emperor Constantine (ca. 280–337) embraced Christianity in the early fourth century. Under Constantine and his sons, the Christian church was elevated from a marginalized and criminalized sect into the favored and protected faith of the imperial family and, eventually, a kind of shadow government whose reach extended throughout the Roman Empire. Once the Roman emperor was a Christian rather than a persecutor of Christians, the condemnation of imperial Rome in the book Revelation no longer made much sense. Indeed, the Christian church now styled itself as "the Church Militant and Triumphant."

For John, the Roman emperor is an agent of the Devil who drinks himself into a stupor on the blood of Christian martyrs. For the Christians who lived under Constantine, by contrast, the Roman emperor is God's regent on earth: "Just as there is only one God, so there is only one emperor," affirms Eusebius, who served as both church chronicler and court historian during Constantine's long reign.[25] John insists that Rome, which he labels as "BABYLON THE GREAT, MOTHER OF HARLOTS AND OF EARTH'S ABOMINATIONS," will be utterly destroyed in the end-times: "Babylon is fallen, that great city," proclaims an angel in one of his visions, "because she made all nations drink of the wine of the wrath of her fornication."[26] But Eusebius "was not troubled overmuch to distinguish Constantine's reign from the time of the messianic kingdom,"[27] and he describes the Roman empire under its first Christian emperor as nothing less than heaven on earth.

"One might have thought it a foreshadowing of Christ's kingdom," enthuses Eusebius, "and a dream rather than reality."[28]

The stark contrast between what John predicted and what had actually come to pass in imperial Rome prompted some pious but also practical men in the Christianized empire to conclude that Revelation must be contained, or cut out of the Bible altogether. The same cognitive dissonance prompted other Christians to go to extraordinary lengths to explain away what seemed to be a collection of misbegotten and wrongheaded visions. Both the attackers and defenders of John's little book were coming at the same awkward problem from opposite directions— the fact that Christian emperors were now sitting on what John sees as the throne of Satan.

Ω

Indeed, the single biggest problem with the book of Revelation is the plain fact that the world did *not* end. John insists that he has been shown "the things which must shortly come to pass"—and yet, as the years, decades, and centuries passed, Rome still ruled the world.[29] For those Christians in late antiquity who regarded the book of Revelation as the revealed word of God, the manifest failure of its prophecies was embarrassing but undeniable.

"As history, in other words, persistently failed to end on time," explains historian and New Testament scholar Paula Fredriksen, "the Church, of necessity, had to come to terms with its own foundational prophecy."[30]

John, of course, is not the only biblical figure whose predictions of the end of the world turned out to be wrong or, at least, grossly premature. The book of Daniel, as we have seen, seems to confidently predict that the end of the world would come exactly 1,290 days after "the abomination of desolation is set up."[31] Of course, the author is maddeningly oblique in describing the event that is supposed to start the countdown clock—the "abomination of desolation" is probably a pagan image that was installed in the Temple at Jerusalem by the Syrian conquerors of Judea in the second century B.C.E.—and he undercuts his own credibility by stating, only one verse later, that the waiting period is actually 1,335 days. But the author assures his readers that such ambiguities and contradictions need not trouble the true believer—a credo of Bible prophecy that is invoked even today.

"None of the wicked shall understand," the author Daniel writes, "but they that are wise shall understand."[32]

Jesus, too, is depicted in the Gospels as announcing that the end is near. In fact, he quotes the book of Daniel—"Therefore when you see the 'abomination of desolation,' spoken of by Daniel the prophet, standing in the holy place (whoever reads, let him understand), then let those who are in Judea flee to the mountains"[33]—and his description of the end-times is equally heart shaking but far more poignant when compared with those in Revelation. "And alas for those who are with child and for those who give suck in those days!" Jesus is shown to say in the Little Apocalypse as it appears in the Gospel of Matthew. "Pray that your flight may not be in winter or on a sabbath. For then there will be great tribulation, such as has not been from the beginning of the world until now."[34]

Jesus, as we have noted, insists that at least some of his contemporaries will be eyewitnesses to the end of the world—eclipses of the sun and moon, stars falling from the sky, "famines and pestilences and earthquakes"[35]— and the arrival of the Son of Man "in the glory of His Father with the holy angels."[36] His assurances, so awkward for later teachers and preachers precisely because they are so plainspoken and yet so plainly wrong, can be found in both Mark—"Truly, I say to you there are some standing here who will not taste death before they see that the kingdom of God has come with power"[37]—and Matthew: "Truly, I say to you, this generation will not pass away till all these things take place."[38]

Indeed, the first Christians lived with the constant and urgent expectation that they would witness the end of the world. Paul's First Epistle to the Thessalonians, for example, describes what has come to be called the "rapture"—that is, the sudden elevation of faithful Christians from earth to heaven upon the second coming of Jesus Christ: "For the Lord Himself will descend from heaven with a shout, with the voice of an archangel, and with the trumpet of God, and the dead in Christ will rise first," says Paul. "Then we who are alive and remain shall be caught up together with them in the clouds to meet the Lord in the air."[39] Paul's unequivocal prediction, in fact, is contained in a letter that may have been composed as early as 49 C.E.—"the earliest datable witness to Christianity that we possess," according to some scholars.[40]

But the New Testament also includes writings that seek to tamp down the apocalyptic expectations of early Christians. Significantly, Paul's Second Epistle to the Thessalonians backs off from the promise that the end is near, which is one reason why it is generally regarded as having been written much later than the First Epistle and by someone other than Paul. "Now concerning the coming of our Lord Jesus Christ and our assembling to meet him, we beg you, brethren, not to be quickly shaken in mind or excited, either by spirit or by word, or by letter purporting to be from us, to the effect that the day of the Lord has come," Paul is made to say in the second letter. And then he adds what appears to be a reference to the end-time scenario of Revelation: "Let no one deceive you in any way; for that day will not come, unless the rebellion comes first, and the man of lawlessness is revealed, the son of perdition."[41]

Jesus himself pointedly rules out any sure knowledge of *when* the world will end. "When you hear of wars and rumors of war, do not be troubled, for such things must happen, but the end is not yet,"[42] Jesus is quoted as saying in a famous passage in the Gospel of Mark. In fact, Jesus specifically warns against "false Christs and false prophets" who will seek to lead good Christians astray by claiming to know the date or details of the end-times.[43] And Jesus insists that no one in heaven or on earth—not even himself!—has been granted a revelation about the date of doomsday. "If anyone says to you, 'Look, here is the Christ!' or, 'Look, He is there!,' do not believe it," Jesus is shown to say. "But of that day and hour no one knows, not even the angels in heaven, nor the Son, but only the Father."[44]

Of course, Jesus may have cautioned his followers against idle speculation on the date of the end of the world, but his words did nothing to stop some readers of the book of Revelation from doing exactly what he tells them not to do. Indeed, the whole effort to crack the code of Revelation has always struck some pious clerics as unseemly and even sinful: "The numerous attempts by His professed followers to attain precise knowledge seem to me to be evidence of serious disloyalty to Him, Who announced that the secrets they vainly try to fathom are reserved for God Himself," writes H. H. Rowley.[45] But such cautions have not prevented countless generations of visionaries, ranging from the prophetesses Prisca and Maximilla to the Bible-thumping televangelists and best-selling authors of our own era, from convincing themselves—and seeking to convince others—that they know when the world will end.

R evelation is not the only ancient writing that was regarded as too hot to handle by some clerics in the early years of the Christian church. At a site in the Egyptian desert called Nag Hammadi, for example, a collection of papyrus texts—the so-called Gnostic Gospels—were buried in the sand by some fearful Christian precisely because they had been declared to be heretical by the authorities of the church. Among the forbidden texts of early Christianity were a great many apocalyptic tracts, including one that preserves a sly parody of perhaps the single most familiar line in the book of Revelation.

"I am the first and the last," goes a passage in *The Book of Thunder,* "I am the honored one and the scorned one, I am the whore and the holy one."[46]

The fate of the Gnostic Gospels suggests what might have happened to the book of Revelation if the would-be censors had been more successful: the Gnostic Gospels remained buried and forgotten for two thousand years until archaeologists retrieved them from Nag Hammadi in the twentieth century and thereby rewrote an early chapter in the history of Christianity. Revelation, too, was in danger of losing its place in the Christian scriptures and perhaps even disappearing from Christian tradition in the same way that Jewish apocalyptic texts like the book of Enoch were written out of rabbinical tradition.

The precarious status of the book of Revelation in the early Christian church, as it turns out, is confirmed in the writings of the church fathers. The ancient historian Eusebius frankly reports that Revelation "was considered genuine by some and spurious by others."[47] At certain moments, the controversy over Revelation was hot enough to divide members of the same family. One early and influential commentator, Gregory of Nazianzus, cites the book of Revelation in his own work, but his cousin, Amphilochius of Iconium, notes that "most call it spurious."[48]

The debate over whether Revelation belonged in the Bible was framed as a question about its authorship. According to one of the litmus tests adopted the early church fathers, only a writing that was regarded as "apostolic"—that is, a writing whose author was an apostle or a disciple of Jesus—was eligible for inclusion in the New Testament. Thus, the identity of the man who calls himself "John" in the book of Revelation turned out to be crucial. If the author was John, son of Zebedee, one of the original twelve disciples of Jesus of Nazareth, then Revelation was worthy of inclusion, but if the author was "another John," as Bishop Dionysius declared in the third century, then it was to be excluded from the Christian scriptures.[49] The fact that the book of Revelation struck Dionsyius as "senseless and without reason" was almost beside the point. "[T]hose things which I do not understand I do not reject," he explained, "but I wonder the more that I cannot comprehend."[50]

One illuminating example of how canonization worked in the early Christian world—and how it might have worked in the case of Revelation—can be seen in the fate of a work called *The Shepherd of Hermas*. Like Revelation, it is a strange text with prophetic and apocalyptic passages, featuring a celestial visitor who bestows upon a human being the power to read and understand a book of divine secrets. It was probably composed sometime after 90 C.E., which means that *The Shepherd of Hermas* may have been roughly contemporaneous with Revelation. And, again as with Revelation, its author is believed to have been a Jewish convert to Christianity. Unlike Revelation, however, it is purely Christian, full of references to church, clergy, Christian rites and rituals, and other elements that are largely or wholly absent from Revelation.

Yet Revelation was ultimately welcomed into the Christian canon, and *The Shepherd of Hermas* was excluded for the simple reason that its author was self-evidently *not* an apostle or a disciple of Jesus Christ. Rather, it was plainly a work of recent authorship by a man who identifies himself as a resident of Rome.[51] The book was a favorite among Christian communities of the second century, but popularity did not matter when it came to canonization. *The Shepherd of Hermas* was excluded from the earliest surviving document that defines the Christian canon—the so-called Muratorian Canon of the late second century—with the simple and sufficient explanation that it was written "in our own times."[52]

As late as the fourth century, the list makers were still divided on the question of whether Revelation ought to be included in Christian scripture. Athanasius (ca. 293–373), bishop of Alexandria and a fiery crusader against Christian heresies of all kinds, includes Revelation in his own catalog of the books of the New Testament, but it is omitted from the lists composed and endorsed by Cyril of Jerusalem (ca. 315–ca. 386) and, by a certain irony, the Council of Laodicea, one of the seven cities to which the author of Revelation addresses himself. Indeed, the book of Revelation was especially suspect in the eastern realm of Christianity, and it is notably absent from the biblical citations that appear in the writings of church fathers residing in such important eastern cities as Antioch and Constantinople.

In fact, Revelation did not make the first cut in the early version of the Bible as it was known and used in eastern Christianity. The Eastern Syrian Church rejected the book of Revelation, and it does not appear at all in the earliest Syriac translation of the Christian scriptures. As late as the ninth century, Revelation was still flagged as a "disputed" book in Byzantine church writings, and it was wholly omitted from a Byzantine list of Christian texts that were embraced as canonical. Not until the tenth century did Revelation begin to appear routinely in Greek manuscripts of the New Testament throughout Christendom.[53]

Revelation may have had a slow and uncertain start in the very place where it was composed, but the western reaches of the Roman Empire were considerably more receptive. The New Testament as it was known and used in the West always included Revelation, and the text turned out to be especially influential in Germany, France, and England. Indeed, as we shall see, Revelation always seems to move ever westward, across Europe and all the way to America—a fact with fateful consequences for its function in our own age.

Ω

Even after Revelation finally secured its place in the Christian scriptures, the book continued to carry a certain bad odor. The bizarre imagery and the blood-shaking carnage favored by John were always off-putting to more-restrained Christian preachers and teachers. Not a word in the whole of Revelation offers any moral instruction about how to live a decent and righteous life *hic et nunc*—here and now. And the higher clergy were always concerned that some new Prisca or Maximilla would be encouraged by what she read in Revelation to start spouting her own visions and prophecies. The book of Revelation was tolerated, but it was also kept at a safe distance by some church authorities.

As one measure of its marginal status in early Christianity, for example, fewer than two hundred manuscripts of Revelation in its original Greek text—compared with more than two thousand manuscripts of the Gospels—survive from antiquity. "These totals," reports Protestant Bible scholar and theologian Ernest Cadman Colwell, "accurately represent the relative prestige of these volumes in Eastern Christendom down through the Middle Ages." Another sign of the same phenomenon can be discerned in one ancient biblical commentary whose author freely rendered passages from Revelation in conversational Greek but left the other books of the New Testament untranslated from the more formal Greek of the original text because, unlike Revelation, "they were too sacred!"[54]

Even as late as the Reformation, when the conflict between Protestants and Catholics was often a matter of life or death, a few theologians on both sides of the struggle agreed on one thing: the book of Revelation was a dangerous text that required cautious handling. "Some gold is purer and better than other," goes a dismissive comment about Revelation by Renaissance theologian Desiderius Erasmus (1469–1536) in a biblical treatise published in the early sixteenth century. "In sacred things also one thing is more sacred than another."[55] And Martin Luther, the Roman Catholic monk who set the Protestant Reformation into motion, was no less skeptical and far less oblique: he confessed his own inclination to wholly exclude the book of Revelation from the Bible on the grounds that it is "neither apostolic nor prophetic."[56]

The front line in the battle over Revelation has always been drawn between the authority of the church and the ragtag army of unruly Bible readers who insist on coming to their own conclusions about its veiled inner meanings. That is why, as we shall see, Revelation has *always* been the "text of choice" for religious eccentrics who see their own time as the end-time, ranging from Montanus in the second century to David Koresh in the twentieth century, and countless others in between.

"There has never been a book provoking more delirium, foolishness, and irrational movements, as if this book contained the possibility of a temptation actually demonic," complains French political scientist and Protestant theologian Jacques Ellul, whose words apply with equal force to the Montanists and the religious fanatics of the third millennium. "Too often the Apocalypse excites our curiosity, unbridles our imagination, arouses our appetite for mystery, and finally hides from us the central truth which ought to be revealed."[57]

At the same time, Revelation turned out to be so crucial to Christian theology that it simply could not be ignored. "Revelation is not a nice book, nor in any conventional sense is it morally edifying," observes historian

and Bible scholar Donald Harman Akenson in his revolutionary reread-
ing of Jewish and Christian scripture, *Surpassing Wonder: The Invention of
the Bible and the Talmuds*. Yet he describes the inclusion of Revelation in
the Christian canon as "an architectural master stroke" precisely because
Revelation fundamentally reorients the rest of Christian scripture. "The
book forces one to read the entire text of the 'New Testament' as an apocalypse," Akenson explains, "which starts with the birth of Jesus and ends
with Christ's kingdom in eternity."[58]

By the fourth century, however, the church authorities decided to do
something about the fact that the book of Revelation continued to work
its powerful and provocative magic on the hearts and minds of the most
excitable men and women among the laity. So they came up with a simple
and convenient rule to govern the reading of Revelation. A good Christian,
they taught, must not commit the error of reading Revelation "carnally"—
that is, taking John's visions of the end-times literally. Instead, the book of
Revelation must be read "spiritually"; that is, Revelation must be understood as an allegory rather than a plain depiction of what will actually happen when the world comes to an end.

The rule represents an earnest effort to defuse the ticking time bomb that
sputters away in the text of Revelation. The full weight of church authority and, eventually, the terrible threat of the Inquisition were brought to
bear in enforcing the rule on the laity, but never with complete success.
Ironically, the willful and unruly Christians who insisted on reading Revelation "carnally" were defying not only the dogma of the Roman Catholic
Church but also the clear instructions of the author himself.

Ω

At a certain crucial moment in the book of Revelation, John describes a
vision of what will take place in an unnamed city in the end-times. The
"Gentiles"—a term used in the Hebrew Bible for non-Jews—will "tread
the holy city underfoot" for a period of forty-two months, John is told
by an angel. Then two anonymous "witnesses" will be given the power to
prophesy for a period of exactly 1,260 days. As soon as the two witnesses are finished with their prophecies, "the beast that ascends from the bottomless pit will make war upon them and conquer them and kill them."
Their bodies will lay unburied in the streets for three and a half days, and
then they will be resurrected and called to heaven by a divine voice.[59]

"At that hour there was a great earthquake, and a tenth of the city fell," writes John, describing the divine catastrophe that he has glimpsed in his visions. "Seven thousand people were killed in the earthquake, and the rest were terrified and gave glory to the God of heaven."[60]

John never actually identifies the place that he sees in his vision, referring only to "the great city, which is spiritually called Sodom and Egypt." Some translators render the word *spiritually* as *allegorically* because, in fact, John is signaling his readers and hearers that both of these place names are purely symbolic. And he reveals the intended meaning of the symbolic names by describing the "great city" as the place where "our Lord was crucified." To put it plainly, when the author of Revelation says "Sodom" and "Egypt," he means Jerusalem—that is, the earthly city under the occupation of pagan Rome—but he says it allegorically rather than literally.[61]

It's hardly the most celebrated line of text in the book of Revelation, but it is arguably among the most illuminating ones. Here, as elsewhere in the book of Revelation, John makes it clear that the names, numbers, colors, and images in his visions are ciphers that must be decoded to yield their actual meanings. Montanus may have expected to see the celestial Jerusalem float down through the clouds above Pepuza and bestir the Phrygian dust when it came to rest on solid ground—but only because he failed to heed John's warning to read the book of Revelation "spiritually."

Indeed, John himself is given a short course in the interpretation of dreams and visions by his own heavenly mentors. At first glance, for example, John is astounded and bewildered by the sight of the seven-headed beast on which the Whore of Babylon rides. "Why marvel?" says an angel. "I will tell you the mystery of the woman and of the beast that carries her." And it turns out that the seven heads of the beast are merely symbols that are meant to represent, among other things, seven earthly kings.[62] And Jesus himself explains the "mystery" of the seven stars and the seven golden lamp stands that John sees in his very first vision: they are merely symbols for the seven earthly churches that John is called upon to address.[63]

Still, John knows how to work a crowd, and he surely means to manipulate the fears and longings of his audience with scenes of sexual excess, violent persecution of Christians by pagan authorities, and equally violent revenge by God against their persecutors. And the early church fathers saw for themselves how the potent words and images of Revelation were capable of moving some men and women to dreams and visions of their own.

When they cautioned good Christians to engage in a "spiritual" rather than a "carnal" reading of Revelation, they were struggling to make it safe for human consumption—and thus began the long, ardent, but failed enterprise that one scholar calls the "taming" of the apocalyptic tradition.[64]

R eading a sacred text as an artful allegory rather than the plain truth was an ancient and honorable notion in the Greco-Roman world, and it was embraced by both Jewish and Christian scholars and theologians, including Philo of Alexandria in Jewish tradition and Origen and Jerome in Christian tradition. Thus, for example, the Bible literalists who projected themselves into the passages in Revelation where the saints and martyrs are shown to reign alongside Jesus Christ in the millennial kingdom—"They think they are to be kings and princes," complains Origen, "like those earthly monarchs who now exist"—were condemned for "refusing the labor of thinking."[65]

But the "spiritual" approach to scripture was given its most complete and commanding expression by a forgotten figure called Tyconius, a late-fourth-century Christian cleric whose writings are now mostly lost but whose teachings cast a long shadow over the book of Revelation. Tyconius taught that the terrible and glorious images and incidents in Revelation—the demonic monsters, the celestial warriors, the final battle between God and Satan, and the thousand-year reign of Jesus—must be understood as symbolic expressions of an ongoing struggle between good and evil rather than a literal account of things to come. For Tyconius, the Whore of Babylon and the Bride of the Lamb were nothing more than convenient glyphs for distinguishing between ordinary human beings whose lives were godly or satanic.

Tyconius himself has been mostly written out of Christian tradition because he was a so-called Donatist, a member of the schismatic faction within the early church that refused to accept the authority of bishops whom they regarded as having been too quick to compromise with the pagan magistrates during the periods of persecution under imperial Rome. The Donatists condemned any Christian who complied with an order to turn over his Bible for burning as a *traditor*—the Latin word that originally meant "one who hands over" but soon acquired the meaning that is associated with its English equivalent, "traitor." In that sense, the Donatists and the author of Revelation were kindred spirits: both were Christian radicals who ruled out any compromise with pagan Rome and detested above all any fellow Christian who collaborated with the Roman authorities.

When it came to reading the book of Revelation, however, Tyconius advocated a restrained and sensible approach, thus "liberating it from the embarrassments of a literal interpretation," as Paula Fredriksen explains.[66] But it fell to someone whose Christian credentials were in better order to elevate the "spiritual" reading of Revelation to the status of a church doctrine—Augustine (354–430), bishop of Hippo in the Roman province of Africa, and perhaps the single most influential theologian in the early church. He urged the readers and hearers of Revelation to regard the battle between God and Satan, so luridly depicted in Revelation, as an allegory for the "moral conflict within each person and in the Church in general"— and he insisted that anyone who did otherwise was merely succumbing to "ridiculous fancies."[67]

Ω

Augustine, who is famous for his quickness in confessing his own failings, admits in *City of God* that he, too, was once tempted to engage in what he calls a "carnal" reading of Revelation.[68] That is, he was willing to entertain the thrilling and consoling idea that flesh-and-blood Christians would, sooner or later, see Jesus Christ descend from the heavens on a cloud and reign as king on earth for one thousand years. But Augustine declares that he later realized the error of his ways, and he calls on his fellow Christians to do the same. Indeed, he derides the popular belief that the resurrected saints would be permitted to resume the pleasures of the flesh during the millennial countdown to the final destruction of the world.

Based on a few spare lines of text in the book of Revelation that describe the thousand-year reign of Christ and the saints, some wishful thinkers painted an elaborate picture of the earthly paradise that resembles nothing to be found in Revelation itself or anywhere else in the Christian scriptures. They insisted, for example, that the dead would awaken in flawless bodies of the approximate age of Jesus at the time of his crucifixion— "thirty-something," as Paula Fredericksen wryly puts it.[69] Fat people would be given slender bodies, and amputees would get back their missing arms and legs. According to Irenaeus, who claims to possess knowledge of divine secrets that John taught but did not write down in Revelation, the millennium will resemble something out of a fairy tale.

"The days will come in which vines will grow, each having ten thousand branches, and in each branch ten thousand twigs, and in each twig ten thousand shoots, and in each shoot ten thousand clusters, and on every cluster ten thousand grapes," he imagines in *Against Heresies*. "And when any of the saints shall lay hold of a cluster, another cluster will cry out, 'I am a better cluster, take me.'"[70]

For ordinary men and women who struggled from day to day to put food on the table—and who lived in constant fear of famine—it is hardly surprising that paradise is imagined as a place where there is plenty to eat. But Augustine finds these fantasies to be naive and infantile, and he openly ridicules the notion that the resurrected saints would spend a thousand years gorging themselves at "immoderate carnal banquets, in which there will be so much to eat and drink that those supplies will break the bounds not only of moderation, but also of credibility."[71]

Augustine insists that the millennium as described in Revelation refers to a celestial paradise rather than an earthly one: "The joys of the saints in that Sabbath shall be spiritual," he insists.[72] And, contrary to the feverish imaginings of men like Montanus, he scoffs at the idea that the heavenly Jerusalem will be seen by human beings in the here and now. Rather, Augustine regards the new Jerusalem as depicted in Revelation as the symbol of "a glory so pervading and so new that no vestige of what is old shall remain"—that is, a phenomenon that is reserved until the world itself is gone.[73] No one will actually witness the thousand-year reign of Christ with mortal eyes, because the millennial kingdom, according to Augustine, is yet another symbol. "The Church," declares Augustine, "is the Kingdom of Christ."[74]

Indeed, Augustine prefers to see all the spooky and scary details in the prophecies of Revelation as a series of elaborate metaphors for a divine truth so ineffable that John is compelled to reduce it to concrete words, numbers, and images because the ordinary human mind could not otherwise comprehend them. John puts the reign of Christ at one thousand years not as a literal measurement of time, according to Augustine, but as "an equivalent for the whole duration of this world": one thousand, Augustine writes, is "the number of perfection." And when John describes how Satan will be bound in chains and cast into an abyss during the thousand-year reign of Christ, Augustine understands "abyss" to mean "the countless multitude of the wicked whose hearts are unfathomably deep in malignity against the Church of God."[75]

Nor is Augustine willing to concede that the final battle between God and Satan, as described so vividly in the book of Revelation, can be recognized in the troubles that were, even as he wrote, afflicting Rome. Some of his contemporaries, for example, argued that when John sees visions of the armies of Satan at war with the armies of God, he is predicting the invasion of the Roman Empire by various "barbarian" peoples, including the Goths and the Moors, who were dubbed Getae and Massengetae in some ancient sources. But Augustine insists that John is only speaking metaphorically about the enemies of the church wherever they may dwell on earth. "For these nations which he names Gog and Magog," writes Augustine, "are not to be understood of some barbarous nations in the some part of the world, whether the Getae and Massangetae, as some conclude from the initial letters, or some other foreign nations not under the Roman government."[76]

Above all, Augustine strikes a stance that one modern scholar calls "radical agnosticism" and another scholar dubs "the eschatological uncertainty principle."[77] Augustine piously affirms the inner truth of the scriptural account of the end-times—but he insists that "the manner in which this shall take place we can now only feebly conjecture, and shall understand it only when it comes to pass."[78] Since Jesus has already cautioned all good Christians that no one knows when the end will come, Augustine suggests, the book of Revelation must be consulted only for its "spiritual" instruction and not as a source of eschatological thrills.

Augustine's strict and narrow reading of Revelation was embraced and enforced by church authorities, and thus served to discourage any open speculation on the colorful details of the Second Coming. "Augustine glowered on Christian millennialists," explains historian Robert E. Lerner, "and made them guard their words." Apocalyptic speculation was so effectively suppressed by the church that, between 400 and 1000, "there is no surviving written product that displays an independent Western millenarian imagination."[79] And those self-styled soothsayers who were audacious enough to fix a certain date for the end of the world, such as the doomsayers who announced with perfect confidence that the Second Coming would take place in the year 500 C.E., were denounced by more cautious Christians as *deliri et insani*—that is, "insane crazies."[80]

"And, of course, in terms of empirical verification, the essence of their argument has been vindicated by the simple passage of time," observes Paula Fredriksen, "which has continued not to end."[81]

Augustine's stern and austere approach to Revelation, however, was never wholly successful in extinguishing the fires that the text was meant to ignite in the hearts and minds of its readers and hearers. Just as John had surely intended, the word-magic of Revelation was irresistible. For men and women who were forced to cope with the daily stresses and intermittent terrors of life in the medieval world, the book of Revelation held out the promise that plague, famine, pestilence, and war would be followed by revenge against one's enemies on earth and the reward of eternal life in a celestial kingdom—and not just someday, but soon.

For the true believer, it is easy to explain the failure of the world to "end on time" without dismissing Revelation a mere allegory or, for that matter, a set of failed prophecies. The *other* way to read the book of Revelation is based on the conviction that divine secrets are surely encoded and enciphered in the text but that the readers of Revelation have so far failed to understand them. After all, the apocalyptic tradition is based on the thrilling notion that the real meanings of Revelation are hidden in plain sight and that "the mind which hath wisdom," as John puts it, will discern and understand the divine secrets.[82]

So the medieval Bible literalists, like their modern counterparts, insisted on reading the book of Revelation as divine prophecy, and they continued their tireless efforts at code breaking. The best example, then as now, is the effort to identify the villain who is described in Revelation as the "beast." As early as the third century, a Roman bishop called Hippolytus (ca. 170– ca. 235) announced that the "beast" of Revelation is the very same arch-demon who is mentioned elsewhere in the New Testament in the epistles attributed to the apostle John: "Little children, it is the last hour! As you have heard the Antichrist is coming, even now many antichrists have come, by which we know that it is the last hour."[83] And thus began the ancient and enduring tradition of doing exactly what Augustine warned pious Christians *not* to do—that is, looking for specific people and events in the real world and matching them up with the characters and incidents in the book of Revelation.

The task is all the more daunting precisely because the book of Revelation, like the Epistles of John, suggests that there will be more than one candidate for the title of Antichrist. Indeed, the author of Revelation comes up with a whole bestiary of satanic creatures. He starts with the red dragon, a creature that he straightforwardly identifies as "that ancient serpent, who is called the Devil and Satan, the deceiver of the whole world."[84] But he also conjures up two more "beasts," a seven-headed beast that rises from the sea and a two-horned beast that crawls up out of the earth, both of them serving as agents of the Devil. To the first beast, "the dragon gave his power and his throne and great authority," and the second beast compels humankind to offer worship to the first beast.[85]

Such ambiguities and complexities have demanded the attention—and taxed the imagination—of the readers of Revelation for the last two thousand years. Of course, one simple and compelling answer suggests itself when the text of Revelation is restored to the historical context in which it was first composed. Most modern scholars agree that John intends the beast from the sea to symbolize imperial Rome, with each of its seven heads representing a different Roman emperor. And he intends the beast from the land to symbolize the provincial gentry in the seven cities of Asia Minor whose aping of their Roman overlords so disgusted the author. Some of the earliest readers of Revelation, like the scholars who came long after them, sought to identify the "beast" with one or another of the reigning Roman emperors of antiquity.

The single most famous and provocative clue to the identity of the Beast of Revelation has always been the alphanumeric code that is expressed in the number 666: "Here is wisdom," explains John. "Let him that hath understanding count the number of the beast: for it is the number of a man; and his number is six hundred threescore and six."[86] The key to the code, as we have seen, is the numerical value of the letters in the Hebrew, Greek, and Latin alphabets. By rendering the letters in a name as a series of numbers, it is possible to come up with "the number of a man"—that is, the numerical value of the letters in his name.

Nero, the first-century Roman emperor who has been depicted as a monster in Jewish, Christian, and pagan sources alike, has always been a favorite candidate because the numerical value of the Hebrew letters that spell "Nero Caesar" is, in fact, 666. The fact that Nero died an apparent suicide in the year 68 has never discouraged some readers of Revelation from regarding him as the Antichrist who is yet to come. John, after all, writes that the Beast "was, and is not, and shall ascend out of the bottomless pit," which has been interpreted to mean that Nero lived, died, and will be raised from the dead to reign again in the end-times.[87] And, in fact, the notion of a resurrected Nero explains an otherwise deeply enigmatic line in Revelation about the seven-headed beast from the sea.

"One of its heads seemed to have a mortal wound," writes John, "but its mortal wound was healed, and the whole earth followed the beast with wonder."[88]

John, who borrows freely from pagan sources, may have been inspired by a tale that was told about Nero in ancient Rome. According to a street rumor that was later elevated to the stature of a myth, Nero did not actually die by a self-inflicted knife wound during the tumult of a general uprising at the end of his reign; rather, the wounded emperor sought refuge with the Parthians, an enemy of ancient Rome, and would be miraculously sustained in life until the day when he would return to reign over Rome again. The tale was turned into a sacred prophecy of resurrection and return in one of the Sibylline Oracles.

"At the last time, there shall come from the ends of the earth a matricide," the Sibyl predicts, identifying Nero by reference to the belief that he murdered his own mother. "He shall gain all power, and that for which he perished he shall seize once again."[89]

So John may have repurposed the pagan myth of Nero *redivivus*—the "returned Nero"—as a vision of the end-times. But Nero is hardly the only historical figure who has been written into the pages of Revelation by its imaginative and enterprising readers. Indeed, the cast of characters in Revelation has been made to play an astounding range of roles, and each generation has churned up new candidates for the title of the Antichrist. The Beast of Revelation, as it turns out, is a man for all seasons.

Ω

Even as Augustine was advocating for a spiritual reading of Revelation, for example, some of his fellow clerics were scaring the wits out of their congregants by conjuring up the monsters and malefactors who stalk its pages and placing them in the here and now. Martin of Tours (316–397)—a visionary who believed that he had once seen the Devil with his own eyes—was convinced that the "beast" of Revelation was alive and well somewhere in the world, the flesh-and-blood spawn of the Devil himself, sired in the womb of an unwitting woman and destined to "assume power as soon as he reached the proper age."[90] One of Martin's disciples, a man called Sulpicius, spread the same chilling message after Martin himself was dead and gone. Indeed, he anticipates the harum-scarum plotline of *The Omen* by a millennium and a half.

"Now, this is the eighth year since we heard these words from his lips," writes Sulpicius in a work that first appeared at the beginning of the fifth century. "You may guess, then, how soon those things which we fear in the future are about to happen."[91]

Signs of the end-times were seen everywhere by those who were looking for them in the fifth century. The barbarians at the gates of Rome, many of whom were baptized Christians, were seen as the armies of Satan whose arrival signaled the Second Coming: "Behold, from Adam all the years have passed," declared one Christian sermonizer when Alaric and the Visigoths sacked the imperial capital in 410, "and now comes the day of judgment!"[92] Earthquakes in Palestine and a solar eclipse that was recorded on July 19, 418, were seen as fulfillments of the prophecies of Revelation: "And I beheld when he had opened the sixth seal, and, lo, there was a great earthquake, and the sun became black as sackcloth, and the moon became as blood."[93]

Indeed, there were even more extravagant examples of the "ridiculous fancies" that Augustine so coolly disdained. Caught up in the apocalyptic panic—or, more likely, preying on those who were—one young man in Spain advertised himself as the resurrected John the Baptist and another man in the eastern reaches of the Roman Empire posed as Elijah, thus invoking the passage in Revelation that predicts the coming of the two "witnesses" who would be the precursors of Christ. And a Christian chronicler of the same era argued that the numerical value of "Genseric," the name of the Vandal king who had placed himself on the throne of Carthage in North Africa, was the dreaded and demonic 666.

The Roman empire may have been in its decline and fall during the tumultuous years of the fifth century—but the world manifestly did *not* end, and the prophecies of Revelation remained unfulfilled. Still, the readers of Revelation continued to look for signs and wonders in the world around them. After the armies of Islam charged out of the Arabian peninsula in the seventh century, for example, the prophet Muhammad emerged as a compelling candidate for the Antichrist. One Spanish visionary, for example, calculated that Muhammad died in the year 666 on the Christian calendar—a fact that he confidently cited as proof that the founding prophet of Islam was the "beast" of Revelation whose death augured the imminent end of the world.

Once it began, of course, the restless and relentless search for a flesh-and-blood Antichrist never ended, and precisely because the world itself never ended. Nero was an attractive candidate for the title of Antichrist among the readers and hearers of Revelation who recalled the first perse-cution of Christians in Rome, but Muhammad was a more credible choice for someone living in the early Middle Ages. During the Crusades, Sala-din was seen as the Antichrist, and when the Turks conquered Constanti-nople in 1453, the Sultan of the Ottoman empire was the Antichrist of the hour. By the sixteenth century, Martin Luther and the pope of the Roman Catholic Church regarded each other as the Antichrist. At any given point between late antiquity and our own times, the usual suspects in the search for the Antichrist have reflected the anxieties of the age.

Ω

"Pin-the-tail-on-the-Antichrist" has always been a popular pastime among some readers of Revelation. But perhaps even more energy and enterprise have been invested in the effort to calculate exactly when the world will end by studying the mystical numbers that are embedded in the text of Revelation. Jesus specifically forbids any such speculation—and Augustine admonishes all good Christians who are inclined to count the years until doomsday to "relax your fingers, and give them a little rest"—but the plain words of the Gospels and the church fathers have never deterred the mys-tical number-crunchers.[94]

Like so much else in the apocalyptic tradition, the numbers game begins in the book of Daniel, where the prophet is granted a vision of the final ordeal of Israel: "It shall be for a time, times, and a half," says one of his celestial mentors, "and when he shall have accomplished to scatter the power of the holy people, all these things shall be finished."[95] By extrapo-lating from other and rather less obscure passages of Daniel—the prophet, as we have seen, refers to a period of 1,290 days or 1,335 days as the count-down clock to final salvation, a period roughly equal to three and a half years—some early readers of the book of Daniel decided that a "time" is a year, and "times" is two years. Thus, "a time, times, and a half" is under-stood to mean three and a half years.

Precisely the same period of time is invoked almost obsessively the book of Revelation. The woman clothed with the sun, for example, flees to the desert to escape the red dragon—and, according to John, she will stay there "a time, and times, and half a time." Elsewhere in Revelation, John specifies that her sojourn will last 1,260 days. He predicts that the Gentiles will trample the holy city of Jerusalem for forty-two months, and the two witnesses will prophesy for 1,260 days. And John later predicts that the "beast from the sea" will reign over earth for forty-two months.[96] All of these periods are equal to three and a half years if we calculate on the basis of a thirty-day month. And, not coincidentally, three and one half is exactly half of John's favorite number, the divine number seven.

According to a certain conventional wisdom that came to be embraced by apocalyptic date-setters, John means to reveal that the end of the world will come exactly three and a half years after the appearance of the Antichrist. A North African bishop called Evodius of Uzala, for example, assured his congregation in 412 that Satan himself will reign over the world as the Antichrist for exactly three and a half years before Jesus Christ returns to earth in triumph, all as predicted in the book of Revelation. The same three-and-a-half-year period was invoked throughout late antiquity and the Middle Ages as the countdown to the end-times.

Once convinced that the arrival of the Antichrist was the triggering event for the countdown to the end of the world, Christian doomsayers were all the more alert and active in searching for likely prospects among the flesh-and-blood kings and conquerors in their own world. The book of Revelation offers both bad news and good news, as we have seen, and here is yet another example: the Antichrist will bring oppression and persecution, to be sure, but he is also the surest sign that Jesus Christ is on his way. And, after all, three and a half years is not such a long time to wait for the rewards that are promised in Revelation—the second coming of Jesus Christ, the millennial kingdom, the final defeat of Satan, the Day of Judgment and, for a happy few, eternal life in the new heaven and the new earth. Apocalyptic true believers have been on the lookout for the Antichrist ever since.

Ω

But on the question of timing, too, the apocalyptic imagination has never been satisfied with simple notions, and far more elaborate theories were proposed in the early Middle Ages for calculating the end-times. The most enduring and pervasive theory is based on an ancient tradition that the history of the world from beginning to end can be divided into seven periods, each one a thousand years in duration. The seed of the idea can be found in a stray line of Jewish scripture—"For a thousand years in your sight are but as yesterday," says the Psalmist to God in the Hebrew Bible—but it sprouted and flowered in some remarkable ways in the hothouse of the apocalyptic tradition.[97]

The same simile, for example, is rephrased in the Christian scriptures in a way that suggests a more literal meaning: "One day is with the Lord as a thousand years," writes the author of the epistles of Peter, "and a thousand years as one day."[98] And the readers of Revelation elaborated on these spare lines of scripture by imagining that the seven days of creation in Genesis are meant to predict the so-called World Week—that is, seven ages of history, each age a thousand years in duration. The seventh and final "day" in the cosmic week of ages—the so-called Sabbath Age—will be the thousand-year reign of Christ on earth as predicted in Revelation.

The seven ages of history have been used to solve some of the more perplexing mysteries within the text of Revelation. John, for example, explains that the seven heads of the beast from the sea are meant to symbolize seven kings, but he does not specify which ones. Some early readers studied *The Twelve Caesars* of the ancient historian Suetonius in the hope of putting names on the seven heads. One faction starts with Julius Caesar and counts the first seven emperors in strict order of succession, and another faction leaves out the more obscure ones like Otho and Vitellius and counts only the most celebrated or notorious Roman emperors. But theologians of late antiquity and the early Middle Ages preferred to see the seven-headed beast of Revelation as a symbol of the seven ages of history, and they thrilled at the notion that they were living in the seventh and final age.

None of these theories, however, and nothing in Revelation itself, suggests that the world will end in a year that ends in three zeroes. The only significance of the millennium in the book of Revelation is the duration of Christ's earthly kingdom and the period of Satan's imprisonment in the bottomless pit. John seems to allow that the millennium might start in *any* year of the calendar. Thus, for example, a Spanish monk called Beatus of Liébana, writing around the year 775, confidently predicted that the Sabbath Age would begin sometime in the year 800—but he cagily downplays the significance of the precise date.

"Every catholic ought to ponder, wait and fear, and to consider these twenty-five years, as if they were not more than an hour, and should weep day and night in sackcloth and ashes for their destruction and the world's," writes Beatus in his thousand-page commentary on Revelation, "but not strive to calculate time."[99]

Far more important than the number of zeroes in any given year on the calendar were the signs and wonders that John warns his readers to expect when the end-times approach. The breaking of the seven seals, the pouring of the seven vials, and the sounding of the seven trumpets are all said to signify plague and pestilence, famine and war, earthquake and eclipse, and even stranger phenomena of nature: "And I beheld when he had opened the sixth seal, and, lo, the sun became black as sackcloth of hair, and the moon became as blood," writes John, "and the stars of heaven fell unto earth, and every mountain and island were moved out of their places." For the watchful Christians of the Middle Ages, then, anything even slightly out of the ordinary—a calf born with a birth defect, a seismic tremor, or a shooting star—might turn out to be a welcome sign of the end-times.

"Alpha and Omega. The beginning and the End," are the words of an inscription from Poitiers in the seventh century. "For all things become every day worse, for the end is drawing near."[100]

$$\Omega$$

Even the most commonplace sights on the landscape of medieval Europe, in fact, were also freighted with apocalyptic meanings for Christians who lived in anticipation of the end-times. And, prompted by the book of Revelation to watch for the signs of the Antichrist, they let their eyes fall on the men and women among them whom John so hatefully characterizes as members of "the synagogue of Satan." Thus did the Jews earn a crucial role in the apocalyptic drama that came to dominate the Christian imagination in the Middle Ages.

Here is yet another dark and dangerous irony. Christianity started as a sect within Judaism. Jesus, the twelve disciples, and all of the first Christians were Jews by birth, of course, and the author of Revelation, too, proudly claims to be an authentic Jew. But Revelation clearly shows the theological fault line along which the two faiths split asunder in the early history of the Christian church. The first Christians, after all, were Jews who saw Jesus of Nazareth as the Messiah, but they were not content with distancing themselves from their fellow Jews who refused to do the same. Following the example of Revelation, the Jews were not merely condemned but demonized, too.

Bishop Hippolytus, writing in the third century, was among the earliest Christian propagandists to characterize the Beast of Revelation as both satanic *and* Jewish: the Antichrist, he insists, will be a descendant of the biblical tribe of Dan, and he will recruit his demonic army from Jewish communities throughout the world. By linking the Antichrist with the tribe of Dan, Hippolytus is offering an intriguing solution to one of the most obscure mysteries of the book of Revelation. John includes a list of the twelve tribes of ancient Israel, but he pointedly omits the biblical tribe of Dan. Perhaps John leaves Dan off the list because he has been granted an undisclosed revelation that the Antichrist will carry that tribe's blood in his veins, or so the early church fathers speculated.

By the fourth century, the depiction of the Antichrist in religious propaganda was even more elaborate—and even more specifically anti-Semitic. Martin of Tours, for example, warned that when the Antichrist finally reveals himself to the world, he will seat himself on a throne in the city of Jerusalem, rebuild the Temple of Solomon, and compel the universal practice of circumcision. And, according to the lascivious details that were added to the profile of the Antichrist in Christian legend and lore, he will be conceived in a Babylonian brothel, the child of the Devil and a Jewish whore; he will be circumcised in Jerusalem, where he will declare himself to be the Messiah; and he will die when he attempts to ascend to heaven from the Mount of Olives but falls into the depths of hell.

The book of Revelation itself, of course, is more restrained. Aside from John's passing reference to "the synagogue of Satan," however hateful it may strike us today, the rest of the text is wholly free of crude anti-Semitism. Indeed, as we have seen, John considers himself an authentic and faithful Jew, and he is deeply attached to Jewish history, ritual, and symbolism. At the only moment in the book of Revelation when he depicts himself as actually participating in a visionary event, for example, John is handed a golden measuring rod by an angel and ordered to survey the celestial Jerusalem in all of its particulars. John pauses in his otherwise wild-eyed and blood-shaking tract to note in meticulous detail that boundaries of the holy city are exactly twelve thousand furlongs (or fifteen hundred miles) in length on each of its four sides.[101] By contrast, Jesus is shown in the Gospel of John to declare that the Temple at Jerusalem will be destroyed and replaced by "the temple of his own body."[102]

Above all, John betrays his Jewish roots when he envisions the thousand-year reign of Jesus Christ. Indeed, it is exactly here that we see the fundamental difference between Judaism and Christianity when it comes to the idea of the Messiah. The Jewish redeemer is imagined to be a flesh-and-blood human being whom God will send to bring security and sovereignty to the Jewish people down here on earth, an era that will last between forty and four hundred years according to some Jewish apocalyptic writings. By contrast, the Christian messiah is the Son of God, and he will reign eternally in heaven after the world has come to a final end. John seems to want it both ways in the book of Revelation: he predicts that Jesus will reign as king on earth in a restored Jerusalem for exactly one thousand years, and then the earthly kingdom of saints and martyrs will be replaced by a celestial one for the rest of eternity.

John is the only author in all of the Christian scriptures who plainly describes Jesus as an earthly king whose reign can be measured in real time. That's one reason why Revelation has been characterized by some scholars as "subchristian or not even Christian."[103] And, in fact, John's awkward embrace of the Jewish messianic idea provided a rhetorical weapon for Christian theologians like Jerome and Augustine who insisted on a "spiritual" rather than a "carnal" reading of Revelation. Only the Jews imagined a messianic kingdom like the one described in Revelation, and Christians must read and understand John's text symbolically rather than literally: the thousand-year reign of Christ on earth as depicted in Revelation represents the authority of the church rather than a prediction that Jesus will actually float down from heaven and seat himself on a throne in the city of Jerusalem.

"The saints will in no wise have an earthly kingdom, but only a celestial one; thus must cease the fable of one thousand years," insists Jerome, who characterizes the literal reading of Revelation as a theological error that only a Jew would make. Indeed, that's the worst accusation and insult that he can lay against any Christian who commits the same error: "To take John's Apocalypse according to the letter," he warns, "is to 'Judaize.'"[104]

John's own ambiguous and highly conflicted attitude toward his Jewish origins will soon disappear under the flood tide of anti-Semitism that washed over Western civilization in the Middle Ages. Future readers will rediscover the theological subtleties at play in Revelation, and they will come to regard themselves as allies and advocates of the Jewish people and even as so-called Christian Zionists. For the next thousand years or so, however, all of the Jews will be consigned to membership in "the synagogue of Satan," and Revelation will serve to inspire and justify some of the worst atrocities committed against them in the name of "the Lion of the tribe of Judah, the Root of David."[105]

A n elaborate mosaic that adorns one medieval church in western Europe reveals something subtle but crucial about the role of Revelation in early Christendom. The oldest portion of the mosaic depicts Jesus seated among the twelve disciples, a scene that was borrowed from the purely pagan motif of a colloquium of philosophers. Later, after Constantine embraced Christianity and the Roman Empire became a Christian empire, the mosaic was embellished with the symbols of imperial authority: the chair on which Jesus sits has been turned into a gem-studded throne, and a golden halo has been added to suggest a kingly crown. And the third and final overlay introduces elements from the distinctive iconography of the book of Revelation—the "four living creatures" who serve God in the divine throne room; the celestial city of Jerusalem; and the Lamb of God, looking as if he were slain and yet standing upright with a sword in his mouth.[106]

By deconstructing the mosaic, scholars have confirmed a curious fact about the book of Revelation. The images of the Apocalypse were used only rarely in Christian art and architecture prior to the fourth century. Then, abruptly, the sword-wielding Lamb of God and other iconic symbols of the end-times begin to appear on sarcophagi, ivory carvings, murals, mosaics, and monumental paintings throughout Christendom. Alpha and omega, the Greek letters that John uses to evoke the creation and destruction of the world, are inscribed on artifacts ranging from a woman's gold ring to a slave collar. So "sudden and profuse" was the eruption of apocalyptic imagery in Christian arts and crafts that one scholar characterizes the phenomenon as an "invasion": the Apocalypse seemed to suddenly seize the imagination of both clergy and laity throughout Christendom, and the vengeful Christ of Revelation displaced the suffering Christ of the Gospels.[107]

The apocalyptic invasion was especially lively and long-enduring in western Europe. But the same phenomenon can be seen in eastern Christendom, where Revelation was received only belatedly and only with a certain trepidation. Thus, for example, a strange text titled *The Revelation of the Holy Theologian John,* which first appeared in the eastern Roman Empire as early as the fifth century, depicts a heavenly encounter between God and the author of Revelation in which the physical features of the satanic "beast" are described in detail: "The appearance of his face is gloomy; his hair is like the points of arrows; his brows rough; his right eye as the rising morning star and the left like a lion's," John is told. "His mouth is a cubit wide, his teeth a span in length, his fingers are like sickles. His footprints are two cubits long, and on his forehead is the writing, 'The Antichrist.'"[108]

The timing of the apocalyptic invasion is highly revealing. John may have intended the book of Revelation to console and exhort the persecuted Christians of his own era, but it was only when Christianity was both militant *and* triumphant that the imagery of the Apocalypse began to proliferate across Europe. Indeed, Revelation achieved its sudden and widespread prominence shortly after Emperor Theodosius formally raised Christianity to the status of the state religion of the Roman Empire in 391.

The apocalyptic invasion also coincides with a powerful change in the Christian perception of the world. The machinery of Roman power that had once been used against the Christians—the constabulary, the courts, the torture chambers, and the execution blocks—were now available to Christian authorities for use against their own enemies both inside and outside the church. So the Christ who is depicted in the Gospels as the victim of torture and execution suddenly seemed less appropriate to the new circumstances of the church than the Christ of Revelation who rides a warhorse, wields a sword, and wears a crown.

At the same time, of course, the Roman Empire was already in decline and fast approaching its ultimate fall. Rome itself and the western reaches of the empire disintegrated into a chaotic assortment of "barbarian" kingdoms soon after the sack of Rome in 410, and the eastern remnant was continually menaced by the pagan armies of Persia. Bubonic plague—the dreaded Black Death that seems to be prefigured in the imagery of Revelation—first appeared in the sixth century and reached epidemic proportions over the next two hundred years. By the eighth century, former

Roman provinces in Spain, North Africa, and the Levant, including the city of Jerusalem itself, had fallen under the banner of militant Islam.

Revelation, however, offered a way to understand even the most catastrophic events as an augury of a greater triumph. Theologians may have debated whether the thousand-year reign of Christ as depicted in Revelation is prophecy or allegory, but whether Revelation is read "carnally" or "spiritually," its unambiguous message is that, sooner or later, the world will be destroyed once and for all, and any Christian soul who is judged worthy by Jesus Christ will live forever in a celestial kingdom. Even Augustine, who declined to take the book of Revelation too literally, was convinced that the end of the world was inevitable.

"Elijah shall come; the Jews shall believe; Antichrist shall persecute; Christ shall judge; the dead shall rise; the good and the wicked shall be separated; the world shall be burned and renewed," Augustine concedes. "All these things, we believe, shall come to pass; but how, or in what order, human understanding cannot perfectly teach us, but only the experience of the events themselves."[109]

Augustine's pointed phrase—"the experience of the events themselves"—reminds us of exactly what prompted a great many otherwise pious Christians to ignore his cautions about reading the book of Revelation as literal truth. For nearly a thousand years, daily life in the here and now seemed to fulfill even the most frightful prophecies of Revelation, and the end of the world seemed to be very near indeed. And yet, on the far side of their tribulation—wars and rumors of war, famine and plague, and all the other biblical afflictions that God promises to bring down on a suffering humanity—the readers of Revelation glimpsed the tantalizing sight of a new heaven, a new earth, and a New Jerusalem whose streets were paved with gold.

For all of the high anxiety and Grand Guignol on display in its pages, in fact, Revelation has always been understood by some readers as a story with the happiest of endings. That's why Revelation can be a soporific drug—"Take it, and eat it up," says an angel to John, urging him to literally consume the "little book"—that leaves the reader in a kind of mystical stupor.[110] Since God's plan for the world is already written down in the pages of Holy Writ—and since God has promised to raise the saints and martyrs to eternal life in the end-times—the credulous readers of Revelation are content to close their eyes to the dangerous world in which they live, dream of the delights to come in the messianic kingdom, and pray that they will wake up in the celestial Jerusalem.

But there is quite another way to experience the book of Revelation. Some men and women across the ages, as we shall see, find Revelation to be a stimulant that fills them with frantic energy. They are fully awake and alert to the workings of the Devil, and they find themselves compelled to *do* something to hasten the final victory of God. Some are moved to preach and prophesy, some are inspired to go in search of the new world that God has promised to bestow on humankind, and some are willing to pick up "the sharp two-edged sword" in willful imitation of Jesus as he is depicted in the book of Revelation and nowhere else in the New Testament.[111]

Five

"Your Own Days, Few and Evil"

The time for vengeance has come,
and the Lord wishes me to unveil new secrets....
GIROLAMO SAVONAROLA

One cherished idea about the Apocalypse holds that the hopes and fears for the end of the world spiked in the year 1000. The turn of the first millennium of the Christian calendar, we are invited to imagine, was the occasion for extraordinary popular delusions and the madness of crowds, all inspired by the sure belief that the end was near—"The Terrors of the Year 1000," according to the phrase embraced by a few overexcited historians.[1]

The scene is memorably suggested in Ingmar Bergman's *The Seventh Seal*, a motion picture whose title alludes to the end-times as depicted the book of Revelation. The Lamb of God is ready to break the seventh seal over a plague-ridden, corpse-strewn, and omen-haunted landscape peopled with penitents and flagellants, doomsaying preachers, and knights on crusade. But the idea of a millennial panic in the year 1000, like so much of the conventional wisdom about the Apocalypse, is wrong.[2]

To be sure, more than a few medieval preachers thrilled at the notion that a thousand years had passed since the birth of Jesus of Nazareth, and they were convinced that *something* remarkable would surely happen. But they did not even agree among themselves whether the momentous year would be 1000, the anniversary of the birth of Jesus, or 1033, the anniversary of the crucifixion of Jesus, or somewhere in between. Indeed, the whole exercise of counting down the end of the world in units of one thousand years was (and is) fundamentally flawed by an error in the calculations of

Dionysius Exiguus, the sixth-century monk who devised the calendar system that uses the markers B.C. ("Before Christ") and A.D. ("*Anno Domini*," or "In the Year of Our Lord"). Dionysius, according to modern scholarship, "got the year of Christ's birth wrong by at least four and possibly as much as six years."[3] As a result, the end of the first millennium had probably passed unnoticed a few years before the calendar year 1000.

Christians who heeded the cautions of Jesus, Paul, and Augustine about such speculation, as it happened, were capable of remaining calm as the year 1000 approached and passed without incident. So did the Bible readers who knew that the book of Revelation does not regard the passage of one thousand years from the birth or death of Jesus as a significant benchmark. Jesus Christ's reign on earth would last one thousand years, of course, but the starting date of the millennial kingdom is not mentioned at all in Revelation. And the church itself continued to insist on a "spiritual" rather than a "carnal" reading of Revelation, a doctrine that tamped down the hotter fires of apocalyptic yearning among compliant Christians.

"When I was a young man I heard a sermon about the End of the world preached before the people in the cathedral of Paris," writes a monk called Abbo of Fleury (d. 1004) about an experience of his own during the countdown to the year 1000. "According to this, as soon as the number of a thousand years was completed, the Antichrist would come and the Last Judgment would follow in a brief time." Abbo, a careful reader of the Jewish and Christian scriptures, was unimpressed by all the doomsaying: "I opposed this idea with what force I could from passages in the Gospels, Revelation, and the Book of Daniel."[4]

Abbo, in fact, is the only contemporary observer who links the year 1000 to the end-time prophecies in the Bible—and he "does so only to dismiss the notion."[5] Still, the good monk fully expected the world to end even if he piously refused to speculate on the precise date. Indeed, the apocalyptic fever in medieval Christendom was chronic rather than acute, and the church had never really been successful in turning back the so-called apocalyptic invasion of the fourth century. The men and women of medieval Christendom, especially in western Europe, were exposed to apocalyptic imagery in the ornamentation and decoration of churches, the monumental architecture and inscription of public buildings, the illuminated manuscripts of holy books, the pronouncements of preachers and pamphleteers, and the secular arts and letters that flourished in the late Middle Ages and the Renaissance.

"The Apocalypse is ubiquitous," write Bernard McGinn and his colleague Richard K. Emmerson, a fellow specialist in apocalypticism during the Middle Ages. "John's powerful revelation seeped into almost every aspect of medieval life."[6]

For people who lived their lives in the precarious world of medieval Europe, a world that teetered between hope and despair, Revelation turned out to be an inspiring and even intoxicating text. The opening of the seven seals, the sounding of the seven trumpets, and the pouring of the seven bowls of God's wrath, for example, offered a way of understanding and enduring the catastrophic events that afflicted Christendom—invasion and conquest, war and revolution, famine and plague, earthquakes and floods. And, at the same time, John's sublime vision of "a new heaven and a new earth" held out a shining promise of redemption and reward that sustained the readers of Revelation even (and especially) in the moments of greatest tumult.

Once imprinted on the Western imagination during the Middle Ages, the iconography and "language arsenal" of Revelation—and its terrifying but also thrilling fantasies of the end-times—would never be wholly erased. Indeed, an obsessive concern with when and how and why the world will come to an end can be seen as a dominant habit of the Western mind, no less in the third millennium than in the first, and no less in popular culture of the twenty-first century than in the religious art and letters of medieval Europe. And the obsession begins here and now.

The thousand-year reign of Jesus Christ on earth, as we have noted, was understood by Augustine and other Christian authors as a purely symbolic reference to the sovereignty of the church itself. "The Church Militant and Triumphant," according to its glorious self-description, *was* the millennial kingdom. One early theologian, for example, fixed 326 as the year when the emperor Constantine raised the church to earthly power and glory in Rome—and so he calculated that the end of the world would come in 1326, exactly one thousand years later, thus fulfilling the prophecy of Revelation.

Other medieval Christians, however, were not so convinced that the Church Militant and Triumphant deserved to be compared to the kingdom of saints and martyrs that is described in Revelation. Rather, they saw something satanic at work in the excesses and abuses of the church, now so rich and so powerful. Priests, bishops, and even popes, for example, took wives or concubines or both—a practice that came to be condemned as "Nicolaitanism." (The term is borrowed from the book of Revelation, where it is used by John to condemn a rival faction in the early church.) Clerical marriage had been commonplace for centuries, of course, even if one church directive of the eighth century restricted a priest to a single wife only. Now, however, the purifiers of the church argued for a strict rule of celibacy.

"The hands that touch the body and blood of Christ must not have touched the genitals of a whore," stormed one preacher in 1059, referring not to prostitutes but to the consecrated wives of the clergy.[7]

But the call for chastity was not purely a spiritual concern; it also served the material and political interests of the church. A bishop with a wife and children, for example, might be inclined to regard the lands, buildings, and treasures of his bishopric as property to be passed down to his sons. Clearly, the wealth and power of the church were at risk unless the clergy were deprived of the temptation and opportunity to sire potential heirs. Such concerns were on the mind of Pope Gregory VII (1020–1085) when he complained of clerical marriage as a "foul plague of carnal contagion" that "[loosened] the reins of lust."[8]

Then, too, the call for the criminalization of clerical marriage owed something to the fear and loathing of women that is writ large in the book of Revelation. Thus, for example, Peter Damian, a white-hot church reformer of the eleventh century, addresses the consecrated wives of married priests as "appetizing flesh of the devil, that castaway from Paradise" and condemns them en masse as "poison of minds, death of souls, companions of the very stuff of sin, the cause of our ruin."[9] Indeed, he saw *all* women as sisters of the Great Whore of Babylon, and he was provoked into rhetorical excesses quite as hateful as the worst passages of Revelation.

"I exhort you, women of the ancient enemy, you bitches, sows, screech-owls, night-owls, blood-suckers, she-wolves," rails Peter. "Come now, hear me, harlots, prostitutes, with your lascivious kisses, you wallowing places for fat pigs, couches for unclean spirits."[10]

Another besetting sin of the medieval church was the practice of simony—that is, the buying and bartering of church offices for profit among the royalty, aristocracy, and gentry as well as the high clergy. Politics were at work here, too; popes were jealous of their power to make and break bishops and cardinals and resented the monarchs who tried to take it away. After all, a bishop who owed his rank and title to a king was less likely to side with a pope in the struggle between church and state that was a commonplace of the late Middle Ages. But it is also true that those who profited from their clerical offices were often tempted to spend their riches on lives of opulence and sensuality. Simony reached all the way to the papacy; Pope Gregory VI (d. 1048), for example, is said to have purchased his seat on the papal throne from the previous pope, Benedict IX, at the stated price of two thousand silver pounds.

Such human flaws and failings among the clergy, high and low, sparked the so-called Gregorian reform, a wide-ranging set of innovations and improvements that reached a critical mass during the reign of Pope Gregory VII. The book of Revelation provided Pope Gregory with the language arsenal to justify his decrees: "For the nearer the time of Antichrist approaches," he declared, "the harder he fights to crush out the Christian faith."[11] And the same impulse toward the purification of Christianity—"a longing for an ideal gospel life built on the imitation of the life lived by Jesus and his followers"[12]— moved Francis of Assisi (1181/82–1226) to found the monastic order that inspired medieval Christians to ask themselves: "What would Jesus do?"

Here was yet another culture war in which the book of Revelation served as a rhetorical weapons dump. While kings and popes contested with each other for worldly power, monks and priests like Francis of Assisi, known as the *Poverello* ("Poor little man"), aspired to simplify and purify Christianity by stripping the church of its corrupting wealth and splendor. Both factions, as we shall see, resorted to the book of Revelation to justify their respective visions of the right way to live as a Christian in the world as we find it rather than the world to come. Indeed, it was the sorry state of the church—rather than war, famine, plague, and the other classic signs of the end of the world—that prompted a revolution in the reading of Revelation.

Ω

The maker of the apocalyptic revolution in medieval Europe was a visionary monk called Joachim of Fiore (ca. 1135–ca. 1202). Joachim was raised and educated to serve as an official in the royal court of the Norman king in southern Italy, but he was drawn to the life of "a wandering holy man," the same calling that sent John to the seven churches of Asia Minor. Joachim took monastic vows and later founded a monastery in the rugged reaches of the Calabrian countryside, where he was inspired to undertake a study of the scriptures in an effort to crack the divine secrets that were hidden away in Holy Writ.[13]

When Joachim started to read the book of Revelation, he hoped to find "the key of things past, the knowledge of things to come," as he puts it, "the opening of what is sealed, the uncovering of what is hidden."[14] But he reached only the tenth verse of the text before the mysteries of Revelation stopped him like "the stone that closed the tomb."[15] Like so many other visionaries, Joachim sought a revelation of his own—and received one. After a year of prayerful longing and meditation, as Joachim himself describes it, the epiphany took place on Easter morning around the year 1184. Not unlike the experience described by Robert Graves eight centuries later, the baffling text miraculously snapped into focus for the medieval monk.

"About the middle of the night's silence, as I think, the hour when it is thought that our Lion of the tribe of Judah rose from the dead, while I was meditating," recalls Joachim, referring to Jesus Christ with the same code words that John uses in Revelation, "I suddenly perceived in my mind's eye something of the fullness of this book and of the entire harmony of the Old and New Testaments."[16]

Once he had been given what he called "the gift of understanding," Joachim extracted all kinds of new and unsuspected meanings from the book of Revelation.[17] He was convinced, for example, that human history is divided into three ages, each one corresponding to a "person" of the Trinity—the Father, the Son, and the Spirit. The first age lasted until the crucifixion of Jesus, the second age was in progress during Joachim's lifetime and would end with the arrival of the Antichrist, and the third age—an age of spiritual peace and perfection—would begin only after the Antichrist is defeated. And, echoing the words of Jesus himself, Joachim expressed his conviction that the final battle between God and Satan was at hand.

"This will not take place in the days of your grandchildren or in the old age of your children," warns Joachim, "but in your own days, few and evil."[18]

Joachim's single most revolutionary innovation was his refusal to confine Revelation to the spiritual realm, thus breaking with the approved reading of the text that dated all the way back to Augustine. Rather, he saw even the strangest visions in Revelation as prophecies of specific people and events in the real world. The seven heads of the satanic red dragon, for example, are understood by Joachim to signify the seven persecutors of the church across the centuries of human history, including Herod, Nero, and Saladin, the celebrated Muslim warrior who took Jerusalem back from the crusaders in 1187. The seventh head, he insisted, was the Antichrist yet (but soon) to come.

Yet Joachim's vision of the end-times can be seen as a bright and cheerful one precisely because he saw the millennial kingdom as the reign of a reformed Christian church right here on earth. "His glorious new era was to occur within history and was therefore more utopia than Millennium," explains British journalist and historian Damian Thompson. "This has led to Joachim being blamed for every failed utopian experiment from Savonarola's Florence to Soviet Communism." Joachim, however, regarded himself as a reformer rather than a revolutionary, and his conception of the New Jerusalem was "an exclusively Catholic vision."[19]

Joachim's new reading of the book of Revelation could be as baffling as the original text itself, and, in fact, his writings did not attract a sizable readership until they were copied out and circulated by his posthumous followers, the so-called Joachimites. Once Joachim had broken Augustine's grip, however, those who came after him dared to interpret the visions of Revelation in ever more audacious ways. The church condemned them as "diviners and dreamers" and dismissed their writings as "false and fantastic prophecies."[20] Not a few of them were burned along with their manuscripts. But Revelation was now, quite literally, an open book.

"The abbot's discovery of a new interpretation that remained influential for centuries," observes Bernard McGinn, "might have made him the patron saint of critics had he been canonized rather than condemned."[21]

Significantly, Joachim's influence was not confined to the scholars and theologians who found their way to his arcane writings. Some of his readers were outraged by his inflammatory rhetoric, including the high clergy who recognized themselves in his denunciation of Christians who "abandoned the bosom of the Chaste Mother and preferred the Whore who rules over the kings of the earth."[22] But other readers, including popes, kings, and crusaders all across Europe, sought him out as a kind of "apocalyptic advisor," and begged him to reveal to them the divine secrets that he had prized out of the scriptures.[23]

No less commanding a figure than Richard the Lion-Hearted, the legendary English king, called on Joachim on his way to the Holy Land during the Third Crusade in 1190–1191 to find out what Revelation might foretell about his own fate. And the old monk obliged the crusader-king by revealing that when John sees "a beast rise up out of the sea" in the book of Revelation, he is actually glimpsing the Saracen army that Richard would soon face in the battle for Jerusalem. Soon thereafter, Joachim assured Richard, Jesus Christ would return to earth to undertake the final crusade against the Antichrist, the long-promised battle of Armageddon.

"And this Antichrist (he sayde) was already borne in the citie of Rome, and should be there exalted in the Apostolical see," Joachim is shown to say to King Richard in a sixteenth-century Protestant tract. "And then shall the wicked man be revealed, whom the Lord shall consume with the spirits of his mouth and shall destroye with the brightness of his coming."[24]

The Antichrist, in other words, would be the pope himself.

Ω

Another reader of Revelation who achieved a kind of superstardom in the eleventh century was Hildegard of Bingen, the Benedictine nun who distinguished herself as a visionary, a preacher, and an author of apocalyptic tracts as well as various texts on medicine, music, and natural history. Indeed, her treatise on the use of herbs to cure illness remains "among the foundational documents of western pharmacy," and her musical compositions "make Hildegard the only medieval figure whose life story must include a discography."[25] Like Joachim of Fiore, Hildegard insisted that the greatest evil in Christendom was to be found within the bosom of the church, where members of the clergy were using their offices to enrich themselves—and then using their riches to satisfy their carnal appetites. With Joachim and Hildegard begins the tradition of using Revelation as a weapon against the church itself.

Hildegard saw some grotesque sights when she slipped into one of her trance states, as we have already noted, including the image of a beautiful woman who gives birth to a misshapen beast in the nave of a church: "In her vagina there appeared a monstrous and totally black head with fiery eyes, ears like the ears of a donkey, nostrils and mouth like those of a lion," Hildegard writes in her account of the vision that came to her as she prayed. "Lo, the monstrous head removed itself from its place with so great a crash that the entire image of the woman was shaken in all of its members."[26]

Hildegard's vision is plainly inspired by the book of Revelation—"a radical conflation" of the woman clothed with the sun and crowned with the stars, who gives birth to the Savior, and the Whore of Babylon, who fornicates with kings and rides on the back of a satanic beast with seven heads.[27] But Hildegard, like her near-contemporary Joachim, assigned new and startling meanings to these symbols: the laboring woman represents the church, and the monster in her womb represents the Antichrist. To put it more plainly, the Antichrist will emerge from within the church itself like an infant from its mother's womb—"a violent expulsion that is like a reverse rape,"[28] according to Bernard McGinn. And Hildegard, who lived chastely as a "bride of Christ" within the walls of a convent, dressing in bridal garb for the rite of communion, resorted to raw and explicit sexual imagery to express her anxieties about the will of God and the fate of humankind in the end-times: "[T]he evil male figure of Satan attacks humanity, the female bride of Christ, progressively figured in Eve, the synagogue, Mary, and the church."[29]

When Hildegard preached in churches and cathedrals—a wholly remarkable role for any woman, but especially a cloistered nun, in medieval Europe—the sins that she found most alarming were the sexual excesses and self-enrichment of the clergy. And she introduced a new understanding of how the final battle between good and evil would manifest itself in the end-times by describing a day in the not so distant future when the "rash populace" and the "greedy princes" would "cast [the clergy] down, chase them, and carry away their riches." Then the world will see the "dawn of justice," and the surviving clergy, once again poor and chaste just as God intended them to be, would "shine like the purest gold."[30]

Significantly, if also surprisingly, Hildegard's preachments were not condemned by the church. Hildegard was so credible and so compelling that the archbishop under whose authority she lived and worked found himself forced to concede that her visions "were from God," and so did the pope himself. Indeed, a monk was assigned to serve as her scribe so that the prophecies issuing from Hildegard's mind and mouth would be promptly and accurately preserved, and she corresponded often and at length with popes, emperors, kings, and churchmen all over Europe. And so Hildegard reminds us, yet again, that a charismatic man or woman might succeed in catching and holding the attention of an audience by invoking the power of Revelation. If John had been graced with the gift of prophecy, they were willing to concede, why not Hildegard, too?

Not every reader of the Revelation, however, was able to complain about the church with the same impunity. For instance, the radical faction of the Franciscan order, the so-called Zealots or Spirituals, followed the example of Joachim and Hildegard in conjuring up the Whore of Babylon and the Antichrist when they condemned the corruption that they beheld within in the church itself. So did the Beguines, a remarkable community of women who took up their own crusade for purification and reform in anticipation of the end-times. And, as their numbers increased and their rhetoric escalated, all of them began to attract the ungentle attention of the Church Militant and Triumphant. Along with Jews, Muslims, and assorted Christian heretics, apocalyptic preachers were persons of special interest to the Holy Office of the Inquisition.

Pope John XXII (ca. 1244–1334) convened a papal court in 1317 to consider one especially aggravating instance of apocalyptic speculation among the Spirituals of the Franciscan order. The defendant was a book rather than a human being—a commentary on the book of Revelation by a Franciscan monk named Peter John Olivi (ca. 1248–1298), who insisted that the church founded by the disciples of Jesus Christ was now "infected from head to toe and turned, as it were, into a new Babylon."[31] The author himself was already dead, but his book was found guilty of heresy on charges that sixty of its tenets "offended the faith."[32] Copies of Olivi's writings were put to the flames, and a few of his flesh-and-blood followers were put to death for the crime of reading and teaching his revolutionary ideas on the end-times.

Olivi was among the most prominent and influential members of the Spirituals. Drawing on the text of Revelation, they saw Francis of Assisi, founder of the Franciscan order, as "the Angel of the Sixth Seal,"[33] and they imagined Francis and Domingo de Guzman (ca. 1170–1221), founder of the Dominican order, as the two witnesses of the end-times. And when

Pope John XXII condemned the Spirituals as heretics, he succeeded only in confirming the zealous friars in their conviction that *he* was the real heretic or, even worse, the Antichrist himself.

Joachim of Fiore may have issued an oblique and intentionally vague warning that the Antichrist would come to sit on the papal throne, for example, but one of the Spirituals, a radical monk named Ubertino da Casale (ca. 1259–ca. 1330) was perfectly willing to name names. Da Casale insisted that the beast from the land and the beast from the sea, the satanic twins described in Revelation, were actually visions of two popes of his own era, Boniface VIII and Benedict XI, both sworn enemies and active persecutors of the Spirituals. And, following the example of the author of Revelation, da Casale worked out the numerical value of the letters in Benedict XI's name as the dreaded number of the Beast, 666.[34]

So the Spirituals were revolutionaries rather than reformers. For example, John of Rupescissa (ca. 1310–ca. 1366), a Franciscan monk from southern France who is sometimes known simply as "Brother John," insisted that all of the afflictions foretold in Revelation would be visited on the world as punishment for the sins of the church. Inspired by visions of his own, he saw the Saracens, Turks, and Tartars who threatened medieval Christendom as the satanic armies that were gathering for the final battle of Armageddon. And he predicted that the last days would bring what he called "a horrendous novelty": the common folk would take their own bloody revenge against both the gentry and the clergy, rising up against the rich and powerful "like earthworms devouring lions" and tearing down the palaces and cathedrals with their own hands.[35]

"The world will be filled with indignation against the ostentation of wealth, and the oppressed peoples will rebel in an unexpected and sudden way," warns John of Rupescissa in *Handbook in Tribulation*. "Many princes, nobles, and mighty ones will fall from the height of their dignities and the glory of their riches, and the affliction of the nobles will be beyond belief."[36]

His prophecy of what we would call a social revolution is decorated with all the eschatological trappings of Revelation. Based on an epiphany that he experienced "while the choir was singing the Te Deum during the Matins liturgy for the feast of the Virgin,"[37] Brother John predicted that a pair of Antichrists would appear, one in the eastern realm of Christianity in 1365 and the other in the west in 1370. A Franciscan monk would be raised to the papal throne, and the new pope would appoint a French king to the throne of a world empire. Together, the pope and the emperor would make war on the two Antichrists, close the schism between the eastern and western churches, and call the Jews into communion with the Christians.

Indeed, John's "greatest prophetic daring" was his conviction that the Jewish people would become "God's new imperial nation." Here was another novelty. At a time when the mystery plays of medieval Europe enshrined the old slander that the Antichrist would be the spawn of the Devil and a Jewish harlot, Brother John predicted an exalted role for the Jewish people in the end-times. Jerusalem would be rebuilt to serve as the glorious capital of a unified and purified faith during the millennial kingdom on earth. With explicit apologies to Augustine, who had warned against taking the reign of Christ on earth too literally, John explained that he had been granted a divine revelation of his own on the subject of the thousand-year Sabbath, and he insisted that his vision of the future was "most certain, infallible and necessary."[38]

Brother John's attacks on the church grew so ferocious that even his superiors in the reformist Franciscan order felt obliged to confine him in one of their own prisons, and he was eventually put on trial by the papal court in Avignon on charges of heresy. Although he was not condemned to death by the cautious church authorities, who were apparently willing to entertain the notion that perhaps he was really in touch with God, the fiery monk remained in prison for the rest of his life, and all of his surviving apocalyptic tracts were written behind bars.[39] Yet copies of *Handbook in Tribulation* circulated throughout Europe in its original Latin text as well as in French, German, Czech, and Castilian translations—an early example of the "medieval 'best-sellers'" that were inspired by the book of Revelation.[40]

Ω

Like Montanus and his pair of prophetesses in the second century, Peter John Olivi, Brother John, and their like-minded brothers and sisters were regarded by the church as dangerous provocateurs. As their sermons and tracts reached ever-larger audiences across medieval Europe, the apocalyptic radicals were seen to pose a direct threat to the high churchmen whom they demonized as tools of Satan and incarnations of the Antichrist. Inevitably, the culture war between the defenders and reformers of the church escalated into an open struggle in which blood was shed and lives were lost.

The Inquisitor's Manual, composed in 1324 by Bernard Gui, singled out the so-called Beguines as an example of what can go wrong when Christians dare to read the book of Revelation for themselves. "They also teach that at the end of the sixth era of the Church, the era in which they say we now are, which began with St. Francis, the carnal Church, Babylon, the great harlot, shall be rejected by Christ, as the synagogue of the Jews was rejected for crucifying Christ," writes Gui. "They teach that the carnal Church, which is the Roman Church, will be destroyed." Such "errors and pernicious opinions," he reports, were discovered "by lawful inquisition and through depositions and confessions"—that is, by interrogation under torture—but the grand inquisitor also allows that "many of them have chosen to die by burning rather than to recant."[41]

Gui, in fact, readily concedes that the Beguines are perfectly confident of their ultimate victory over the "spiritual or mystical" Antichrist—that is, the church itself—and "the real, greater Antichrist," who "has already been born" and will reveal himself in 1325, "according to some of them," or perhaps 1330, or possibly 1335. "They say that the first Antichrist is that pope under whom is now occurring the persecution and condemnation of their sect," explains Gui. "Also, they say that after the death of Antichrist, the Spirituals will convert the whole world to the faith of Christ and the whole world will be good and merciful, so that there will be no malice or sin in the people of that era, with the possible exception of venial sin in some."[42]

Behind the rantings of the grand inquisitor is an intriguing example of what passed for heresy in the medieval church. The Beguines were women who lived communally, observed strict chastity, earned their livelihoods in nursing and teaching, and spent the rest of their days in fasting and self-mortification, mystical contemplation, and apocalyptic speculation. The houses of the Beguines, which appeared in Belgium, France, Germany, and Italy, offered a practical solution to the plight of single women who were otherwise unattached and unprotected. Not surprisingly, the Beguines aroused the suspicions of the Inquisition, but not only because they boldly condemned the church as "Babylon" and "the great harlot." Just as threatening to men like Bernard Gui was the simple fact that they were women who had placed themselves beyond the authority of fathers and husbands.[43]

"We have been told that certain women commonly called Beguines, afflicted by a kind of madness, discuss the Holy Trinity and the divine essence, and express opinions on matters of faith and sacraments contrary to the catholic faith, deceiving many simple people," a church council concluded in 1312. "We have therefore decided and decreed that their way of life is to be permanently forbidden and altogether excluded from the Church of God."[44]

Among the women who fell afoul of the Inquisition was Marguerite Porete (d. 1310), author of *The Mirror of the Simple Soul*—an ironic title, as it turned out. She is reputed to have been a Beguine, but she apparently lived and worked as a wandering preacher, "solitary and itinerary" and "essentially homeless."[45] Inevitably, she came to the attention of the church authorities, and when she defied their warnings to silence herself, Marguerite was turned over to the Inquisition, imprisoned in Paris for eighteen months, and finally brought before a tribunal consisting of twenty-one theologians on the faculty of the University of Paris. Her sole defender was a man styled as the "Angel of Philadelphia" after a figure from Revelation—"Behold, I have set before thee an open door," John writes of the angel, "and no man can shut it"[46]—but he was rewarded for his efforts on her behalf with his own charge of heresy. Marguerite's advocate recanted in order to save his own life, but she was convicted and burned at the stake.

The same fate befell a mystic called Na Prous Boneta (1290–1325), who assured her followers that Jesus had carried her to heaven "in spirit" on Good Friday in 1321. According to her visions, Francis of Assisi is the angel described in Revelation as "having the seal of the Living God," and Peter John Olivi is the angel with a "face like the sun" who declares that "there should be time no longer."[47] Jesus had sent these two holy men as apocalyptic witnesses, she asserted, but his divine will was foiled by the Antichrist in his incarnation as Pope John XXII. Na Prous Boneta insisted that the third and final age of human history was imminent: the Antichrist would be defeated, and the papacy itself would be "annulled for perpetuity" along with all sacraments except holy matrimony.[48]

Significantly, everything we know about Na Prous Boneta is preserved in the meticulous minutes of her interrogation and trial. Like so many other readers of Revelation about whose lives we can only speculate, she would have slipped through the cracks of history if she had escaped the attention of the Inquisition. "Having been warned, called, and urged many times in court and elsewhere, to revoke and adjure all the aforesaid things as erroneous and heretical," the inquisitors concluded, "she persevered in them, claiming that in the aforesaid, as in the truth, she wishes to live and die." Her final wish, so principled and so courageous, was granted, and Na Prous Boneta was burned at the stake along with her sister, Alisette, and one of their companions.[49]

The tragic fate of these women offers an example of the price that more than a few true believers have been called upon to pay for their idiosyncratic readings of Revelation. Long after they were dead and gone, many others would also literally go down in flames because they were inspired by Revelation to act out their own end-time fantasies. But they also remind us that Revelation has always seemed to exert an especially powerful attraction for the female reader, ranging from the prophetesses Prisca and Maximilla through the visionary nun Hildegard of Bingen and not excluding the female Bible scholars who figure so importantly in the modern study of Revelation. Here is yet another irony that has attached itself to Revelation, a book whose author seems to regard all fleshly women with fear and loathing.

Women do not fare well in the book of Revelation itself. Its author, as we have already noted, is appalled by *all* human sexuality and betrays a distinct "hatred and fear" of women in particular.[50] Among the most vivid figures in Revelation—and an all-purpose symbol of satanic evil among sermonizers and propagandists over the last twenty centuries—is the Great Whore of Babylon. By contrast, the only flesh-and-blood woman whom the author actually identifies by name in the book of Revelation, the prophetess he calls Jezebel, is singled out for condemnation "for beguiling my servants to practice immorality."[51] And yet flesh-and-blood women were among the most ardent readers of Revelation at a time when it was rare for women to read at all.

Unlike Hildegard—or her less fortunate sisters such as Marguerite Porete and Na Prous Boneta—most of the medieval women who opened the book of Revelation were seeking spiritual self-improvement or entertainment of the chills-and-thrills variety rather than revelations of their own. Deluxe editions of the text, richly illuminated and lavishly illustrated, were specially commissioned by wealthy women for their private contemplation. Thus, for example, *The Birth and Time of the Antichrist,* a treatise on the end-times, was composed in the tenth century by a monk especially for a woman called Gerberga, the wife of the Frankish king Louis IV. And the book was yet another medieval best seller, copied out and circulated throughout western Europe over the next several centuries.

The story line of Revelation, such as it is, can be approached as a romantic tale, full of intrigue and suspense, or so scholars have suggested. Many of the same characters and incidents that are found in medieval accounts of chivalrous knights and damsels in distress can also be found in Revelation. The woman clothed with the sun is stalked by a bloodthirsty dragon who seeks to devour her newborn son, and she is ultimately rescued by a dragon-slaying champion. Jesus Christ is presented as a crowned prince on a white charger who rides into battle to defend her honor. And the happy ending of Revelation includes the wedding feast of the King of Kings and his bride, an occasion that marks the founding of a kingdom that will, quite literally, last forever.

Even more popular than the challenging biblical text itself were abridged, simplified, and illustrated versions of Revelation, the medieval version of a Classics Illustrated comic book. Picture books were especially appealing to Christians who could not actually read the Bible in its original Greek text or in its Latin translation, the only versions of the Christian scriptures generally available in the Middle Ages, or who could not read at all, a category that included a great many women. Above all, the book of Revelation, with its angels and demons, monsters and marvels, signs and wonders, was an early and enduring favorite of artists ranging from Albrecht Dürer to Hieronymus Bosch. The strange visions that the author of Revelation saw in his mind's eye were readily and repeatedly transferred to canvas, fresco, or woodcut, where they came to define the Christian imagination of the end-times down to our own times.

Ω

Apocalyptic speculation, then, was never confined to the musings of cloistered monks or the disputations among contesting theologians. Augustine's call for a sober reading of Revelation, as it turned out, was mostly ignored by the preachers and pamphleteers, artists and scribes, who addressed a far larger and noisier audience than the clerical insiders ever managed to reach. And they borrowed freely from the legend and lore that appear nowhere in the Bible but had come to be attached to the book of Revelation in the popular imagination. As rich and strange as Revelation may be, still richer and stranger ideas and images boiled up out of the apocalyptic imagination of these "dreamers and diviners," whose sermons and tracts passed into the popular culture of medieval Europe.

Among the most exotic reworkings of Revelation, for example, was a text that supposedly originated with the so-called Sibyl of Tivoli. The sibyls were legendary women of pagan antiquity who were believed by the ancients to channel the voices of the gods and deliver messages from on high: "The Sibyl with frenzied lips, uttering words mirthless, unembellished, unperfumed," writes Heraclitus (ca. 500 B.C.E.), "penetrates through the centuries by the powers of the gods."[52] The original Sibylline Oracles, a collection of the various enigmatic sayings of the Sibyls, were purely pagan. Later, however, both Jewish and Christian authors composed their own editions of the Sibylline Oracles in an effort to turn the pagan world to the worship of the One True God. The Sibyl of Tivoli, for example, was styled by some anonymous Christian author as a seeress who is summoned to the court of the emperor Trajan in the early second century to interpret a dream that had miraculously disturbed the sleep of one hundred Roman senators in the same night.

The dream, as deciphered by the Sibyl of Tivoli, is an elaborate prophesy of the end-times that puts a wholly new spin on the visions of Revelation. She sees the arrival of a tall and handsome man, "well put together in all of his parts," who will call the Jews and pagans to baptism and unite the "Greeks and Romans"—that is, the eastern and western halves of the Roman Empire (or, from a medieval perspective, the eastern and western realms of Christendom). The Sibyl predicts that he will defeat the armies of Gog and Magog and rule over a world empire for exactly 112 years, an era of miraculous abundance: "A measure of wheat, a measure of wine, and a measure of oil would all come at the price of one denarius." But, according to the Sibyl, his empire will end with the enthronement of the Antichrist in "the House of the Lord" in Jerusalem.[53]

"After this he will come to Jerusalem, and having put off the diadem from his head and laid aside the whole imperial garb, he will hand over the empire of the Christians to God the Father and to Jesus Christ his Son," go the words of the oracle. "The Lord will shorten those days for the sake of the elect, and the Antichrist will be slain by the power of God through Michael the Archangel on the Mount of Olives."⁵⁴

The Sibyl of Tivoli may have originated in a lost manuscript of the fourth century, but the medieval version of the text began to attract a sizable readership only in the eleventh century. Some 150 manuscripts of the oracles of the Tiburtine Sibyl, as she is also known, survive from the Middle Ages, about the same number of manuscripts as those of *The Travels of Marco Polo,* another medieval best-seller. And the comparison is telling: both of these books reveal that medieval readers were curious about the origin and destiny of the world in which they lived.

Not everyone who lived in or after the year 1000, in other words, was gripped with despair and terror when they contemplated the end-times. Indeed, some looked forward to the millennial kingdom with hope and joy—an approach to reading Revelation that turned out to be one of the great and enduring theological innovations in the long history of John's little book.

Ω

Embedded in the visions of the Tiburtine Sibyl is one of the assorted apocalyptic improvisations that came to be added to the story line of Revelation in the Middle Ages—the idea of the Last World Emperor. A single all-powerful monarch, as the Sibyl suggests, would reign over the world in the last days, and the idea prompted much speculation about which of the contending kings of medieval Europe would play the role of Last World Emperor in the end-times that were surely and soon to come. The notion is found nowhere in the book of Revelation, of course, but it turned out to be yet another convenient rhetorical weapon in an era when the vocabulary of the Apocalypse was readily put to use in politics and propaganda.

For example, Frederick II (1194–1250), the German crusader-king, "was not averse to making personal use of messianic legends about the Last World Emperor as the restorer of Christianity and reformer of the church when it suited him."⁵⁵ Pope Gregory IX, by contrast, referred to his rival as "the beast that rises from the sea"—"What other Antichrist should we await when, as is evident in his works, he is already come in the person of Frederick?"⁵⁶—and excommunicated him in 1227 when the emperor delayed in setting off for the Holy Land. Frederick, as it turned out, was disqualified for both titles after he died unheroically of dysentery and the world went on without him, although it was later predicted that Frederick, like Nero, would be resurrected.[57]

Another apocalyptic innovation of the thirteenth century is the notion of the *Pastor Angelicus* or "Angelic Pope," a wholly benign figure who would replace the venal characters who had occupied the papal throne and caused so much consternation among the church reformers. One of the earliest references to the idea is found in the writing of Roger Bacon (ca. 1220–1292), the English Franciscan who is perhaps better known for his prescient interest in gunpowder, flying machines, and experimental science. "Forty years ago it was prophesied, and there have been many visions to the same effect, that there will be a pope in these times who will purify Canon Law and the Church of God," he writes. "Because of the goodness, truth, and justice of this pope the Greeks will return to the obedience of the Roman Church, the greater part of the Tartars will be converted to the faith, and the Saracens will be destroyed."[58]

The title of Pastor Angelicus was applied to various reformers who sat on the papal throne, including a remarkable man called Celestine V who was elected by the College of Cardinals in 1294, "either by desperation or by revelation," after more than two years of stalemate.[59] He was an unlikely candidate in an era when the pope was as much a political and diplomatic figure as a spiritual one: Celestine was a venerable hermit-monk of the Benedictine order who shunned the lavish digs that he was entitled to occupy and lived instead in a modest hut that he built with his own hands on the palace grounds. Celestine reigned only from July to December, then abdicated, and ended up a prisoner of his successor, Pope Boniface VIII, who promptly declared open war on the Spirituals.

So Revelation may have been regarded by pious Christians as a book whose real author was Jesus Christ, but its hard-won status as a work of Holy Writ did not prevent generation upon generation of artists and storytellers, fantasists and fabulists, preachers and propagandists, from adding their own touches to the biblical scenario. It's a practice that began in antiquity, reached a certain flowering in the High Middle Ages, but—as we shall see—never really ended. Indeed, the phantasmagorical quality of Revelation itself seems to provoke and invite the reader to come up with visions of his or her own.

Ω

Then, too, the book of Revelation offered a way to make sense of the exotic peoples, places, and phenomena that came to the attention of western Christendom through the adventures (and misadventures) of crusaders, merchants, and explorers in the late Middle Ages. Here is another crack in the wall of conventional wisdom that has been built up around the so-called Dark Ages: the medieval world was hardly confined to the walled towns, feudal estates, and cloistered monasteries of Europe itself, and the medieval imagination resorted to old and familiar texts like Revelation when it encountered something new and unfamiliar.

A medieval manuscript titled *Mandeville's Travels*, for example, elaborates upon a tale told about the satanic armies of Gog and Magog: they had been confined in a defile in the Caucasus Mountains of Asia by Alexander the Great, or so the legend goes, and that's why the wall that holds them back is dubbed "Alexander's Gate." Gog and Magog are actually the Lost Ten Tribes of Israel, the author continues, and he insists that the Hebrew language has been preserved and studied by the Jewish communities of Europe so that they could communicate with their long-lost brethren when the Antichrist releases them to fight in the battle of Armageddon. For the readers of *Mandeville's Travels*, however, the account was more than a mere folktale: Gog and Magog were recognizable as the Tartar hordes and Saracen armies that threatened Christendom on its eastern frontier.

The same dreamy conflation of biblical prophesy and baffling reality can be found in *The Fifteen Signs of Doomsday*, a checklist of the signs and wonders—earthquakes, eruptions, falling stars, and various other oddities and curiosities—that would supposedly signal the arrival of the end-times. The text, which was traditionally ascribed to Jerome but first appeared in Ireland in the tenth century, survives in more than 120 manuscripts and a number of languages. And it suggests that any natural phenomenon—but especially a freak of nature—was likely to provoke a new apocalyptic thrill among those who waited and watched for the end of the world.

If a cow or a donkey gave birth to an offspring with catastrophic birth defects, for example, the medieval reader of Revelation might see apocalyptic meanings in the appearance of the misshapen creature. The so-called "Monk-Calf" and "Papal Ass" were famously touted as miraculous signs of "the abominations of the Roman Church and the nearness of the judgment."[60] And the sighting of the celestial light show that later came to be called Halley's Comet was understood as a fulfillment of John's visions in

Revelation: "And the fifth angel sounded, and I saw a star fall from heaven unto earth," writes John, "and to him was given the key of the bottomless pit."[61]

Apocalyptic fancies, no matter how weird or woozy, were capable of taking on the quality of revealed truth. The so-called Tripoli Prophecy, also known as the Cedars of Lebanon Prophecy, first appears in English chronicles of the early thirteenth century as a reading of astrological signs. To the modern reader, the words of the prophecy are near-gibberish:

> The lofty cedar of Lebanon will be cut down. Mars will prevail over Saturn and Jupiter, and Saturn will lie in wait for Jupiter in all things. There will be one God, that is, one bishop. The second God will depart. The sons of Israel will be freed from captivity within eleven years. A wandering people considered to be without a leader will come. Woe to the clergy—a new order will grow strong! Woe to the Church—should it fail! There will be changes of belief, of laws, of kingdoms.[62]

But the credulous readers of the Middle Ages came to see the Tripoli Prophecy as an eerily accurate vision of the Mongol armies that crossed into Russia from the Steppes of Central Asia in 1237—and as a fulfillment of biblical prophecies of the end-times: "And the sixth angel poured out his vial upon the great river Euphrates," goes the text of Revelation, "and the water thereof was dried up, that the way of the kings of the east might be prepared."[63]

The sure and urgent expectation of the end-times was, quite literally, a fact of life in the Middle Ages. That is why the author of *Mirror of History,* an encyclopedia published in 1250, presented the nightmarish visions of Hildegard of Bingen—who came to be called "the German Sibyl"[64]—as "future history" rather than mere mystical speculation. Among the book's other entries were a biography of the Antichrist, a checklist of the signs of the end-times, and a description of the last judgment.[65] Neither Christ nor the Antichrist actually showed up, of course, but the long narrative title of a work by a German visionary named Nicholas Raimarus, first published in Nuremberg in 1606, is plain evidence that the end of the world was always regarded as inevitable and imminent: *Chronological, Certain, and Irrefutable Proof, from the Holy Scripture and Fathers, That the World Will Perish and the Last Day Will Come Within 77 Years.*[66]

Ω

No incident of life, in fact, was too mundane or too intimate to put someone in mind of the book of Revelation and its promise that the end of
the world is near. "Concern with the last things was not limited to fanatics or heretics," explains Richard K. Emmerson, "but was an essential part
of what it meant to be in living in *novissimis diebus*"—that is, in the last
days.[67]

After William the Conqueror put himself on the throne of England
in 1066, for example, he famously ordered a survey of his new realm.
The result was a book of lists—landowners and land holdings, freemen
and slaves and livestock—that is most accurately described as a census
tract. The common folk of England, however, were reminded of one of
John's haunting visions of judgment day in the book of Revelation: "And
I saw the dead, small and great, standing before God; and the books were
opened," writes John, "and the dead were judged out of those things which
were written in the books, according to their works."[68] The royal census
"could hardly be further removed from the apocalyptic cataclysms of Judgment Day," observes Penn Szittya, a specialist in medieval literature, but
William's new subjects spontaneously dubbed it the Domesday Boke (that
is, "Doomsday Book") in "an unspoken analogy" to those fateful books.[69]

Even a scandalous love affair might be seen to reveal apocalyptic meanings. When Peter Abelard, a charismatic teacher of theology, seduced,
impregnated, and secretly married his young student, Héloïse, the star-
crossed lovers were condemned by her uncle, a high churchman in the
cathedral of Paris. The outraged uncle contrived to punish Peter with cas-
tration, and, as if that were not enough, he kept the lovers apart by confin-
ing Héloïse in a convent and sending Abelard into a monastery. The letters
exchanged by Abelard and Héloïse are famous, of course. Rather less celebrated is a letter written by one of their contemporaries, who saw the defiant Abelard as the forerunner of Satan: "Peter Abelard already goes before
the face of Antichrist to prepare his ways."[70]

Apocalyptic imagery was so pervasive and so powerful that the finger-
prints of the author of Revelation, however faint, can be found on the arts
and letters of western Europe throughout the Middle Ages, the Renaissance, and beyond, ranging from Caedmon and the Venerable Bede in the
seventh and eighth centuries to Petrarch and Chaucer in the fourteenth

century and Donne and Milton in the seventeenth century. The villainous Mordred of the Arthurian legend, for example, was seen as a stand-in for the Antichrist, and Merlin the Magician was credited with apocalyptic foresight: "Woe to the red dragon," Merlin is made to say in a work dating to the twelfth century, "for his destruction is nigh."[71] Even Shakespeare, who preferred to draw his plot lines from classical pagan sources rather than the Bible, conjures up a vision of the end-times that was very much on the minds of his audience in the waning years of the sixteenth century.

> O let the vile world end,
> And the promised flames of the last day
> Knit earth and heaven together.[72]

Indeed, the Apocalypse shows up in some altogether unlikely and unexpected places. The medieval manuscript known as the *Carmina Burana*, a collection of ribald songs and satires and religious poetry dating back to the thirteenth century, includes a ritual of exorcism that invokes a "twisted venomed snake" with a sweeping tail[73]— an oblique reference to the "great red dragon" of Revelation whose "tail swept down a third of the stars of heaven, and cast them to earth."[74] And Jan Vermeer, who depicts the mundane scene of a Dutch matron at work with a jeweler's balance in *A Lady Weighing Pearls* (ca. 1660), pointedly includes a painting of the Last Judgment on the wall behind her—a wink and a nod to readers of Revelation who know that one of the Four Horsemen of the Apocalypse carries a pair of balances as a symbol of the day of judgment that awaits all men and women in the end-times.

Perhaps the single best example of how Revelation was recycled for various artistic, political, and theological purposes is *The Divine Comedy*. Dante (ca. 1265–1321) was inspired by not only the canonical book of Revelation but also by some of the more obscure apocalyptic writings of the Pseudepigrapha, including the so-called *Apocalypse of Paul*, where the apostle is taken on a tour of heaven and hell that resembles the one depicted in Dante's masterpiece. Dante borrows and uses the familiar imagery of Revelation, including the Great Whore, the woman clothed with the sun, the four living creatures, the seven-headed dragon, the seven lamps, and the twenty-four elders. And he engages in the same kind of apocalyptic projection that can be found in Revelation itself, suggesting obliquely that King Philip of France is the Antichrist and the papal court at Avignon—a rival papacy known in church history as "the Babylonian Captivity"[75]—is the Mother of Harlots.

"It was shepherds such as you that the Evangelist had in mind," he writes in the *Inferno,* addressing the pope at Avignon, "when she that sitteth upon the waters was seen by him committing fornication with the kings."[76]

Dante also follows the example of Revelation by ornamenting his text with a mystical number code and challenging his readers to discern the historical figure whom it is meant to signify: "For I see surely ... stars already close at hand ... that shall bring us a time wherein a Five Hundred, Ten, and Five, sent by God," writes Dante in *Purgatorio,* "shall slay the thievish woman [and] that giant who sins with her." The alphanumeric code is understood by scholars to represent the numerical value of the letters in the name of Henry VII of Luxembourg, a now-obscure monarch who was Dante's own candidate for the role of the Last World Emperor as predicted by the Tiburtine Sibyl.[77]

Dante, of course, offers only one example of how Revelation served as a kind of lending library of stock scenes and characters, shorthand words and phrases, mystical codes and ciphers, and various other apparatus. By the time he set his hand to *The Divine Comedy* in the early fourteenth century, the reimagining and repurposing of the original text of Revelation was already an old if not always honorable tradition, and not only among pious theologians and self-styled seers.

Indeed, the author of Revelation, who envisioned the terrors and marvels of the near future, surely could not have imagined what would become of the words he spoke aloud to a little congregation of Christians in the provincial backwater of Roman Empire so many centuries before. Once set into motion in the Middle Ages, however, the enterprise of recycling the book of Revelation for new, startling, and sometimes reckless purposes turned into an engine of art, politics, and propaganda that is still running in high gear today.

Yet it was the author of Revelation who assured the longevity of his little book by offering an all-purpose arsenal of excoriation by which one's adversaries could be readily, thoroughly, and colorfully abused. The powerful inner logic of Revelation—and whole of the apocalyptic tradition—abandons all effort at persuasion, erases all ambiguities and uncertainties, and threatens the gravest punishment for even the slightest deviation or difference of opinion. By the lights of Revelation, a human being is either right or wrong, good or evil, godly or satanic. And, in the world according to the Apocalypse, anyone who disagrees with the author in the slightest degree is worthy of one or more of the convenient labels that the text provides in abundance: the Beast, the Great Whore, Satan and the Devil, among many others.

Some readers of Revelation were slower than others in realizing how useful Revelation could be in a culture war or, for that matter, a shooting war. Like Joachim of Fiore and Hildegard of Bingen, Martin Luther (1483–1546) was appalled by what he saw as the corruption of the Roman papacy. By 1517, when Luther famously nailed his defiant writings on the door of the Castle Church in Wittenberg, he was ready to break with Roman Catholic dogma and, soon enough, the church itself. But Luther—a monk in the order of St. Augustine—also distanced himself from the book of Revelation.

"There is one sufficient reason for the small esteem in which I hold it," writes Luther in 1522, "that Christ is neither taught in it nor recognized."[78]

Eight years passed before Luther figured out how to deploy the book of Revelation as a rhetorical weapon in his own war against the Roman Catholic Church—and so "the Reformer performed a *volte-face*."[79] Luther, like the author of Revelation, saw his enemies as not merely wrongheaded but purely evil and even diabolical, and he gave himself permission to draw on its ideas and imagery in his own sermons, tracts, and missives. "[I]t is meant as a revelation of what is to come," Luther now writes of the Apocalypse, "and especially of coming tribulations and disasters for the Church." No longer quite so troubled by the absence of Christ in its text, Luther declares that the satanic beast whose coming is predicted in the book of Revelation is the papacy itself.[80]

"[T]he true Antichrist . . . is reigning in the Roman Curia," proposes Luther. "I do not know whether the pope himself be Antichrist or his apostle, so miserably is Christ (i.e., the Truth) corrupted and crucified by him."[81]

The author of Revelation may have radicalized the language of abuse, but Luther found new and ever more outrageous ways of using Revelation as a cudgel against his adversaries. Luther, for example, is only following the example of earlier reformers when he characterizes the papacy as the "Babylonian Captivity" of the church and Rome as "Babylon, Mother of Whores." But he plays with the metaphor in genuinely shocking ways: "We too were formerly stuck in the behind of this hellish whore, this new church of the pope," Luther rails in one of his notoriously scatological tracts. "We supported it in all earnestness, so that we regret having spent so much time and energy in that vile hole. But God be thanked that he rescued us from the scarlet whore."[82]

Not every Protestant reformer was equally enamored with Revelation, and a few of them were as alarmed as the earliest church fathers had been by its potent and provocative imagery. Across the Rhine in Switzerland, for example, Ulrich Zwingli (1484–1531) and John Calvin (1509–1564) restricted the use of the inflammatory text "in order not to awaken visionary demons."[83] A synod in Saumur, a center of Protestant activism in western France, issued a decree in 1596 that flatly prohibited making any comment on the book of Revelation without formal approval from the church authorities. But Revelation turned out to be so useful and so compelling to the Protestant cause that literally hundreds of new commentaries were composed and published in the century following Luther's declaration of war on the Roman Catholic Church, and Revelation soon established itself as the "text of choice" for Protestant doomsayers down through the ages.

Protestant preachers, in fact, were even more readily convinced than their Catholic counterparts that they knew when the world would end—and, of course, they were just as wrong. Michael Stifel, a German mathematician, mounted the pulpit in Luther's church to announce his calculation that the end-times would begin promptly at 8:00 AM on October 19, 1533. More than two hundred years later, undiscouraged by any of the earlier failed prophecies, an English preacher named George Bell declared with equal certainty that Jesus Christ would descend from heaven to earth on February 28, 1763. On the night of the promised Second Coming, John Wesley, the founder of Methodism, preached all night long in an effort to calm the agitated crowds and prepare them for the disappointment of what he correctly presumed would be the dawning of yet another unremarkable day.

Ω

The apocalyptic tradition embraces two very different approaches to the proper conduct of pious men and women in times of tribulation. The book of Daniel, as we have seen, teaches the "wise ones" to suffer in silence until God is ready to revenge himself on their oppressors—but *The Animal Apocalypse* praises the true believers who pick up the sword and go to war. Significantly, the book of Revelation, for all of its rhetorical fireworks, actually sides with Daniel. As John sees it, the suffering saints are meant to wait patiently for their martyrdom and look forward to the happy day when the Word of God, "clothed with a vesture dipped in blood" and bearing a sword in its mouth,[84] will return to wreak a bloody vengeance.

Not every of reader of Revelation in the medieval world, however, was able to check the powerful emotions that were stirred up by the words and images to be found in the last book of the Bible. A longing for the end-times—and a willingness to hasten them along—burned hotly among "the underprivileged, the oppressed, the disoriented, and the unbalanced," as Norman Cohn puts it, all of whom populated what he calls "the obscure underworld of popular religion."[85] Not a few of them, like the sword-wielding lambs in *The Animal Apocalypse,* were inspired to take matters into their own hands. Indeed, that's exactly why Revelation has always been regarded as a dangerous text by the more sober clerics, early and late.

One striking example of the power of Revelation is found in the Crusades. The popes who called on Christian soldiers to take back Jerusalem from its Muslim overlords—and the princes and kings who harkened to the call—may have embraced the rhetoric of Revelation, but their motives can be seen as geopolitical rather than religious: "The Great Crusade," declares Bernard McGinn, "was fundamentally a papal plan for the reestablishment of the Mediterranean Christian empire under the leadership of the pope."[86] But a great many ordinary Christians understood the call to take up the cross as a fulfillment of the prophecies of Revelation. The so-called People's Crusade and, even more poignantly, the Children's Crusade were spontaneous upwellings of apocalyptic fervor that inspired men, women, and children to set off for the Holy Land and take back Jerusalem from the Antichrist.

"Many portents appeared in the sky as well as on the earth, and excited not a few who were previously indifferent to the Crusade," writes

Ekkehard of Aura in *Jerusalem Journey,* an account from the eleventh century. "Some showed the sign of the cross stamped by divine influence on their foreheads or clothes or on some parts of their body, and by that mark they believed themselves to be ordained for the army of God. In the midst of all of this, more people than can be believed ran to the churches in crowds, and the priests blessed and handed out swords, clubs and pilgrim wallets in a new ritual."[87]

Some of the Crusaders were so agitated that they could not wait until they reached the Holy Land to unsheathe their swords. As they crossed the European countryside, they set upon the Jewish communities that lay in their line of march, inflicting a kind of proto-Holocaust on those whom they had been taught to hate as members of the Synagogue of Satan. Indeed, the "folk eschatology" of medieval Europe, as we have seen, included the notion that the Antichrist would be the offspring of Satan and a Jewish whore, and so the crusaders were unsentimental about slaughtering Jewish men, women, and children alike, any one of whom might be the Antichrist himself.[88]

The same apocalyptic impulse was triggered in the poor and disempowered folk who, from time to time, rose up against their masters just as Hildegard and Brother John had predicted. Thus, for example, Wat Tyler's Rebellion of 1381—a bloody rebellion by English workers and farmers against the gentry and the clergy—was seen as a sign of the end-times, and the armed mob was likened to the apocalyptic armies of Gog and Magog. The Taborites, a movement composed of Bohemian peasants and the urban poor of Prague, set up their own armed communes in the fifteenth century in anticipation of the millennial kingdom that would replace kings and priests alike. By 1452, a punitive expedition succeeded in capturing the last stronghold of the Taborites in what turned out to be only a toy-box version of the Apocalypse.

"Liberate us from the evil Antichrist and his cunning army," they chanted as they prepared for Armageddon. "Accursed be the man who withholds his sword from shedding the blood of the enemies of Christ."[89]

The tremors and eruptions that followed in the wake of the Protestant Reformation included an armed peasant uprising in Germany under the leadership of Thomas Müntzer (ca. 1488–1525), a minister who was persuaded that God had chosen him as the new revelator on the very eve of the end-times. "Harvest-time is here, so God himself has hired me for his harvest," declared Müntzer, alluding to the Grim Reaper as depicted in

Revelation. "I have sharpened my scythe, and my lips, hand, skin, hair, soul, body, life curse the unbelievers." He saw his faithful followers as the "Elect," and everyone else as the minions of the Devil. "For the ungodly have no right to live," he insisted, "save what the Elect choose to allow them." Like so many other messianic warriors, he was hunted down, tortured, and beheaded by the very princes whom he boldly condemned as "godless scoundrels."[90]

Another upwelling of "apocalyptic activism" was prompted by the crusade that Louis XIV carried out in the late seventeenth century against the Protestants of France, the Huguenots.[91] Long accustomed to persecution and oppression by the Catholic monarch, they rallied to the charismatic "child-prophets" who assured their elders that the latest outrages were sure signs of the Second Coming. And some Huguenot preachers, embracing the popular notion that the French "Babylon" would be destroyed in 1690, succeeded in setting off a guerilla war by the so-called Camisard rebels against the army of the Sun King. Fatefully, the war ended with the withdrawal of all civil and religious liberties and the self-exile of nearly a half million Huguenots.

But the acting out of the apocalyptic impulse reached its fullest expression in 1534 with the establishment of a self-proclaimed messianic kingdom in the German city of Münster. A radical faction of Anabaptists managed to convince themselves that the whole world *except* their hometown would shortly be destroyed. Münster, they believed, would be the New Jerusalem and the site of "a kingdom of a thousand years," and they anointed a former tailor and sometime actor named Jan Bockelson (also known as Jan van Leiden) as "Messiah of the Last Days."[92] And the first public act of the charismatic, handsome, and high-spirited young man was a characteristically showy one.

"He ran naked through the town in a frenzy and then fell into a silent ecstasy which lasted three days," writes Norman Cohn, an influential British historian specializing in medieval studies, in *The Pursuit of the Millennium*. "When speech returned to him he called the population together and announced that God had revealed to him that the old constitution of the town, being the work of men, must be replaced by a new one which would be the work of God."[93]

The townsfolk were required to surrender their gold and silver, submit to rebaptism, and comply with a strict code of sexual morality that was meant to purify all good Christians in anticipation of the Day of Judgment. Later, however, Bockelson revised the code to permit the practice of polygamy in imitation of the Hebrew patriarchs and kings—and he promptly took a gaggle of young women, "none older than twenty," as his own wives. Anyone who defied his authority was subject to capital punishment: "Now I am given power over all nations of the earth, and the right to use the sword to the confusion of the wicked and in defence of the righteous," he declared. "So let none in this town stain himself with crime or resist the will of God, or else he shall without delay be put to death with the sword."[94] Bockelson, seated on a golden throne, presided over the beheadings that were conducted in the town square with the "Sword of Justice"—and the King of the New Jerusalem himself lopped off more than a few heads. Among the victims was a woman who had committed the crime of "denying her husband his marital rights."[95]

"The glory of all the Saints is to wreak vengeance," declared one of the royal propagandists. "Revenge without mercy must be taken on all who are not marked with the Sign (of the Anabaptists)."[96]

The "kingdom of a thousand years," of course, was doomed from the start. The local bishop called upon the surrounding cities and states to contribute arms, men, horses, and money to mount a campaign against Münster, and the town was blockaded and besieged. Bockelson and his royal court continued to dine on the meat and drink that he had requisitioned from his subjects, but everyone else was reduced to eating dogs and cats, mice and rats, then "grass and moss, old shoes and the whitewash on the walls," and finally "the bodies of the dead."[97] At last, in 1535, the town was taken by the besieging army in a final surprise attack, and the defenders were put to a general slaughter that lasted several days. Bockelson and his cohorts were tortured at length with red-hot irons, and their broken bodies were put on public display as a warning against any other like-minded readers of Revelation who might be tempted to engage in a similar "horrendous novelty."

Ω

So it was that a sermonizer might seek to set his audience afire with terrors and yearnings and end up in the flames of his own making. Such was the fate of a man who has been called "a martyr of prophecy," Girolamo Savonarola (1452–1498), perhaps the single most famous (or notorious)

Gold coins from the reign of Nero (54–68). When the author of Revelation invokes "the mark of the beast" ("No one can buy or sell unless he has the mark, that is, the name of the beast or the number of his name" [Rev. 13:17, rsv]), he is probably referring to the name and image of a deified Roman emperor as they appeared on imperial coinage. The most likely candidate is Nero, shown above both early and late in his reign, and scholars believe that he uses "666" as an alphanumeric code to identify the first persecutor of Christians.

Detail from illuminated manuscript of Revelation (France, early fourteenth century). The author of Revelation suggests that his visions are to be understood "spiritually" rather than "carnally"—and so the Church decreed after Augustine—but readers in every age have insisted on approaching the text as literal truth. Here, Satan incarnated as a seven-headed dragon bestows authority upon the seven-headed "beast rising out of the sea" that symbolizes imperial Rome. (Rev. 13:1–4, RSV)

Woodcut from* The Revelation of St. John *by Albrecht Dürer (1498). Already a best-seller in the Middle Ages, Revelation reached an ever-larger audience with the advent of printing. Even men and women who could not read at all thrilled at the scenes depicted in a series of fifteen woodcuts created and published by Albrecht Dürer, including the "war in heaven" between the celestial armies captained by the archangel Michael and Satan in the guise of a seven-headed dragon. (Rev. 12:7, KJV)

Detail from the **Apocalypse of Angers** *by Nicolas Bataille (France, late fourteenth century).* The author of Revelation betrays something dark and disturbing in his own sexual imagination when he conjures up the Great Whore of Babylon, the famous seductress who rides the seven-headed beast and carries "a golden cup full of the impurities of her fornication." (Rev. 17:4, RSV) "How the apocalypticists would have loved to drink of her cup!" commented D. H. Lawrence. "And since they couldn't how they loved smashing it!"

Detail from the **Silos Apocalypse** *by Beatus of Liébana (Spain, c. 1109).* Despite the so-called Terrors of the Year 1000, the first millennium of the Common Era did not bring the end of the world. By then, however, an obsessive concern with the end-times had already become a dominant habit of the Western mind. The Four Horsemen of the Apocalypse, for example, offered one way of understanding and explaining such commonplaces of life in the Middle Ages as famine, plague, and war.

Detail from illuminated manuscript of Revelation (France, thirteenth century).
From Martin of Tours to Martin Luther to Daniel Berrigan, the promised destruction of Babylon by earthquake and fire has been repurposed by generation after generation of preachers, pamphleteers, and propagandists who use the punishing text of Revelation as a "language arsenal" to attack their adversaries. "And God remembered great Babylon, to make her drain the cup of the fury of his wrath." (Rev. 16:19, RSV)

The Last Judgment as rendered by Hieronymus Bosch (1504). Revelation imprinted itself deeply on Western art and letters and continued to inspire new interpretations over the twenty centuries since it was first composed. Perhaps no scene has been more compelling to artists than Judgment Day, when we are told that the faithful will be elevated to "a new heaven and a new earth" and the rest of humanity will be cast into "a lake of fire." (Rev. 20:15, 21:1, KJV)

The Last Judgment as rendered by Michelangelo (1537–1541). Even as
Michelangelo borrowed from the book of Revelation in order to glorify the papacy, some of his contemporaries saw the pope himself as the Antichrist. Here was yet
another culture war in which Revelation served as a rhetorical weapons dump, and
both factions resorted to the same ancient text to justify their respective visions of the
right way to live as a Christian in the world as we find it rather than the world
to come.

The Last Judgment as rendered by William Blake (1808). Revelation moved ever westward and exerted its greatest power in the hearts and minds of the Anglo-Saxons on the far western fringe of Europe, including the visionary artist and poet William Blake, who imagined the building of New Jerusalem "in England's green and pleasant land." The Puritans carried the text from England to the New World, where it was transformed yet again in what one scholar calls "the Americanization of the apocalyptic tradition."

Detail from illuminated manuscript of Dante's **Purgatory** *(fifteenth century).*
Revelation belongs to a genre of apocalyptic writing that includes various texts,
known as Pseudepigrapha ("false writings"), that were wholly excluded from the
Bible. *The Apocalypse of Paul,* for example, features a tour of heaven and hell that
resembles the one depicted in Dante's masterpiece. The author of Revelation, too,
may have known and used some of these more exotic apocalypses.

Plate from Scivias *by Hildegard of Bingen (Romanesque, twelfth century).* The author of Revelation may be distrustful and disdainful of women, but his work has always commanded an ardent female readership. Among the earliest and most influential was Hildegard of Bingen (1098–1179), a nun whose apocalyptic prophecies commanded the attention of kings and popes. But other medieval women who dared to offer their own interpretations of Revelation ended up hanging from gallows or burned at the stake.

Detail from illuminated manuscript of **Jerome's Commentary on Daniel**
(France, twelfth century). Only two of the many apocalypses composed in antiquity found their way into Jewish and Christian scripture—Daniel in the Hebrew Bible and Revelation in the New Testament. The book of Daniel is perhaps the single most important of the various "models and sources" that the author of Revelation seems to have invoked in his own writings, and it continues to serve as the "text of choice" for modern doomsayers and date-setters.

Wing of triptych by Hans Memling depicting St. John the Evangelist on the island of Patmos (1474–1479). By pious tradition, the author of Revelation was thought to be the disciple known as John, son of Zebedee. Starting in antiquity, however, discerning readers have argued that the text was actually composed by "another John." Some modern scholars suggest the author was a Jew by birth and education, a war refugee from Judea, and perhaps an eyewitness to the conquest of Jerusalem and the destruction of the Temple by a Roman army of occupation.

Photo: Foto Marburg/Art Resource, NY

Engraving of the burning of Anabaptists at Münster (date unknown). Some readers of Revelation have always been tempted to take matters into their own hands and hasten the end of the world, and that's exactly why it has always been regarded as a dangerous text. The acting out of the apocalyptic impulse reached its fullest expression in 1534 with the establishment of a self-proclaimed messianic kingdom by Anabaptists in the German city of Münster. And, like David Koresh and the Branch Davidians, some apocalyptic warriors end up in the flames of their own making.

Painting of the execution of Savonarola in Florence (Italian, sixteenth century). Perhaps the single most famous (or notorious) of the apocalyptic radicals was Girolamo Savonarola (1452–1498), a self-appointed soldier in a culture war against the worldly ways of life and art that are seen today as the glory of the Renaissance. Ironically, he was burned at the stake in the same public square where he had once organized the "Bonfire of the Vanities," where penitent men and woman were commanded to cast their finery and frippery into the flames.

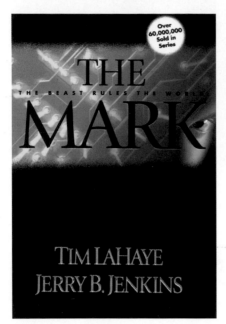

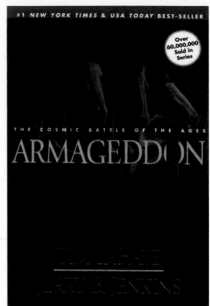

Titles in the Left Behind series. Some of the earliest commentaries on Revelation have been characterized as "medieval best-sellers," and the most recent example of the same phenomenon is the Left Behind series, a sensationally successful media enterprise that demonstrates the power of the apocalyptic idea in its purest and simplest form. "In the world of Left Behind," writes critic Gershom Gorenberg, "there exists a single truth, based on a purportedly literal reading of Scripture; anyone who disagrees with that truth is deceived or evil."

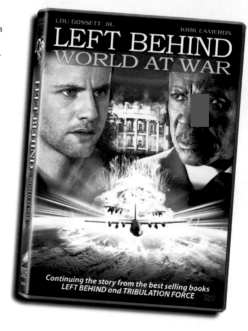

of the apocalyptic radicals.[98] Florence was destined to be the New Jerusalem, or so Savonarola believed and preached, and he saw it as his divine mission to make it so. At a moment in history when Europe was afflicted by "presages, phantoms and astrological conjunctions of dreadful import," as one contemporary chronicler put it, the Florentines were a ready and willing audience.[99]

Like the author of Revelation, Savonarola was a self-appointed soldier in a culture war. The Dominican friar detested what he called "the perversities and the extreme evil of these blind peoples amongst whom virtue is reduced to zero and vice triumphs on every hand"[100]—that is, the worldly ways of life and art that are seen today as the glory of the Renaissance. And, just as John denounced the pleasures and treasures of Roman paganism ("Cargo of gold, silver, jewels and pearls, fine linen, purple, silk and scarlet . . ."),[101] Savanarola condemned the opulent lives of the Roman Catholic clergy.

"You have been to Rome," he declared. "Well, then, you must know something of the lives of these priests. They have courtesans, squires, horses, dogs. Their houses are filled with carpets, silks, perfumes, servants. Their pride fills the world. Their avarice matches their pride. All they do, they do for money."[102]

Savonarola, again like the author of Revelation, was a gifted and powerful preacher, and his sermons "ignited a fireball of religious panic that heated even the city's most urbane minds," according to cultural historian Robin Barnes.[103] His public lectures on the book of Revelation were so popular, in fact, that he was forced to move to ever-larger quarters in order to accommodate the crowds. They took to heart his warning that the end of the world was near: "torrents of blood," "a terrible famine," and "a fierce pestilence" awaited the sinners.[104] And they surely thrilled at the sight of a seer in action: "My reasons for announcing these scourges and calamities are founded on the Word of God," ranted Savonarola in one of his white-hot sermons. "I have seen a sign in the heavens. Not a cross this time, but a sword. It's the Lord's terrible swift sword which will strike the earth!"[105]

Above all, Savonarola commanded his congregation to forgo the pleasures of the flesh in anticipation of the Day of Judgment. "Sodomy is Florence's besetting sin," declared Savonarola, who complained that "a young boy cannot walk in the streets without of falling into evil hands."[106] But he was no less punishing when it came to the sexual excesses of women, real or imagined. "Big flabby hunks of fat you are with your dyed hair, your high-rouged cheeks and eyelids smeared with charcoal," he railed. "Your perfumes poison the air of our streets and parks. Not content with being the concubines of laymen and debauching young boys, you are running after priests and monks in order to catch them in your nets and involve them in your filthy intrigues."[107] And he laid the same charge against the pope and the clergy: "Come here, you blasphemy of a church!" he sermonized, making good use of the catchphrases of Revelation. "Your lust has made of you a brazenfaced whore. Worse than beasts are you, who have made yourself into an unspeakable monster!"[108]

The most remarkable and enduring moment in Savonarola's war on the humanism and high art of the Renaissance was the so-called Bonfire of the Vanities, a pyre on which he urged the penitent men and women of Florence to toss their finery and frippery, wigs and gowns, perfumes and face powders, mirrors and rouge pots, dice and playing cards, and "certain musical instruments whose tone was deemed to be of an excitant nature."[109] Some of the fuel for the bonfire can be described as pornography or worse—"marble statues of lewd posture, mechanized dolls of impure gesturing, as well as all articles apt or calculated to excite lust"[110]— but paintings by Botticelli and books by Petrarch and Boccaccio were also pitched into the flames.[111] The reward for the self-sacrifice of the Florentines, he promised, would be the elevation of the city of Florence to the stature of the New Jerusalem, a model of Christian purity and the capital of the millennial kingdom.

Like so many other apocalyptic preachers, Savonarola saw no meaningful distinction between religion and politics. Indeed, his vision of the end-times was deeply rooted in the soil of realpolitik. Thus, for example, he condemned the papacy in Rome on moral grounds: "They have turned their churches into stalls for prostitutes," he declared, "I shall turn them into stalls for hogs and horses because these would be less offensive to God."[112] And his moral revulsion prompted him to side with the French king, Charles VIII, who was contesting with the pope for political sovereignty over Italy. Nor was Savonarola troubled by the bloodshed and chaos that he invited and even instigated. When Pope Alexander reportedly tried to make a separate peace with Savonarola by offering to raise him to the rank of cardinal, whose badge of office was a scarlet miter, the pope badly misjudged the temper of the true believer.

"I want nothing but what you, O Lord, have given to your saints, namely death," Savonarola retorted. "A red hat, yes, but red with blood—that's what I wish for."[113]

Savonarola may have won over the guilt-ridden and panic-stricken souls who rallied to his potent sermons, but he also managed to alienate those among the wealthy and powerful of Florence who sided with the pope and who, not incidentally, were offended and embarrassed by Savonarola's denunciation of their riches and privileges. "Fra Girolamo either sees spooks," cracked one of his adversaries, referring to him by his title and first name, "or he drinks too much."[114] Savonarola's enemies in Florence, acting in concert with the pope in Rome, arranged for his arrest, torture, and trial, and he was condemned on charges of heresy and schism.

"I separate you from the Church Militant and Triumphant," said the bishop who conducted the formal ritual of excommunication. "From the Church Militant, not from the Church Triumphant," retorted the defiant Savonarola. "That is not within your competence."[115]

The "proto-messianic republic" that Savonarola founded in Florence lasted only three years.[116] On May 24, 1498, Savonarola was stripped of his monk's robe, his head was shaved to destroy his tonsure, and he was hanged by the neck from a gibbet. Then his broken body was put to the flames in the same crowded and clamorous public square where he had once kindled his own dangerous fires.

"Prophet," taunted an ironist in the noisy mob, "now is the time for a miracle!"[117]

Still, the apocalyptic idea is not always or only a matter of gloom and doom. For readers who are so inclined, the book of Revelation—and all of the apocalyptic writings in both Judaism and Christian traditions—can be understood as a story with the happiest of endings. To be sure, John warns that our benighted world will end in fire and brimstone, but he also promises a new heaven and a new earth. "Behold," says God at the end of Revelation, "I make all things new."[118] That is why the apocalyptic tradition has been aptly described as "bipolar": the bad news is that the earth will be destroyed and humankind will be exterminated, but the good news is that the saints will live forever in paradise.[119]

At the very moment when Savonarola's apocalyptic visions (and Savonarola himself) were going up in flames, for example, another celebrated reader of Revelation was looking forward to a much happier fate for himself and all of humankind. Of course, Christopher Columbus (1451–1506) is remembered for his historic voyages of discovery rather than for his apocalyptic speculation. Long before Columbus embarked on the first of his momentous voyages, however, the Admiral of the Ocean Seas had already found his way to the ancient mystical texts, all of which he read with the greatest curiosity and credulity. Between his second and third sailings to America, Columbus compiled his own collection of apocalyptic and prophetic passages that he had extracted from the Bible, the writings of the church fathers, and various medieval commentaries, a work that he titled *The Book of Prophecies.*

His goal was to make the case for royal sponsorship of a very different but no less ambitious enterprise. The Holy Land remained under Islamic sovereignty, but Columbus was encouraged by what he had read in the apocalyptic texts to see a role for himself in achieving what the crusaders had repeatedly failed to accomplish—the defeat of the Muslim overlords of Jerusalem. Indeed, he was convinced that God bestowed the gold and silver of the Americas on Christendom in order to finance the reconstruction of the Temple in Jerusalem, "the apocalyptic city *par excellence.*"[120]

Columbus himself witnessed a fresh upwelling of apocalyptic frenzy. His royal patron, Ferdinand of Aragon, was seen as a worthy candidate for the title of Last World Emperor, and the victory of the Spanish crown over the last Islamic kingdom on the Iberian Peninsula was regarded as a sign of the approaching millennial kingdom. And, since the New Jerusalem was a crucial element of the end-times as they were predicted in the book of Revelation, Columbus was inspired to offer his services in bringing it into existence.

Among the texts that he consulted were the writings of Joachim of Fiore, and he recognized himself in the prophesies that he found there. "Jerusalem and Mount Zion are to be rebuilt by the hand of a Christian, [and] Abbot Joachim said that he was to come from Spain," writes Columbus in an account of his final voyage to America in the opening years of the sixteenth century. "Who will offer himself for this work? If our Lord brings me back to Spain, I pledge myself, in the name of God, to bring him there in safety."[121]

Columbus, like Savonarola, lived in a state of "psychological imminence"—that is, "the conviction that the final events of history are already under way even though we cannot determine how near or far off the last judgment may actually be."[122] Both men, of course, died without seeing the fulfillment of their apocalyptic visions, but it turns out that Columbus had a far better sense of "future history." Fatefully, the next generation of visionaries took it upon themselves to create the millennial kingdom that is promised in the book of Revelation, not in the Holy Land but on the new continent that Columbus had found when he sailed westward in search of a faster route to India. And when Revelation took its next quantum leap, from the benighted shores of Europe to the raw wilderness of North America, the apocalyptic idea was fully and fatefully transformed.

"Then I saw a new heaven and a new earth," writes the author of Revelation at the climax of his apocalyptic visions. "God made me the messenger of the new heaven and the new earth of which he spoke in the Apocalypse of St. John," affirms Columbus, "and he showed me the spot where to find it."[123]

Notably, the phrase that is rendered as "the new earth" in most English translations of the Bible—and as "the new land" in the writings of Columbus—appears in the Vulgate as *terra nova*. But the most familiar translation of the same Latin phrase is "New World." And, as we shall see, it is only in America that the book of Revelation would reach its richest, strangest, and most enduring expression.[124]

Six

To Begin the World Over Again

We are the pioneers of the world, the advance guard,
sent on through the wilderness of untried things,
to break a new path in the new World that is ours.
HERMAN MELVILLE, *White Jacket* (1850)

When the *Arabella* sailed from England in 1630, the little ship carried a contingent of Puritan families who were setting out to colonize the raw North American wilderness. The passengers gathered on deck to hear a sermon delivered by a fiery Puritan minister, John Cotton (1585–1652), who stirringly characterized their destination as "the new promised land," a place that had been "reserved by God for his elect people as the actual site for a new heaven and a new earth."[1] Thus transplanted to the rich soil of the Massachusetts Bay Colony, the Apocalypse flowered in new, remarkable, and enduring ways.

"Christ by a wonderful Providence hath dispossessed Satan, who reigned securely in these Ends of the Earth, for Ages the Lord knoweth how many," declared another Puritan minister, Increase Mather (1639–1723), after his arrival in America, "and here the Lord has caused as it were *New Jerusalem* to come down from Heaven."[2]

The author of Revelation may have set down his visions on an island off the coast of Asia, but his remarkable little book promptly began to move ever westward. The eastern realm of Christianity, as we have seen, nearly excluded it from the biblical canon, but Revelation earned a place in the earliest biblical lists of western Christendom. The so-called apocalyptic invasion reached its fullest expression in the arts, letters, and architecture of France and Germany. And Revelation worked its strange magic with even greater power in the hearts and minds of the Anglo-Saxons on the far western fringe of Europe. They came to entertain the thrilling idea that Jesus Christ himself once walked "upon England's mountains green," as visionary artist and poet William Blake (1757–1827) puts it in the poem "Jerusalem," and would one day set the New Jerusalem "among these dark satanic mills."[3] Blake himself was an obsessive reader and reinterpreter of Revelation, and his poem later became a British national hymn.

I will not cease from mental fight
Nor shall my sword sleep in my hand,
Till we have built Jerusalem
In England's green and pleasant land.[4]

Still, the most radical of the Protestant reformers, whom we know as the Puritans, refused to sing hymns to England, its church, or its monarch. By their lights, the priestcraft and high ceremonials of the Church of England were as corrupt as those of the Roman Catholic Church. They regarded the kings of England, whose royal titles included "Defender of the Faith," as the latest and likeliest candidates for the role of Antichrist. And the Puritans found the rich and sometimes ribald culture of England in the seventeenth century—scandalous plays and love poems, hedonistic masques and musicales, high-spirited bouts of feasting and drinking, extravagant fashions and manners, and much else besides—to be as offensive as Roman paganism had been to the author of Revelation and Renaissance humanism had been to Savonarola. That is one reason why the wilderness on the far side of the Atlantic, even though it was occupied by native-dwelling tribes whom they saw as minions of the Devil, struck the Puritans as a much worthier site for the New Jerusalem than those satanic mills of Old England.[5]

So began the next leg of the westward movement of Revelation, a remarkable phenomenon that historian Stephen J. Stein calls "the Americanization of the apocalyptic tradition."[6] When the Puritans arrived in the New World—"flying from the Depravations of Europe," as they saw it, "to the American Strand"—they promptly unpacked and polished up the old apocalyptic texts. John Winthrop (1588–1649), a passenger on the *Arabella* and the first governor of the Massachusetts Bay Colony, famously invoked the New Jerusalem when he likened the Puritan settlement to "a City upon a Hill." And, significantly, "The Day of Doom," a poem by Michael Wigglesworth (1631–1705), was "the first best seller in the annals of the American book trade."[7]

But the Puritans and those who came after them also felt at liberty to tinker with the scenario of Revelation and come up with story lines wholly of their own invention. Indeed, they insisted on accentuating the positive in Revelation, and they gave the apocalyptic idea a uniquely American spin that has persisted into our own anxious age. Remarkably, the end of the world and the destruction of humankind, if viewed in the right way, could be seen as a *good* thing.

The world that the Puritan colonists left behind was still shadowed by all of the old terrors that are given such vivid names, faces, and figures in the book of Revelation. The shattering events of the Civil War in England, when the Puritan leader Oliver Cromwell (1599–1658) and the parliamentary army drove King Charles I from the throne and then took off his head, brought the apocalyptic fantasies into even sharper focus. Amid chaos and crisis—war and revolution, torture and execution, witch burning and book burning—the readers of Revelation teetered between the old certainty that the end of the world was nigh and the new conviction that a better world was at hand.

The followers of Cromwell, for example, saw the conflict between the parliamentary and royalist armies as a struggle between Christ and Antichrist, and they regarded the defeat of King Charles I as a sign that the millennial kingdom of Jesus Christ was soon to begin: "The Eternall and shortly-expected King," writes poet (and Puritan pamphleteer) John Milton (1608–1674), "shall open the Clouds to judge the severall Kingdomes of the World."[8] And the enemies of Cromwell, too, invoked the book of Revelation. One royalist pamphleteer, who dubbed Cromwell "Rex Oliver Lord Protector," insisted that the title was an alphanumeric code that added up to the demonic 666, but only if he conveniently dropped the letter "L" from the word "Lord."

"These are days of shaking," observed one English preacher in 1643, "and this shaking is universal."[9]

At one precarious moment in 1653, in fact, Parliament nearly fell under the control of the so-called Fifth Monarchy Men, a radical faction of soldiers, clergy, and poor folk whose name refers to the divine kingdom that is predicted to follow the four earthly monarchies described in the book of Daniel. These self-styled "saints" looked forward to an apocalyptic revolution of the kind predicted by Hildegard of Bingen: church and government alike, and the rich and powerful along with them, would be replaced once and for all by a biblical theocracy under King Jesus himself. Cromwell deemed it necessary to suppress the Fifth Monarchy Men by force of arms in 1656: "Lord, appear, now or never," they cried as a detachment of soldiers broke up one of their public rallies and escorted them to prison.[10] Needless to say, the Lord was once again a no-show.

The strict and censorious Puritans and their worldly adversaries had long been engaged in a culture war, too. A Puritan sermonizer, adopting one of the rhetorical quirks of Martin Luther, condemned the Anglican clergy as "the excrement of Antichrist."[11] A bon vivant like playwright and poet Ben Jonson (1572–1637), by contrast, poked fun at the dire apocalyptic expectations of the Puritans when he created a character in *Bartholomew Fair* called Zeal-of-the-Land-Busy, a self-convinced seer who sees an unfamiliar musical instrument on display at a country fair and promptly leaps to the conclusion that he has spied the Beast of Revelation. The drum of the instrument, according to Jonson, is "the broken belly of Antichrist, and thy bellows there are his lungs, and these pipes are his throat, those feathers are his tail, and thy rattles the gnashing of his teeth."[12]

The apocalyptic fancies that Jonson found so laughable penetrated even the loftiest circles of the scientific revolution that was already in progress. Scottish mathematician John Napier (1550–1617), originator of the logarithm, applied his arithmetical genius to a treatise on Revelation in which he argued that the seventh and final age of human history had begun in 1541 and would end in 1786. And Isaac Newton (1642–1727), who achieved enduring greatness in mathematics and physics, also found time to engage in his own apocalyptic number-crunching: "Sir Isaac Newton wrote his comment upon the Revelation," cracks French philosopher Voltaire (1664–1777), "to console mankind for the great superiority he had over them in other respects."[13]

But the apocalyptic idea may have reached its apogee in the Old World just as the Puritans were making their way to the New World. As Voltaire's joke at the expense of Isaac Newton seems to suggest, the book of Revelation had already started its descent into the netherworld of religious oddities and curiosities. The Great London Fire of 1666, for example, brought a fresh wave of doomsaying, thanks to the appearance of the old demonic number on the calendar: "Every thunderstorm," wrote George Fox, a leader of the Quakers, "produced expectations of the end."[14] And yet, by 1696, an English scientist named William Whiston was ready to argue that a wholly natural celestial phenomenon like Halley's Comet may have caused the Great Flood as described in Genesis, and proposed that "the earth's prophesied destruction by fire would be by the same means."[15]

"Whiston's end-time drama included no Second Coming, no Last Judgment," as Perry Miller, a distinguished historian of Puritanism, points out.[16] Here was perhaps the earliest stirring of an idea that would take on ever more ominous meanings in our own times—a vision of the end of the world that allowed no role at all for God. And even those Christian true believers who continued to read the book of Revelation with perfect credulity began to see wholly new and unsuspected meanings in the ancient text. Those ideas, too, would move westward to America, where Yankee ingenuity was applied to Holy Writ with revolutionary consequences.

Ω

An early example of the Americanization of the Apocalypse is found in the remarkable life and work of Cotton Mather (1663–1728), son of Increase Mather, grandson of John Cotton, and minister of the Old North Church in Boston. He was capable of holding an earnest belief in the efficacy of both witchcraft as supposedly practiced by the women of Salem *and* the efficacy of the newfangled science of smallpox inoculation. He penned a panic-making treatise on satanic possession that played a role in the witch trials—"Go tell the world what it is these Monsters love to do"—and yet he also arranged for his own young son to be inoculated, an act so controversial in colonial Boston that it prompted one outraged citizen to throw a bomb (or "a Fired Granado," as Mather himself describes it) through the window of his lodging room.[17]

"But, *this Night there stood by me the Angel of GOD*," Mather writes in his journal to explain why the grenade failed to explode, "*whose I am and whom I serve.*"[18]

The apparent contradictions that coexisted within the heart and mind of Cotton Mather can be readily explained by his conviction that he was beholding, at once, the shuddering death of the old earth and the birth pangs of the new one. "In fact, Mather's blend of optimism and paranoia is entirely characteristic of the millennial vision," explains historian Damian Thompson in *The End of Time*. "Fear of witches is above all evidence of End-time anxiety, since it was believed that the Last Days would see a terrible loosing of the powers of darkness." At the same time, Mather saw the prosperity of the American colonies—"great increase in the blessings of land and sea"—as a evidence that "God had surely intended 'some great thing' when he planted these American heavens and earth."[19]

Indeed, Cotton Mather saw himself as "Herald of the Lord's Kingdome now approaching,"[20] and he shared the conviction of his famous father and grandfather that America was the place where the prophecies of Revelation would be fulfilled. He was so fixated on Revelation, in fact, that he convinced himself that "evil angels," speaking through a young woman whom he believed to be the victim of demonic possession, once scolded him for neglecting a certain passage from the book of Revelation in his sermons. The demons wanted him to preach on Rev. 13:8 ("All that dwell upon the earth shall worship [the beast]"), but he defied them by choosing Rev. 20:15 instead: "And whosoever was not found written in the book of life was cast into the lake of fire."[21]

On the subject of doomsday, Mather was inspired by both religion and science. He conceded that the New Jerusalem would appear in North America only after the world was destroyed in a vast conflagration, just as John had predicted in Revelation, but he was also mindful of the latest discoveries of the earth sciences when he described the end-times. Volcanoes, he suggested, will be the instrument of the divine will: "Subterraneous *Combustions,* and such Amassments of *Igneous Particles,*" he writes, "which are an *Eternal Fire.*"[22] And, significantly, he looked beyond the days of terror and tribulation to the shining moment when the New Jerusalem floats down from the heavens.

"[O]ur glorious LORD will have an Holy city in AMERICA," Mather declares in 1709, adopting a phrase that became (and remains) an American credo, "a *City,* the Street whereof will be *Pure* Gold."[23]

A century or so after Mather uttered these words, men, women, and children by the millions would begin to arrive in America—"huddled masses yearning to breathe free," according to the poem by Emma Lazarus that is famously inscribed on the Statue of Liberty—and they, too, came in search of streets paved with gold.[24] Even if they were wholly ignorant of the book of Revelation, they were following in the footsteps of the Puritan fathers who failed to foresee what would become of their apocalyptic fancies.

Ω

The Puritan colonists, of course, were no democrats. Rather, they aspired to the kind of government that is deeply implicit in both Jewish and Christian scripture and especially the book of Revelation—"a *theocracy,* as near as might be, to that which was the glory of Israel," according to John Mather.[25] That's why the earliest Puritan colonists in America, who aspired to create a religious utopia, felt thoroughly justified in denying citizenship to anyone who was *not* a member of a Puritan congregation, banishing religious dissenters, and even sending a few Quakers to the gallows.

Happily for the health of the American democracy, the Puritans were soon eclipsed by new arrivals to North America who did not feel obliged to impose their religious beliefs and practices on their fellow citizens. The Founding Fathers, for example, drew more inspiration from the proto-democracies of pagan Greece and Rome than they did from the divine monarchy that is celebrated so lushly in Revelation. Indeed, they were perfectly willing to tinker with Holy Writ itself. Thomas Jefferson, for example, disdained the book of Revelation and boldly took it upon himself to rewrite the Gospels to suit the spirit of a revolutionary and democratic age, keeping only what he regarded as "the very words only of Jesus" and cutting away "the artificial vestments in which they have been muffled by priests, who have travestied them into various forms as instruments of riches and power for themselves."[26]

Still, the glowing theological core of Revelation—the sure promise that a new and better world was coming soon—appealed to even the most secular of the American patriots. Thus, for example, the apocalyptic vocabulary of abuse was put to good use by pamphleteers in the struggle for American independence. King George III was denounced as the Antichrist, and the Stamp Act of 1765, which required the American colonists to affix a tax stamp bearing the king's name and image to their papers and publications, was linked to the prophecy in Revelation that Satan would command all of mankind to display the mark of the Beast.

To be sure, many American patriots were also pious Christians, but when colonial preacher Samuel West sermonized on "that terrible denunciation of divine wrath against the worshippers of the beast and his image," he was referring to the British lion rather than the satanic seven-headed dragon of Revelation.[27] And the American version of the New Earth in 1776 was a place where every human being—or, at least, every adult white male—enjoyed the "inalienable rights" of Life, Liberty, and the Pursuit of Happiness, free of the dictates of kings *or* priests. *Novus Ordo Seculorum* is the Latin motto that was adopted in 1782 and placed on the great seal of the United States: "A new order of the ages." Even a red-hot revolutionary like Thomas Paine, who may have stripped his rhetoric of all religious trappings, expressed himself in terms of the millennial ideal that can be traced all the way back to the apocalyptic tradition of distant antiquity. And the destiny of American democracy, as Paine defined it, owes something to the words that were written down in John's little book in biblical antiquity.

"We have it in our power," he declared, "to begin the world over again."[28]

Ω

Of course, the old ideas about the apocalyptic kingdom of Christ on earth were never wholly abandoned in colonial America. Now and then, the banked embers of religious true belief would burst into flame as preachers stoked the fears and longings of their congregations with the kind of hard-sell sermonizing that is the trademark of American evangelism. Again and again, the spirit of Christian revival attracted the crowds to church halls and tent meetings and whipped them into a spiritual frenzy—so often, in fact, that certain stretches of western New York State came to be called the Burned-Over District precisely because its populace was so susceptible to each new wave of religious enthusiasm.

The revival movement in America was "the forerunner of something vastly great," according to Jonathan Edwards (1703–1758), the Puritan minister whose preaching sparked the so-called First Great Awakening in the mid–eighteenth century. Not incidentally, Edwards was the author of a vast commentary on Revelation titled *Notes on the Apocalypse*.[29] Starting with the prophecy in Revelation that the Antichrist will reign for 1,260 "days," which he interpreted to mean "years," Edwards decided that the reign of the arch-demon had begun in 606 and calculated that it would end sometime around 1866. And he saw the convulsions of the Great

Awakening as "signs of the millennium lately begun in Northampton"—
that is, the Massachusetts town where his own pulpit was located.[30]

Some of the more sober clergy, however, were skeptical of spontaneous
mass conversions, and they fretted that the men and women who experienced such powerful revelations during the revival meetings of the Great
Awakening "had fallen prey to dangerous enthusiasms and delusions."[31]
When another wave of revivalism erupted in the 1790s, the Second Great
Awakening, the religious idealism of some Christians in America began
to express itself in quite a different way. A new generation of Christians
was inspired to agitate for the abolition of slavery and the emancipation
of women as a way of hastening the millennial kingdom. Here, too, were
the first stirrings of a distinctively American version of the apocalyptic
idea, a "high-octane blend of millennial fervor and patriotic enthusiasm,"
according to American cultural historian Paul Boyer, that expressed itself
in efforts to improve the quality of American democracy.[32]

Indeed, the gloom and doom of Revelation were far less compelling to
the high-spirited and high-minded American nation builders than, say,
the promise in Matthew that the kingdom of heaven was open to anyone who clothed the naked, fed the hungry, and sheltered the homeless.
Thus, Christian piety was translated into what later came to be called the
Social Gospel—that is, a call "to build on American soil a society worthy
of the exalted vision of the new Jerusalem found in the book of Revelation," including principled crusades for the abolition of slavery and alcohol, the reform of prisons, and the opening of shelters for the homeless and
the hungry and asylums for the ailing—"the least of these my brethren,"
as Jesus Christ puts it.[33]

"Christianity is primarily concerned with this world," explained one
theologian, "and it is the mission of Christianity to bring to pass here a
kingdom of righteousness and to rescue from the evil one and redeem all
our social relations."[34]

Even those who still believed that the end is near began to subtly repur-
pose the text of Revelation in ways that meshed with sturdy and vigor-
ous American values of Yankee ingenuity, material comfort, and personal
self-improvement. Samuel Hopkins, the abolitionist pastor of a Congrega-
tional church in Rhode Island in the late eighteenth century, imagined the
millennial kingdom as a place where "all utensils, clothing, buildings &c
will be formed and made in a better manner and with much less labor,"

thanks to improvements in "all useful branches of the arts and sciences that promote spiritual and bodily comforts in this life." Only two or three hours of work each day will be required to earn a livelihood, he predicted, and leisure hours will be spent in "reading and conversation," all of which would be conducted in a universal language that all of humankind will speak. All of these prophecies, Hopkins promised, would be fulfilled in not more than a couple of centuries.[35]

By the 1850s, the dividing line between faith in God and faith in progress was even murkier. A Methodist women's magazine, for example, praised the invention of the telegraph as "the means of extending civilization, republicanism and Christianity over the earth," which amounted to a new and thoroughly modern definition of the kingdom of Christ on earth: "Then shall come to pass the millennium."[36] And the westward expansion of the United States—an enterprise that has been likened to a war of genocide against the people who were already here when the Puritans showed up—was seen as nothing less than a divine mandate.

"We are entering on its untrodden space, with the truths of God in our minds, beneficent objects in our hearts, and with a clear conscience unsullied by the past," writes John O'Sullivan in the 1839 article that inserted the doctrine of "Manifest Destiny" into the American political vocabulary. "In its magnificent domain of space and time, the nation of many nations is destined to manifest to mankind the excellence of divine principles; to establish on earth the noblest temple ever dedicated to the worship of the Most High—the Sacred and the True."[37]

A fault line runs between these two ways of understanding of the apocalyptic idea, one embraced by revivalists and the other embraced by reformers. On one side are the true believers who lift their eyes heavenward and search the skies for a sign of the Second Coming. On the other side are the more practical believers who hunker down to the task of building the millennial kingdom with their own hands right here on earth. A great many earnest men and women, of course, were capable of straddling the line and trying to do both at once. But, as we shall see, the landscape of American democracy would be shaken again and again by the tremors that result when these two tectonic plates collide.

Ω

The apocalyptic idea, as we have seen, is supposedly linked to oppression and persecution. The victims, we are told, console themselves with visions of revenge like the ones that are described so rousingly in the pages of Revelation. The fact is, however, that the text is capable of stirring up the passions of ordinary men and women who suffer from nothing more than overactive imaginations. Even in the New World, for example, and even in an era of peace and prosperity, the prospect of the second coming of Jesus Christ and the end of the world was a thrilling notion to otherwise comfortable and complacent Americans like an upstate New York farmer whose name was William Miller (1782–1849).

Miller was a Baptist from the Burned-Over District, wholly untutored in Bible scholarship and backsliding in the direction of deism. While serving as an officer in the War of 1812, however, he experienced a battlefield conversion, and when he returned to civilian life on the family farm, he devoted himself to the study of the Bible. His eye fell on a passage in the book of Daniel where the prophet is told in one of his visions that twenty-three hundred days shall pass, and "then the sanctuary shall be cleansed."[38] Like the author of Revelation and countless other biblical finger-counters, Miller was convinced that he had stumbled across a line of scripture that contained a coded reference to the end of the world, and he spent the next two years trying to crack the code.

Miller figured that the biblical reference to twenty-three hundred *days* actually means twenty-three hundred *years*—of course!—and he fixed the starting point for the countdown clock in 457 B.C.E., which he calculated as the year when the exiled Jews commenced the rebuilding of the Temple of Yahweh in Jerusalem. The "sanctuary," he decided, was a code word for the world. Then, simply by doing the math, he calculated that the second coming of Jesus Christ and the beginning of the end of the world would take place "sometime around 1843."[39]

"I believe," wrote Miller, "that the Scriptures do reveal unto us in plain language that Jesus Christ will appear again on this earth, that he will come in the glory of God, in the clouds of heaven, with all his Saints and angels."[40]

Miller "did not rant or rave," preferring to patiently explain his approach to the scriptures "in a low-keyed schoolmasterish fashion."[41] At first, he confided only in his friends and neighbors. By the 1830s, however, Father Miller, as he had come to be called, was attracting the attention of evangelical ministers and their small-town congregations around New England. Among his followers were some capable and imaginative men who understood how to put a message across to a mass audience, and they resolved to let the rest of America know what awaited them in the very near future.

Like the revivalists of the Great Awakening, the leaders of the so-called Millerites organized tent meetings that attracted earnest seekers by the thousands. And, like the televangelists of our own era, they made good use of the latest information technology of the mid–nineteenth century, the high-speed printing press, to produce the elaborately illustrated publications, tracts, and broadsheets—including periodicals titled *Midnight Cry* and *Signs of the Times*—that explained Miller's complex theories of biblical prophecy in simple and colorful terms.

Some of Miller's hard-charging handlers encouraged him to commit himself to a more specific prediction than "sometime around 1843." By redoing his calculations according to what he called "ancient Jewish reckoning," Miller came up with a somewhat narrower prophecy: Jesus Christ would return sometime between March 21, 1843, and March 21, 1844. When the new deadline passed without any sign of the Second Coming, one of his enterprising followers claimed to have found a calculational error and fixed D-day for October 22, 1844. And then, at last, Father Miller and his followers put down their pencils and waited for the day that would surely bring the fulfillment of the ancient prophecies of Revelation about the second coming of Jesus Christ.

"If he does not come within 20 or 25 days," Miller announced at the beginning of October 1844, "I shall feel twice the disappointment I did this spring."[42]

As the glorious day approached, the Millerites prepared to greet Jesus Christ when he descended from heaven to the soil of the New World. They spurned the petty concerns of the old earth in preference to the new one that seemed so close at hand: "Some left their jobs, boarded up their businesses, confessed to unsolved crimes, sold their farms and everything they owned, and let their crops go unharvested," writes American historian and theologian Timothy P. Weber, "so that they could spread the word of Christ's coming and meet him with clean consciences and free of debt."[43] The most ardent true believers donned white "ascension" robes, according to some contemporary accounts, and gathered on rooftops and hilltops all over the Burned-Over District of western New York and elsewhere around America to greet the Lamb of God as he descended from heaven on a cloud.

The great day turned out to be the Great Disappointment, as historians have dubbed it. "Our fondest hopes and expectations were blasted, and such a spirit of weeping came over us as I never experienced before," recalled a farmer named Hiram Edson, one of the disappointed Millerites. "We wept, and wept, till the day dawn."[44] And their skeptical friends and neighbors did nothing to console them in their grief: "What! Not gone up yet? We thought you'd gone up! Aren't you going up soon?" one scoffer was heard to say. "Wife didn't leave you behind to burn, did she?"[45]

A few Millerites were so distraught that they went mad or took their own lives, or so it was reported. Others repented of their hasty decisions during the last days and filed lawsuits to reclaim the property that they had so rashly given away. And some only blamed themselves: God's secret plan for the end of the world is surely concealed within the scriptures, they continued to believe, and they had merely failed to find it.

"I still believe that the day of the Lord is near, even at the door," insisted Father Miller himself, who entertained the reassuring notion that the spectacular public failure of his own prophecy had been God's way of sending lukewarm Christians back to their Bibles in search of divine truth. As an authentic American visionary, Father Miller looked on the sunny side even when contemplating the end of the world.[46]

Ω

Among the undiscouraged Millerites was a young woman named Ellen White (*née* Harmon) (1827–1915). During the year of the Great Disappointment, at the age of seventeen, White experienced the first of a series of divine visions that eventually numbered some two thousand in all. She was convinced that Miller had been right about the year but wrong about what would actually happen. Jesus Christ, she believed, chose 1844 as the year to fulfill a prophecy in Revelation that she interpreted as an act of preparation for the Second Coming and the Day of Judgment: "And the temple of God was opened in heaven, and there was seen in his temple the ark of his testament: and there were lightnings, and voices, and thunderings, and an earthquake, and great hail."[47]

As she continued to read and reinterpret the book of Revelation, with its obsessive references to the number seven, Ellen White came to believe that God was calling upon Christians to observe the Jewish Sabbath as the holiest day of the week. She insisted that anyone who hoped to be numbered among the saints on judgment day must prepare for salvation by renouncing coffee, tea, alcohol, and tobacco, abstaining from masturbation, and embracing sexual purity and vegetarianism. (White herself "battled heroically against her own addiction to Southern fried chicken.")[48] By 1863, Ellen White and her husband, a preacher named James White, founded a church of their own, the Seventh-day Adventists. Their "text of choice" was the book of Revelation.[49]

The Seventh-day Adventists were only the largest and most successful of the apocalyptic churches that proliferated and prospered in the wake of the Great Disappointment. The United Society of Believers in Christ's Second Appearing, better known as the Shakers, for example, and the Zion Watch Tower Tract Society, later renamed the Jehovah's Witnesses, also harkened to "the state of emergency announced in the final words in the Book of Revelation: 'And behold, I come quickly.'"[50] And yet, mindful of the fate that had befallen the Millerites, they were always forced to confront the plain fact that the world still failed to "end on time."

Thus, for example, the early followers of Joseph Smith, founder of the Church of Jesus Christ of Latter-day Saints (and, perhaps not coincidentally, a childhood resident of the Burned-Over District), resolved to build a kingdom of saints with their own hands on the American frontier. Indeed, the Mormons were fearless and tireless pioneers who pulled their own handcarts across the vast stretches of the desert wilderness to reach the New Zion in Utah. Yet they were also convinced that various ills and afflictions of the world around them were sure signs of "that great day fast approaching when this scene of wickedness shall close," according to a Mormon newspaper called *The Evening and Morning Star*.[51]

"When they learned to tolerate that tension—knowing the end was near, but not knowing how near—they came a lot closer to the sensibility of the earliest Christians," observes historian Richard Wrightman Fox in *Jesus in America*.[52]

Far more ominous examples of the apocalyptic impulse can also be discerned in the tumultuous years leading up to the Civil War. An African-American slave named Nat Turner (1800–1831), a lay Baptist preacher with a strong visionary bent, came to believe that he had been called to bring down God's wrath on the slave owners of the American South. He regarded a solar eclipse in 1831 as a sign from on high, and he was inspired to lead a band of fifty armed slaves in what turned out to be the single bloodiest slave insurrection in American history. Not unlike apocalyptic revolutionaries in other times and places, Turner was hunted down and not merely executed but obliterated: his corpse was skinned, and his remains were boiled down into grease.

Still, it is significant that the Great Awakenings were followed by the Great Disappointment. Americans clearly seemed to prefer the pursuit of life, liberty, and happiness in the here and now to the contemplation of the horrors and terrors of doomsday. Even Christian believers saw the perfection of American democracy through social and political reform as a more worthy enterprise than watching out for signs of the end. "[M]ainstream Protestants still believed that the world would have an end," explains American church historian James H. Moorhead, "but they would not admit that it should arrive with unseemly haste."[53]

Only on the ragged edges of Christian true belief in America was Revelation still being read as a book of "future history." By now, however, the apocalyptic idea—and the provocative rhetoric of Revelation—were deeply woven into the fabric of American culture. Inevitably, the old impulses of thought and language reasserted themselves when the very existence of the United States was placed at risk in the conflagration that we call the Civil War, which was not only a clash of arms but a social revolution and a Kulturkampf, too.

Ω

Americans had always looked to the future with bully optimism and stout self-confidence. Even the otherwise dour and censorious Puritans, as we have seen, were capable of visualizing the New Jerusalem as a bustling American metropolis. But the coming of the Civil War, with its industrial-scale carnage and the threat it posed to the very existence of American democracy, reminded even the most cheerful Americans of the dire events that are predicted in the book of Revelation. And so Revelation served yet again as a "language arsenal" for combatants on both sides of the struggle.

Julia Ward Howe, for example, pointedly invokes the iconography of Revelation in "The Battle Hymn of the Republic" when she glorifies "the fateful lightning of His terrible swift sword" and conjures up "the vintage where the grapes of wrath are stored," an oblique allusion to the passage in Revelation where "the angel thrust in his sickle into the earth, and gathered the vine of the earth, and cast it into the great winepress of the wrath of God."[54] A less celebrated line of the same famous song offers an even more literal reference to the passage in Revelation that describes the final battle between the Lamb of God and the Devil in the guise of a red dragon: "Let the Hero, born of woman, crush the serpent with His heel."[55]

Indeed, the book of Revelation provided a template for sermonizers and propagandists in both the Union and the Confederacy who sought to rally the troops and strengthen the resolve of the civilians back home. "The Lord is mustering the nations to the last great struggle between freedom and slavery, truth and error," insisted one preacher whose text was reproduced and circulated to Union soldiers in an anthology of speeches and sermons titled *Christ in the Army.* "We are entering, fellow-citizens, upon a period foretold by prophets of old—looked for and longed for by lovers of their country in past generations—which kings and prophets waited to see, and have not seen—a period of the overthrow of despotism, and the downfall of Anti-Christ."[56]

When the Civil War ended, however, America found itself in a world that was wholly unforeseen by the prophets of old. Americans began to leave farms and small towns for the big cities in ever greater numbers. Village workshops were replaced by the smoke-belching factories of the kind that Blake called "satanic mills." Horse-drawn carriages and ox-drawn Conestoga wagons were left behind in the smoke of locomotives. Communications flashed across the continent, first over telegraph lines and then over telephone lines. America had been an immigrant nation since the first Pilgrim Father stepped onto Plymouth Rock, of course, but now Ellis Island and Angel Island were beginning to teem with new arrivals from exotic places all over Europe and Asia.

All of these phenomena were proof of the success of the American experiment, but not everyone welcomed the newcomers *or* the new ways of life. Here was a new culture war in the making: the changing face of America was seen as the march of progress by some observers and as the decline and fall of civilization by others. And one way of understanding—and resisting—the brave new world in which Americans now lived was the religious stance that came to be called "fundamentalism"—that is, a return to what were imagined to be older and more authentic values in culture, politics, and religion. Thus, for example, the latest generation of Bible literalists, known as "premillennialists" because they believed that they were living in the final age before the Second Coming and the millennial kingdom of Jesus Christ, came to be convinced that they were witnessing the signs of the end-times as predicted in Revelation.

"[A]ll premillennialists seemed to have a real stake in the unraveling of modern life," explains Timothy P. Weber. "As far as premillennialists were concerned, the turbulent and troublesome decades after the Civil War were proof positive that everything was right on schedule."[57]

"Premillennialism," and a related if more nuanced term, "dispensational premillennialism," are used to describe the eschatological stance of one strain of Christian fundamentalism—the belief that Jesus Christ will return to earth and reign over the millennial kingdom exactly as described in the book of Revelation.[*] That is, the premillennialists refuse to content themselves with an allegorical reading of Revelation, and they are convinced that they will behold with their own mortal eyes the sight of Jesus Christ descending from heaven on a cloud, seating himself on an earthly throne, and reigning over a kingdom of saints for a thousand years. For premillennialists, then, the second coming of Jesus Christ is a "real, literal, personal bodily coming."[58]

Strictly speaking, premillennialism is based on the belief that Jesus Christ will return to earth *before* the establishment of the millennial kingdom. By contrast, "postmillennialism" is based on the conviction that Jesus Christ will return only *after* the millennial kingdom has been established through "the triumph and rule of the true church" and "human progress and moral advance achieved through the prayerful efforts of Christian believers in the present age."[59] Thus, as a general if not invariable rule, postmillennialists tend to focus on good works in the here and now, and premillennialists tend to cast their eyes heavenward in the hope of spotting Jesus Christ coming on a cloud of glory. To put it another way, the followers of Father Miller were premillennialists, and the adherents of the Social Gospel were postmillennialists. Both camps, however, embraced the apocalyptic idea, and they disagreed only on the timing of the end of the world.

---

[*] See the Glossary on page 317 for a brief explanation of these terms.

"The theory put the end indefinitely far away," confesses postmillenni-
alist theologian William Newton Clarke (1841–1912), "and yet I listened
trembling for the trump of God in every thunder-storm."[60]

None of these notions were wholly new when they surfaced in America
in the years after the Civil War. Indeed, as we have already seen, the debate
between those who read Revelation "carnally" and those who read it "spiritually" goes all the way back to Augustine. Now, however, the banked fires
of apocalyptic true belief burst into flames yet again, and they burned as
hotly in the New World as they had at any time since Montanus and his
prophetesses first announced that the New Jerusalem would descend out
of the clouds at any moment.

Yet the apocalyptic true believers in nineteenth-century America insisted on putting a new spin on the oldest texts. Ironically, the Bible literalists
were perfectly willing to tinker with Holy Writ when it came to the troubling prospect of what will happen to good Christians in the end-times.
The plot twist that they introduced into the gloom-and-doom scenario of
Revelation was the single greatest innovation in the apocalyptic tradition
since John first described the visions that came to him on the isle of Patmos. Remarkably, the apocalyptic preachers rewrote the history of the end
of the world with the happiest of endings.

A plain reading of Revelation suggests that everyone on earth in the end-
times—men, women, and children, saints and sinners alike—will be
compelled to endure the suffering to be inflicted on humankind by the
Antichrist during the final years of persecution and oppression known as
the Tribulation. Only after the Tribulation is over will the dead saints and
martyrs be raised from the grave and allowed to enjoy their just rewards in
the kingdom to come.

Certain cheerful Christians in nineteenth-century America, however,
refused to believe that they would be called upon to endure such afflictions, and they insisted on embracing a new and highly inventive version
of the end of the world. Christians who are worthy of salvation, they preferred to believe, will be miraculously plucked up and elevated to heaven
before the Tribulation begins in earnest. Seated in the galleries of heaven,
they will be privileged to look down and watch as everyone who has been
left behind on earth suffers and dies under the Antichrist. Only when the

Tribulation is over will they return to earth in the company of Jesus Christ to dwell in the millennial kingdom. Their comforting theological innovation came to be called the Rapture.

Neither the word nor the concept of the Rapture is mentioned anywhere in Revelation. Rather, the whole notion of the Rapture is based on a couple of lines of biblical text in the First Letter to the Thessalonians, the earliest of Paul's writings and perhaps the single oldest document in the New Testament. And, significantly, Paul seems to believe that the remarkable events he describes will take place in his own lifetime rather than at some unknown point in the future.

> For the Lord himself will descend from heaven with a cry of command, with the archangel's call, and with the sound of the trumpet of God. And the dead in Christ will rise first; then we who are alive, who are left, shall be caught up together with them in the clouds to meet the Lord in the air; and so we shall always be with the Lord.[61]

But it was only in the late nineteenth century—and principally in America—that the idea of the Rapture was elevated into an article of faith among Christian fundamentalists. Indeed, the whole idea has been credited to an Anglo-Irish preacher named John Nelson Darby (1800–1882), who found an appreciative audience for his new teaching over the course of seven lecture tours to America between 1859 and 1877. Some scholars trace various elements of Darby's new apocalyptic doctrine back to sources ranging from Joachim of Fiore to Increase Mather, and Darby has even been accused of stealing the whole idea of the Rapture from a young woman named Margaret McDonald, a fifteen-year-old Scottish religious ecstatic. Darby himself insisted that "the doctrine virtually jumped out of the pages of Scripture."[62] Whatever the ultimate source of his inspiration, however, the fact remains that Darby was an authentic innovator who managed to find a credulous and enthusiastic audience in the New World.

Darby is yet another one of those freelance preachers and self-appointed prophets who populate the history of the apocalyptic tradition. At the age of twenty-five, Darby had been ordained as a priest in the Church of Ireland, the Irish counterpart of the Church of England, but he soon broke away and eventually founded his own tiny congregation of religious dissenters known as the Plymouth Brethren. Starting in 1840, Darby began to sermonize on the shiny new idea of the Rapture, first in Switzerland and then in the United States. His comforting promise that Christian believers would be spared the ordeal of the Tribulation—"a neat solution to a thorny problem," as Timothy Weber points out—was received and repeated by his colleagues among the Christian fundamentalist clergy in America.[63]

"The teaching," enthused Darby after his seventh and final visit to America, "is spreading wonderfully."[64]

Ω

Among those who propagated Darby's teachings throughout America was a preacher named Dwight L. Moody (1837–1899), who has been described as "the evangelist who did more than anyone else in America to spread premillennial views of an imminent end."[65] Like the Millerites, who made good use of the latest printing technology to produce vast quantities of tracts and broadsheets, the Moody Bible Institute preached the new strain of Christian true belief through its own publishing house and, later, a powerful radio station that prefigured the television evangelism of the late twentieth century.

"I look on this world as a wrecked vessel," explained Moody. "God has given me a lifeboat, and said to me, 'Moody, save all you can.'"[66]

The other crucial American convert to Darby's reading of Revelation was Cyrus R. Scofield (1843–1921), a veteran of the Confederate army who spent some time in jail on charges of forgery before experiencing a religious conversion and undertaking his life's work of explaining the prophetic meanings that he found in the Bible. The so-called *Scofield Reference Bible*, an edition of the King James Version to which Scofield added his own marginal annotations, was first published in 1909 and ultimately sold more than 10 million copies before it was revised and republished later in the century. So influential was Scofield, observes Paul Boyer, that many evangelical Christians "had difficulty remembering precisely where they had acquired a particular idea: from the sacred text itself, or from Scofield's notes."[67]

Between Moody and Scofield, in fact, the newfangled idea of the Rapture and the various other theological innovations of John Nelson Darby achieved the status of received truth in the early years of the twentieth century: "My hope is built on nothing less," went one parody of a gospel song, "than Scofield's notes and Moody Press."[68] And Christian fundamentalism of the kind espoused by men like Moody and Scofield defined the skirmish line in a culture war against what they regarded as the minions of Satan at work in America—"the ultimate antidote for all infidelity," according to Reuben A. Torrey (1856–1928), superintendent of the Moody Bible Institute and a far-ranging revivalist preacher, "and the impregnable bulwark against liberalism and false cults," by which he meant all of the unwelcome phenomena of the modern world.[69]

"I don't find any place where God says the world is to grow better and better," insisted Moody himself. "I find that the earth is to grow worse and worse."[70]

What the rest of the world celebrated as the march of civilization, the fundamentalists condemned as the secret workings of a diabolical conspiracy. "Satan has organized the world of unbelieving mankind upon his cosmic principles of force, greed, selfishness, ambition and pleasure," ranted Scofield in his annotations to the book of Revelation in *The Scofield Reference Bible*. "[T]he present world-system ... is imposing and powerful with armies and fleets; is often outwardly religious, scientific, cultured, and elegant; but, seething with national and commercial rivalries and ambitions, is upheld in any real crisis only by armed force, and is dominated by Satanic principles."[71]

Just as the author of Revelation detested the buying and selling of goods in the Roman marketplace and distrusted the pagan guilds that a Christian craftsman might be tempted to join, for example, some Christian fundamentalists in America decried the "congested wealth" of big business—"a whirlpool of mad and maddening excess," according to one evangelical preacher[72]—and saw union labels on factory goods as "the mark of the beast." And, just as John was deeply offended by the pleasures of Roman civilization, the fundamentalists denounced the entertainments and diversions of popular culture in modern America. The Reverend Torrey, for example, was willing to concede that "dancing was not a sin—as long as men and women did not do it together," but certain fashionable dances, including the fox-trot, the shimmy, and the Charleston, were regarded as "nothing less than obscene."[73]

"Many of the couples performing these dances should have a marriage license before stepping out on the ballroom floor," complained one outraged Christian observer, "and if they had a marriage license, there would be no excuse for committing such acts in public."[74]

Still, the Protestant fundamentalists in America always looked on the sunny side of doomsday. Back in the Old World, an ardent Catholic reader of Revelation like the French nun Thérèse of Lisieux thrilled at the prospect of the Tribulation: "When thinking of the torments which will be the lot of Christians at the time of Anti-Christ, I feel my heart leap with joy and I would that these torments be reserved for me."[75] But here in America, some Christians preferred to believe that they would be spared all such torments when they were first "raptured" to heaven and then restored to earth to reign over the millennial kingdom alongside the King of Kings.

"Let us remember one thing," John Darby had announced back in the mid–nineteenth century, "we Christians are sheltered from the approaching storm."[76] And Reuben Torrey affirmed the same reassuring message in the opening years of the twentieth century: "The storm will be brief," he declared, "and beyond the storm there is a golden day, such as philosophers and poets never dreamed of."[77]

Curiously, and even rather touchingly, some of the apocalyptic enthusiasts who were delighted at the prospect of watching the Tribulation from on high were also troubled by the fate that would surely befall those benighted souls who still clung to what John calls "the synagogue of Satan." Attentive readers of Revelation were reassured that 144,000 male virgins from the tribes of Israel would be "sealed" in the end-times, but what about the rest of the Jewish people? Here, too, John Darby offered a startling new way to understand the story of Revelation and, especially, the special fate that was reserved for the Jewish people in the end-times.

Ω

Of all the ironies that have come to be attached to the book of Revelation, none is quite so strange as the love-hate relationship between its fundamentalist readers in America and the Jewish people. The author of Revelation, as we have seen, condemns his Jewish contemporaries for rejecting the messiahship of Jesus of Nazareth and suggests that Jews will spend eternity in the company of pagans and lukewarm Christians in a lake of fire. And yet some of the most ardent readers of Revelation in America proudly call themselves Zionists—and they are inspired to do so by their most cherished apocalyptic beliefs.

"Christian Zionism" sometimes seems like an oxymoron precisely because the Christian apocalyptic tradition has always carried an ugly stain of anti-Semitism. Starting in late antiquity, as we have seen, the folklore of the Apocalypse came to include the scandalous notion that the Antichrist will be a Jewish man sired by the Devil and a Jewish harlot in a Babylonian brothel. At best, some otherwise anti-Semitic readers of Revelation held out the faint hope that at least some Jews would spare themselves the fires of hell by belatedly embracing Jesus Christ as the Messiah.

Joachim of Fiore, author of a tract frankly titled *Against the Jews,* insists that the Jewish people will follow the Antichrist until the end of days, when a few of them will convert to Christianity at the last possible moment. The same idea was carried forward into Protestant theology by Martin Luther. If the Jews accept Jesus Christ, Luther allows in a tract of his own titled *Against the Jews and Their Lies,* "we will be glad to forgive them," but if not, "we should not tolerate and suffer them."[78]

Apocalyptic legend and lore imagined that the Jewish people would return to the land of Israel at the end of days—but only with deadly consequences. For example, a text titled *Christ and Antichrist,* which dates back to the third century, insists that the Antichrist will rebuild the Temple in Jerusalem, call back the Jewish people from their places of exile, and then commence a new persecution of Christians that will end only "when Christ, heralded by Elijah and John the Baptist, comes again in glory."[79] As the author of Revelation suggests, the blood of the defeated Jewish army of the Antichrist will rise to the height of a horse's bridle in the streets of Jerusalem.

A much brighter picture was painted by the apocalyptic preachers of the New World. Increase Mather predicted in *The Mystery of Israel's Salvation Explained and Applied* (1669) that the Jewish people would be "brought into their own land again" and that, once they returned to the site of ancient Israel, they would convert to Christianity and become "the most glorious nation in the world."[80] One Presbyterian minister actually undertook to build dock houses and wharves in New Haven as a place of embarkation for the Jewish emigrants: "The return of the Jews to their own land," he declared in 1800, "is certain."

But, like the Rapture, the repatriation of the Jewish people took on a new degree of power and authority in the teachings of John Darby. He came away from his study of the Hebrew Bible with a new idea about the role of the Jewish people in the end-times, a notion that has been called one of the "most distinctive and controversial features" of his doctrine.[81]

To sum up Darby's elaborate theory, he taught that God has devised one fate for the Jewish people and a different fate for the Christian church—but the two phases of the divine plan for the end of the world are interrelated, and so the final salvation of Christians depends on the destiny that God has assigned to the Jewish people.

Since Darby was convinced that all biblical prophecy must be fulfilled, including the prophecies in the Hebrew Bible that were addressed to the Israelites, he concluded that God will keep his promise to restore the land of Israel to the Chosen People and rebuild the Temple in Jerusalem *before* bringing the world to an end. Indeed, the gathering of the Jewish people in their ancient homeland in Palestine came to be seen as both a sign and a necessary precondition of the Second Coming, the defeat of Satan, and the creation of the New Heaven and the New Earth. Thus did the Jewish people come to play an unwitting but decisive role in the end-times as imagined so vividly by the apocalyptic true believers in America.

Ω

By a fateful coincidence, the divine plan for the Jewish people in Darby's scenario of the end-times coincided with the emergence of modern political Zionism in the mid–nineteenth century. The Zionist movement was motivated by political rather than religious impulses; the Zionists sought to rescue Jewish men, women, and children from the dangers of anti-Semitism in Europe, and they believed that Jewish statehood was essential to Jewish survival. Indeed, the Zionist movement in Russia and eastern Europe was rooted in the thoroughly secular doctrines of socialism and nationalism rather than the pious yearning of the Jewish people for a return to Zion in the days of the Messiah. Thus, for example, Theodor Herzl (1860–1904), a highly assimilated Jewish journalist from Vienna who came to be seen as the father of modern Zionism, was perfectly willing to accept Argentina or Uganda as the site of a Jewish homeland if the biblical land of Israel was unavailable.

The most ardent enemies of early Zionism, in fact, were the Jewish true believers who insisted that the Jewish people will be restored to their homeland only when God, in his own good time, finally sends the Messiah to bring them there. To be sure, a few highly observant Jews had always made their way to Palestine, long a provincial backwater of the Ottoman empire, to spend their last years in prayer and to be buried in holy ground when they died. But the audacious idea of Jews betaking themselves en masse to the Holy Land to pioneer a modern and sovereign Jewish state was regarded by pious Jews as apostasy and blasphemy—the sin of "forcing the end." For that reason, Zionism was regarded by the most observant Jews as "the ultimate heresy."[82]

Here we are reminded of a striking difference between the apocalyptic ideas of Judaism and Christianity. The defeat of the Bar Kochba revolt by the Roman overlords of Judea in the second century, as we have already seen, cooled the messianic expectations of the Jewish people. By sharp contrast to the promise of Jesus Christ in the book of Revelation—"Surely I come quickly"[83]—one of the thirteen articles of Jewish faith as framed by Maimonides acknowledges that the Messiah is *not* coming anytime soon: "I believe with perfect faith in the coming of the Messiah, and though he may tarry, I will wait daily for his coming."[84]

The catastrophic consequences of "forcing the end" were symbolized in Jewish history by the unhappy example of the messianic pretender called Shabbatai Zevi (1626–1676). Starting in 1666, Shabbatai Zevi played on the hopes of the Jewish people by suggesting that he was, in fact, the long-awaited but long-tarrying Messiah who would deliver them from their persecution and oppression. And, rather like the Millerites in America two centuries later, the most ardent followers of Shabbatai Zevi abandoned their houses, shops, and farms all over Europe in the perfect faith that he would "carry them on a cloud to Jerusalem" at any moment.[85]

"The day of revenge is in my heart, and the year of redemption hath arrived," announced Shabbatai Zevi, striking a bloodthirsty note that will not be unfamiliar to readers of Revelation. "Soon will I avenge you and comfort you."[86]

Shabbatai Zevi set himself up in a mansion outside of Constantinople, a Jewish pilgrimage site that soon outdrew the Wailing Wall in Jerusalem, and his provocative claims caught the attention of the Ottoman authorities. Not unlike Pontius Pilate, who regarded the messianic claims of Jesus of Nazareth as a political threat to the Roman Empire, the Grand Sultan was unsettled by the prospect of Shabbatai Zevi reigning as a king in a province of the Ottoman empire. The would-be Messiah was arrested, hung with chains, and offered a choice between conversion to Islam or death—and he broke the hearts of his Jewish followers by choosing to convert rather than die. After the public apostasy of Shabbatai Zevi, anyone who seemed to be "forcing the end" was regarded with skepticism and even contempt in Jewish traditions.

The Christian true believers, by contrast, were instructed by their apocalyptic doctrine that the repatriation of the Jewish people, by whatever means necessary, was one sure sign of the coming of the Messiah. For them, of course, it was the *second* coming of the Messiah as prophesied in the book of Revelation, and he was known by the Christian equivalent of the word Messiah: "Christ." And so, as it happened, some of the earliest efforts of the secular and even antireligious Zionists to reclaim the land of Israel for the Jewish people were carefully monitored in Christian apocalyptic circles in America.

Christian newspapers and magazines in America reported with interest and enthusiasm on the publication of *The Jewish State,* Herzl's manifesto of political Zionism; the flare-up of anti-Semitic incidents in Russia and France; and the planting of the first Jewish colonies and kibbutzim on the soil of Palestine. Christian correspondents were present in Basel for the Zionist Congress in 1898, and they "often speculated about when the Jewish immigrants would start contemplating the construction of a new temple in Jerusalem"—a notion that would have shocked and scandalized any religious Jew and one that would never have occurred to the Jewish socialists and nationalists.[87]

Some Christian Zionists, in fact, were already hard at work on the project of Jewish nation building long in advance of their Jewish counterparts. William Eugene Blackstone (1841–1935), a real-estate developer who turned to apocalyptic preaching, was so convinced that the Jews must return to Zion in order to bring the Second Coming that he set himself the task of making it a matter of American foreign policy. Blackstone secured the signatures of more than four hundred prominent American politicians and moguls on a petition that called on President Benjamin Harrison to champion the cause of a Jewish homeland. On March 5, 1891—five years before Herzl composed *The Jewish State* and six years before he convened the first Zionist Congress—Blackstone delivered his petition to the White House.

"Why not give Palestine back to them again?" implored Blackstone. "Let us now restore to them the land of which they were so cruelly despoiled by our Roman ancestors."[88]

Blackstone, in a sense, was more Zionist than the founder of modern Zionism. When Herzl openly entertained the pragmatic notion that a Jewish colony in British East Africa would suffice so long as Palestine remained out of reach, Blackstone boldly sent him a copy of the Hebrew Bible in which he had carefully marked—"in typical premillennialist fashion," as Timothy Weber points out—the specific lines of biblical text that had convinced Darby and his followers that the restoration of the Jews to Palestine was both a divine promise and a divine mandate. For his efforts, Blackstone himself was acclaimed as a "Father of Zionism" at a Jewish conference in Philadelphia in 1918.[89]

Still, Blackstone was more forthright than many other Christian supporters of Zionism in revealing the theological basis of his commitment to a Jewish homeland in Palestine. Like Joachim of Fiore and Martin Luther and Increase Mather, Darby taught—and Blackstone believed—that the Jews who returned to the land of Israel were destined to suffer and die during the reign of the Antichrist and to burn in hell for the rest of eternity. Only the Jews who converted to Christianity before it was too late, they insisted, would be restored to life in the New Jerusalem.

At a mass meeting of Zionists in Los Angeles in 1918, for example, Blackstone once again proclaimed himself to be "an ardent advocate of Zionism"—and yet he also revealed his belief that any Jew who embraces *only* Zionism is treading on a path that "leads through unequaled sorrows." The better path, he insisted, "is to become a true Christian, accepting Jesus as Lord and Savior, which brings not only forgiveness and regeneration, but insures escape from the unequaled time of tribulation which is coming upon all the earth."[90]

"Oh, my Jewish friends, which of these paths shall be yours?" he witnessed to an audience that must have been amazed at his frank words. "Study this wonderful Word of God, and see how plainly God Himself has revealed Israel's pathway unto the perfect day."[91]

Ω

Witnessing to the poor benighted souls who were not yet believers was regarded as a crucial mission in the culture war that was fought under the banner of fundamentalism. That's what Dwight Moody meant when he quoted God's instructions: "Moody, save all you can." And that's what motivated William Blackstone to join in founding one of several Christian missionary societies whose goal was the conversion of the Jewish immigrants who arrived in America in great numbers in the late nineteenth century. Surely, they were convinced, the end-times will be hastened by calling the Jewish people to Jesus Christ.

One such effort was the so-called Hope of Israel Mission, whose principal missionary, Arno C. Gabelein (1861–1945), started preaching on Saturdays in the Jewish neighborhood on the Lower East Side in New York City. Gabelein, a Methodist immigrant from Germany, studied both Yiddish and Hebrew so that he could answer the rabbis who came out to defend their faith. "In fact, he acquired such an expertise in the Talmud and other rabbinic literature and spoke such flawless Yiddish," reports Timothy Weber, "that he often had a difficult time convincing many in his audiences that he was not a Jew trying to 'pass' as a gentile."[92]

But the Jews turned out to be a hard sell. When students from the Moody Bible Institute in Chicago ventured into a Jewish neighborhood to sermonize, for example, they succeeded only in attracting an angry mob that covered them with "an avalanche of watermelon rinds, banana peelings, overripe tomatoes, and other edible fruit."[93] Some missionaries adopted a kind of protective coloration, referring only to "the Messiah" and never to its Greek-derived equivalent, "Christ." And one earnest missionary found out for himself why it was unwise to start canvassing a Jewish tenement from the ground up. By the time he reached the top floor, the apartment dwellers on the lower floors had read the literature he was handing out and greeted him on the way back down with curses and insults, hot soup, and rotten vegetables.

"Thus I learned that the next time I went into a tenement house," the young man explained, "I must start on the top floor and work down."[94]

For some Christian fundamentalists, the resistance of the Jewish people to their efforts at conversion was seen as a sign of something wicked. *The Protocols of the Elders of Zion*, a crude anti-Semitic forgery that imagines a satanic Jewish conspiracy at work in the world, was read with credulity in certain Christian circles in the early years of the twentieth century, and Arno Gabelein openly praised Henry Ford for publishing the *Protocols* in his newspaper. Indeed, the notion of a secret cabal of Jewish malefactors was perfectly plausible to many readers of Revelation: "Premillennial eschatology is, after all, a conspiracy theory of cosmic proportions," explains Weber.[95]

To their credit, many other fundamentalists were moved to denounce those of their fellow Christians who engaged in acts or expressions of anti-

Semitism. Thus, for example, James M. Gray, a minister with the Moody Bible Institute, condemned anti-Semitism as "one of the most despicable, brutal and dangerous forms of racial hatred and antagonism known to mankind." At the same time, however, he frankly acknowledged that his religious convictions instructed him to regard the Jews as doomed: "It is true that Jehovah has awfully cursed Israel for her sins, and His curse rests upon her today," Gray declared. "But it is one thing for God to curse her and another thing for us to do so."[96]

Then, too, some frustrated missionaries were encouraged by what they read in the book of Revelation to take a kind of smug satisfaction in the fate of those who resisted conversion, Jews and Christians alike. The author of Revelation, as we have seen, burns with resentment toward the "lukewarm" Christians who prefer the good life to what he sees as the righteous life, and he seems to take pleasure in imagining the revenge that God will take on anyone who does not share his faith. And the same gloating can be seen in latter-day readers of Revelation, too. Thus, for example, a revivalist preacher writing in 1918 insisted that God will literally chortle with delight over the suffering of everyone who has not been "raptured" to heaven before the end-times.

"Often had these left-behind ones been warned, but in vain," wrote the preacher. "Servants of God had faithfully set before them their imperative need of fleeing from the wrath to come only to be laughed at for their pains. And now the tables will be turned. God will laugh at them, laugh at their calamity and mock at their fear."[97]

To be sure, the God of Israel is famously depicted as a jealous and wrathful deity in certain horrific passages of the Hebrew Bible. "Vengeance will I wreak on my foes," promises God in the book of Deuteronomy. "I will make my arrows drunk with blood as my sword devours flesh."[98] But here we see exactly how God is transformed in the new readings of Revelation from judge, king, and warrior into a cackling killer who takes pleasure in avenging himself on the men, women, and children whom he created in the first place.

At the same time that Christian fundamentalists were seeking to save Jewish souls, they were also engaged in a bitter struggle with some of their fellow Christians over the right way to read the book of Revelation.

The same debate that had divided Christians in late antiquity—whether to read Revelation "spiritually" or "carnally"—was now setting traditionalists against modernists in the opening years of the twentieth century.

Revelation, according to one Christian commentator writing in 1907, was "a 'queer bird' hatched from 'visions of the impossible,'" and he insisted that a majority of modern Christians had abandoned the whole apocalyptic enterprise in favor of "saner and more spiritual conceptions." Other critics resorted to the old argument that the book of Revelation tempted Christians to engage in the error of "Judaizing" the biblical text: "A product of 'highly imaginative Jewish thought,'" as James H. Moorhead sums up the argument, "apocalypticism seduced the early Christian community for a time but was never consistent with the basic thrust of the church's message."[99]

Against the overheated doomsday scenario of the premillennialists, the Christian progressives advocated what came to be characterized as postmillennialism—that is, the notion that the second coming of Jesus Christ will take place only *after* the world is perfected by human effort. Advocates of the Social Gospel, for example, believed that "the kingdom of God would come as Christians joined others of goodwill in supporting labor unions, battling child labor, campaigning for laws to protect factory workers and immigrant slum dwellers, and otherwise joining the struggle for social justice in urban-industrial America."[100] In a real sense, they were engaged in precisely the kind of spiritual reading of Revelation that Augustine had recommended: "The Kingdom of God is always coming," writes Walter Rauschenbusch (1861–1918) in *A Theology for the Social Gospel* (1917).[101]

Ironically, the most progressive ideas in Christianity appealed to some of the most wealthy and powerful Christians. For example, it was John D. Rockefeller Jr. (1874–1960), son of the founder of Standard Oil and a major American philanthropist, who financed the so-called Interchurch World Movement, an early effort to engage the Christian churches with the grave and ever-growing problems of the modern world. "I see it literally establishing the Kingdom of God on earth," he affirmed in an article in the *Saturday Evening Post,* thus embracing the most fundamental tenet of the Social Gospel.[102]

But the Christian fundamentalists were able to recruit a few captains of industry of their own. In 1910, for example, the two brothers who owned Union Oil Company, Lyman and Milton Stewart, sponsored the free distribution of 3 million copies of *The Fundamentals,* a series of pamphlets designed to win Protestant clergy across America to the credo of Christian fundamentalism. And the Stewart brothers also paid for the distribution of some seven hundred thousand copies of William E. Blackstone's apocalyptic manifesto, *Jesus Is Coming,* to the same influential readership.

Such lavish efforts prompted a kind of third great awakening in the opening years of the twentieth century—"more than three hundred separate denominational bodies," according to Paul Boyer, "all committed to belief in Christ's premillennial return."[103] The ancient apocalyptic ideas of the book of Revelation, as revised and reinvigorated by the teachings of John Darby, attracted men and women across the spectrum of Christian belief and practice, ranging from the old-line Protestant churches to the Pentecostalists, who embraced such practices as speaking in tongues and the laying on of hands.

One notable example of the fresh outbreak of apocalyptic fever began with Charles Taze Russell (1852–1916), a haberdasher from Pennsylvania whose reading of Revelation and the other apocalyptic texts convinced him that the first stirrings of the millennium had already commenced. At any moment, he believed, God will snatch 144,000 "saints" off the face of the earth, and they will soon return in the company of Jesus Christ to fight the battle of Armageddon against the armies of Satan. Russell's followers, numbering some thirty thousand by the beginning of the twentieth century, were first organized as the Watchtower Society and later changed the name of their church to the Jehovah's Witnesses.

"Millions now living," Russell assured them, echoing the words of Jesus and Paul as first recorded in Christian scriptures nearly twenty centuries earlier, "will never die."[104]

Russell, like so many other apocalyptic preachers before and after him, was daring enough to set a date for doomsday. He fixed 1874 as the starting date of the countdown clock, and he predicted that the reign of Jesus Christ would begin forty years later—that is, in 1914. For that reason, when the opening shots of the First World War were fired, his prophecy took on sudden and urgent meaning, not only for his own followers but for a great many other apocalyptic true believers.

"War! War! War!!!" enthused one Pentecostal journal. "The Nations of Europe Battle and Unconsciously Prepare the Way for the Return of the Lord Jesus."[105]

Ω

By the late summer of 1914, America was still clinging to the happy notion that goodwill, enterprise, and ingenuity are all that humankind needs to achieve the secular equivalent of the millennial kingdom right here on earth. "The word *machine*," as Paul Fussell puts it in *The Great War and Modern Memory,* "was not yet invariably coupled with the word *gun*."[106] Such bright hopes were among the first casualties of the First World War, which demonstrated that the promising new technology of the twentieth century was capable of killing and maiming young men by the millions. For the readers of Revelation, however, the ghastly spectacle of modern combat only confirmed their conviction that they were witnessing nothing less than the battle of Armageddon.

Ironically, the First World War was dubbed "the war to end all wars" by optimistic and high-minded propagandists—a phrase that certainly applies to Armageddon—but the conflagration turned out to be neither the end of war nor the end of the world. Still, the terror and tumult of the Great War sparked the same kind of apocalyptic speculation that had attended every war in Western history since the sack of Rome in the fifth century. The latest generation of seers studied the ancient texts and decided that the world was witnessing the events that had been prophesied in the book of Daniel: "And a mighty king shall stand up, that shall rule with great dominion, and do according to his will, and his kingdom shall be broken, and shall be divided toward the four winds of heaven."[107]

Indeed, the First World War was so traumatic—and the postwar world so terrifying—that it scared the bejesus out of men and women who had placed themselves on the cutting edge of the modern world. Thus, for example, Christabel Pankhurst (1880–1958) was transformed by the experience of the First World War from a famously militant feminist into a stump speaker for the premillennialist cause and "the promised return of Jesus as King of Kings and Lord of Lords," as she witnessed in one of her own works of biblical prophecy.[108]

"Like so many others, I had lived in an atmosphere of illusion, thinking that once certain obstacles were removed, especially the disenfranchisement of women, it would be full steam ahead for the ideal social and international order," Pankhurst declared. "But when, in 1918, I really faced the facts, I saw that the war was not a war to end war—but was, despite our coming victory, a beginning of sorrows."[109]

Viewed through the lens of biblical prophecy, in fact, the shattering events of the First World War made perfect sense to the apocalyptic mind. Russia was identified as the biblical kingdom of Gog, and the toppling of the czar by the Bolsheviks in 1917 was seen as the fulfillment of a prophecy in the book of Ezekiel: "Thus saith the Lord God: Behold, I am against thee, O Gog."[110] The Balfour Declaration of 1917, which committed Great Britain to the establishment of a Jewish homeland in Palestine, and the liberation of Jerusalem from the Turks in 1918 by the British army, were interpreted as "the beginning of a series of events that are destined to establish God's kingdom here upon earth," according to an enthusiastic Bible commentator named E. L. Langston.[111]

"The Jews and the land of Palestine are like charts to the mariner," Langston explains. "As we study the prophecies concerning 'the people' and 'the land' we hold the key to the mysteries of God's plan and purpose for the world."[112]

Like Daniel in Babylon, like John in pagan Rome, men and women in twentieth-century America were ready to see signs of the approaching end all around them. "Wars and rumors of war" produced a constant and mounting thrum of anticipation in Christian circles. For them, as for readers of Revelation across the last twenty centuries, even the bad news could be seen as good news.

Ω

Thus did Revelation begin to work its old magic on the hearts and minds of otherwise modern men and women. At various points in the long history of the ancient text, as we have seen, the number 666 was understood to identify Nero, Alaric, Muhammad, or Napoleon. Now the same number was variously understood by the latest generation of apocalyptic codebreakers to reveal the names of Lenin and Stalin, Hitler and Mussolini, even Franklin Delano Roosevelt—all depending on the specific political stance of the beholder.

Some of the apocalyptic excess on display in the wake of the Great War was downright scandalous. The Pentecostal preacher Aimee Semple McPherson (1890–1944) was capable of moving her congregation and her radio audience to moments of rapture with high-spirited sermons on the

Second Coming. Clad in colorful if also bizarre costumes and backed by a fifty-piece stage orchestra, she purported to engage in acts of faith healing and "spirit slaying." A verse from the book of Revelation appeared on the masthead of *The Bridal Call,* a publication of McPherson's International Church of the Foursquare Gospel: "And the Spirit and the bride say, Come …"[113] But she ended up a victim of her own passions: a mysterious sojourn in the desert was rumored to be nothing more than a shackup with her lover, a radio technician on the church staff, and she died of an overdose of barbiturates.

Other examples are comical. One apocalyptic sect called the House of David, for example, sought to gather the lost twelve tribes in anticipation of the coming millennial kingdom. The House of David fielded a baseball team whose players sported long beards that were meant to suggest Old Testament prophets, and the team put on exhibition games across the country to raise money and attract new members. Advertised as a celibate community, the House of David attracted its own scandal when its founder, who styled himself as King Benjamin and his wife as Queen Mary, landed in jail on charges of fraud and seduction.

Still other uses of the iconography of Revelation were purely rhetorical and wholly secular. Sportswriters in the mid-1920s dubbed the four players who made up the backfield of coach Knute Rockne's football team at Notre Dame as "The Four Horsemen," and the same term was applied to four conservative members of the Supreme Court who voted to strike down various components of the New Deal during the Roosevelt administration in the 1930s. When one apocalyptic preacher in Los Angeles claimed that the "mark of the beast" was actually the stylized blue eagle that served as the logo of the National Recovery Administration—the centerpiece of the New Deal—even otherwise pious observers were forced to crack a smile.

"Who that has seen it," wrote Ernest Cadman Colwell in 1937, "can ever forget the rapt expression of the interpreter who found the explanation of the Beast of Revelation in the N.R.A.?"[114]

Yet some of the most inventive interpreters of Revelation were utterly earnest when it came to the new meanings that they prized out the ancient biblical text. They were so respectful of the apocalyptic tradition that they regarded Benito Mussolini as a more likely Antichrist than Adolf Hitler precisely because Mussolini reigned in the city of Rome, the seat of ancient Roman paganism and the object of such fear and loathing in the book of

Revelation. Indeed, Mussolini caught the attention of Christian apocalyptic observers when he first came to power in the 1920s, and *Il Duce* remained in their crosshairs long after *Der Führer* had proved himself to be far more beastly.

"I am not prepared to say Stalin, Hitler, or Mussolini is the beast," declared the pastor of a Baptist church in New York City, "but I have no hesitation in saying they are his forerunners and are beating the trail for him to come upon the scene. Mussolini, above them all, bears the earmarks."[115]

Thus, for example, the salute that was originated by Mussolini's Fascist Party (and only later adopted by the Nazis), with its open palm and upraised arm, was linked to the passage in Revelation where it is said that the Beast "causeth all to receive a mark in their right hand."[116] According to evangelist W. D. Herrstrom, "it is certain that the people of the world will be required to raise their right hands with a movement similar to the present Fascist salute in order to show the mark during the reign of the beast."[117] And the fasces that appeared on the American dime in the 1930s—the bundle of rods with a projecting ax blade that originally represented the magisterial authority of ancient Rome and later served as a symbol of the Fascist party in Italy—was seen as yet another example of "the mark of the beast."

On at least one occasion, in fact, such apocalyptic speculation prompted a face-to-face confrontation with Mussolini himself. A husband-and-wife team of Christian journalists from Belgium, Mr. and Mrs. Ralph Norton, managed to secure an audience with *Il Duce,* and they asked in the course of their interview whether he intended to reestablish the Roman Empire. When he replied that it would be impossible to do so, they boldly witnessed to the Fascist dictator about the prophecy that Rome, symbolized in Revelation as "Babylon, the Mother of Harlots and Abominations of the Earth,"[118] would be reborn and then destroyed in the end-times.

"Is that really described in the Bible?" asked the astounded Mussolini. "Where is it found?"[119]

Mussolini, of course, was no laughing matter. The atrocities of the Second World War and the Holocaust beggared even the apocalyptic imagination, and they readily suggested a kind of Armageddon. "Human history [is] moving toward a climax in which evil becomes more and more naked and unashamed," conceded theologian Reinhold Niebuhr in 1940.[120] Yet the theological calculus of Revelation prompts the true believer to see even the worst atrocities—and *especially* the worst atrocities—as a sign that the Second Coming is fast approaching.

"Suddenly, in the midst of the brilliant civilization of the twentieth century, all the worst attributes of humanity have come to the front; all the most evil passions have been unleashed; all the evil spirits some thought were exorcized centuries ago have returned sevenfold, more loathsome and diabolical than of old," wrote Arthur Maxwell, editor of the prophetic journal of the Seventh-day Adventists, in *History's Crowded Climax.* "All the strange and terrible developments of these tremendous times … are indeed but a further indication that we are in the midst of the crowning crisis of the ages."[121]

Tragically, some of the same Christian fundamentalists who saw the creation of a Jewish state in Palestine as a precondition to the Second Coming were also capable of extraordinary callousness toward the Jewish victims of the Holocaust. "God may be permitting Satan to use a Hitler, Goebels [*sic*] or a Stalin to chasten His People and thus make them discontent in their wealth and prosperity," argued one Christian tract when the machinery of the Holocaust was already in full operation. "The Jew is gradually being forced to go back to his promised land. He is not wanted in very many lands."[122]

Then, too, the very prospect of victory over the Axis by force of arms was something of a disappointment to the apocalyptic doomsayers precisely because the defeat of a mortal enemy, no matter how barbarous and cruel, was not equivalent to the defeat of Satan. "Uncle Sam will be no match for the Antichrist," insisted the *Christian Digest* in 1942, alluding to the Armageddon yet to come and delighting in the knowledge that only the Lamb of God will be able to vanquish the ultimate villain. But neither Hitler nor Mussolini was the Beast: "The worst is yet to appear."[123]

Ironically, the apocalyptic idea can be seen on both sides of the struggle between democracy and totalitarianism in World War II. The Nazis, like the first readers of Daniel and Revelation, "believed that they had arrived at the crucial moment in human history," explains Damian Thompson. "A new heaven and a new earth was within the grasp of the Elect—so long as they did not yield to the forces of the enemy." The Nazi leaders of Germany may have disdained the kind and gentle Jesus of the Gospels—"National

Socialism and Christianity are irreconcilable," declared Martin Bormann in 1941[124]—but Hitler plainly understood the terrible power of the millennial ideal: "There can be little doubt that the thousand-year reign of the saints lies behind the vision of a thousand-year Reich," observes Thompson.[125]

Nazi Germany provides a case study of the terrible things that can happen when apocalyptic passion and true belief are fused in the hearts and minds of otherwise civilized human beings. "It is a grotesque irony that Nazism should have unconsciously adopted the structure of belief partly developed, though not necessarily invented, by the Jews," Thompson points out, referring to the fact that the apocalyptic tradition in Judaism begins in the book of Daniel. "But in terms of blood or sheer malignant hatred of the enemy, Daniel and the earliest apocalypses do not begin to rival the Nazis' apocalyptic struggle; for that we must got to the book of the Revelation." For the Nazis, as for the author of Revelation, the adversary was imagined to be "pure evil . . . in human form" and "so resilient that he can be defeated only in a cosmic war," a conviction on which they relied in carrying out the crimes of the Holocaust.[126]

Indeed, the "millenarian roots of Nazism" can be discerned in Norman Cohn's masterful study of apocalyptic violence in the Middle Ages, *The Pursuit of the Millennium*. Cohn looked all the way back to such apocalyptic excesses as the mass murder of Jews during the First Crusade—but he was provoked into undertaking his work when, as an intelligence officer in World War II, he was called upon to interrogate captured SS men and thereby found himself face-to-face with "a mind-set 'in which one can actually feel it is a *good* thing to shove small children into ovens or to send millions of people to starve and freeze to death.'"[127]

Still, the Second World War produced something wholly new in the apocalyptic tradition. The authors of Daniel and Revelation were capable of imagining the end of the world, but human experience seemed to confirm that the world was not so easily destroyed. After all, the extermination of humankind and the destruction of human civilization had proved to be far beyond the will or the power of the barbarians, the armies of Islam, the Spanish armada, or the Napoleonic battalions, all of which were seen as the work of Satan. Over and over again, the world had persistently refused to end.

At 5:30 AM on July 16, 1945, the detonation of the world's first atomic bomb in the desert of New Mexico gave proof that the power to destroy the world actually exists. The successful test-firing of a nuclear weapon, code-named "Trinity," produced a curious phenomenon: the silica in the desert sand was fused into solid glass for a distance of eight hundred yards in every direction from ground zero. For the reader of Revelation, the spectacle calls to mind one of the visions of the throne of God as it is described in the ancient text.

> From the throne issue flashes of lightning, and voices and peals of thunder, and before the throne burn seven torches of fire, which are the seven spirits of God; and before the throne there is, as it were, a sea of glass like unto crystal.[128]

Indeed, the sight of the first thermonuclear explosion in the history of the world inspired an apocalyptic vision in J. Robert Oppenheimer, the so-called Father of the Atomic Bomb, but he borrowed from Hindu tradition to describe what he glimpsed in the smoke and fire: "I am become Death," Oppenheimer later mused, quoting the words of Vishnu, "the destroyer of worlds."[129]

To discern *any* deity in the iconic mushroom cloud at Trinity, however, misstates the significance of what Oppenheimer was beholding at that moment—a scientific experiment that demonstrated the power of humankind to destroy itself. With the detonation of the first atomic bomb, the Apocalypse took a quantum leap into a new and previously unimaginable realm, and humankind was suddenly forced to confront the awful knowledge that the end of the world does not require God at all.

Seven

The Godless Apocalypse

Things fall apart; the centre cannot hold
Mere anarchy is loosed upon the world.

Surely some revelation is at hand....
　　WILLIAM BUTLER YEATS, *The Second Coming*

An intimate apocalypse is played out in the final scenes of *On the Beach,* a 1959 motion picture that imagines a nuclear war with no survivors at all. An exchange of atomic bombs has created a toxic cloud of radioactivity that drifts around the globe, silently killing all living creatures in its path, and the last human survivors are awaiting the same fate in distant Australia. Every single man, woman, and child on earth—including Gregory Peck in the role of a U.S. nuclear submarine captain and Ava Gardner as his Australian love interest—will die of radiation sickness, slowly, surely, and horribly, unless they figure out a way to take their own lives first.

At first glance, *On the Beach* might seem to be yet another variation on the apocalyptic theme that can be detected in the countless books and movies of the late 1940s and 1950s in which the end of the world is depicted. Sometimes the agent of destruction is an extraterrestrial invasion or an ecological catastrophe, but more often it is an atomic war or a monster who exists only because of a genetic mutation caused by the radioactive hell on earth. All of these artifacts of pop culture, like *On the Beach* itself, share the same sense of gloom and doom that was first injected into the American consciousness by Hiroshima and Nagasaki and only mounted as the United States and the Soviet Union competed with each other

to achieve parity in their ever-growing nuclear arsenals—a policy of recip-
rocal nuclear deterrence later known as "mutual assured destruction" or,
more simply and aptly, "MAD."

But *On the Beach* is not a restaging of Revelation in modern dress, and
neither God nor the Devil is given a role in the end of the world. Rather, blame is placed solely and squarely on human beings: "The whole
damned war was an accident," explains a scientist, played by an aging and
world-weary Fred Astaire, who is poisoned with remorse over his role in
the design of atomic weaponry long before he faces the prospect of death
by radiation sickness. "In the end, somehow granted time for examina-
tion, we shall find that our so-called civilization was gloriously destroyed
by a handful of vacuum tubes and transistors." And then he adds in a bitter aside: "Probably faulty."

God is invoked only twice in *On the Beach,* and only rhetorically. A Salvation Army preacher delivers a final sermon to a sparse crowd that gath-
ers on the street where government-issue suicide pills are being handed out.
"O Lord, give us strength," he intones. "Help us to understand the reason
for this madness on earth, the reason why we have destroyed ourselves."[1]
And an earnest young naval officer, played by Anthony Perkins, reflexive-
ly invokes the deity while anguishing over his fatherly duty to administer a
dose of poison to his infant daughter when the first symptoms of radiation
sickness appear: "God," he mutters, "God forgive us."

Indeed, *On the Beach* strays from apocalyptic tradition in both Judaism
and Christianity for the simple reason that the movie holds out no hope
for survival even by a few saints and martyrs: everyone on earth will surely die, whether by suicide or by radiation sickness, and history will come
to an end, final and unredeemed. Indeed, that's what distinguishes *On
the Beach* from most of the other books and movies of the postwar era in
which the story line focuses on the undaunted survivors. One of the most
affecting moments, in fact, is the scene in which the young naval officer,
having already administered a fatal dose to his baby, prepares a cup of
poison-laced tea for his negligee-clad wife. So far, she has refused to accept
the fact that the world will end, but now she is resigned to her fate: "Dar-
ling, I'm ready for my tea" are her last words, a coded expression of utter
hopelessness and helplessness.

Here, then, is a God-less apocalypse in which human beings have no
one to blame except themselves—and, crucially, no one to whom they

may turn for rescue or redemption. The point is made in the last frame of *On the Beach,* where we see for a second time the inspirational banner that was previously displayed at the Salvation Army rally. The banner, now tattered and windblown, flies over a street that is utterly devoid of human life, and its encouraging message is shown to have been wholly and tragically wrong: "THERE IS STILL TIME, BROTHER."[2]

Even if the Apocalypse according to Hollywood allows no role for God, the fact remains that *On the Beach* carries a few strands of the theological DNA that can be found in Revelation and Daniel. Some of the same shocks and thrills that men and women once found in altarpieces or block prints of an earlier age—Michelangelo's scenes of the Last Judgment on the ceiling of the Sistine Chapel, for example, or Dürer's illustrated edition of *The Apocalypse of St. John*—are now displayed and contemplated on the silver screen. All of these products of the human imagination, from Daniel and Revelation to the latest apocalyptic movie or miniseries, ask the same old and scary questions: When and how will the world come to an end, and what will happen next?

Ω

On the Beach is perhaps the single most despairing expression of an apocalyptic state of mind that seized the American imagination in the 1940s and 1950s—"the postwar 'doom boom,'" according to Stephen D. O'Leary, a scholar and critic who specializes in the study of the apocalyptic idea in modern politics and popular culture.[3] Rather than avenging archangels like Gabriel and Michael, however, the celestial figures in the pop-culture version of the end-times are men from Venus or Mars, and instead of the satanic beasts of Revelation, the monsters are reptilian creatures like Godzilla or mutant insects like the oversize ants in *Them.* But it is also true that apocalyptic science fiction is concerned with exactly the same hopes and fears that are addressed in the book of Revelation—and, like Revelation (but unlike *On the Beach*), most of the books and movies that imagine the end of the world also imagine a New Heaven and a New Earth in which the Elect will survive and thrive.

"Science fiction films are not about science. They are about disaster, which is one of the old subjects of art," observes critic and cultural observer Susan Sontag in her essay "The Imagination of Disaster." "[S]cience fiction allegories are one of the myths about—that is, one of the ways of accommodating to and negating—the perennial human anxiety about death. (Myths of heaven and hell, and of ghosts, had the same function.)"[4]

Significantly, God appears not at all in the bulk of apocalyptic science fiction in the postwar era. Even *Deus Irae,* by Philip K. Dick and Roger Zelazny, a theologically sophisticated novel about the quest for God by the limbless survivor of a nuclear holocaust, ends with the shattering revelation that the "God of Wrath" whom he seeks is, in fact, the government scientist who devised "the evil instruments which had shown up the 'God' of the Christian Church for what he was"—that is, an impotent if not wholly imaginary deity.[5]

"The final enemy which Paul had recognized—death—had had its victory after all; Paul had died for nothing," write Dick and Zelazny, referring to the biblical apostle. "Death was not an antagonist, the last enemy, as Paul had thought; death was the release from bondage to the God of Life, the Deus Irae. In death one was free from Him—and only in death."[6]

Salvation in apocalyptic science fiction, when it is available at all, comes not from God but from human beings. The title of *The Omega Man,* of course, refers obliquely to the book of Revelation ("I am the Alpha and the Omega, the first and the last"), but the hero of the movie is a mortal man, played by the ruggedly handsome Charlton Heston, who manages to defeat the deformed and slightly demonic survivors of a catastrophic biological war only because he possesses a submachine gun, an electrical generator, a supply of gasoline, and a laboratory where he succeeds in concocting a cure for the plague that killed or maimed everyone else on earth. The movie ends with a distinctly Christological image—the character played by Heston, struck down by a spear, dies in the posture of Jesus on the cross—and the last hope for the survival of humankind is a flask of his own blood, but only because it contains the vital antibodies that will preserve the lives of the rest of the survivors.

"Christ, you could save the world," says one of the hopeful survivors to the thoroughly human savior, and one of the last children on earth asks: "Are you God?"[7]

The same theme—scientist as savior—could be discerned among flesh-and-blood scientists who felt themselves called to a kind of secular prophecy in the postwar world. The *Bulletin of Atomic Scientists,* for example, devised the so-called "Doomsday Clock" as a consciousness-raising device to call the attention of politicians, generals, and the citizenry to the deadly implications of nuclear proliferation. But the Doomsday Clock, an icon of the Cold War era, played on the same anxieties that have afflicted the human imagination since biblical antiquity: "Like the first followers of Jesus and John the Baptist," observes Stephen D. O'Leary, "the scientists who attempted to enter the political arena in the late 1940s were animated by the urgent conviction that time was short and destruction was sure unless our course could be changed."[8]

The decoupling of God and the end-times in politics and popular culture was complete by the mid-1960s, and it was even possible to regard the end of the world as an appropriate object of gallows humor. *On the Beach,* released in 1959 and set in 1964, contemplates the end of the world with utter despair. By 1964, of course, the world was still intact, and when Stanley Kubrick took a second look at the same scenario, he saw it as a laughing matter. The world ends once and for all in *Dr. Strangelove, or How I Learned to Stop Worrying and Love the Bomb,* but now it is the occasion for the blackest of black comedies.

Human failings alone are once again to blame in *Dr. Strangelove.* A rogue U.S. Air Force general launches a nuclear strike on the Soviet Union in the mad hope of convincing the president to order a full-scale attack. "Well, boys, I reckon this is it," says one of the B-52 pilots as he trades his helmet for a battered cowboy hat. But it turns out that the Soviets have secretly deployed a "doomsday device" that is programmed to respond to an American attack by detonating a mammoth cache of thermonuclear explosives and thereby creating "a doomsday shroud"—"a lethal cloud of radioactivity which will encircle the earth for ninety-three years" and "destroy all human and animal life." If a single bomb falls on Soviet soil, the world will be inevitably and irretrievably destroyed.

Kubrick and his collaborators on *Dr. Strangelove* do not mention God or the Devil at all, but they may have been mindful of the end-time scenario of Revelation when they devised the final scene of the movie. Faced with the utter destruction of humankind, the demented scientific genius called Dr. Strangelove holds out the bright hope of a New Heaven and a New Earth. A few hundred thousand men and women—"a nucleus of human specimens"—can be sheltered "at the bottom of some of our deeper mine shafts" for a century or so. Men would be selected for their potency and women for their sexual allure. Like the ancient readers of Revelation who imagined the millennial kingdom as an era of abundance, the postnuclear New Earth would be a sensual paradise for those who survived to see it.

"Naturally, they would breed prodigiously," explains Dr. Strangelove. "But with the proper breeding techniques and a ratio of, say, ten females to each male, I would guess that they could then work back to the present gross national production within, say, twenty years." And when the survivors finally emerge from the abyss, the men and women who had been judged worthy to live in the New Earth will be ready for the brave new world that they will find on the surface: "The prevailing emotion will be one of nostalgia for those left behind," he concludes, "combined with a spirit of bold curiosity for the adventure ahead."[9]

At precisely the moment of greatest optimism, however, a single American aircraft reaches its target in the Soviet Union, the doomsday device is triggered, and the atmosphere is suddenly filled with a series of mushroom-shaped clouds, the iconic image of the atomic age. Like *On the Beach*—and, again, quite unlike the other books and movies in the apocalyptic genre—*Dr. Strangelove* ends with no hope of human survival. "We'll meet again, don't know where, don't know when," goes the song that plays beneath the final fugue of thermonuclear detonations. The song would be an appropriate soundtrack to the book of Revelation, but now the words are purely and bitterly ironic.

Not everyone in America in the postwar era, however, shared the secular and cynical outlook that characterizes *Dr. Strangelove*. For a great many men and women, the comforting certainties of old-time religion—including the end of the world as it is depicted in the premillennialist reading of Revelation—remained very much alive. Indeed, two different and contesting apocalyptic ideas coexist in America, one based on science and the other based on religion. For the religious true believer, the prospect that the world might end in a nuclear conflagration is perfectly consistent with the belief that God, rather than humankind, will be its author.

"Some day we may blow ourselves up with all the bombs, [b]ut I still believe that God's going to be in control," declared the Reverend Charles Jones, pastor of a Baptist church in Amarillo, Texas, whose congregants included many of the men and women who worked at the nearby Pantex hydrogen-bomb assembly plant. "If He chooses to use nuclear war, then who am I to argue with that?"[10]

Christian fundamentalism, in fact, produced its own pop-culture version of the Apocalypse, including books, movies, comics, posters, and miscellaneous items of inspirational merchandise. The true believer might buy and wear a "Rapture watch" whose face carried a message to remind the wearer that the end is nigh—"One hour nearer the Lord's return"—or display a dashboard plaque that was meant to alert passengers that the driver might be "raptured" to heaven at any moment: "If you hear a trumpet, grab the wheel."[11]

Visions of what will happen when Christians are suddenly removed to heaven might be horrific—"bursting graves, crashing planes, and cars careening out of control"—or rhapsodic. "In one Rapture painting," writes Paul Boyer, "the lawnmower-pushing suburban husband gapes in wonder as his aproned wife soars over the clothesline to meet Jesus."[12] And the modern counterpart of a medieval best seller like *Fifteen Signs of Doomsday* was a handbook titled *How to Recognize the Antichrist.*

Youngsters in fundamentalist households were reared from early childhood in constant and urgent anticipation of the end of the world. "Many who were raised as premillennialists can tell horror stories," explains Timothy P. Weber, "about coming home to empty houses or finding themselves suddenly alone in department stores or supermarkets and instinctively concluding that Jesus has come and left them behind."[13] And novelist Rhoda Huffey, whose mother and father were both Pentecostal preachers, recalls the mind-set of an anxious eleven-year-old girl growing up with the conviction that she would be left behind when her parents were raptured to heaven:

"If the Christians had left, there was still one more way, which involved chopping off your head," writes Huffey in her semiautobiographical novel, *The Hallelujah Side.* "This was in Revelation, the horrible book. The Antichrist rode up on his dark horse to brand your forehead with the Mark of the Beast, 666. If you refused, he cut off your head with a hatchet and you went to heaven immediately. So there was nothing to be afraid of."[14]

But the apocalyptic subculture was not confined to sermons, tracts, and comic books, however colorful and imaginative. Like the Millerites, who made good use of the latest high-speed printing presses in the mid–nineteenth century, the doomsayers of the twentieth century were quick to embrace the latest technologies of mass communications. As early as 1936, for example, one enthusiastic preacher pondered the famous prophecy in Revelation—"Behold, he cometh with the clouds; and every eye shall see him"[15]—and then offered his own explanation of what the biblical author really means to say: "In the past we had to fall back on the explanation that it does not necessarily mean that all should see the Lord coming in the clouds of heaven at the same time," the preacher explained, "but now we know that by Television, that beatific sight can be seen the world over at one and the same moment."[16]

Some of the very first programs to be broadcast over the newfangled invention called radio were devoted to old-time religion. The Moody Bible Institute, for example, started broadcasting in the early 1930s over its own powerful radio station, and a hard-preaching radio show called the *Old-Fashioned Revival Hour,* originating in Long Beach, California, was heard over some 450 stations across the United States by the 1940s. Even the CBS radio network carried a weekly program on religion hosted by Donald Grey Barnhouse (1895–1960), the editor of an apocalyptic magazine titled *Revelation.* "If atomic bombs fall upon our cities," declared Barnhouse, "we shall be in heaven the next second."[17]

Some of the most charismatic pulpit preachers discovered the power of television and thereby turned themselves into authentic superstars in Christian circles. Oral Roberts (b. 1918) and Billy Graham (b. 1918) can be credited with the invention of televangelism; both started their ministries as tent revivalists but moved on to radio in the 1940s and television in the 1950s. A whole generation of fundamentalist preachers followed their example, the most famous (or notorious) of which include Pat Robertson (b. 1930), Rex Humbard (b. 1919), Timothy LaHaye (b. 1926), Jimmy Swaggart (b. 1935), Jim Bakker (b. 1939), and Jerry Falwell (b. 1933), the latter of whom came to be described as "the prince of the electronic church."[18]

All of them couched their preaching (and their fund-raising appeals) in distinctly apocalyptic terms, playing on the fears and hopes of their electronic flocks in precisely the same way that the author of Revelation addressed his first readers and hearers. Ironically, both the daily newspapers and the Saturday-afternoon science-fiction flicks seemed to reinforce even the most urgent prophecies about the end of the world. "We may have another year, maybe two years to work for Jesus Christ," warned

Billy Graham during his 1950 crusade, "and [then] ladies and gentlemen, I believe it is all going to be over."[19]

Ω

The apocalyptic idea in Christian fundamentalism has always remained on the far side of a certain cultural divide in America. Like the author of Revelation, who detested the classical civilization in which he lived and preached, the latter-day readers of Revelation condemned some of the most celebrated features of American civilization. They feared big business, big government, and big labor; they were revolted by the entertainment that was available in the local movie houses, over the radio, or on television; and they adopted the "language arsenal" of Revelation to denounce the sinful and satanic world in which they found themselves.

A few American doomsayers, of course, have always accentuated the positive when it comes to the end of the world. The millennial kingdom, for example, is sometimes advertised as a celestial version of the American dream: "Everyone will be self-employed and will enjoy the full fruitage of his own labor," declared one preacher. "Every single inhabitant of the world in that age will be independent, own his own property and his own home, and provide for his own family in abundance." Another preacher optimistically calculated that "the ratio between the eternally lost and saved would be 1 in 17,476." And an evangelist associated with the Moody Bible Institute conceded that "the Lord is going to judge America some day," but he insisted that "we are justified in hoping our country will be spared and that Americans will share the joy of the kingdom."[20]

But the embers of resentment and revenge that burn at the core of Revelation always seem to explode into flames. "The United States has departed a-whoring after strange gods," declared pioneering radio preacher Donald Grey Barnhouse shortly after the end of World War II. "The greed of the labor unions, the lust of Hollywood, the debauchery of the masses cry to high Heaven for judgment."[21] One preacher, sermonizing in 1949, blamed the public schools—"Godless, Bibleless, Christless"—for "clearing the path for Antichrist."[22] And M. R. DeHaan, the author of a 1963 apocalyptic novel titled *The Days of Noah,* attributed the moral decay of America to "women leaving their homes and children to enter factories and shops and offices" and described "people going almost completely crazy under [the] spell" of popular music: "Squeaks and squawks and empty groans and baby talking and monkey moans."[23]

Stripped of its sugarcoating, the apocalyptic vision of America is a weapon in the culture war between fundamentalism and the modern world: "God is going to judge America for its violence, its crimes, its backslidings, its murdering of millions of babies, its flaunting of homosexuality and sadomasochism, its corruption, its drunkenness and drug abuse, its lukewarmness toward Christ, its rampant divorce and adultery, its lewd pornography, its child molestation, its cheatings, its robbings, its dirty movies, and its occult practices," declared evangelist David Wilkerson in 1985. "America today is one great holocaust party, with millions drunk, high, shaking their fist at God, daring him to send the bombs."[24]

All of the perceived ills of contemporary America were stitched together by some apocalyptic preachers into one vast web of conspiracy, with Satan planted invisibly but unmistakably at the center. At one time or another, the elements of the "cosmic conspiracy to install the Antichrist" have been said to include bankers, biofeedback, credit cards, computers, the Council on Foreign Relations, feminism, Freudian psychology, the human-potential movement, Indian gurus, "international Jews," lesbianism, the Masons, Montessori schools, secular humanism, the Trilateral Commission, Universal Product Codes, and the United Nations—and the list is certainly not comprehensive.[25] Even *The Protocols of the Elders of Zion*, long ago proven to be a work of crude anti-Semitic propaganda concocted by the secret police of imperial Russia, still surfaces now and then in apocalyptic circles.

Indeed, the conspiracy theory begins in the text of Revelation, where the author alerts his readers and hearers to the dangers of "the deep things of Satan" and warns them against the invisible working of Satan's will through the creatures who are his agents and deputies.[26] And so each new and unfamiliar phenomenon in postwar America could be seen by apocalyptic true believers as yet another manifestation of the same satanic conspiracy. Thus, for example, the technological revolution that brought computers into every aspect of American life inspired some readers of Revelation to regard credit-card numbers and pricing bar codes as "the mark of the beast." After all, as the author of Revelation writes, "no one can buy or sell unless he has the mark, that is, the name of the beast or the number of its name"[27] A few visionaries even insisted that "Antichrist would *be* a computer."[28]

But, paradoxically, the conspiracy theories were actually a source of comfort—"an anchor ... in a world of uncertainty and doubt" for men and women who were confused and disturbed by the cultural and political upheavals of postwar America.[29] Where a secular observer sees a "subtext of conspiracy, paranoia, and social alienation" in apocalyptic preaching, the true believer sees a revelation that invests history with "drama and meaning," according to Paul Boyer. Indeed, otherwise comfortable and complacent Americans whose only afflictions are boredom and ennui are attracted to the chills and thrills of Revelation, and they find meaning in an otherwise meaningless world by embracing the old apocalyptic idea that "history is following a clear trajectory determined by God and that it is headed toward an ultimate, glorious consummation."[30]

Still, the antics and alarms of Christian doomsayers in postwar America were all but invisible to the audiences that laughed out loud at *Dr. Strangelove* when it was released in 1964. Of course, even a worldly or wholly secular family might be called upon by a pair of Jehovah's Witnesses going door-to-door with a supply of free literature. *Revelation: Its Grand Climax at Hand!*, one publication of the Watchtower Bible and Tract Society, features comic-book illustrations of the whole unlikely bestiary of Revelation. And anyone who switched through the channels on the television dial on any Sunday morning in the 1950s or the 1960s would encounter the preachments of Oral Roberts or Billy Graham or countless other fledgling televangelists. But, by and large, the old ideas about the end of the world were confined to a kind of Christian ghetto while the rest of America accustomed itself to the idea that doomsday will be strictly a human enterprise.

As with so much else in postwar America, however, the old ways of thinking and talking about the end of the world were about to change in profound and enduring ways. America was swept by wave after wave of radical new ideas and unsettling new experiences in the 1960s and 1970s— war, riot, and assassination, of course, but also the civil rights movement and the antiwar movement, the sexual revolution and the computer revolution, Beatlemania and Woodstock, the birth-control pill and men on the moon. The times they were a-changing, according to Bob Dylan's anthem, and Christian fundamentalism caught the same the winds of change. The New World was the site of yet another apocalyptic invasion that carried the book of Revelation out of the Christian ghetto and into the heart of American politics and popular culture.

Ω

The self-made apocalyptic seer who literally put the apocalyptic idea on the best-seller lists of America was a colorful and charismatic preacher named Hal Lindsey (b. 1930). He was working as a tugboat captain on the Mississippi in the 1950s when he experienced a powerful religious conversion. After studying at the Dallas Theological Seminary, a center of premillennialist doctrine, Lindsey went on the road as a preacher for the Campus Crusade for Christ. Inspired by the lively response to the sermons on Bible prophecy that he delivered in the late 1960s, Lindsey and his collaborator, C. C. Carlson, went public with his prediction that the end was near with the publication of *The Late Great Planet Earth* in 1970.

Like the "medieval best sellers" of an earlier age, Lindsey's book repurposed and reinterpreted the text of Revelation and other apocalyptic passages of the Bible in terms that made sense to contemporary readers. And Lindsey was rewarded with best-seller status that far exceeded even the *Scofield Reference Bible* and, significantly, reached far beyond the customary readership of Christian fundamentalist texts and tracts. *The Late Great Planet Earth* sold more than 20 million copies, and Lindsey was hailed by the *New York Times* as "the best-selling author of the 1970s."[31] Bart Ehrman goes even further and declares that Lindsey is "probably the single most read author of religion in modern times."[32]

Lindsey comes across in *The Late Great Planet Earth* as media savvy and thoroughly modern, but he is only the latest in a long line of apocalyptic preachers that reaches all the way back to the author of Revelation himself. He is a supercharged culture warrior, setting himself against all the bogeymen that he discerns in the counterculture and the so-called New Age—astrology, extrasensory perception, meditation, mysticism, spiritualism, witchcraft, hallucinogenic drugs, progressive politics, Christian ecumenicalism, and what he calls "oriental religions."[33] And, again like the author of Revelation, he condemns all ideas about religion except his own, and he suggests that diversity and toleration in matters of faith are, quite literally, the tools of Satan.

"Satan loves religion, which is why he invades certain churches on Sunday," Lindsey writes, hinting but never stating exactly which churches he regards as the "throne of Satan." "Religion is a great blinder of the minds of men."[34]

Above all, he insists that God's plan for the imminent end of the world is to be found in "the tested truths of Bible prophecy." *The Late Great Planet Earth,* in fact, is essentially a restatement of the doctrine of dispensational premillennialism as framed by John Darby in the nineteenth century. "Some time in the future there will be a seven-year period climaxed by the visible return of Jesus Christ," Lindsey begins, and he proceeds to describe the standard version of the end-time scenario that he learned at the Dallas Theological Seminary. In fact, some of his former fellow seminarians, surely a bit envious of his remarkable success, "complained that Lindsey had simply repackaged his lecture notes!"[35]

The "seven-year countdown" to the Second Coming will be triggered by the reconstruction of the Temple in Jerusalem and the resumption of animal sacrifice by the Jewish people. Next will come the world dictatorship of the Antichrist and the period of persecution known as the Tribulation—but not before Christian true believers are raptured to heaven. At the end of the Tribulation, Jesus Christ will return to fight the battle of Armageddon, reign over a peaceable kingdom on earth for a thousand years, and then, at last, defeat Satan once and for all, sit in judgment over all humankind, and reward the Christian saints with eternal life in a new heaven and a new earth.

"Someday, a day that only God knows, Jesus Christ is coming to take away all those who believe in Him," writes Lindsey about the Rapture. "Without benefit of science, space suits, or interplanetary rockets, there will be those who will be transported into a glorious place more beautiful, more awesome, than we can possibly comprehend."[36]

What distinguishes Lindsey from doomsayers with more modest book sales is his undeniable genius for hot-wiring the book of Revelation to the geopolitical realities of the contemporary world. Here, too, Lindsey is following the example of earlier readers of Revelation; indeed, as we have seen, the author of Revelation himself apparently sees the Roman emperor Nero as the Antichrist, and successive generations have come up with their own suspects, ranging from Muhammad to Mussolini. And, like exegetes in every age, Lindsey offers his readers and hearers a way to make sense of the baffling and frightening world in which they find themselves. For Lindsey, it is a world haunted by the realpolitik of the Cold War and the constant threat of nuclear annihilation.

The Antichrist, according to Lindsey, will be a flesh-and-blood politician who rises to a position of leadership in what he calls "the revived Roman

Empire"—that is, the Common Market, the community of nations that was the forerunner of today's European Union.[37] Magog, he insists, is the Soviet Union, and Gog is its head of state. The "kings of the east," briefly mentioned in Revelation as combatants in the battle of Armageddon, are meant to identify the People's Republic of China.[38] And the final conflagration, described in Revelation in terms of stars falling from heaven and monstrous creatures rising from the abyss, is actually meant to be a global nuclear war—"an all-out attack of ballistic missiles upon the great metropolitan areas of the world."[39]

Lindsey insists that God granted visions of the far distant future to the ancient prophets that were wholly unintelligible to them or the readers and hearers to whom they preached during their own lifetimes. Thus, for example, Lindsey quotes from the book of Zechariah—"Their flesh shall consume away while they stand upon their feet, and their eyes shall consume away in their holes, and their tongues shall consume away in their mouths"[40]—and then he credits the Hebrew prophet with a vision of events that would come to pass only in the atomic age: "Has it occurred to you that this is exactly what happens to those who are in a thermonuclear blast?" asks Lindsey. "It appears that this will be the case at the return of the Christ."[41]

Then, too, Lindsey adopts a "language arsenal" of his own making in *The Late Great Planet Earth,* a vocabulary that is intended to capture the attention of jaded readers who would not otherwise pick up a book of Christian witness or Bible prophecy. Thus, for example, the Bible itself is "the Best Seller." The Antichrist is called "the 'Future Fuehrer,'" and the Great Whore of Babylon is "Scarlet O'Harlot." Armageddon is "World War III." Those 144,000 male virgins from the twelve tribes of Israel who are said to be "sealed" by Jesus Christ in the end-times are dubbed "Jewish Billy Grahams"—that is, "physical, literal Jews who are going to believe with a vengeance that Jesus is the Messiah." (All other Jews, he suggests, will be dead and gone.) And Lindsey, after having condemned the use of hallucinogenic substances, proceeds to describe the experience of the Rapture as "The ultimate trip."[42]

"If you are a believer, chapters 4 and 5 of Revelation describe what you will be experiencing in heaven," Lindsey writes. "Talk about mind expansion drugs!"[43]

Fatefully, Lindsey is unable to resist the same temptation that has resulted in the embarrassment of every previous doomsayer from Montanus to Father Miller—the cardinal sin of date setting. The countdown clock for doomsday, Lindsey argues, began with the establishment of the modern state of Israel, and he interprets various fragments of biblical text to confirm that the end will come within the lifetime of the generation that witnessed its rebirth in 1948. On the assumption that a generation is equivalent to forty years, Lindsey suggests in *The Late Great Planet Earth*, first published in 1970, that the Rapture will take place in 1981, followed by seven years of persecution under the Antichrist and then, in 1988, the battle of Armageddon and the second coming of Jesus Christ.

Lindsey, of course, was proven wrong. As the year 1981 approached and the Rapture seemed no nearer, he rechecked his end-time calculations and offered a slightly revised schedule in *The 1980s: Countdown to Armageddon* (1980). After the collapse of the Soviet bloc in the early 1990s, however, he was inspired to offer a new end-time scenario in *Planet Earth 2000 A.D.* (1994): Islamic fundamentalism rather than the Red Army will be the final adversary of Jesus Christ at the battle of Armageddon, although he insists that "the 'collapse' of Communism is part of a masterful game of deceit engineered by Mikhail Gorbachev and the Soviet KGB."[44] Still later, Lindsey offered another insight into the workings of Satan: UFO sightings, he argued, are "deceptive ruses by demons, who will soon stage a massive UFO landing to mislead earthlings into believing in life on other planets."[45]

Lindsey himself, like Father Miller, remained cheerful and unchastened even though his prophecies proved to be wrong and his revisionist works failed to achieve the same stellar sales that had been racked up by *The Late Great Planet Earth*. As it turned out, Lindsey had achieved something new, significant, and enduring in spite of the manifest failure of his prophecies: he played a crucial role in leveraging the apocalyptic idea out of the fundamentalist churches and into the mainstream of American civilization. Among his 20 million readers, for example, was a man who would take the book of Revelation out of the tent meeting and into the White House.

Ω

Revelation achieved its first penetration into American politics with the unlikely rise of Ronald Reagan, first as governor of California and later as president of the United States. Raised in a church with roots that reached all the way back to the era of the Second Great Awakening—and reportedly an early reader of *The Late Great Planet Earth*—Reagan was perhaps the first national figure outside of fundamentalist circles to openly and unapologetically affirm his belief in the imminent fulfillment of Bible prophecy.

"Apparently never in history have so many of the prophecies come true in such a relatively short time," said Ronald Reagan, then serving as governor of California, in an interview that appeared in 1968 in *Christian Life* magazine.[46] And he was even more forthcoming at a political dinner in Sacramento in 1971 when he commented on the significance of a recent coup in Libya: "That's a sign that the day of Armageddon isn't far off," declared Reagan. "Everything's falling into place. It can't be long now."[47]

Reagan, in fact, was able to cite chapter and verse to support his prediction. The incident in Libya apparently put him in mind of a Sunday-school lesson on the apocalyptic prophecies of the Hebrew Bible: "For the day is near, even the day of the Lord is near," goes a passage in the book of Ezekiel. "Ethiopia, and Libya, and Lydia, and all the mingled people ... shall fall with them by the sword." And Reagan, apparently inspired by the sight of waiters igniting bowls of cherries jubilee in the darkened dining room, was mindful of God's vow to bring down on Gog, the biblical enemy of Israel, "great hailstones, fire, and brimstone."[48] Reagan alluded to these passages during his table talk and concluded: "That must mean they'll be destroyed by nuclear weapons."[49]

Reagan carried those Sunday-school lessons all the way to Washington. "We may be the generation that sees Armageddon," he told televangelist Jim Bakker in 1980.[50] "You know, I turn back to your ancient prophets in the Old Testament and the signs foretelling Armageddon, and I find myself wondering if we're the generation that's going to see that come about," he told a Jewish lobbyist in 1983. "I don't know if you've noted any of those prophecies lately, but believe me, they certainly described the times we're going through."[51]

Reagan surrounded himself in the White House with men who shared the same beliefs. "I have read the Book of Revelation," affirmed Caspar Weinberger, his secretary of defense, "and yes, I believe the world is going to end—by an act of God, I hope—but every day I think that time is running out." And James Watts, Reagan's interior secretary, demurred to a question about his plans for protecting the environment for the benefit of future generations by invoking the Second Coming: "I do not know how many future generations we can count on before the Lord returns."[52]

Reagan appears to have been a convinced reader of *The Late Great Planet Earth*. "Every one of Lindsey's proposals for domestic and foreign policy," insists Stephen D. O'Leary, "was part of Reagan's campaign platform."[53] To hear Lindsey himself tell it, Reagan was eager to win over the American military establishment to apocalyptic true belief. With the president's blessing, Lindsey asserts, he was invited to brief Pentagon war planners on the divine implications of nuclear combat with the Soviet Union. And Reagan invited televangelist Jerry Falwell, another prominent and outspoken apocalyptic preacher, to attend briefings of the National Security Council and deliver the same sermon.

Such notions were wholly unremarkable in the fundamentalist churches of America—and they reached an even wider audience through the radio and television broadcasts of various apocalyptic preachers, both famous and obscure—but they were deeply unnerving in the mind and mouth of a man who is accompanied wherever he goes by the launch codes of the American nuclear arsenal. If the president of the United States is a true believer who is convinced that "the day of Armageddon isn't far off," would he not be tempted to take it upon himself to rain fire and brimstone down on the latest enemy to be seen as the Antichrist?

That troubling question was raised by network correspondent Marvin Kalb during the televised debates of the 1984 presidential campaign. Nancy Reagan could be heard to mutter "Oh no!" in the background, but the president himself was prepared with a reasonable and even statesmanlike answer. Reagan conceded that he had a "philosophical" interest in the biblical prophecies about the battle of Armageddon, and he argued that "a number of theologians" had suggested that "the prophecies are coming together that portend that." But he concluded that it was impossible to know whether Armageddon "is a thousand years away or day after tomorrow." And he insisted that he "never seriously warned and said we must plan according to Armageddon."[54]

Still, the issue did not go away. The *New York Times* editorialized on the peril posed by the "Armageddonist" advisers in the inner circle of the Reagan administration. Self-styled "gonzo" journalist Hunter S. Thompson, noting that "the president is very keen on the Book of Revelation" and pointing out a few of the weirder sights that are described in the biblical text, observed that "a lot of acid freaks have been taken away in white jackets with extremely long sleeves for seeing things like that."[55] On a more sober note, a committee of one hundred clergy joined in imploring the president to "disavow the dogma that nuclear holocaust is foreordained in the Bible."[56]

Reagan, however, continued to affirm his own true belief in the end-time scenario of Revelation when he famously and memorably branded the Soviet Union as the "evil empire." The phrase meant one thing to fans of *Star Wars* but something quite different to readers of Revelation, who were inevitably reminded of the satanic empire that is described in biblical code as "Babylon the Great, the Mother of Harlots and Abominations of the Earth."[57] Indeed, Reagan said as much in an address to the National Association of Evangelicals in 1983, when he referred to the Soviet Union as "the focus of evil in the modern world" and predicted that both the evil empire and history itself will soon end.

"There is sin and evil in the world, and we're joined by Scripture and the Lord Jesus to oppose it with all our might," the president witnessed. "I believe that communism is another sad, bizarre chapter in human history, whose last pages are even now being written."[58]

Reagan was only half right, of course. The fact that the Soviet Union ended—but the world did not—posed an awkward problem for the doomsayers and, especially, the date setters. And yet, as we have seen over and over again, the true believer is not much troubled by the demonstrable failure of a prophecy, which can always be recalibrated and reissued to suit the latest turn of events. Once injected into politics and statecraft by Ronald Reagan, the book of Revelation achieved a degree of stature and influence that it had not enjoyed since Joachim of Fiore and Hildegard of Bingen served as apocalyptic advisers to the popes and kings of the medieval world.

The new respectability of the apocalyptic idea in American politics seems to coincide with its sudden popularity in American popular culture, where the imagery of Revelation began to appear in artifacts ranging from a punk-rock song by the Sex Pistols titled "I Am Antichrist" to a jingle in a Pizza Hut commercial: "Beware of 666! It's the Anti-Pizza!"[59] And surely it is no coincidence that the best-seller status of *The Late Great Planet Earth* in the early 1970s was quickly followed by the release of *The Omen,* an apocalyptic thriller about an American diplomat who discovers that he is the unwitting adoptive father of the Antichrist.

"When the Jews return to Zion, and a comet rips the sky," goes a bit of doggerel that figures prominently in the plot of *The Omen* (and neatly sums up the apocalyptic scenario according to John Nelson Darby), "the Holy Roman Empire rises, then you and I must die."[60]

Tellingly, *The Omen* does not actually concern itself with the end of the world. Rather, the moviemakers concoct a wholly spurious plot line that requires the hero, played by Gregory Peck, to kill the satanic child with seven daggers that have been excavated from the ruins of Megiddo, the supposed site of the Battle of Armageddon. "The book of Revelation predicted it all," announces a doomsaying priest—but Revelation predicts no such thing.[61] Indeed, *The Omen* "can be read as reflecting the baby boomers' own ambivalence about parenting," according to Stephen D. O'Leary, rather than anything that is actually to be found in Revelation.[62]

Still, *The Omen* was successful enough at the box office to spawn a series of sequels, including *Damien: Omen II* in 1978 and *The Final Conflict* in 1981, and the screenwriter of *The Omen* returned to the apocalyptic well yet again for a network miniseries titled *Revelation* in 2005. A remake of *The Omen* in 2006 was promoted with the slogan: "You have been warned! 6-6-06." And the memorable scene in *The Omen* in which the ambassador detects a birthmark in the form of three sixes on the skull of the young Antichrist conveyed the satanic meaning of 666 to millions of Americans who had never cracked open the book of Revelation. Thus did the corpus of urban legend in America come to include anecdotes about supermarket customers who refuse to accept change in the amount of $6.66 or automobile owners who send back license plates that include the number 666.

"Watching, waiting and working for the millennium," observes church historian and pop theologian Leonard Sweet, "has become, even more than baseball, America's favorite pastime."[63]

The pop-culture version of the apocalypse, however, fails to convey the soul-shaking hopes and terrors that have been inspired in the readers and hearers of Revelation since it was first composed twenty centuries ago. The end of the world according to Revelation has been depicted, literally and luridly, in a series of movies—including *Image of the Beast, Early Warning, The Final Hour,* and *The Road to Armageddon*—that were produced by Christian fundamentalists and screened only in church basements and classrooms. But whenever a secular moviemaker sets out to deal with Revelation in a straightforward way, the absence of true belief always gets in the way.

For example, Michael Tolkin's independent feature film *The Rapture* is torn between a fascination with the iconography of Revelation and a horror of religious fundamentalism. To be sure, *The Rapture* comes much closer to what is actually depicted in Christian scripture than any of the major studio releases in the Omen series. The hero and heroine—an agnostic cop and a jaded telephone operator who favored group sex with strangers before she was born again—end up being chased down a desert highway in California by the Four Horsemen of the Apocalypse and then rising into the heavens on the day of the Rapture. (The director used a smoke machine and a camera dolly on a darkened soundstage to create the crude effect.) But Tolkin also depicts the heroine, played by Mimi Rogers, as a religious fanatic who murders her own young daughter with a gunshot to the head in order to hasten the weeping child into heaven. As a result, the movie is a theological muddle that seems to suggest that even nonbelievers and child killers will be "raptured" on the last day. No true believer would have committed such a grave doctrinal error.

For consumers of pop culture, then, the apocalyptic idea is sometimes just another item in the smorgasbord of religious beliefs and practices on offer in contemporary America: "[T]he latest surge in prophetic interest began in the early 1970s, at the same time that Americans began showing interest in the occult, parapsychology, ouija boards, Eastern religions, and UFOs," observes Timothy Weber. "They may simply be an example of Americans' insatiable appetite for the unusual, spectacular and exotic."[64] And another scholarly observer wonders if the phenomenon is "just another merchandising ploy, a cult of 'chic bleak' herding us into bookstores and cinemas and revival meetings to buy the latest wares of the latest self-selected messiah."[65]

The Omen may have been Revelation Lite, but that's about as much as America was ready to embrace in the 1970s. Even *The Late Great Planet Earth* was a sugarcoated and caffeine-charged version of the hellfire-and-damnation sermons that were still confined to the church halls and Christian broadcasting. As the end of the second millennium approached, however, the book of Revelation would come to be used yet again as a weapon in the culture war that was being fought by Christian fundamentalists for the heart and soul of America.

Ω

No American president after Ronald Reagan has been quite so outspoken about his personal belief that the end of the world is nigh. At the same time, however, *every* American president since Reagan has declared himself to be a "born-again" Christian. George Herbert Walker Bush, for example, may have been affiliated with the United Nations, the Trilateral Commission, and the Council on Foreign Affairs at various points in his long career—all of them condemned as tools of Satan by apocalyptic conspiracy theorists on the far right wing of Christian fundamentalism—but he proudly proclaimed himself to be a born-again Christian, too: "I'm a clearcut affirmative to that."[66]

The perceived need of American politicians to affirm their religious credentials may have less to do with their spiritual beliefs than with the sea change in American politics that took place during the Reagan presidency. Televangelists like Jerry Falwell, founder of the Moral Majority, and Pat Robertson, founder of the Conservative Coalition, among many others, sought to deploy the faithful as a voting bloc and a source of financial support for politicians who adhered to certain articles of faith in Christian fundamentalism, which include criminalizing abortion and legalizing prayer in the public schools.

With 46 percent of all Americans declaring themselves to be evangelical or born-again Christians, according to a 2002 Gallup poll, the so-called Christian Right came to play a crucial role in the political strategy that ultimately achieved a Republican majority in Congress and a Republican president in the White House.[67] By 1984, for example, the Republican party deemed it appropriate to invite televangelist James Robison to give the invocation at the convention where Reagan was renominated—and Robison deemed it appropriate to deliver a white-hot apocalyptic sermon to the enthusiastic delegates: "Any teaching of peace prior to [Christ's] return is heresy," said Robison. "It's against the word of God. It's Antichrist."[68]

A certain high-water mark of political activism by Christian fundamentalists in America came in 1988, when Pat Robertson, founder of the Christian Broadcasting Network, declared himself to be a candidate for the Republican presidential nomination. He was already on record as predicting that the end was near—"I guarantee you by the fall of 1982 there is going to be a judgment on the world," he wrote in 1980[69]—but now he found it appropriate to tone down the apocalyptic rhetoric: "There is no way I feel I'm going to help the Lord bring the world to an end," he told the *Wall Street Journal* in 1985, perhaps already thinking of his own presidential ambitions.[70]

The willingness of preachers like Falwell and Robertson to enter the political arena was something new in Christian fundamentalism. The apocalyptic idea suggests that politics are essentially pointless because human beings can do nothing to change or postpone God's divine plan for the end of the world, and so saving souls is the only sound occupation for a good Christian. That's why Christian fundamentalists in the early twentieth century regarded the Social Gospel with such contempt, and the same disdain for doing good works in the here and now continues to characterize many of the doomsayers who are convinced that the end is near.

"God didn't send me to clean the fishbowl," is how Hal Lindsey put it. "He sent me to fish."[71]

The woes of the world, in fact, are nothing but good news in the eyes of apocalyptic true believers who look forward to a new heaven and a new earth. "We are not to weep as the people of the world weep when there are certain tragedies or breakups of the government or systems of the world," explained Pat Robertson in an unguarded moment. "We are not to wring our hands and say, 'Isn't that awful.' That isn't awful at all. It's good. That is a token, an evident token of our salvation, of where God is going to take us."[72]

Other Christian fundamentalists, however, are inspired to "give the Devil 'all the trouble [they] can till Jesus comes,'" a calling that prompts them to crusade for creationism, school prayer, and family values and against abortion, gay marriage, and pornography, among various other causes.[73] Pat Robertson, for example, condemns feminism as "a socialist, anti-family political movement that encourages women to leave their husbands, kill their children, practice witchcraft, destroy capitalism, and become lesbians." And when Disney World hosted a privately sponsored weekend gathering called "Gay Days," he insisted that the toleration of homosexuality in America will result in hurricanes, earthquakes, tornadoes, and "possibly a meteor," citing chapter and verse from Revelation to support his prediction.[74]

Some Christians, of course, seek to trouble the Devil by following the lofty moral example of the Gospels. Jimmy Carter, for example, is a born-again Baptist—a church whose members, by and large, embrace the hard-edged apocalyptic doctrine of dispensational premillennialism—and he famously invoked the strictest expression of Christian morality when he confessed to *Playboy* in 1976 that he "committed adultery in my heart many times," an allusion to the Sermon on the Mount: "Whosoever looketh on a woman to lust after her," says Jesus in the Gospel of Matthew, "hath committed adultery with her already in his heart."[75] But Carter is also famous for picking up a hammer and pounding nails under the auspices of Habitat for Humanity, an act that wordlessly but eloquently alludes to the Little Apocalypse as it appears in Matthew: "For I was hungry and you gave Me food; I was thirsty and you gave Me drink; I was a stranger and you took Me in."[76]

Some fundamentalist preachers endorse both faith *and* works. "[E]very person who is a follower of Christ is responsible to do something for the hungry and sick in the world," writes Billy Graham in *Approaching Hoofbeats: Four Horsemen of the Apocalypse.* "We must do what we can, even though we know that God's ultimate plan is the making of a new earth and a new heaven." Yet Graham also insists that all of the afflictions of the modern world that might be remedied through good works, ranging from AIDS to global warming, are sure signs that the end is near. "The Bible teaches that peoples and nations have brought this pain upon themselves by humanistic religion and man-made war," he insists. "Almost every headline, almost every television news flash, almost every radio bulletin proclaims one truth: the rider who brings death is on his way and hell is close behind."[77]

Apocalyptic true believers, in other words, are instructed by their faith to consult the Bible to discover the inner meaning of the events, great and small, that unfold around us every day. When they do, however, they are likely to conclude that it is too late to do anything except pray that they will be among the saved when the Antichrist reveals himself. It's an approach to problem-solving that links the author of Revelation with Ronald Reagan and, for that matter, millions of other Americans. Thus, for example, when they consider one of the most explosive human conflicts on earth—the struggle between Arabs and Jews over sovereignty in what three faiths regard as the Holy Land—some Christians cast their eyes to heaven rather than contemplating facts on the ground. For them, the fate of the modern Middle East is a matter of theology rather than geopolitics, and the birthplace of Daniel and John is now the stage on which the final act of the divine drama of the end-times is being played out.

Just as an earlier generation of Christian Zionists had thrilled at the Balfour Declaration and the liberation of Jerusalem by the British army in 1918, their latter-day counterparts celebrated Israel's lightning victory in the Six Day War of 1967 and, above all, the liberation of the Old City of Jerusalem. Here stands the Temple Mount, the site of the original Temple of Yahweh as described in the Bible and the place where, according to the beliefs of both Jewish and Christian fundamentalists, the Third Temple will be built in the end-times. Significantly, the Temple Mount now passed under Jewish sovereignty for the first time since the Second Temple was destroyed by a Roman army in 70 C.E.

"The hands on Israel's prophecy clock leaped forward on June 8, 1967," writes Tim LaHaye in *The Beginning of the End,* an apocalyptic tract that long predates the Left Behind series, "when the Israeli troops marched into the Old City of Jerusalem."[78]

According to some Christian Zionists, as we have seen, the beginning of the end would commence in the fortieth year after the establishment of the modern state of Israel. A former NASA rocket engineer named Edgar Whisenant argued the case in *88 Reasons Why the Rapture Will Be in 1988,* where he predicts that the Tribulation would begin on October 3, 1988—Rosh Hashanah, the first day of the new year on the Jewish ritual calendar—and the Battle of Armageddon would break out exactly seven years later. One enterprising preacher offered a package tour to Israel that was timed to coincide with the day when faithful Christians would be "raptured" to heaven. The price of the package was $1,850, including "return if necessary."[79]

"We stay at the Intercontinental Hotel on the Mount of Olives," the brochure announced. "And if this is the year of our Lord's return, as we anticipate, you may even ascend to Glory from within a few feet of His ascension."[80]

As it turned out, of course, the tour members were compelled to make use of their return tickets, but the failure of the Rapture to arrive on time did nothing to cool the ardor of Christian Zionists. The so-called Jerusalem Temple Foundation, headquartered in Los Angeles and addressing its fund-raising appeals to Christian fundamentalists across America, raised a reported $10 million to fund the construction of the Third Temple in Jerusalem. Christian fundamentalists on tour in Israel delight in the spectacle of Jewish fundamentalists who gather to slaughter goats in preparation for the resumption of animal sacrifice in the rebuilt Temple, and they take home souvenirs in the form of the half-shekel coins, freshly minted in pure silver, that one Jewish entrepreneur is coining to fill the treasury of the Third Temple when it is finally built.

Yet another attraction for doomsday-minded Christians, at least for a short while, was the dairy farm in northern Israel where a cow called Melody was born in 1996. The Holstein calf was bright red at birth, a fact that sparked a fresh wave of messianic anticipation: the offering of an unblemished red heifer is mentioned in the book of Numbers,[81] and the availability of a cow that was suitable for the long-abandoned ritual of animal sacrifice suggested to both Jewish and Christian fundamentalists that the end was near. Until Melody's red coat began to show patches of white hair, thus rendering her ritually impure and unfit for sacrifice, Melody attracted busloads of Christian tourists, and apocalyptic preachers wondered out loud whether she was destined to be the first animal to be offered to God on the altar of the Third Temple.

"Could Melody's ashes be used for Temple purification ceremonies," mused televangelist Jack Van Impe, "as early as 2000?"[82]

Such yearnful apocalyptic fancies have been likened by journalist and author Gershom Gorenberg to the cargo cults of the South Pacific islanders, who watched in envy as ships and planes arrived, seemingly out of nowhere, to bring abundant quantities of both essentials and luxuries to newly arrived European and American missionaries and soldiers. Starting in the late nineteenth century and continuing through World War II, the islanders imitated the well-provisioned newcomers by fashioning their own crude versions of docks and control towers out of reeds and fronds in the hope that ships and planes would magically appear and deliver cargo to them, too. Here is yet another variant of the millennial kingdom of peace and plenty as envisioned by men and women who knew the book of Revelation, if at all, only from Christian missionaries.

"For some fundamentalists, Jewish and Christian—often educated people—the Temple has become the great Cargo ship," explains Gorenberg in *The End of Days.* "[M]inting silver half-shekels is akin to building the dock."[83]

Magical thinking, of course, has always figured in the religious imagination in general and the apocalyptic idea in particular. The author of Revelation, as we have seen, delights in the revenge fantasy of "Babylon" and its cargo going up in flames: "And the merchants of the earth weep and mourn for her, since no one buys their cargo any more, cargo of gold, silver and pearls...."[84] But magical thinking can be literally life threatening when it is applied to an enterprise as delicate and as dangerous as peacemaking in the Middle East.

Ω

Christian Zionists, in fact, tend to regard the prospect of peace between Israel and its Arab neighbors as an obstacle to the second coming of Jesus Christ and, therefore, the work of the Devil. Peaceful coexistence between Arabs and Jews, as they see it, would only hold back the hands on "Israel's prophecy clock" by postponing the fateful day when Israel is restored to its most expansive biblical boundaries and the Jewish people return en masse to their homeland.

"In spite of the rosy and utterly unrealistic expectations by our government, this treaty will not be a lasting treaty," said Jerry Falwell in condemning the Camp David accords between Israel and Egypt in 1979. "You and I know that there's not going to be any real peace in the Middle East until the Lord Jesus sits down upon the throne of David in Jerusalem."[85]

Such sentiments have endeared the Christian Zionists to the hawks and hard-liners in Israel. "Your devotion to our country," Prime Minister Yitzhak Shamir declared to a gathering of evangelical ministers in 1988, "will become a strong arm in our arsenal of defense."[86] On an official visit to Washington, D.C., in the 1990s, Benjamin Netanyahu, then prime minister of Israel, pointedly closeted himself with Jerry Falwell before calling on President Bill Clinton. "It is my belief," Falwell once announced on *60 Minutes,* "that the Bible Belt in America is Israel's only safety belt right now."[87]

Some gestures of support for Israel by Christian Zionists, of course, are purely whimsical when they are not downright weird. When Israel asserted sovereignty over all of Jerusalem after the liberation of the Old City in 1967, for example, most nations of the world declined to move their embassies from Tel Aviv to Jerusalem. The diplomatic rebuke inspired a Dutch minister named Jan Willem van der Hoeven to establish the so-called International Christian Embassy in Jerusalem. The "embassy" is nothing more than a public-relations gimmick, but several prime ministers of Israel, ranging from the rightist Benjamin Netanyahu to the leftist Yitzhak Rabin, found it appropriate to address its annual gatherings.

"My messiah is not going to come to a Mosque of Omar," declared van der Hoeven at one such gathering, "but a Third Temple which God will let be built."[88]

Other efforts in support of Israel, however, are more substantial. The International Fellowship of Christians and Jews, headed by an Orthodox rabbi named Yechiel Eckstein, has raised in excess of a quarter-billion dollars from some four hundred thousand Christian donors in support of its various programs, including the promotion of Jewish emigration to Israel. "No Jew since Jesus has commanded this kind of gentile following," cracked commentator Zev Chafets in the *New York Times*.[89] And the Christian Friends of Israeli Communities encourages churches across America to "adopt" Jewish settlements on the West Bank: "Those pioneers are now fulfilling the covenant to Abraham, Isaac and Jacob," it is explained in one pamphlet, "regarding the restoration of *all* the land God has allocated to Israel."[90]

Benjamin Netanyahu once affirmed Israel's solidarity with Christian fundamentalism—and answered those who regard Christian and Jewish Zionists as strange bedfellows—in elevated and even rhapsodic terms while addressing an annual event called the National Prayer Breakfast for Israel. "A sense of history, a sense of poetry, and a sense of morality imbued the Christian Zionists who more than a century ago began to write, and plan, and organize for Israel's restoration," said Netanyahu, then serving as Israel's ambassador to the United Nations. "So those who are puzzled by what they consider the new-found friendship between Israel and its Christian supporters reveal an ignorance of both. But we know better."[91]

What's puzzling goes far beyond the superficial irony of Christians befriending Jews even though they believe that their Jewish friends have already damned themselves to hell by refusing to embrace Jesus of Nazareth as the Messiah. That's the same grievance, of course, that prompts the author of Revelation to refer to *his* Jewish acquaintances as "the synagogue of Satan." But the end-time scenario that motivates Christian Zionists to support Israel in the political arena also instructs them that the Jewish state will ultimately ally itself with the Antichrist—but only until the Antichrist goes to war against his allies and "slaughter[s] two-thirds of all Jews in a Holocaust worse than anything unleashed by Hitler."[92] Only the remnant of Jews who convert to Christianity in the last days will be spared, they believe, and the rest will burn forever in the lake of fire along with Satan himself.

Only rarely do Christian Zionists speak out loud about the role that they envision for the Jewish people in the end-times. Jerry Falwell, for example, once made the tactical mistake of observing in public that "many evangelicals believe the Antichrist will, by necessity, be a Jewish male."[93] He deemed it necessary to issue a public apology two weeks later at a prayer breakfast in support of Israel. But Falwell pointedly refused to disavow his remark and expressed regret only for the fact that it reached the public record. "I apologize not for what I believe," said an unrepentant Falwell, "but for my lack of tact and judgment in making a statement that serves no purpose whatsoever."[94]

Such awkward and ugly beliefs are understandably off-putting to Jewish sensibilities—but these beliefs are also mostly overlooked by many Jewish leaders who welcome the political support of Christian Zionists. "Some [Christians] are motivated theologically, in that for the Second Coming of the Messiah, one of the prerequisites is for Jews to be safe and secure in the Holy Land," concedes Abraham Foxman, executive director of the Anti-Defamation League. "That's not a reason for us to reject them. I believe that when the Jews are safe and secure in the Holy Land, the Messiah will come for the first time. So what?"[95]

Still, at least some Jewish observers are willing to comment on the strange bedfellowship of fundamentalist Christians and Jews. "This is a grim comedy of mutual condescension," Leon Wieseltier, literary editor of the *New Republic,* told the *New York Times.* "The evangelical Christians condescend to the Jews by offering their support before they convert or kill them. And the conservative Jews condescend to Christians by accepting their support while believing that their eschatology is nonsense. This is a fine example of the political exploitation of religion."[96]

Apocalyptic activism, in fact, has reached the highest levels of American politics and policy-making. When the Senate debated whether Israel ought to withdraw the Jewish settlements on the West Bank, for example, Senator James Inhofe, a Republican from Oklahoma, relied on the Bible to justify the continued occupation of Hebron: "It is at this place where God appeared to Abram and said, 'I am giving you this land,'" he declared on the floor of the Senate, quoting the book of Genesis. "This is not a political battle at all. It is a contest over whether or not the word of God is true."[97]

Very few politicians, diplomats, or generals who hold such beliefs are courageous (or foolish) enough to speak about them so openly. For that reason, it is all too easy to dismiss as a religious eccentric someone who advocates the use of the Bible as a document of American foreign policy. But, as Senator Inhofe reminds us, true belief and Bible literalism have never been confined to backwater churches where the congregants handle snakes and speak to each other in tongues. Every now and then, the apocalyptic idea explodes into the headlines and reminds the rest of us that it has been lurking in the shadows all along.

B ack in the 1930s, a congregation of Seventh-day Adventists in Los Angeles found itself with an awkward problem after welcoming a new member named Victor Houteff, a Bulgarian-born washing-machine salesman. Houteff had come to believe that the Christian scriptures were composed in a secret code that only he had succeeded in solving, and he offered his own strange teachings in place of those sanctioned by the church. At last, in 1935, Houteff was barred from the congregation, and he led a dozen families to a self-imposed exile on a remote hilltop compound in Waco, Texas, where he fully expected to witness the end of the world in the company of the 144,000 followers that he hoped to gather there.

Nowadays, of course, Waco calls to mind an incident that proves how tenacious and how dangerous the apocalyptic idea can be. Back in the 1930s, however, Houteff and his followers were merely one more obscure and exceedingly odd religious community whose day-to-day lives in a remote Texas backwater were wholly invisible to the rest of America. Yet the seeds of the deadly standoff between the Branch Davidians and federal law-enforcement agents that took place in 1993 reach all the way back to the earliest stirrings of the apocalyptic tradition in the New World and, arguably, the worst excesses of Jan Bockelson, the messiah-king of medieval Münster.

Houteff adopted "Mount Carmel" as the name of his community in an allusion to the site where, according to the Bible, the prophet Elijah orders the seizure and slaughter of 450 priests of the pagan god Baal in an act of carnage that is meant to glorify the God of Israel.[98] For Houteff and his followers, as for Elijah and the author of Revelation, the choice between the One True God and all other beliefs and practices is, quite literally, a matter of life or death: "It should be ever kept in mind that the very name 'Mt. Carmel,'" wrote one observer who visited the compound in 1937, "indicates a place where we are being severely tested as to whether we will serve God or Baal."[99]

Houteff, like other doomsayers, was convinced that the return of the Jewish people to their ancient homeland was a precondition to the Second Coming, and he called his followers "Davidians" in anticipation of the restoration of the throne of King David. To keep them in "a state of perpetual readiness for the End," he ordered that a clock in the headquarters of the Davidians at Mount Carmel be fixed at eleven o'clock "as a reminder that time was nearing its conclusion."[100] Thus roused to an unremitting state of "psychological imminence," Houteff and the rest of the Davidians waited for the world to end on time.

Houteff, of course, did not live to see any of the remarkable events that he was able to discern in the coded passages of the Bible. Upon his death in 1955, the community shattered into contending factions, and the one that ended up in possession of the Waco property called itself the Branch Davidians. On April 22, 1959, they gathered at Mount Carmel to witness the fulfillment of a new prophecy by Houteff's widow, Florence: "the faithful would be slaughtered, resurrected and carried up to heaven." A journalist who covered the spectacle reported on the "pitiful" display of disappointment by those who found themselves still alive and well at the end of the day. "Of the thousand there, more or less, only one person was relieved," he wrote. "Me."[101]

By the mid-1980s, Mount Carmel was very nearly moribund, but the Branch Davidians were reinvigorated by the arrival of a charismatic young man called Vernon Howell, a "semi-literate rock guitarist with fantastically detailed knowledge of the Bible and an overwhelming urge to uncover its secrets."[102] Howell was blessed with a glib tongue, a lively sense of humor, and "a gift for self-parody."[103] Indeed, he slyly called himself a "sinful messiah," and he recruited a brood of "wives" out of a self-proclaimed duty to sire as many children as possible.[104] As he rose to the leadership of the Branch Davidians, he acknowledged his new role by taking a new name— David Koresh.

Ω

The name that Vernon Howell chose for himself is dense with biblical meanings. The first name, of course, was meant to remind the Branch Davidians of the biblical king of Israel whose blood is said to have flowed in the veins of Jesus: "Lo, the Lion of the tribe of Judah, the Root of David," writes the author of Revelation, "has conquered, so that he can open the scroll and its seven seals."[105] And "Koresh" is the Hebrew name of the Persian emperor, Cyrus, who permitted the exiled Jews to return to Judea and rebuild the Temple in Jerusalem, thereby earning for himself the biblical title of "Messiah." Thus did Vernon Howell make a coded claim to his own messiahship.

Like Houteff, David Koresh was convinced that he alone was capable of retrieving the hidden secrets of the Bible, especially the meaning of the seven seals of Revelation. Like Jan Bockelson, he prescribed a strict code of sexual morality that applied to everyone but himself, and he openly snacked on forbidden foods like ice cream and candy while his followers were confined to a vegetarian diet "whose rules about food combination changed frequently." Like Father Miller, he engaged in the dangerous practice of date setting. The Tribulation, Koresh predicted, would begin in 1995, exactly ten years after his "coronation" as leader of the Branch Davidians.[106] And, like the author of Revelation, he insisted that he had been "taken up into the heavens by angelic beings," which Koresh described as "a 'spaceship' that 'travels by light, the refraction of light.'"[107]

Koresh was convinced that the world was witnessing the fulfillment of the prophecies that are expressed in Revelation as the breaking of the seven seals. He understood his own calling to the leadership of the Branch Davidians as the prophecy of the first seal: "And I saw, and behold a white horse: and he that sat on him had a bow; and a crown was given unto him: and he went forth conquering, and to conquer."[108] By 1992, Koresh had come to believe that one of the spookiest and most unsettling prophecies in the book of Revelation, the opening of the fifth seal, was imminent:

And when he had opened the fifth seal, I saw under the altar
the souls of them that were slain for the word of God,
and for the testimony which they held:
And they cried with a loud voice, saying, How long, O Lord,
holy and true, dost thou not judge and avenge our blood
on them that dwell on the earth?[109]

David Koresh might well have lived out his life in obscurity as a self-appointed "prophet" if he had not also embarked on a fateful plan to arm the Davidians with automatic weapons. He had already amassed an arsenal, and now he began to purchase the kits that would enable him to convert a cache of semiautomatic rifles into weapons with a far greater rate of fire. That's why agents of the U.S. Bureau of Alcohol, Tobacco and Firearms began to take an active interest in what was happening inside the compound at Mount Carmel. On February 23, 1993, federal agents launched an abortive raid, the beginning of a siege that lasted fifty-one days and ended only with a final conflagration that burned Mount Carmel to the ground and cost the lives of more than eighty Branch Davidians, including Koresh himself.

At one point during the siege, the FBI was given some curious but insightful advice by a pair of professors of religion who insisted that a close reading of Revelation held the key to ending the standoff with the heavily armed Davidians. Koresh was apparently convinced that the Davidians were the ones destined to be "slain for the word of God" when, according to Revelation, the fifth seal is broken. But the two scholars sought to persuade Koresh, by means of a radio broadcast, that he should read and heed the very next line in the book of Revelation: "And it was said unto them, that they should rest yet for a little season."[110] If Koresh could be convinced that "God intended the 'little' season to last until after the end of the siege, giving him time to stand trial and then resume a worldwide ministry," explains Damian Thompson, "then the standoff would end peacefully."[111]

FBI negotiators, in fact, took the advice seriously enough to play a tape of the radio broadcast over the telephone for Koresh, and he reportedly agreed to abandon his stronghold at Mount Carmel once he had composed his own treatise on the meaning of the seven seals. But the FBI was not willing to wait long enough for Koresh, who was capable of sermonizing at extraordinary length, to complete his latest exegesis. "[T]hey were unfamiliar with religion's ability to drive human behaviour to the point of sacrificing all other loyalties," explains Thompson, writing of an era when the world did not yet fully understand what motivates suicide bombers.[112]

The role of Revelation in the siege of Mount Carmel was mostly overlooked at the time it was taking place, and entirely forgotten thereafter. The whole sorry affair has been written off as an unfortunate encounter between overeager law-enforcement agents and overzealous religious cranks, all of whom were spoiling for a shoot-out. But the tragedy would never have taken place—and the Branch Davidians would not have come into existence at all—but for the strange power of the apocalyptic idea. The book of Revelation carries some "dangerous baggage," as we have seen already and will see again, and even the brightest and shiniest dreams of a new heaven and a new earth have a dark side.

Consider, for example, the remarkable media phenomenon known as the Left Behind series, which exploded into American popular culture even as the ugly memories of Waco were beginning to fade away.

When Tim LaHaye published a tract titled *The Beginning of the End* in 1972, he was yet another hard-preaching doomsayer who urgently sought to persuade his readers that the end of the world was nigh. Indeed, he offered a strong dose of dispensational premillennialism that differed not at all from what John Nelson Darby or Father Miller preached in their own day. "[W]e could well be the generation that sees the culmination of the ages and the ushering in of the Kingdom of Christ," he writes. "Certainly we have more historical evidence for such a possibility than any generation of Christians in almost 2,000 years. In fact, I believe the Bible teaches that we are already living in the beginning of the end."[113]

By 1995, however, LaHaye put himself in a very different place on the cultural landscape when he penned (with coauthor Jerry B. Jenkins) a slick apocalyptic thriller titled *Left Behind*. The message is exactly the same, but the medium is wholly different. Styled as a contemporary potboiler, *Left Behind* features the stock characters, exotic settings, and fast-paced plot that we would expect to find in a best seller by Robert Ludlum. Aside from the fact that *Left Behind* was published by Tyndale House, a leading publisher of fundamentalist Christian titles, nothing on the front or back cover reveals that it is actually a thinly disguised theological tract. But the very first passage slyly introduces the reader to the doctrine of the Rapture when the hero, a commercial airline pilot called Rayford Steele, discovers that half of the passengers on his Boeing 747 have somehow exited the aircraft in midflight.

"I'm not crazy! See for yourself!" screams a distraught flight attendant. "All over the plane, people have disappeared."

"It's a joke. They're hiding, trying to—"

"Ray! Their shoes, their socks, their clothes, everything was left behind. These people are gone!"[114]

Thus began a sensationally successful media enterprise that demonstrates the power of the apocalyptic idea in its purest and simplest form. The Left Behind series, a protracted account of the Tribulation and the antics of the Antichrist, spawned not merely a string of novels but a multimedia empire, including books, comics, newsletters, audios, videos, and a Web site called "The Left Behind Prophecy Club." Significantly, the publisher spun off a separate series especially for young readers, titled *Left Behind: The Kids,* which now consists of an additional forty titles. While Hal Lindsey was hailed as the best-selling author of the 1970s for selling 20 million copies of *The Late Great Planet Earth,* the Left Behind series has reportedly sold more than 50 million copies since the first title was published in 1995. And the end—surely to the disappointment of its authors—is nowhere in sight.

Indeed, LaHaye's motives in repurposing Revelation as a thriller are not merely mercenary. Before he took up his new calling as a best-selling novelist, LaHaye enjoyed a long and active career as a pastor and an educator, a televangelist and a leading figure in Christian politics. LaHaye is credited by Jerry Falwell as "the motivation behind the birth of the Religious Right,"[115] and he served as cochairman of the failed presidential campaign of conservative Republican Jack Kemp, at least until he was asked to resign after he was quoted as calling Roman Catholicism "a false religion."[116]

Aside from the Left Behind series, LaHaye's fifty books include tracts that condemn the United Nations, gay sexuality, "secular humanism," and various other bogeymen of Christian fundamentalism. "He's basically provided an agenda for conservatives on a range of issues from abortion and pornography to creationism, prayer in schools, and public education as a hotbed of secularism and liberalism," according to Paul Boyer.[117] And LaHaye himself readily acknowledges that the Left Behind series is a yet another weapon in the struggle for the hearts and minds of his fellow Americans.

"We are in a cultural war in this country, and there are two world-views—one built on the writings of man and one on the writing of God," LaHaye explained to one interviewer. "Those two views of what is going to help America and the world are 180 degrees in opposition."[118]

That's exactly why the books in the Left Behind series embrace the same dualistic theology—and the same revenge-seeking rhetoric—that burn so hotly in the book of Revelation. All of the complexities of the modern world are swept away and replaced by the simple conflict between God and Satan—another borrowing from the book of Revelation. As the Tribulation begins, according to the plot line of the Left Behind series, a handful of Christians who missed out on the Rapture are inspired to join the struggle against the Antichrist, who is depicted as a slick Jewish politician with headquarters in modern Iraq, the site of ancient Babylon.

"They promote conspiracy theories; they demonize proponents of arms control, ecumenicalism, abortion rights and everyone else disliked by the Christian right," complains Gershom Gorenberg in a review of the Left Behind series that appeared in the *American Prospect*.[119] "Their anti-Jewishness is exceeded only by their anti-Catholicism. Most basically, they reject the very idea of open, democratic debate. In the world of Left Behind, there exists a single truth, based on a purportedly literal reading of Scripture; anyone who disagrees with that truth is deceived or evil."[120]

Not coincidentally, the Left Behind series peaked at the very moment when the Western world awakened to the new peril that had replaced the "evil empire" of the Reagan era—the challenge of militant Islam and, especially, the spectacle of religious terrorism on an unprecedented scale. Suddenly, everything old was new again; after all, the prophet Muhammad had been seen as a candidate for the Antichrist by the Christian world more than a thousand years before the Bolshevik Revolution. And when America went to war against Iraq, the struggle that George W. Bush called a "clash of ideologies" could be readily seen, yet again, as the war between the Lamb and the Beast.

Ω

By the time George W. Bush put himself in pursuit of the presidency, in fact, the bonding of politics and religion in America was nearly complete. Converted to born-again Christianity by Billy Graham after a drunken weekend at the Bush family compound in 1985, he had come to rely on the fundamentalist voting bloc as his core constituency. When asked during a debate among Republican presidential candidates in 1999 to cite his favorite political philosopher, for example, he answered "Christ," and went on to explain: "When you turn your heart and your life over to Christ, when you accept Christ as the Savior, it changes your heart and changes your life."[121] And, once he reached the White House in 2001, Bush promptly launched a "faith-based initiative" that funded the social-welfare programs of various religious organizations.

"The nation's founders, smarting still from the punitive pieties of Europe's state religions, were adamant about erecting a wall between organized religion and political authority," wrote journalist Ron Suskind in the *New York Times*. "But, suddenly, that seems like a long time ago. George W. Bush ... has steadily, inexorably, changed the office itself. He has created the faith-based presidency."[122]

Bush is not given to making apocalyptic pronouncements of the kind that fell so readily from the lips of Ronald Reagan. He prefers the phrase "cultural change" to "culture war."[123] Bush, however, is plainspoken about what he sees as the targets of "culture change," including abortion, gay marriage, embryonic stem-cell research, and the constitutional ban on prayer in public schools. In fact, he adopts a strikingly warlike tone in describing his self-appointed mission: "So the faith-based initiative recognizes that there is an army of compassion that needs to be nurtured, rallied, called forth, and funded," he explained during an interview with representatives of various religious publications, "without causing the army to have to lose the reason it's an army in the first place.[124]

If Bush does not speak in the familiar vocabulary of apocalyptic fundamentalism, it is mostly because a new and updated "language arsenal" has been deployed in contemporary America. What was once called "creationism," for example, is now known as "intelligent design"—a code phrase that means essentially the same thing—and Bush has advocated that both "intelligent design" and the scientific theory of evolution ought to be taught in public schools. What doctors call "end-of-life care" is now condemned as "euthanasia," and Bush has called for a national commitment to "a culture of life, where all Americans are welcomed and valued and protected, especially those who live at the mercy of others."

The fact that Bush is *not* a Bible thumper is itself a cause for concern among observers on both sides of the culture war precisely because they suspect that he is only concealing his true beliefs. "The nation's executive mansion is currently honeycombed with prayer groups and Bible study cells, like a white monastery," wrote historian and biographer Garry Wills in the *New York Times*. "A sly dig there is 'Missed you at Bible study.'"[125] Bush, as far as we know, does not display the placard that could be seen in the office of former Republican congressman Tom DeLay—"This Could Be the Day!"[126]—but the unspoken suspicion among some of Bush's critics is that he may secretly share the same urgent expectation.

Ironically, such suspicions are mirrored among Bush's adversaries on the ragged edge of Christian fundamentalism. Bush *père,* for example, may have boasted of being a born-again Christian, but his insider status at the United Nations, the Central Intelligence Agency, and the Trilateral Commission only confirmed the worst fears of the conspiracy theorists. And when Bush *fils* came along, the fact that both father and son had been members of Skull and Bones, a club for undergraduates at Yale that is often called a "secret society," took on satanic meanings. "Indeed, it may be that men of goodwill such as Woodrow Wilson, Jimmy Carter, and George Bush," writes Pat Robertson in *The New World Order,* "are in reality unknowingly and unwittingly carrying out the mission and mouthing the phrases of a tightly knit cabal whose goal is nothing less than a new order for the human race under the domination of Lucifer and his followers."[127]

Any politician who embraces the apocalyptic idea, whether openly or secretly, is treading on the same trap door that has opened under the feet of presidents like George Bush, both father and son. "Millennarian movements cannot help but fall into conspiracy thinking, for they rigorously divide the world into the good and evil, the saved and the damned," explains political scientist Michael Barkun. "Evil constitutes an ever-present threat. Only the final consummation of history will remove it."[128] But the question of whether one is good or evil, saved or damned, is wholly in the eye of the beholder, as both of the Bushes have discovered.

Ω

Today, some twenty centuries after the book of Revelation first appeared in our tormented world, the words of Jerome are even more appropriate than when he first uttered them in the fourth century: "Revelation has as many mysteries as it has words."[129] To which we might add: and as many dangers, too.

To be sure, some readers understand the book of Revelation as a stirring manifesto of freedom and a call to self-liberation in the here and now. "Martin Luther King Jr.'s *Letter from a Birmingham Jail,* for instance, reflects experiences and hopes similar to the theology of Revelation," insists Catholic scholar Elizabeth Schüssler Fiorenza, a feminist theologian who sees "a glimpse of the new Jerusalem" in the resonant phrase of King's 1963 sermon at the Lincoln Memorial, "I have a dream."[130] And poet and radical priest Daniel Berrigan, after being arrested for digging a grave on the White House lawn as an act of political protest, was inspired to write a commentary of his own on Revelation in a jail cell in Washington, D.C. Father Berrigan, too, urges us to regard Revelation as a liberating rather than a fearful and hateful text.

"The book of Revelation ought to be burned, it is positively subversive!" he exults in *Nightmare of God,* striking a note of sarcasm. "The corporate state wastes the earth, dislocates minds, corrupts all areas of science, in its expanding military and economic adventurism—behold the Rome of Revelation. Behold also America!"[131]

Other readers elevate the book of Revelation to a still loftier and more ethereal plane. Theologian Jacques Ellul, for example, has been credited with a wholly redemptive reading of Revelation that purges the text of all its terror: "Rather than announcing the catastrophic end of history as our fate," explains Darrell J. Fasching, a religious scholar who specializes in the study of religion and violence, "the Apocalypse is, he argues, the revelation of God's freedom at work in history as mediated by radical human hope." When contrasted with such refined and elegant readings of Revelation, the crass apocalyptic speculation on display in Hal Lindsey's writings, according to Fasching, "is nothing short of obscene."[132]

"[Hal Lindsey] engages in a form of scriptural exegesis that Augustine once appropriately condemned as *fantastica fornicatio,*" writes Fasching in *The Ethical Challenge of Auschwitz and Hirsoshima,* "which might be politely translated 'mental masturbation,' or less politely as 'fucking the sacred symbols.'"[133]

What's at stake in the reading of Revelation, however, is far more than a matter of mental masturbation. The intentionally provocative text, as we have seen, is capable of moving some men and women to madness, some to acts of violence, and some to both at once. Perhaps it was meant to do so. "It is hard to know whether gloomy speculations with the apocalypse represent real fear of its occurrence or a kind of perverse fascination with it," observes Michael Barkun in *Disaster and the Millennium.* "It may, on the other hand, serve in some subtle fashion as a self-fulfilling prophecy which drags in train the very dreaded events themselves."[134] No better explanation has been offered for the malign influence of Revelation on a man like David Koresh and the little apocalypse that took place in Waco.

That's why some readers recoil in horror at the scenes of carnage that leave Revelation with such a bitter and even toxic aftertaste. "[T]here is no other document in either the Old or New Testament so inhuman, so spiritually irresponsible," writes Jewish biblical scholar and translator Robert Alter, a discerning critic who has extracted new and illuminating insights from the ancient text. "There is no room for real people in apocalypses, for when a writer chooses to see men as huddled masses waiting to be thrown into sulphurous pits, he hardly needs to look at individual faces...."[135] And the very phrase that Alter chooses to describe what he sees in the book of Revelation—"huddled masses waiting to be thrown into pits"—is surely meant to remind us of Babi Yar and the other killing fields of the Holocaust.

The linkage between Revelation and the Holocaust, in fact, has been noticed by more than one modern reader. The apocalyptic idea, stripped of its biblical trappings and expressed in a wholly new vocabulary, was embraced by both fascists and Marxists in the mid–twentieth century. Hitler and Stalin, for example, were both true believers who convinced themselves that they were ordained to create a paradise on earth by ruthlessly destroying the old order and building a new one in its place. And so, as unsettling as it may be to pious Jews and Christians, some revisionists draw a line that runs from the very first apocalyptic true believers in the Judeo-Christian tradition—the readers and hearers of Daniel and Revelation—to the mass murderers who targeted the Jewish people during the Holocaust.

"It is a grotesque irony that Nazism should have unconsciously adopted a structure of belief partly developed, though not necessarily invented, by Jews," argues Damian Thompson. "There can be little doubt that the thousand-year reign of the saints lies behind the vision of a thousand-year Reich; but a far more important influence on the Nazis was Revelation's portrayal of the Antichrist—an enemy so resilient that he can be defeated only in a cosmic war."[136]

The apocalyptic idea, in fact, has been blamed for both of the horrors that have come to symbolize the human potential for catastrophic violence in the modern world—the murder of 6 million Jewish men, women, and children during the Holocaust, and the deaths of several hundred thousand Japanese men, women, and children when one atomic bomb was dropped on Hiroshima and a second bomb was dropped on Nagasaki in what turned out to be the last days of World War II. The victims were wholly innocent of any wrongdoing. Yet once we come to regard any adversary as a satanic beast rather than a fellow human being—as Revelation plainly teaches us to do—then killing can be seen as a justifiable and even a sanctified act of vengeance.

The apocalyptic idea and its dangerous baggage are not confined to the Judeo-Christian tradition. "The Hour is coming," goes one verse of the Koran, which describes a stalking beast and various "cosmic cataclysms"— "the rolling up of the sun, the darkening of the stars and the movement of the mountains, the splitting of the sky, and the inundation of the seas"—as signs of the day of resurrection "when the tombs are overthrown." The Koranic version of the end-times, according to Saïd Amir Arjomand, a scholar specializing in the history and sociology of Islam, may have been specifically inspired by the vision of the sixth seal in the book of Revelation.[137]

Whether it originates in Islam, Christianity, or Judaism, however, the apocalyptic imagination has always moved some men and women to act out their revenge fantasies by taking the lives of their fellow human beings. Osama bin Laden alerted the world to his own homicidal intentions when he recited a traditional saying attributed to Muhammad during an interview that took place two years before horrors of 9/11: "Judgment day shall not come," goes the hadith that bin Laden quoted, "until the Muslims fight the Jews, where the Jews will hide behind the trees and stones, and the tree and the stone will speak and say, 'Muslim, behind me is a Jew. Come and kill him.'"[138]

Here, then, is yet another example of the dark side of the apocalyptic idea—the fear and loathing of the "other," and the insistence that the "other" must convert or die. The fact that the bloodthirsty tale was told by Osama bin Laden is chilling, of course, but the same idea can be teased out of both Jewish and Christian apocalyptic tradition. Indeed, Jerry Falwell was embracing the same hateful notion when he wondered out loud whether God had permitted the terrorists to carry out their attacks on 9/11 in order to punish America for its unforgivably easygoing attitude toward pagans, abortionists, feminists, gays, lesbians, the ACLU and the People for the American Way.[139]

"Mass movements can rise and spread without belief in a god," observed longshoreman and folk philosopher Eric Hoffer (1902–1983) during the most anxious days of the Communist witch hunts of the McCarthy era, "but never without belief in a devil."[140]

The book of Revelation, as we have seen, insists that humankind has always been confronted with a simple choice—good or evil, the Lamb or the Beast, God or Satan, and the wrong choice is punishable not merely by death but by eternal damnation. Like other expressions of religious true belief, which looks on the remarkable diversity of human faith and practice and declares all but one as error, sin, and crime, the apocalyptic idea may be hardwired into the human imagination. But the long, strange, and ultimately tragic history of the book of Revelation—the history of a delusion—proves that it is always a cruel idea and sometimes a deadly one.

$$\Omega$$

Not every apocalyptic cult, of course, expresses itself in the familiar words and phrases of Revelation. The so-called Ghost Dance movement, which arose among the Native American tribes on the western frontier in the late nineteenth century, focused on a home-grown version of the millennial kingdom: "The spirits of the dead would return, the buffalo would once again be plentiful, and the earth would tremble."[141] At its peak, the self-styled prophet of the Ghost Dancers, a messianic figure called Wovoka, taught his followers that their exertions would inspire the ancestral spirits to drive off the white settlers who threatened the Native Americans with both cultural and physical extermination.

Even the Ghost Dancers, however, owed something to the apocalyptic and messianic traditions of Judaism and Christianity, which they apparently picked up from the preaching of Christian missionaries and then translated into their own spiritual vernacular. And, notably, the Ghost Dancers discovered for themselves the peril that has always threatened apocalyptic preachers and their followers, including the Maccabees, the Zealots, and the early Christians. The military authorities who were charged with maintaining law and order on the frontier regarded the Ghost Dance movement as a spooky and dangerous form of insurrection, and they resolved to wipe it out in a series of punitive expeditions that culminated in the notorious massacre at Wounded Knee in 1890.

The Ghost Dancers, in fact, fit neatly into the theoretical model that has been applied to Daniel, Revelation, and the other ancient apocalyptic writings. The promise that the end of the world is nigh, as we have seen, is supposedly intended to "hearten the faithful in the time of affliction and persecution" and to console "those engulfed by suffering and overwhelmed by dread."[142] And these words accurately describe the predicament of the Native Americans who performed the Ghost Dance to drive off the white settlers who were conducting not merely a culture war but a war of extermination. Indeed, the Ghost Dancers are far more appropriately described as the victims of affliction and persecution than, say, the Puritans, the Millerites, or the Christian fundamentalists of our own era, all of whom have been privileged to live their lives in perfect comfort and safety.

That is why scholars have found it necessary to fine-tune the apocalyptic model by pointing out that persecution may be entirely in the mind of the beholder. "Whatever his actual economic situation," writes Adela Yarbro Collins about the man who wrote the book of Revelation, "the author or editor seems to *feel* that he is a victim of injustice."[143] Or the self-imagined victim seethes with resentment toward someone he regards as better off than himself, a phenomenon that scholars call "relative deprivation" or "status anxiety."[144] Or the victim is unsettled by some cultural or political change that her zealous true belief will not allow her to accommodate, a description that probably best describes the first readers and hearers of Revelation as well as the otherwise comfortable Christian fundamentalists in modern America. And sometimes the whole apocalyptic phenomenon is more nearly a psychiatric disorder than a spiritual calling.

"Classic millenarians, from self-flagellating medieval peasants to Sioux Ghost Dancers," quips Damian Thomson, "are often people who, if not clinically mad, have reached what George Rosen has called 'the wilder shores of sanity.'"[145]

Thus, for example, the members of the Heaven's Gate cult in Southern California came to believe that a spacecraft was hidden in the tail of the Hale-Bopp comet, full of aliens on a mission to destroy the world, and they convinced themselves that they would be able to escape the apocalypse by elevating themselves to a higher plane. Thirty-nine members of the cult packed their bags, put on new tennis shoes, stuffed their pockets with five-dollar bills and rolls of quarters, and then supped on applesauce spiced with phenobarbital before putting plastic bags over their heads to ensure death by suffocation if the self-administered poison did not kill them first. Their source of inspiration was science fiction rather than scripture, of course, but Heaven's Gate, too, demonstrates the terrible power of the apocalyptic idea (and the mass media) on a disordered mind.

"We watch a lot of *Star Trek,* a lot of *Star Wars,*" says one cheerful member of Heaven's Gate in the videotaped messages that they left behind in 1997. "It's time to put into practice what we have learned."[146]

Now and then, it is simply impossible to make any meaningful distinction between apocalyptic vision, psychological dysfunction, and mass murder. The Japanese cult called Aum Shinrikyo, for example, embraces a strange blend of Buddhist, Hindu, and Taoist beliefs along with "predictions from the book of Revelation and a dose of anti-Semitic conspiracy theory."[147] The founder, Shoko Asahara, reportedly taught his followers that Armageddon was fast approaching, and ordered them to assemble their own arsenal of chemical and biological weapons. In 1995, they put their weaponry to a practical test by setting off canisters of sarin nerve gas in the subways of Tokyo, thus taking the lives of twelve victims and injuring thousands more.

"For ye have the poor with you always," says Jesus, and he might have said the same of the doomsayers.[148] Most of them will remain invisible to the rest of us, caught up in their own complicated and impenetrable fancies about the coded meanings of the Bible. Many others will continue to advertise their own visions in the public prints, on radio and television, and over the Internet; a Google search for "Book of Revelation," for example, retrieves more than 1.6 million "hits." And a few, of course, will always succeed in claiming the attention of the whole world, if only for fifteen minutes, because of some ghastly act, whether suicidal or homicidal, that is meant to hasten the end of the world.

Ω

I know the ending, to paraphrase the credo that appears in the very first sentence of the book you are now reading, but whether or not God wins is somewhat less certain nowadays.

The world will end, or so are assured with absolute certainty by the findings of modern astrophysics. One day, sooner or later, the sun will run out of hydrogen, its primary solar fuel. When it does, the sun will turn into what scientists call a red giant as its superheated atmosphere expands across open space to embrace the near planets, including our own, thereby incinerating every living thing on earth. At that moment, perhaps 5 billion years from now, history as we understand it will be over and done. Then the sun will turn into a white dwarf, cold and dark, but human beings will be long gone from the cosmos.

The sure and precise knowledge of when and how the world will end can be terrifying to contemplate, as I mused out loud to a friend and colleague of mine, science writer K. C. Cole, on an otherwise bright and cheerful day in sunny Southern California.

"Oh, I can tell you about much worse things," remarked Cole with a laugh, "that could happen much sooner."[149]

With the insistent truth telling that is the stock-in-trade of science, Cole reminded me of the whole catalog of God-less apocalypses that are worth worrying about. If we survive the accidental or intentional use of the tens of thousands of chemical, biological, and nuclear weapons that are stockpiled in arsenals around the world, we might still suffer the catastrophic consequences of pandemic disease, climatic catastrophe, or overpopulation of Malthusian proportions. And even if we manage to survive all of these potential doomsdays, some stray asteroid might still collide with our little planet and put an end to life on earth while the solar furnace is still fully functional.

Scientific doomsaying changes nothing at all for apocalyptic true believers. The end of the world, whether caused by accident, error, disaster, or the slow but sure process of solar combustion, is still seen as the fulfillment of the divine prophecies that are described in Revelation. If God is capable of creating the earth, the argument goes, then God is also capable of destroying it, whether by means of nuclear weaponry, infectious disease, global warming, or the exhaustion of the solar fuel that allows the sun to shine. That's exactly why the Christian scriptures begin with Genesis and end with Revelation, and that's what the Lamb of God means when he is quoted as saying "I am the Alpha and the Omega, the beginning and the ending."[150]

But any contemplation of the end-times, whether it is rooted in religion or science or some combination of the two, poses the same moral risk that has always confronted human beings who seek a revelation in the original sense of unveiling what is concealed. The apocalyptic texts of both Judaism and Christianity tempt us to occupy ourselves with fantasies of revenge and redemption while watching for signs and wonders that augur the end of the world. And more than a few readers and hearers of these texts have taken it upon themselves to do God's work of revenge and to hasten the end-times. But the most exalted and exalting passages of the Bible, both in its Jewish and Christian redactions, plainly instruct us to put aside the pursuit of "secret things" and call on us to answer the urgent needs of the hungry and the homeless, the prisoner and the patient, all in the here and now.[151]

Some true believers, as we have seen throughout the history of the end of the world, are willing to stand and fight over the right way and the wrong way to understand the Bible. The rest of us, however, still regard ourselves as free to choose how to read the scriptures or, for that matter, whether to read them at all. But the choice is not without consequences. That is one way to understand what the biblical author means by the oft-quoted and highly provocative words of Deuteronomy: "I have set before thee life and death, the blessing and the curse, therefore choose life."[152]

Some Bible readers, of course, are instructed by the book of Revelation to read these words as a death sentence pronounced by God himself against men and women who make the wrong choice. Others read the same words as a challenge to "do justice, and to love goodness, and to walk modestly with your God," according to Micah, and they ignore the apocalyptic preachers in favor of the biblical prophets who, like Isaiah, urge us "to share your bread with the hungry, and to take the wretched poor into your home."[153] The fact that both teachings—and many others, too—can be extracted from between the covers of the same book is what has always made Bible reading such a crazy-making experience.

Nowadays, of course, the apocalyptic idea works its powerful magic on plenty of people who never open a Bible, and for them, God is no longer necessary or sufficient to solve the mystery of when and how the end will come. On one point, however, we all seem to agree: somehow and someday, sooner or later, whether by the hand of God or the hand of humankind or the mindless workings of the cosmos, the earth itself and all living things upon it will pass away. Ultimately, we are compelled to decide for ourselves how to make sense of our lives as we continue to wait—as men and women have always waited—for the world to end on time.

Appendix

The Book of Revelation

AUTHOR'S NOTE: The entire text of the book of Revelation, exactly as it appears in the King James Version with conventional divisions into chapters and verses, is reproduced here. For the convenience of the reader, I have added headings to indicate major themes, figures, and incidents.

CHAPTER 1

[Things Which Must Shortly Come to Pass]

1:1 The Revelation of Jesus Christ, which God gave unto him, to shew unto his servants things which must shortly come to pass; and he sent and signified it by his angel unto his servant John:

1:2 Who bare record of the word of God, and of the testimony of Jesus Christ, and of all things that he saw.

1:3 Blessed is he that readeth, and they that hear the words of this prophecy, and keep those things which are written therein: for the time is at hand.

[John's Greetings to the Seven Churches of Asia]

1:4 John to the seven churches which are in Asia: Grace be unto you, and peace, from him which is, and which was, and which is to come; and from the seven Spirits which are before his throne;

1:5 And from Jesus Christ, who is the faithful witness, and the first begotten of the dead, and the prince of the kings of the earth. Unto him that loved us, and washed us from our sins in his own blood,

1:6 And hath made us kings and priests unto God and his Father; to him be glory and dominion for ever and ever. Amen.

1:7 Behold, he cometh with clouds; and every eye shall see him, and they also which pierced him: and all kindreds of the earth shall wail because of him. Even so, Amen.

[I am Alpha and Omega]

1:8 I am Alpha and Omega, the beginning and the ending, saith the Lord, which is, and which was, and which is to come, the Almighty.

1:9 I John, who also am your brother, and companion in tribulation, and in the kingdom and patience of Jesus Christ, was in the isle that is called Patmos, for the word of God, and for the testimony of Jesus Christ.

1:10 I was in the Spirit on the Lord's day, and heard behind me a great voice, as of a trumpet,

1:11 Saying, I am Alpha and Omega, the first and the last: and, What thou seest, write in a book, and send it unto the seven churches which are in Asia; unto Ephesus, and unto Smyrna, and unto Pergamos, and unto Thyatira, and unto Sardis, and unto Philadelphia, and unto Laodicea.

[One like unto the Son of Man]

1:12 And I turned to see the voice that spake with me. And being turned, I saw seven golden candlesticks;

1:13 And in the midst of the seven candlesticks one like unto the Son of man, clothed with a garment down to the foot, and girt about the paps with a golden girdle.

1:14 His head and his hairs were white like wool, as white as snow; and his eyes were as a flame of fire;

1:15 And his feet like unto fine brass, as if they burned in a furnace; and his voice as the sound of many waters.

1:16 And he had in his right hand seven stars: and out of his mouth went a sharp two-edged sword: and his countenance was as the sun shineth in his strength.

1:17 And when I saw him, I fell at his feet as dead. And he laid his right hand upon me, saying unto me, Fear not; I am the first and the last:

1:18 I am he that liveth, and was dead; and, behold, I am alive for evermore, Amen; and have the keys of hell and of death.

1:19 Write the things which thou hast seen, and the things which are, and the things which shall be hereafter;

1:20 The mystery of the seven stars which thou sawest in my right hand, and the seven golden candlesticks. The seven stars are the angels of the seven churches: and the seven candlesticks which thou sawest are the seven churches.

CHAPTER 2

[Letter to the Church of Ephesus]

2:1 Unto the angel of the church of Ephesus write; These things saith he that holdeth the seven stars in his right hand, who walketh in the midst of the seven golden candlesticks;

2:2 I know thy works, and thy labour, and thy patience, and how thou canst not bear them which are evil: and thou hast tried them which say they are apostles, and are not, and hast found them liars:

2:3 And hast borne, and hast patience, and for my name's sake hast laboured, and hast not fainted.

2:4 Nevertheless I have somewhat against thee, because thou hast left thy first love.

2:5 Remember therefore from whence thou art fallen, and repent, and do the first works; or else I will come unto thee quickly, and will remove thy candlestick out of his place, except thou repent.

[The Nicolaitans]

2:6 But this thou hast, that thou hatest the deeds of the Nicolaitans, which I also hate.

2:7 He that hath an ear, let him hear what the Spirit saith unto the churches; To him that overcometh will I give to eat of the tree of life, which is in the midst of the paradise of God.

Letter to the Church in Smyrna

2:8 And unto the angel of the church in Smyrna write; These things saith the first and the last, which was dead, and is alive;

[The Synagogue of Satan]

2:9 I know thy works, and tribulation, and poverty, (but thou art rich) and I know the blasphemy of them which say they are Jews, and are not, but are the synagogue of Satan.

2:10 Fear none of those things which thou shalt suffer: behold, the devil shall cast some of you into prison, that ye may be tried; and ye shall have tribulation ten days: be thou faithful unto death, and I will give thee a crown of life.

2:11 He that hath an ear, let him hear what the Spirit saith unto the churches; He that overcometh shall not be hurt of the second death.

[Letter to the Church in Pergamos]

2:12 And to the angel of the church in Pergamos write; These things saith he which hath the sharp sword with two edges;

2:13 I know thy works, and where thou dwellest, even where Satan's seat is: and thou holdest fast my name, and hast not denied my faith, even in those days wherein Antipas was my faithful martyr, who was slain among you, where Satan dwelleth.

[Balaam]

2:14 But I have a few things against thee, because thou hast there them that hold the doctrine of Balaam, who taught Balac to cast a stumblingblock before the children of Israel, to eat things sacrificed unto idols, and to commit fornication.

2:15 So hast thou also them that hold the doctrine of the Nicolaitans, which thing I hate.

2:16 Repent; or else I will come unto thee quickly, and will fight against them with the sword of my mouth.

2:17 He that hath an ear, let him hear what the Spirit saith unto the churches; To him that overcometh will I give to eat of the hidden manna, and will give him a white stone, and in the stone a new name written, which no man knoweth saving he that receiveth it.

[Letter to the Church in Thyatira]

2:18 And unto the angel of the church in Thyatira write; These things saith the Son of God, who hath his eyes like unto a flame of fire, and his feet are like fine brass;

2:19 I know thy works, and charity, and service, and faith, and thy patience, and thy works; and the last to be more than the first.

[Jezebel]

2:20 Notwithstanding I have a few things against thee, because thou sufferest that woman Jezebel, which calleth herself a prophetess, to teach and to seduce my servants to commit fornication, and to eat things sacrificed unto idols.

2:21 And I gave her space to repent of her fornication; and she repented not.

2:22 Behold, I will cast her into a bed, and them that commit adultery with her into great tribulation, except they repent of their deeds.

2:23 And I will kill her children with death; and all the churches shall know that I am he which searcheth the reins and hearts: and I will give unto every one of you according to your works.

2:24 But unto you I say, and unto the rest in Thyatira, as many as have not this doctrine, and which have not known the depths of Satan, as they speak; I will put upon you none other burden.

2:25 But that which ye have already hold fast till I come.

2:26 And he that overcometh, and keepeth my works unto the end, to him will I give power over the nations:

2:27 And he shall rule them with a rod of iron; as the vessels of a potter shall they be broken to shivers: even as I received of my Father.

2:28 And I will give him the morning star.

2:29 He that hath an ear, let him hear what the Spirit saith unto the churches.

CHAPTER 3

[Letter to the Church in Sardis]

3:1 And unto the angel of the church in Sardis write; These things saith he that hath the seven Spirits of God, and the seven stars; I know thy works, that thou hast a name that thou livest, and art dead.

3:2 Be watchful, and strengthen the things which remain, that are ready to die: for I have not found thy works perfect before God.

3:3 Remember therefore how thou hast received and heard, and hold fast, and repent. If therefore thou shalt not watch, I will come on thee as a thief, and thou shalt not know what hour I will come upon thee.

3:4 Thou hast a few names even in Sardis which have not defiled their garments; and they shall walk with me in white: for they are worthy.

3:5 He that overcometh, the same shall be clothed in white raiment; and I will not blot out his name out of the book of life, but I will confess his name before my Father, and before his angels.

3:6 He that hath an ear, let him hear what the Spirit saith unto the churches.

[Letter to the Church in Philadelphia]

3:7 And to the angel of the church in Philadelphia write; These things saith he that is holy, he that is true, he that hath the key of David, he that openeth, and no man shutteth; and shutteth, and no man openeth;

3:8 I know thy works: behold, I have set before thee an open door, and no man can shut it: for thou hast a little strength, and hast kept my word, and hast not denied my name.

3:9 Behold, I will make them of the synagogue of Satan, which say they are Jews, and are not, but do lie; behold, I will make them to come and worship before thy feet, and to know that I have loved thee.

3:10 Because thou hast kept the word of my patience, I also will keep thee from the hour of temptation, which shall come upon all the world, to try them that dwell upon the earth.

3:11 Behold, I come quickly: hold that fast which thou hast, that no man take thy crown.

3:12 Him that overcometh will I make a pillar in the temple of my God, and he shall go no more out: and I will write upon him the name of my God, and the name of the city of my God, which is new Jerusalem, which cometh down out of heaven from my God: and I will write upon him my new name.

3:13 He that hath an ear, let him hear what the Spirit saith unto the churches.

[Letter to the Church in Laodicea]

3:14 And unto the angel of the church of the Laodiceans write; These things saith the Amen, the faithful and true witness, the beginning of the creation of God;

3:15 I know thy works, that thou art neither cold nor hot: I would thou wert cold or hot.

3:16 So then because thou art lukewarm, and neither cold nor hot, I will spue thee out of my mouth.

3:17 Because thou sayest, I am rich, and increased with goods, and have need of nothing; and knowest not that thou art wretched, and miserable, and poor, and blind, and naked:

3:18 I counsel thee to buy of me gold tried in the fire, that thou mayest be rich; and white raiment, that thou mayest be clothed, and that the shame of thy nakedness do not appear; and anoint thine eyes with eyesalve, that thou mayest see.

3:19 As many as I love, I rebuke and chasten: be zealous therefore, and repent.

3:20 Behold, I stand at the door, and knock: if any man hear my voice, and open the door, I will come in to him, and will sup with him, and he with me.

3:21 To him that overcometh will I grant to sit with me in my throne, even as I also overcame, and am set down with my Father in his throne.

3:22 He that hath an ear, let him hear what the Spirit saith unto the churches.

CHAPTER 4

[I Will Show Thee Things Which Must Be Hereafter]

4:1 After this I looked, and, behold, a door was opened in heaven: and the first voice which I heard was as it were of a trumpet talking with me; which said, Come up hither, and I will shew thee things which must be hereafter.

4:2 And immediately I was in the spirit: and, behold, a throne was set in heaven, and one sat on the throne.

4:3 And he that sat was to look upon like a jasper and a sardine stone: and there was a rainbow round about the throne, in sight like unto an emerald.

[Twenty-Four Elders]

4:4 And round about the throne were four and twenty seats: and upon the seats I saw four and twenty elders sitting, clothed in white raiment; and they had on their heads crowns of gold.

4:5 And out of the throne proceeded lightnings and thunderings and voices: and there were seven lamps of fire burning before the throne, which are the seven Spirits of God.

[Four Beasts]

4:6 And before the throne there was a sea of glass like unto crystal: and in the midst of the throne, and round about the throne, were four beasts full of eyes before and behind.

4:7 And the first beast was like a lion, and the second beast like a calf, and the third beast had a face as a man, and the fourth beast was like a flying eagle.

4:8 And the four beasts had each of them six wings about him; and they were full of eyes within: and they rest not day and night, saying, Holy, holy, holy, Lord God Almighty, which was, and is, and is to come.

4:9 And when those beasts give glory and honour and thanks to him that sat on the throne, who liveth for ever and ever,

4:10 The four and twenty elders fall down before him that sat on the throne, and worship him that liveth for ever and ever, and cast their crowns before the throne, saying,

4:11 Thou art worthy, O Lord, to receive glory and honour and power: for thou hast created all things, and for thy pleasure they are and were created.

CHAPTER 5

[A Book with Seven Seals]

5:1 And I saw in the right hand of him that sat on the throne a book written within and on the backside, sealed with seven seals.

5:2 And I saw a strong angel proclaiming with a loud voice, Who is worthy to open the book, and to loose the seals thereof?

5:3 And no man in heaven, nor in earth, neither under the earth, was able to open the book, neither to look thereon.

5:4 And I wept much, because no man was found worthy to open and to read the book, neither to look thereon.

[Behold, the Lion of the Tribe of Judah]

5:5 And one of the elders saith unto me, Weep not: behold, the Lion of the tribe of Judah, the Root of David, hath prevailed to open the book, and to loose the seven seals thereof.

[A Lamb As It Had Been Slain]

5:6 And I beheld, and, lo, in the midst of the throne and of the four beasts, and in the midst of the elders, stood a Lamb as it had been slain, having seven horns and seven eyes, which are the seven Spirits of God sent forth into all the earth.

5:7 And he came and took the book out of the right hand of him that sat upon the throne.

5:8 And when he had taken the book, the four beasts and four and twenty elders fell down before the Lamb, having every one of them harps, and golden vials full of odours, which are the prayers of saints.

5:9 And they sung a new song, saying, Thou art worthy to take the book, and to open the seals thereof: for thou wast slain, and hast redeemed us to God by thy blood out of every kindred, and tongue, and people, and nation;

5:10 And hast made us unto our God kings and priests: and we shall reign on the earth.

5:11 And I beheld, and I heard the voice of many angels round about the throne and the beasts and the elders: and the number of them was ten thousand times ten thousand, and thousands of thousands;

5:12 Saying with a loud voice, Worthy is the Lamb that was slain to receive power, and riches, and wisdom, and strength, and honour, and glory, and blessing.

5:13 And every creature which is in heaven, and on the earth, and under the earth, and such as are in the sea, and all that are in them, heard I saying, Blessing, and honour, and glory, and power, be unto him that sitteth upon the throne, and unto the Lamb for ever and ever.

5:14 And the four beasts said, Amen. And the four and twenty elders fell down and worshipped him that liveth for ever and ever.

CHAPTER 6

[The Opening of the Seven Seals]

6:1 And I saw when the Lamb opened one of the seals, and I heard, as it were the noise of thunder, one of the four beasts saying, Come and see.

[The Four Horsemen]

6:2 And I saw, and behold a white horse: and he that sat on him had a bow; and a crown was given unto him: and he went forth conquering, and to conquer.

6:3 And when he had opened the second seal, I heard the second beast say, Come and see.

6:4 And there went out another horse that was red: and power was given to him that sat thereon to take peace from the earth, and that they should kill one another: and there was given unto him a great sword.

6:5 And when he had opened the third seal, I heard the third beast say, Come and see. And I beheld, and lo a black horse; and he that sat on him had a pair of balances in his hand.

6:6 And I heard a voice in the midst of the four beasts say, A measure of wheat for a penny, and three measures of barley for a penny; and see thou hurt not the oil and the wine.

6:7 And when he had opened the fourth seal, I heard the voice of the fourth beast say, Come and see.

6:8 And I looked, and behold a pale horse: and his name that sat on him was Death, and Hell followed with him. And power was given unto them over the fourth part of the earth, to kill with sword, and with hunger, and with death, and with the beasts of the earth.

[The Souls Under the Altar]

6:9 And when he had opened the fifth seal, I saw under the altar the souls of them that were slain for the word of God, and for the testimony which they held:

6:10 And they cried with a loud voice, saying, How long, O Lord, holy and true, dost thou not judge and avenge our blood on them that dwell on the earth?

6:11 And white robes were given unto every one of them; and it was said unto them, that they should rest yet for a little season, until their fellow servants also and their brethren, that should be killed as they were, should be fulfilled.

6:12 And I beheld when he had opened the sixth seal, and, lo, there was a great earthquake; and the sun became black as sackcloth of hair, and the moon became as blood;

6:13 And the stars of heaven fell unto the earth, even as a fig tree casteth her untimely figs, when she is shaken of a mighty wind.

6:14 And the heaven departed as a scroll when it is rolled together; and every mountain and island were moved out of their places.

6:15 And the kings of the earth, and the great men, and the rich men, and the chief captains, and the mighty men, and every bondman, and every free man, hid themselves in the dens and in the rocks of the mountains;

6:16 And said to the mountains and rocks, Fall on us, and hide us from the face of him that sitteth on the throne, and from the wrath of the Lamb:

6:17 For the great day of his wrath is come; and who shall be able to stand?

CHAPTER 7

7:1 And after these things I saw four angels standing on the four corners of the earth, holding the four winds of the earth, that the wind should not blow on the earth, nor on the sea, nor on any tree.

7:2 And I saw another angel ascending from the east, having the seal of the living God: and he cried with a loud voice to the four angels, to whom it was given to hurt the earth and the sea,

7:3 Saying, Hurt not the earth, neither the sea, nor the trees, till we have sealed the servants of our God in their foreheads.

[The Sealing of 144,000 of the Tribes of Israel]

7:4 And I heard the number of them which were sealed: and there were sealed an hundred and forty and four thousand of all the tribes of the children of Israel.

7:5 Of the tribe of Judah were sealed twelve thousand. Of the tribe of Reuben were sealed twelve thousand. Of the tribe of Gad were sealed twelve thousand.

7:6 Of the tribe of Aser were sealed twelve thousand. Of the tribe of Nepthalim were sealed twelve thousand. Of the tribe of Manasses were sealed twelve thousand.

7:7 Of the tribe of Simeon were sealed twelve thousand. Of the tribe of Levi were sealed twelve thousand. Of the tribe of Issachar were sealed twelve thousand.

7:8 Of the tribe of Zabulon were sealed twelve thousand. Of the tribe of Joseph were sealed twelve thousand. Of the tribe of Benjamin were sealed twelve thousand.

7:9 After this I beheld, and, lo, a great multitude, which no man could number, of all nations, and kindreds, and people, and tongues, stood before the throne, and before the Lamb, clothed with white robes, and palms in their hands;

7:10 And cried with a loud voice, saying, Salvation to our God which sitteth upon the throne, and unto the Lamb.

7:11 And all the angels stood round about the throne, and about the elders and the four beasts, and fell before the throne on their faces, and worshipped God,

7:12 Saying, Amen: Blessing, and glory, and wisdom, and thanksgiving, and honour, and power, and might, be unto our God for ever and ever. Amen.

[Those Who Came Out of Great Tribulation]

7:13 And one of the elders answered, saying unto me, What are these which are arrayed in white robes? and whence came they?

7:14 And I said unto him, Sir, thou knowest. And he said to me, These are they which came out of great tribulation, and have washed their robes, and made them white in the blood of the Lamb.

7:15 Therefore are they before the throne of God, and serve him day and night in his temple: and he that sitteth on the throne shall dwell among them.

7:16 They shall hunger no more, neither thirst any more; neither shall the sun light on them, nor any heat.

7:17 For the Lamb which is in the midst of the throne shall feed them, and shall lead them unto living fountains of waters: and God shall wipe away all tears from their eyes.

CHAPTER 8

[The Seventh Seal and a Silence in Heaven]

8:1 And when he had opened the seventh seal, there was silence in heaven about the space of half an hour.

8:2 And I saw the seven angels which stood before God; and to them were given seven trumpets.

8:3 And another angel came and stood at the altar, having a golden censer; and there was given unto him much incense, that he should offer it with the prayers of all saints upon the golden altar which was before the throne.

8:4 And the smoke of the incense, which came with the prayers of the saints, ascended up before God out of the angel's hand.

8:5 And the angel took the censer, and filled it with fire of the altar, and cast it into the earth: and there were voices, and thunderings, and lightnings, and an earthquake.

[The Seven Trumpets]

8:6 And the seven angels which had the seven trumpets prepared themselves to sound.

8:7 The first angel sounded, and there followed hail and fire mingled with blood, and they were cast upon the earth: and the third part of trees was burnt up, and all green grass was burnt up.

8:8 And the second angel sounded, and as it were a great mountain burning with fire was cast into the sea: and the third part of the sea became blood;

8:9 And the third part of the creatures which were in the sea, and had life, died; and the third part of the ships were destroyed.

[A Star Called Wormwood]

8:10 And the third angel sounded, and there fell a great star from heaven, burning as it were a lamp, and it fell upon the third part of the rivers, and upon the fountains of waters;

8:11 And the name of the star is called Wormwood: and the third part of the waters became wormwood; and many men died of the waters, because they were made bitter.

8:12 And the fourth angel sounded, and the third part of the sun was smitten, and the third part of the moon, and the third part of the stars; so as the third part of them was darkened, and the day shone not for a third part of it, and the night likewise.

8:13 And I beheld, and heard an angel flying through the midst of heaven, saying with a loud voice, Woe, woe, woe, to the inhabiters of the earth by reason of the other voices of the trumpet of the three angels, which are yet to sound!

CHAPTER 9

[The Key to the Bottomless Pit]

9:1 And the fifth angel sounded, and I saw a star fall from heaven unto the earth: and to him was given the key of the bottomless pit.

9:2 And he opened the bottomless pit; and there arose a smoke out of the pit, as the smoke of a great furnace; and the sun and the air were darkened by reason of the smoke of the pit.

[The Plague of Locusts]

9:3 And there came out of the smoke locusts upon the earth: and unto them was given power, as the scorpions of the earth have power.

9:4 And it was commanded them that they should not hurt the grass of the earth, neither any green thing, neither any tree; but only those men which have not the seal of God in their foreheads.

9:5 And to them it was given that they should not kill them, but that they should be tormented five months: and their torment was as the torment of a scorpion, when he striketh a man.

9:6 And in those days shall men seek death, and shall not find it; and shall desire to die, and death shall flee from them.

9:7 And the shapes of the locusts were like unto horses prepared unto battle; and on their heads were as it were crowns like gold, and their faces were as the faces of men.

9:8 And they had hair as the hair of women, and their teeth were as the teeth of lions.

9:9 And they had breastplates, as it were breastplates of iron; and the sound of their wings was as the sound of chariots of many horses running to battle.

9:10 And they had tails like unto scorpions, and there were stings in their tails: and their power was to hurt men five months.

[The Angel of the Bottomless Pit]

9:11 And they had a king over them, which is the angel of the bottomless pit, whose name in the Hebrew tongue is Abaddon, but in the Greek tongue hath his name Apollyon.

9:12 One woe is past; and, behold, there come two woes more hereafter.

9:13 And the sixth angel sounded, and I heard a voice from the four horns of the golden altar which is before God,

9:14 Saying to the sixth angel which had the trumpet, Loose the four angels which are bound in the great river Euphrates.

9:15 And the four angels were loosed, which were prepared for an hour, and a day, and a month, and a year, for to slay the third part of men.

[The Army of Horsemen]

9:16 And the number of the army of the horsemen were two hundred thousand thousand: and I heard the number of them.

9:17 And thus I saw the horses in the vision, and them that sat on them, having breastplates of fire, and of jacinth, and brimstone: and the heads of the horses were as the heads of lions; and out of their mouths issued fire and smoke and brimstone.

9:18 By these three was the third part of men killed, by the fire, and by the smoke, and by the brimstone, which issued out of their mouths.

9:19 For their power is in their mouth, and in their tails: for their tails were like unto serpents, and had heads, and with them they do hurt.

9:20 And the rest of the men which were not killed by these plagues yet repented not of the works of their hands, that they should not worship devils, and idols of gold, and silver, and brass, and stone, and of wood: which neither can see, nor hear, nor walk:

9:21 Neither repented they of their murders, nor of their sorceries, nor of their fornication, nor of their thefts.

CHAPTER 10

[The Little Book]

10:1 And I saw another mighty angel come down from heaven, clothed with a cloud: and a rainbow was upon his head, and his face was as it were the sun, and his feet as pillars of fire:

10:2 And he had in his hand a little book open: and he set his right foot upon the sea, and his left foot on the earth,

10:3 And cried with a loud voice, as when a lion roareth: and when he had cried, seven thunders uttered their voices.

10:4 And when the seven thunders had uttered their voices, I was about to write: and I heard a voice from heaven saying unto me, Seal up those things which the seven thunders uttered, and write them not.

10:5 And the angel which I saw stand upon the sea and upon the earth lifted up his hand to heaven,

10:6 And sware by him that liveth for ever and ever, who created heaven, and the things that therein are, and the earth, and the things that therein are, and the sea, and the things which are therein, that there should be time no longer:

10:7 But in the days of the voice of the seventh angel, when he shall begin to sound, the mystery of God should be finished, as he hath declared to his servants the prophets.

10:8 And the voice which I heard from heaven spake unto me again, and said, Go and take the little book which is open in the hand of the angel which standeth upon the sea and upon the earth.

10:9 And I went unto the angel, and said unto him, Give me the little book. And he said unto me, Take it, and eat it up; and it shall make thy belly bitter, but it shall be in thy mouth sweet as honey.

10:10 And I took the little book out of the angel's hand, and ate it up; and it was in my mouth sweet as honey: and as soon as I had eaten it, my belly was bitter.

10:11 And he said unto me, Thou must prophesy again before many peoples, and nations, and tongues, and kings.

CHAPTER 11

[The Measurement of the Temple of God]

11:1 And there was given me a reed like unto a rod: and the angel stood, saying, Rise, and measure the temple of God, and the altar, and them that worship therein.

11:2 But the court which is without the temple leave out, and measure it not; for it is given unto the Gentiles: and the holy city shall they tread under foot forty and two months.

[The Two Witnesses]

11:3 And I will give power unto my two witnesses, and they shall prophesy a thousand two hundred and threescore days, clothed in sackcloth.

11:4 These are the two olive trees, and the two candlesticks standing before the God of the earth.

11:5 And if any man will hurt them, fire proceedeth out of their mouth, and devoureth their enemies: and if any man will hurt them, he must in this manner be killed.

11:6 These have power to shut heaven, that it rain not in the days of their prophecy: and have power over waters to turn them to blood, and to smite the earth with all plagues, as often as they will.

11:7 And when they shall have finished their testimony, the beast that ascendeth out of the bottomless pit shall make war against them, and shall overcome them, and kill them.

11:8 And their dead bodies shall lie in the street of the great city, which spiritually is called Sodom and Egypt, where also our Lord was crucified.

11:9 And they of the people and kindreds and tongues and nations shall see their dead bodies three days and an half, and shall not suffer their dead bodies to be put in graves.

11:10 And they that dwell upon the earth shall rejoice over them, and make merry, and shall send gifts one to another; because these two prophets tormented them that dwelt on the earth.

11:11 And after three days and an half the Spirit of life from God entered into them, and they stood upon their feet; and great fear fell upon them which saw them.

11:12 And they heard a great voice from heaven saying unto them, Come up hither. And they ascended up to heaven in a cloud; and their enemies beheld them.

[The Great Earthquake]

11:13 And the same hour was there a great earthquake, and the tenth part of the city fell, and in the earthquake were slain of men seven thousand: and the remnant were affrighted, and gave glory to the God of heaven.

11:14 The second woe is past; and, behold, the third woe cometh quickly. 11:15 And the seventh angel sounded; and there were great voices in heaven, saying, The kingdoms of this world are become the kingdoms of our Lord, and of his Christ; and he shall reign for ever and ever.

11:16 And the four and twenty elders, which sat before God on their seats, fell upon their faces, and worshipped God,

11:17 Saying, We give thee thanks, O Lord God Almighty, which art, and wast, and art to come; because thou hast taken to thee thy great power, and hast reigned.

11:18 And the nations were angry, and thy wrath is come, and the time of the dead, that they should be judged, and that thou shouldest give reward unto thy servants the prophets, and to the saints, and them that fear thy name, small and great; and shouldest destroy them which destroy the earth.

11:19 And the temple of God was opened in heaven, and there was seen in his temple the ark of his testament: and there were lightnings, and voices, and thunderings, and an earthquake, and great hail.

CHAPTER 12

[The Woman Clothed with the Sun]

12:1 And there appeared a great wonder in heaven; a woman clothed with the sun, and the moon under her feet, and upon her head a crown of twelve stars:

12:2 And she being with child cried, travailing in birth, and pained to be delivered.

[The Red Dragon]

12:3 And there appeared another wonder in heaven; and behold a great red dragon, having seven heads and ten horns, and seven crowns upon his heads.

12:4 And his tail drew the third part of the stars of heaven, and did cast them to the earth: and the dragon stood before the woman which was ready to be delivered, for to devour her child as soon as it was born.

12:5 And she brought forth a man child, who was to rule all nations with a rod of iron: and her child was caught up unto God, and to his throne.

12:6 And the woman fled into the wilderness, where she hath a place prepared of God, that they should feed her there a thousand two hundred *and* threescore days.

[War in Heaven Between Michael and the Dragon]

12:7 And there was war in heaven: Michael and his angels fought against the dragon; and the dragon fought and his angels,

12:8 And prevailed not; neither was their place found any more in heaven.

12:9 And the great dragon was cast out, that old serpent, called the Devil, and Satan, which deceiveth the whole world: he was cast out into the earth, and his angels were cast out with him.

12:10 And I heard a loud voice saying in heaven, Now is come salvation, and strength, and the kingdom of our God, and the power of his Christ: for the accuser of our brethren is cast down, which accused them before our God day and night.

12:11 And they overcame him by the blood of the Lamb, and by the word of their testimony; and they loved not their lives unto the death.

12:12 Therefore rejoice, ye heavens, and ye that dwell in them. Woe to the inhabiters of the earth and of the sea! for the devil is come down unto you, having great wrath, because he knoweth that he hath but a short time.

12:13 And when the dragon saw that he was cast unto the earth, he persecuted the woman which brought forth the man child.

12:14 And to the woman were given two wings of a great eagle, that she might fly into the wilderness, into her place, where she is nourished for a time, and times, and half a time, from the face of the serpent.

12:15 And the serpent cast out of his mouth water as a flood after the woman, that he might cause her to be carried away of the flood.

12:16 And the earth helped the woman, and the earth opened her mouth, and swallowed up the flood which the dragon cast out of his mouth.

12:17 And the dragon was wroth with the woman, and went to make war with the remnant of her seed, which keep the commandments of God, and have the testimony of Jesus Christ.

CHAPTER 13

[The Beast of the Sea]

13:1 And I stood upon the sand of the sea, and saw a beast rise up out of the sea, having seven heads and ten horns, and upon his horns ten crowns, and upon his heads the name of blasphemy.

13:2 And the beast which I saw was like unto a leopard, and his feet were as the feet of a bear, and his mouth as the mouth of a lion: and the dragon gave him his power, and his seat, and great authority.

13:3 And I saw one of his heads as it were wounded to death; and his deadly wound was healed: and all the world wondered after the beast.

13:4 And they worshipped the dragon which gave power unto the beast: and they worshipped the beast, saying, Who is like unto the beast? who is able to make war with him?

13:5 And there was given unto him a mouth speaking great things and blasphemies; and power was given unto him to continue forty and two months.

13:6 And he opened his mouth in blasphemy against God, to blaspheme his name, and his tabernacle, and them that dwell in heaven.

13:7 And it was given unto him to make war with the saints, and to overcome them: and power was given him over all kindreds, and tongues, and nations.

13:8 And all that dwell upon the earth shall worship him, whose names are not written in the book of life of the Lamb slain from the foundation of the world.

13:9 If any man have an ear, let him hear.

13:10 He that leadeth into captivity shall go into captivity: he that killeth with the sword must be killed with the sword. Here is the patience and the faith of the saints.

[The Beast of the Earth]

13:11 And I beheld another beast coming up out of the earth; and he had two horns like a lamb, and he spake as a dragon.

13:12 And he exerciseth all the power of the first beast before him, and causeth the earth and them which dwell therein to worship the first beast, whose deadly wound was healed.

13:13 And he doeth great wonders, so that he maketh fire come down from heaven on the earth in the sight of men,

13:14 And deceiveth them that dwell on the earth by the means of those miracles which he had power to do in the sight of the beast; saying to them that dwell on the earth, that they should make an image to the beast, which had the wound by a sword, and did live.

13:15 And he had power to give life unto the image of the beast, that the image of the beast should both speak, and cause that as many as would not worship the image of the beast should be killed.

[The Mark of the Beast—666]

13:16 And he causeth all, both small and great, rich and poor, free and bond, to receive a mark in their right hand, or in their foreheads:

13:17 And that no man might buy or sell, save he that had the mark, or the name of the beast, or the number of his name.

13:18 Here is wisdom. Let him that hath understanding count the number of the beast: for it is the number of a man; and his number is Six hundred threescore and six.

CHAPTER 14

[144,000 Virgins]

14:1 And I looked, and, lo, a Lamb stood on the mount Sion, and with him an hundred forty and four thousand, having his Father's name written in their foreheads.

14:2 And I heard a voice from heaven, as the voice of many waters, and as the voice of a great thunder: and I heard the voice of harpers harping with their harps:

14:3 And they sung as it were a new song before the throne, and before the four beasts, and the elders: and no man could learn that song but the hundred and forty and four thousand, which were redeemed from the earth.

14:4 These are they which were not defiled with women; for they are virgins. These are they which follow the Lamb whithersoever he goeth. These were redeemed from among men, being the firstfruits unto God and to the Lamb.

14:5 And in their mouth was found no guile: for they are without fault before the throne of God.

14:6 And I saw another angel fly in the midst of heaven, having the everlasting gospel to preach unto them that dwell on the earth, and to every nation, and kindred, and tongue, and people,

14:7 Saying with a loud voice, Fear God, and give glory to him; for the hour of his judgment is come: and worship him that made heaven, and earth, and the sea, and the fountains of waters.

[Babylon Is Fallen]

14:8 And there followed another angel, saying, Babylon is fallen, is fallen, that great city, because she made all nations drink of the wine of the wrath of her fornication.

14:9 And the third angel followed them, saying with a loud voice, If any man worship the beast and his image, and receive his mark in his forehead, or in his hand,

14:10 The same shall drink of the wine of the wrath of God, which is poured out without mixture into the cup of his indignation; and he shall be tormented with fire and brimstone in the presence of the holy angels, and in the presence of the Lamb:

14:11 And the smoke of their torment ascendeth up for ever and ever: and they have no rest day nor night, who worship the beast and his image, and whosoever receiveth the mark of his name.

14:12 Here is the patience of the saints: here are they that keep the commandments of God, and the faith of Jesus.

14:13 And I heard a voice from heaven saying unto me, Write, Blessed are the dead which die in the Lord from henceforth: Yea, saith the Spirit, that they may rest from their labours; and their works do follow them.

[Thrust in Thy Sickle, and Reap]

14:14 And I looked, and behold a white cloud, and upon the cloud one sat like unto the Son of man, having on his head a golden crown, and in his hand a sharp sickle.

14:15 And another angel came out of the temple, crying with a loud voice to him that sat on the cloud, Thrust in thy sickle, and reap: for the time is come for thee to reap; for the harvest of the earth is ripe.

14:16 And he that sat on the cloud thrust in his sickle on the earth; and the earth was reaped.

14:17 And another angel came out of the temple which is in heaven, he also having a sharp sickle.

14:18 And another angel came out from the altar, which had power over fire; and cried with a loud cry to him that had the sharp sickle, saying, Thrust in thy sharp sickle, and gather the clusters of the vine of the earth; for her grapes are fully ripe.

14:19 And the angel thrust in his sickle into the earth, and gathered the vine of the earth, and cast it into the great winepress of the wrath of God.

14:20 And the winepress was trodden without the city, and blood came out of the winepress, even unto the horse bridles, by the space of a thousand and six hundred furlongs.

CHAPTER 15

[Seven Last Plagues]

15:1 And I saw another sign in heaven, great and marvellous, seven angels having the seven last plagues; for in them is filled up the wrath of God.

15:2 And I saw as it were a sea of glass mingled with fire: and them that had gotten the victory over the beast, and over his image, and over his mark, and over the number of his name, stand on the sea of glass, having the harps of God.

15:3 And they sing the song of Moses the servant of God, and the song of the Lamb, saying, Great and marvellous are thy works, Lord God Almighty; just and true are thy ways, thou King of saints.

15:4 Who shall not fear thee, O Lord, and glorify thy name? for thou only art holy: for all nations shall come and worship before thee; for thy judgments are made manifest.

15:5 And after that I looked, and, behold, the temple of the tabernacle of the testimony in heaven was opened:

15:6 And the seven angels came out of the temple, having the seven plagues, clothed in pure and white linen, and having their breasts girded with golden girdles.

[Seven Golden Vials Full of the Wrath of God]

15:7 And one of the four beasts gave unto the seven angels seven golden vials full of the wrath of God, who liveth for ever and ever.

15:8 And the temple was filled with smoke from the glory of God, and from his power; and no man was able to enter into the temple, till the seven plagues of the seven angels were fulfilled.

CHAPTER 16

16:1 And I heard a great voice out of the temple saying to the seven angels, Go your ways, and pour out the vials of the wrath of God upon the earth.

16:2 And the first went, and poured out his vial upon the earth; and there fell a noisome and grievous sore upon the men which had the mark of the beast, and upon them which worshipped his image.

16:3 And the second angel poured out his vial upon the sea; and it became as the blood of a dead man: and every living soul died in the sea.

16:4 And the third angel poured out his vial upon the rivers and fountains of waters; and they became blood.

16:5 And I heard the angel of the waters say, Thou art righteous, O Lord, which art, and wast, and shalt be, because thou hast judged thus.

16:6 For they have shed the blood of saints and prophets, and thou hast given them blood to drink; for they are worthy.

16:7 And I heard another out of the altar say, Even so, Lord God Almighty, true and righteous are thy judgments.

16:8 And the fourth angel poured out his vial upon the sun; and power was given unto him to scorch men with fire.

16:9 And men were scorched with great heat, and blasphemed the name of God, which hath power over these plagues: and they repented not to give him glory.

16:10 And the fifth angel poured out his vial upon the seat of the beast; and his kingdom was full of darkness; and they gnawed their tongues for pain,

16:11 And blasphemed the God of heaven because of their pains and their sores, and repented not of their deeds.

16:12 And the sixth angel poured out his vial upon the great river Euphrates; and the water thereof was dried up, that the way of the kings of the east might be prepared.

[Three Unclean Spirits Like Frogs]

16:13 And I saw three unclean spirits like frogs come out of the mouth of the dragon, and out of the mouth of the beast, and out of the mouth of the false prophet.

16:14 For they are the spirits of devils, working miracles, which go forth unto the kings of the earth and of the whole world, to gather them to the battle of that great day of God Almighty.

[Behold, I Come as a Thief]

16:15 Behold, I come as a thief. Blessed is he that watcheth, and keepeth his garments, lest he walk naked, and they see his shame.

[The Battle of Armageddon]

16:16 And he gathered them together into a place called in the Hebrew tongue Armageddon.

16:17 And the seventh angel poured out his vial into the air; and there came a great voice out of the temple of heaven, from the throne, saying, It is done.

16:18 And there were voices, and thunders, and lightnings; and there was a great earthquake, such as was not since men were upon the earth, so mighty an earthquake, and so great.

16:19 And the great city was divided into three parts, and the cities of the nations fell: and great Babylon came in remembrance before God, to give unto her the cup of the wine of the fierceness of his wrath.

16:20 And every island fled away, and the mountains were not found.

16:21 And there fell upon men a great hail out of heaven, *every stone* about the weight of a talent: and men blasphemed God because of the plague of the hail; for the plague thereof was exceeding great.

CHAPTER 17

[The Great Whore of Babylon]

17:1 And there came one of the seven angels which had the seven vials, and talked with me, saying unto me, Come hither; I will shew unto thee the judgment of the great whore that sitteth upon many waters:

17:2 With whom the kings of the earth have committed fornication, and the inhabitants of the earth have been made drunk with the wine of her fornication.

17:3 So he carried me away in the spirit into the wilderness: and I saw a woman sit upon a scarlet coloured beast, full of names of blasphemy, having seven heads and ten horns.

17:4 And the woman was arrayed in purple and scarlet colour, and decked with gold and precious stones and pearls, having a golden cup in her hand full of abominations and filthiness of her fornication:

17:5 And upon her forehead was a name written, MYSTERY, BABYLON THE GREAT, THE MOTHER OF HARLOTS AND ABOMINATIONS OF THE EARTH.

17:6 And I saw the woman drunken with the blood of the saints, and with the blood of the martyrs of Jesus: and when I saw her, I wondered with great admiration.

17:7 And the angel said unto me, Wherefore didst thou marvel? I will tell thee the mystery of the woman, and of the beast that carrieth her, which hath the seven heads and ten horns.

17:8 The beast that thou sawest was, and is not; and shall ascend out of the bottomless pit, and go into perdition: and they that dwell on the earth shall wonder, whose names were not written in the book of life from the foundation of the world, when they behold the beast that was, and is not, and yet is.

17:9 And here is the mind which hath wisdom. The seven heads are seven mountains, on which the woman sitteth.

17:10 And there are seven kings: five are fallen, and one is, and the other is not yet come; and when he cometh, he must continue a short space.

17:11 And the beast that was, and is not, even he is the eighth, and is of the seven, and goeth into perdition.

17:12 And the ten horns which thou sawest are ten kings, which have received no kingdom as yet; but receive power as kings one hour with the beast.

17:13 These have one mind, and shall give their power and strength unto the beast.

17:14 These shall make war with the Lamb, and the Lamb shall overcome them: for he is Lord of lords, and King of kings: and they that are with him are called, and chosen, and faithful.

17:15 And he saith unto me, The waters which thou sawest, where the whore sitteth, are peoples, and multitudes, and nations, and tongues.

17:16 And the ten horns which thou sawest upon the beast, these shall hate the whore, and shall make her desolate and naked, and shall eat her flesh, and burn her with fire.

17:17 For God hath put in their hearts to fulfil his will, and to agree, and give their kingdom unto the beast, until the words of God shall be fulfilled.

17:18 And the woman which thou sawest is that great city, which reigneth over the kings of the earth.

CHAPTER 18

[Babylon the Great Is Fallen]

18:1 And after these things I saw another angel come down from heaven, having great power; and the earth was lightened with his glory.

18:2 And he cried mightily with a strong voice, saying, Babylon the great is fallen, is fallen, and is become the habitation of devils, and the hold of every foul spirit, and a cage of every unclean and hateful bird.

18:3 For all nations have drunk of the wine of the wrath of her fornication, and the kings of the earth have committed fornication with her, and the merchants of the earth are waxed rich through the abundance of her delicacies.

[Her Plagues Come in One Day]

18:4 And I heard another voice from heaven, saying, Come out of her, my people, that ye be not partakers of her sins, and that ye receive not of her plagues.

18:5 For her sins have reached unto heaven, and God hath remembered her iniquities.

18:6 Reward her even as she rewarded you, and double unto her double according to her works: in the cup which she hath filled fill to her double.

18:7 How much she hath glorified herself, and lived deliciously, so much torment and sorrow give her: for she saith in her heart, I sit a queen, and am no widow, and shall see no sorrow.

18:8 Therefore shall her plagues come in one day, death, and mourning, and famine; and she shall be utterly burned with fire: for strong is the Lord God who judgeth her.

Rejoice over her, for God hath avenged you on her.

18:9 And the kings of the earth, who have committed fornication and lived deliciously with her, shall bewail her, and lament for her, when they shall see the smoke of her burning,

[And the Merchants of the Earth Shall Weep]

18:10 Standing afar off for the fear of her torment, saying, Alas, alas, that great city Babylon, that mighty city! for in one hour is thy judgment come.

18:11 And the merchants of the earth shall weep and mourn over her; for no man buyeth their merchandise any more:

18:12 The merchandise of gold, and silver, and precious stones, and of pearls, and fine linen, and purple, and silk, and scarlet, and all thine wood, and all manner vessels of ivory, and all manner vessels of most precious wood, and of brass, and iron, and marble,

18:13 And cinnamon, and odours, and ointments, and frankincense, and wine, and oil, and fine flour, and wheat, and beasts, and sheep, and horses, and chariots, and slaves, and souls of men.

18:14 And the fruits that thy soul lusted after are departed from thee, and all things which were dainty and goodly are departed from thee, and thou shalt find them no more at all.

18:15 The merchants of these things, which were made rich by her, shall stand afar off for the fear of her torment, weeping and wailing,

18:16 And saying, Alas, alas, that great city, that was clothed in fine linen, and purple, and scarlet, and decked with gold, and precious stones, and pearls!

18:17 For in one hour so great riches is come to nought. And every shipmaster, and all the company in ships, and sailors, and as many as trade by sea, stood afar off,

18:18 And cried when they saw the smoke of her burning, saying, What city is like unto this great city!

18:19 And they cast dust on their heads, and cried, weeping and wailing, saying, Alas, alas, that great city, wherein were made rich all that had ships in the sea by reason of her costliness! for in one hour is she made desolate.

18:20 Rejoice over her, thou heaven, and ye holy apostles and prophets; for God hath avenged you on her.

[A Great Millstone Cast into the Sea]

18:21 And a mighty angel took up a stone like a great millstone, and cast it into the sea, saying, Thus with violence shall that great city Babylon be thrown down, and shall be found no more at all.

18:22 And the voice of harpers, and musicians, and of pipers, and trumpeters, shall be heard no more at all in thee; and no craftsman, of whatsoever craft he be, shall be found any more in thee; and the sound of a millstone shall be heard no more at all in thee;

18:23 And the light of a candle shall shine no more at all in thee; and the voice of the bridegroom and of the bride shall be heard no more at all in thee: for thy merchants were the great men of the earth; for by thy sorceries were all nations deceived.

18:24 And in her was found the blood of prophets, and of saints, and of all that were slain upon the earth.

CHAPTER 19

[A Great Voice in Heaven, Saying, Hallelujah!]

19:1 And after these things I heard a great voice of much people in heaven, saying, Alleluia; Salvation, and glory, and honour, and power, unto the Lord our God:

19:2 For true and righteous are his judgments: for he hath judged the great whore, which did corrupt the earth with her fornication, and hath avenged the blood of his servants at her hand.

19:3 And again they said, Alleluia. And her smoke rose up for ever and ever.

19:4 And the four and twenty elders and the four beasts fell down and worshipped God that sat on the throne, saying, Amen; Alleluia.

19:5 And a voice came out of the throne, saying, Praise our God, all ye his servants, and ye that fear him, both small and great.

19:6 And I heard as it were the voice of a great multitude, and as the voice of many waters, and as the voice of mighty thunderings, saying, Alleluia: for the Lord God omnipotent reigneth.

[The Marriage of the Lamb and His Wife]

19:7 Let us be glad and rejoice, and give honour to him: for the marriage of the Lamb is come, and his wife hath made herself ready.

19:8 And to her was granted that she should be arrayed in fine linen, clean and white: for the fine linen is the righteousness of saints.

19:9 And he saith unto me, Write, Blessed are they which are called unto the marriage supper of the Lamb. And he saith unto me, These are the true sayings of God.

19:10 And I fell at his feet to worship him. And he said unto me, See thou do it not: I am thy fellowservant, and of thy brethren that have the testimony of Jesus: worship God: for the testimony of Jesus is the spirit of prophecy.

[The White Horse and His Rider]

19:11 And I saw heaven opened, and behold a white horse; and he that sat upon him was called Faithful and True, and in righteousness he doth judge and make war.

19:12 His eyes were as a flame of fire, and on his head were many crowns; and he had a name written, that no man knew, but he himself.

19:13 And he was clothed with a vesture dipped in blood: and his name is called The Word of God.

19:14 And the armies which were in heaven followed him upon white horses, clothed in fine linen, white and clean.

19:15 And out of his mouth goeth a sharp sword, that with it he should smite the nations: and he shall rule them with a rod of iron: and he treadeth the winepress of the fierceness and wrath of Almighty God.

[King of Kings, Lord of Lords]

19:16 And he hath on his vesture and on his thigh a name written, KING OF KINGS, AND LORD OF LORDS.

19:17 And I saw an angel standing in the sun; and he cried with a loud voice, saying to all the fowls that fly in the midst of heaven, Come and gather yourselves together unto the supper of the great God;

19:18 That ye may eat the flesh of kings, and the flesh of captains, and the flesh of mighty men, and the flesh of horses, and of them that sit on them, and the flesh of all men, both free and bond, both small and great.

19:19 And I saw the beast, and the kings of the earth, and their armies, gathered together to make war against him that sat on the horse, and against his army.

19:20 And the beast was taken, and with him the false prophet that wrought miracles before him, with which he deceived them that had received the mark of the beast, and them that worshipped his image. These both were cast alive into a lake of fire burning with brimstone.

19:21 And the remnant were slain with the sword of him that sat upon the horse, which sword proceeded out of his mouth: and all the fowls were filled with their flesh.

CHAPTER 20

[The Bottomless Pit and the Binding of Satan]

20:1 And I saw an angel come down from heaven, having the key of the bottomless pit and a great chain in his hand.

20:2 And he laid hold on the dragon, that old serpent, which is the Devil, and Satan, and bound him a thousand years,

20:3 And cast him into the bottomless pit, and shut him up, and set a seal upon him, that he should deceive the nations no more, till the thousand years should be fulfilled: and after that he must be loosed a little season.

20:4 And I saw thrones, and they sat upon them, and judgment was given unto them: and I saw the souls of them that were beheaded for the witness of Jesus, and for the word of God, and which had not worshipped the beast, neither his image, neither had received his mark upon their foreheads, or in their hands; and they lived and reigned with Christ a thousand years.

20:5 But the rest of the dead lived not again until the thousand years were finished. This is the first resurrection.

20:6 Blessed and holy is he that hath part in the first resurrection: on such the second death hath no power, but they shall be priests of God and of Christ, and shall reign with him a thousand years.

20:7 And when the thousand years are expired, Satan shall be loosed out of his prison,

20:8 And shall go out to deceive the nations which are in the four quarters of the earth, Gog and Magog, to gather them together to battle: the number of whom is as the sand of the sea.

20:9 And they went up on the breadth of the earth, and compassed the camp of the saints about, and the beloved city: and fire came down from God out of heaven, and devoured them.

[The Lake of Fire]

20:10 And the devil that deceived them was cast into the lake of fire and brimstone, where the beast and the false prophet are, and shall be tormented day and night for ever and ever.

20:11 And I saw a great white throne, and him that sat on it, from whose face the earth and the heaven fled away; and there was found no place for them.

20:12 And I saw the dead, small and great, stand before God; and the books were opened: and another book was opened, which is the book of life: and the dead were judged out of those things which were written in the books, according to their works.

20:13 And the sea gave up the dead which were in it; and death and hell delivered up the dead which were in them: and they were judged every man according to their works.

20:14 And death and hell were cast into the lake of fire. This is the second death.

20:15 And whosoever was not found written in the book of life was cast into the lake of fire.

CHAPTER 21

[A New Heaven, a New Earth, and the New Jerusalem]

21:1 And I saw a new heaven and a new earth: for the first heaven and the first earth were passed away; and there was no more sea.

21:2 And I John saw the holy city, new Jerusalem, coming down from God out of heaven, prepared as a bride adorned for her husband.

21:3 And I heard a great voice out of heaven saying, Behold, the tabernacle of God is with men, and he will dwell with them, and they shall be his people, and God himself shall be with them, and be their God.

21:4 And God shall wipe away all tears from their eyes; and there shall be no more death, neither sorrow, nor crying, neither shall there be any more pain: for the former things are passed away.

[Behold, I Make All Things New]

21:5 And he that sat upon the throne said, Behold, I make all things new. And he said unto me, Write: for these words are true and faithful.

21:6 And he said unto me, It is done. I am Alpha and Omega, the beginning and the end. I will give unto him that is athirst of the fountain of the water of life freely.

21:7 He that overcometh shall inherit all things; and I will be his God, and he shall be my son.

21:8 But the fearful, and unbelieving, and the abominable, and murderers, and whoremongers, and sorcerers, and idolaters, and all liars, shall have their part in the lake which burneth with fire and brimstone: which is the second death.

21:9 And there came unto me one of the seven angels which had the seven vials full of the seven last plagues, and talked with me, saying, Come hither, I will shew thee the bride, the Lamb's wife.

21:10 And he carried me away in the spirit to a great and high mountain, and shewed me that great city, the holy Jerusalem, descending out of heaven from God,

21:11 Having the glory of God: and her light was like unto a stone most precious, even like a jasper stone, clear as crystal;

21:12 And had a wall great and high, and had twelve gates, and at the gates twelve angels, and names written thereon, which are the names of the twelve tribes of the children of Israel:

21:13 On the east three gates; on the north three gates; on the south three gates; and on the west three gates.

21:14 And the wall of the city had twelve foundations, and in them the names of the twelve apostles of the Lamb.

21:15 And he that talked with me had a golden reed to measure the city, and the gates thereof, and the wall thereof.

21:16 And the city lieth foursquare, and the length is as large as the breadth: and he measured the city with the reed, twelve thousand furlongs. The length and the breadth and the height of it are equal.

21:17 And he measured the wall thereof, an hundred and forty and four cubits, according to the measure of a man, that is, of the angel.

21:18 And the building of the wall of it was of jasper: and the city was pure gold, like unto clear glass.

21:19 And the foundations of the wall of the city were garnished with all manner of precious stones. The first foundation was jasper; the second, sapphire; the third, a chalcedony; the fourth, an emerald;

21:20 The fifth, sardonyx; the sixth, sardius; the seventh, chrysolite; the eighth, beryl; the ninth, a topaz; the tenth, a chrysoprasus; the eleventh, a jacinth; the twelfth, an amethyst.

21:21 And the twelve gates were twelve pearls; every several gate was of one pearl: and the street of the city was pure gold, as it were transparent glass.

21:22 And I saw no temple therein: for the Lord God Almighty and the Lamb are the temple of it.

21:23 And the city had no need of the sun, neither of the moon, to shine in it: for the glory of God did lighten it, and the Lamb is the light thereof.

21:24 And the nations of them which are saved shall walk in the light of it: and the kings of the earth do bring their glory and honour into it.

21:25 And the gates of it shall not be shut at all by day: for there shall be no night there.

21:26 And they shall bring the glory and honour of the nations into it.

21:27 And there shall in no wise enter into it any thing that defileth, neither whatsoever worketh abomination, or maketh a lie: but they which are written in the Lamb's book of life.

CHAPTER 22

[Behold, I Come Quickly]

22:1 And he shewed me a pure river of water of life, clear as crystal, proceeding out of the throne of God and of the Lamb.

22:2 In the midst of the street of it, and on either side of the river, was there the tree of life, which bare twelve manner of fruits, and yielded her fruit every month: and the leaves of the tree were for the healing of the nations.

22:3 And there shall be no more curse: but the throne of God and of the Lamb shall be in it; and his servants shall serve him:

22:4 And they shall see his face; and his name shall be in their foreheads.

22:5 And there shall be no night there; and they need no candle, neither light of the sun; for the Lord God giveth them light: and they shall reign for ever and ever.

22:6 And he said unto me, These sayings are faithful and true: and the Lord God of the holy prophets sent his angel to shew unto his servants the things which must shortly be done.

22:7 Behold, I come quickly: blessed is he that keepeth the sayings of the prophecy of this book.

22:8 And I John saw these things, and heard them. And when I had heard and seen, I fell down to worship before the feet of the angel which shewed me these things.

22:9 Then saith he unto me, See thou do it not: for I am thy fellowservant, and of thy brethren the prophets, and of them which keep the sayings of this book: worship God.

22:10 And he saith unto me, Seal not the sayings of the prophecy of this book: for the time is at hand.

22:11 He that is unjust, let him be unjust still: and he which is filthy, let him be filthy still: and he that is righteous, let him be righteous still: and he that is holy, let him be holy still.

22:12 And, behold, I come quickly; and my reward is with me, to give every man according as his work shall be.

22:13 I am Alpha and Omega, the beginning and the end, the first and the last.

22:14 Blessed are they that do his commandments, that they may have right to the tree of life, and may enter in through the gates into the city.

22:15 For without are dogs, and sorcerers, and whoremongers, and murderers, and idolaters, and whosoever loveth and maketh a lie.

22:16 I Jesus have sent mine angel to testify unto you these things in the churches. I am the root and the offspring of David, and the bright and morning star.

22:17 And the Spirit and the bride say, Come. And let him that heareth say, Come. And let him that is athirst come. And whosoever will, let him take the water of life freely.

22:18 For I testify unto every man that heareth the words of the prophecy of this book, If any man shall add unto these things, God shall add unto him the plagues that are written in this book:

22:19 And if any man shall take away from the words of the book of this prophecy, God shall take away his part out of the book of life, and out of the holy city, and from the things which are written in this book.

22:20 He which testifieth these things saith, Surely I come quickly. Amen. Even so, come, Lord Jesus.

22:21 The grace of our Lord Jesus Christ be with you all. Amen.

Notes

AUTHOR'S NOTE: I have taken the liberty of omitting some words and phrases from some quoted material, and changing capitalization and punctuation, without using brackets and ellipses to indicate the omissions and changes. Whenever I have done so, I use the word "adapted" in the note that identifies the source of the quotation. In all instances, the omissions and changes do not affect the meaning of the quoted material.

For most biblical citations, I have used *BibleWorks 5: Software for Biblical Exegesis and Research,* version 5.0.020w, a collection of more than 100 versions of the Bible in the original Hebrew and Greek as well as in various translations, including Latin and English. Complete bibliographic information for the versions cited below is available in the BibleWorks program. The following abbreviations are used in the notes to identify the specific versions from which brief quoted passages have been taken:

BBE   The Bible in Basic English (1949–1964)

JPS   Jewish Publication Society (1917)

KJV   King James Version (1611–1769)

NKJ   New King James Version (1982)

NLT   New Living Translation [n.d.]

RSV   Revised Standard Version (1952)

TNK   Jewish Publication Society Tanakh (1985)

I have also quoted briefly from J. Massyngberde Ford's translation of Revelation in the Anchor Bible, which is cited in notes as AB. See below for complete bibliographic information for this source.

CHAPTER 1: SOMETHING RICH AND STRANGE

 1. Rev. 2:9 (KJV).
 2. Schüssler Fiorenza, *Apocalypse*, 8.
 3. *The Seventh Seal.*
 4. See, e.g., Schüssler Fiorenza, *Book of Revelation*, 40–41.
 5. Rev. 1:1 (KJV).
 6. Rev. 9:16 (KJV); Lindsey is quoted in Boyer, *When Time Shall Be*, 127 ("... some kind of mobile ballistic missile launcher ...").
 7. Richard K. Emmerson, "Introduction: The Apocalypse in Medieval Culture," in Emmerson and McGinn, *Apocalypse*, 293.
 8. Farrar, *Rebirth of Images*, 6 (adapted).
 9. Schüssler Fiorenza, *Book of Revelation*, 15 ("apocalyptic pornography"); Frye, *Great Code*, 137 ("insane rhapsody"); Yarbro Collins, *Crisis and Catharsis*, 154 ("imagination of a schizophrenic"); Thomas Jefferson, quoted in E. S. Gaustad, "Religion," in Merrill D. Peterson, ed., *Thomas Jefferson*, 287 ("merely the ravings").
10. Rev. 1:3 (RSV; adapted).
11. Schüssler Fiorenza, *Apocalypse*, 20.
12. Schüssler Fiorenza, *Book of Revelation*, 85.
13. Farrar, *Rebirth of Images*, 98.
14. Rev. 1:10, 11 (KJV; adapted).
15. Quoted in Bernard McGinn, "Revelation," in Alter and Kermode, *Literary Guide*, 529.
16. Quoted in Bernard McGinn, "Revelation," in Alter and Kermode, *Literary Guide*, 523.
17. From C. G. Jung, *Memories, Dreams, Reflections*, quoted in Barnwell, *Meditations on the Apocalypse*, 1.
18. Barclay, *Letters*, 11.
19. Barclay, *Letters*, 11 (adapted).
20. Rev. 3:16 (RSV; adapted).
21. Rev. 22:7 (RSV; adapted).
22. Rev. 1:8, 21:6 (KJV). See also John Spencer Hill, "Themes and Images," in Drane, *Revelation*, 18 ("Scriptural reference to *alpha* and *omega*, the first and last letters of the Greek alphabet, is confined to Revelation....").
23. Rev. 1:18 (NKJ).
24. Rev. 1:13–16 (KJV).
25. Rev. 5:6 (RSV).
26. Rev. 19:16 (RSV).
27. Rev. 12:3, 12:9 (RSV).

28. Rev. 13:11 (RSV).
29. Rev. 17:2, 17:3, 17:4, 17:6 (RSV).
30. Rev. 12:3–9 (KJV).
31. Rev. 6:8, 6:12–13 (RSV; adapted).
32. Rev. 9:6 (RSV).
33. Rev. 19:18 (RSV).
34. Rev. 20:10 (RSV; adapted).
35. Rev. 21:1, 14:12, 21:8 (RSV; adapted).
36. Rev. 14:20 (KJV), 7:14 (NKJ).
37. Rev. 21:4 (RSV).
38. Rev. 21:14 (KJV).
39. Rev. 6:10–11, 3:11 (RSV).
40. Rev. 1:1 (KJV).
41. Paula Fredriksen, "Tyconius and Augustine on the Apocalypse," in Emmerson and McGinn, *Apocalypse,* 20–21.
42. Mark 13:7 (RSV).
43. Rev. 2:24 (RSV).
44. Lev. 19:18 (KJV), Matt. 5:44 (RSV; adapted).
45. Lawrence, *Apocalypse,* 9, 33.
46. Rev. 18:8, 18:20, 19:2 (KJV).
47. Rev. 18:6, 18:7 (NLT).
48. Paul D. Hanson, "Introductory Overview," in "Apocalypses and Apocalypticism," in Freedman, *Anchor Bible Dictionary,* 1:282.
49. Schüssler Fiorenza, *Book of Revelation,* 8 (adapted).
50. Quoted in Cohn-Sherbok and Cohn-Sherbok, *Jewish and Christian Mysticism,* 145.
51. James H. Moorhead, "Apocalypticism in Mainstream Protestantism, 1800 to the Present," in Stein, *Apocalypticism,* 103.
52. Weber, *Living in the Shadow,* 239.
53. Janice Rogers Brown, quoted in Wallstein, "Faith 'War' Rages," A-10.
54. Quoted in Boyer, *When Time Shall Be,* 142.
55. Schüssler Fiorenza, *Book of Revelation,* 135.

CHAPTER 2: SPOOKY KNOWLEDGE AND LAST THINGS
1. Watts, *Nature of Consciousness,* Tape 2.
2. Exod. 33:20 (JPS).
3. Num. 12:6 (JPS).
4. Deut. 29:29 (JPS).
5. 2 Cor. 12:1–2, 1 Cor. 13:12 (KJV).
6. 2 Cor. 12:1–2, 12:4 (KJV).
7. John J. Collins, "From Prophecy to Apocalypticism: The Expectation of the End," in Collins, *Origins of Apocalypticism,* 138, describing the Book of Enoch.
8. Schüssler Fiorenza, *Book of Revelation,* 40–41.

9. Quoted in Hubert Cancik, "The End of the World, of History, and of the Individual in Greek and Roman Antiquity," in Collins, *Origins of Apocalypticism*, 89 ("The eternal return …").
10. Rennie B. Schoepflin, "Apocalypse in an Age of Science," in Stein, *Apocalypticism*, 428–29.
11. Yarbro Collins, *Crisis and Catharsis*, 90, citing Suetonius.
12. Anders Hultgård, "Persian Apocalypticism," in Collins, *Origins of Apocalypticism*, 39. Hultgård insists that "an apocalyptic eschatology is firmly attested in Zoroastrianism already in the sixth century B.C.E.," but concedes that the dating of some Persian texts is subject to scholarly debate (79).
13. James C. VanderKam, "Messianism and Apocalyticism," in Collins, *Origins of Apocalypticism*, 196, 197.
14. 1 Sam. 29:4 (JPS).
15. Rowley, *Relevance of Apocalyptic*, 53 (adapted).
16. Job 2:6 (JPS).
17. Ezek. 38: 2 (JPS). (Elsewhere in the Hebrew Bible, both Gog and Magog are the names of individuals rather than nations. Magog is identified as one of the grandsons of Noah in Gen. 10:9 and 1 Chron. 1:5. Gog is one of the sons of an Israelite man named Joel in 1 Chron. 5:4. These individuals are apparently unrelated to the *nations* identified as Gog and Magog in Revelation, or to the monarch called "Gog of the land of Magog" in Ezekiel).
18. Ezek. 38:23 (TNK).
19. Ezek. 39:26 (TNK).
20. Ezek. 39:28 (TNK).
21. Amos 8:2, 9 (TNK; adapted).
22. Amos 9:14–15 (TNK).
23. Ezek. 1:5–10 (TNK).
24. Ezek. 1:19 (KJV).
25. Rowley, *Relevance of Apocalyptic*, 13.
26. Bernard McGinn, "Introduction: John's Apocalypse and the Apocalyptic Mentality," in Emmerson and McGinn, *Apocalypse*, 7.
27. Rev. 12:9 (KJV).
28. Deut. 28:58, 28:34 (RSV).
29. Deut. 28:59, 28:27, 28:28, 28:49 (TNK).
30. Deut. 28:30, 28:32 (RSV).
31. Deut. 28:56–57 (TNK).
32. Jer. 5:19 (RSV).
33. Isa. 45:1, 45:4 (TNK; adapted).
34. Quoted in Gorenberg, *End of Days*, 203.
35. Dubnow, *Short History*, 89.
36. Graetz, *Popular History*, 1:331.
37. Graetz, *Popular History*, 1:336.
38. Rowley, *Relevance of Apocalyptic*, citing 2 Macc. 4:7 ff.
39. Graetz, *Popular History*, 326.

40. S. Schwartz, quoted in Gruen, *Heritage and Hellenism,* 5 n. 8.
41. "Kulturkampf" was first used to refer to the struggle in the late nineteenth century between the government of Germany and the Roman Catholic Church over the right to control the schools and churches.
42. Flavius Josephus, *The Works of Josephus,* trans. William Whitson (Peabody, MA: Hendrickson Publishers, 1987), *Antiquities of the Jews,* 12.5, 4, 324.
43. John J. Collins, "From Prophecy to Apocalypticism: The Expectation of the End," in Collins, *Origins of Apocalypticism,* 158, 159.
44. Rowley, *Relevance of Apocalyptic,* 47.
45. Rowley, *Relevance of Apocalyptic,* 47.
46. Dan. 1:4 (JPS).
47. Dan. 2:20, 2:22 (JPS; adapted).
48. Dan. 7:18 (TNK).
49. Dan. 7:7, 7:9, 7:10, 7:13, 7:14 (JPS).
50. Dan. 7:15–16 (TNK).
51. Dan. 7:17 (TNK).
52. Dan. 7:27 (JPS).
53. Dan. 3:25 (JPS).
54. Dan. 8:25 (RSV); Dan. 12:1 (KJV).
55. Dan. 9:24 (KJV; adapted).
56. Dan. 12:2 (KJV); Dan. 12:3 (RSV; adapted).
57. Rowley, *Relevance of Apocalyptic,* 13 ("child of prophecy"); Bernard McGinn, "Introduction: John's Apocalypse and the Apocalyptic Mentality," in Emmerson and McGinn, *Apocalypse,* 9–10 ("mother of Christianity").
58. Dan. 7:10 (TNK).
59. Dan. 12:1 (KJV).
60. Job 25:6 (TNK).
61. Dan. 7:13–14 (JPS; adapted).
62. Jer. 29:10, 29:11 (JPS).
63. Dan. 9:21, 9:24 (RSV; adapted).
64. Dan. 12:11, 12:12 (NKJ).
65. John J. Collins, "From Prophecy to Apocalypticism: The Expectation of the End," in Collins, *Origins of Apocalypticism,* 144.
66. Rowley, *Relevance of Apocalyptic,* 50.
67. Moshe Idel, "Jewish Apocalypticism: 760–1670," in McGinn, *Apocalypticism,* 207. (Idel also cites "the drama of redemption in Exodus" as one of the sources of Western apocalypticism.)
68. Bernard McGinn, "The Last Judgment in Christian Tradition," in McGinn, *Apocalypticism,* 367.
69. Paul D. Hanson, "Introductory Overview," in "Apocalypses and Apocalypticism," in Freedman, *Anchor Bible Dictionary,* 1:280.
70. Quoted in John J. Collins, "From Prophecy to Apocalypticism: The Expectation of the End," in Collins, *Origins of Apocalypticism,* 137.
71. Gen. 5:24 (JPS).

72. Gen. 6:4.
73. Adela Yarbro Collins, "The Book of Revelation," in Collins, *Origins of Apocalypticism*, 407, quoting 1 Enoch 9:8.
74. Dan. 4:13 (KJV).
75. 1 Enoch 7:2, 8:1–2, quoted in John J. Collins, "From Prophecy to Apocalypticism: The Expectation of the End," in Collins, *Origins of Apocalypticism*, 136–37.
76. 1 Enoch 10:4–7, quoted in John J. Collins, "From Prophecy to Apocalypticism: The Expectation of the End," in Collins, *Origins of Apocalypticism*, 137–38.
77. Ford, *Revelation*, 31.
78. John J. Collins, "From Prophecy to Apocalypticism: The Expectation of the End," in Collins, *Origins of Apocalypticism*, 140–41.
79. Dan. 9:26 (JPS).
80. 1 Enoch 60, quoted in Ehrman, *Jesus*, 147 (adapted).
81. John J. Collins, "Early Jewish Apocalypticism," in "Apocalypses and Apocalypticism," in Freedman, *Anchor Bible Dictionary*, 1:286.
82. Rowley, *Relevance of Apocalyptic*, 65.
83. John J. Collins, "Early Jewish Apocalypticism," in "Apocalypses and Apocalypticism," in Freedman, *Anchor Bible Dictionary*, 1:286.
84. Collins, "Early Jewish Apocalypticism," in "Apocalypses and Apocalypticism," in Freedman, *Anchor Bible Dictionary*, 1:287.
85. Dan. 7:7, 7:9, 7:10, 7;13, 7:14 (JPS).
86. Josephus, *The Jewish War*, 6.312, quoted in John J. Collins, "From Prophecy to Apocalypticism: The Expectation of the End," in Collins, *Origins of Apocalypticism*, 151. ("Josephus argues that it actually predicted the rise of Vespasian, who was proclaimed emperor on Jewish soil.")
87. Quoted in John J. Collins, "Early Jewish Apocalypticism," in "Apocalypses and Apocalypticism," in Freedman, *Anchor Bible Dictionary*, 1:287. (See Josephus, *The Jewish War*, 2.13.4 sec. 258–60.)
88. Josephus, *The Jewish War*, 2.261–62, quoted in John J. Collins, "From Prophecy to Apocalypticism: The Expectation of the End," in Collins, *Origins of Apocalypticism*, 150–51.
89. Josephus, *The Jewish War*, quoted in Yarbro Collins, *Crisis and Catharsis*, 67.
90. Shem Tov Ibn Gaon, *Migdal Oz*, Hilkhot Melachim 11:3, quoted in Aviezer Ravitsky, "The Messianism of Success in Contemporary Judaism," in Stein, *Apocalypticism*, 211.
91. Quoted in Neusner, *Yohanan Ben Zakkai*, 141, citing, inter alia, TP Taanit 4.7 (adapted).
92. Ehrman, *Jesus*, x, 3.
93. Mark 9:1 (RSV).
94. 1 Thess. 4:16–17 (RSV)

95. Isa. 11:1 (JPS).
96. Armstrong, *Jerusalem,* 153.
97. Rom. 1:3 (KJV).
98. Matt. 27:37 (KJV).
99. Paula Fredriksen, "Tyconius and Augustine on the Apocalypse" in Emmerson and McGinn, *Apocalypse,* 20–21.
100. Rev. 22:20 (KJV).

CHAPTER 3: THE HISTORY OF A DELUSION
1. Jer. 36:4 (JPS).
2. Yarbro Collins, *Crisis and Catharsis,* 33.
3. Rev. 1:1 (AB; adapted).
4. Richard K. Emmerson, "Introduction: The Apocalypse in Medieval Culture," in Emmerson and McGinn, *Apocalypse,* 293.
5. Rev. 1:9 (AB; adapted).
6. Irenaeus, *Against Heresies,* V.xxx.iii, quoted in Ladd, *Revelation of John,* 8 n. 1.
7. Adela Yarbro Collins, "Revelation, Book of," in Freedman, *Anchor Bible Dictionary,* 5:702; quoted in Bernard McGinn, "Introduction: John's Apocalypse and the Apocalyptic Mentality," in Emmerson and McGinn, *Apocalypse,* 18 ("of which many good Christians . . ."); Schüssler Fiorenza, *Book of Revelation,* 87 ("could not have been written . . .").
8. Schüssler Fiorenza, *Book of Revelation,* 86.
9. John 5:24, 11:26 (RSV; adapted). See also John 3:18, 14:3, and 16:7 for examples of a "realized" eschatology. By contrast, see John 6:39–40, 6:54, 12:58, 12:25, 14:3, 14:18, and 14: 28 for examples of a "futuristic" eschatology.
10. Rev. 10:7 (RSV; adapted).
11. Schüssler Fiorenza, *Book of Revelation,* 93.
12. Yarbro Collins, *Crisis and Catharsis,* 28.
13. Rev. 21:14 (RSV). Adela Yarbro Collins finds it "unlikely that a living apostle would speak in such a way." Adela Yarbro Collins, "Revelation, Book of," in Freedman, *Anchor Bible Dictionary,* 5:702.
14. Rowley, *Relevance of Apocalyptic,* 125, summarizing the arguments of R. H. Charles.
15. Quoted in Schüssler Fiorenza, *Book of Revelation,* 87.
16. Ehrman, *Jesus,* 45, citing Acts 4:13; Schüssler Fiorenza, *Book of Revelation,* 88. Ehrman points out that the literal meaning of the Greek word used in Acts 4:13 to describe Peter and John is "illiterate," although it is often translated into English as "uneducated."
17. N. Middle, quoted in Schüssler Fiorenza, *Book of Revelation,* 86. The discussion to which Middle refers is the debate over the authorship of all five books of the New Testament that have been attributed to the apostle John and not merely the authorship of Revelation.

18. Quoted in Yarbro Collins, *Crisis and Catharsis,* 30.
19. Yarbro Collins, *Crisis and Catharsis,* 30.
20. Ford, *Revelation,* 3, 4, 7, 18, 40 (emphasis added). Ford counts "approximately" fourteen references to "Jesus" and "Jesus Christ" in Revelation.
21. Ford, *Revelation,* 40.
22. Ford, *Revelation,* 15.
23. Ford, *Revelation,* 37, 18.
24. Farrer, *Rebirth of Images,* 98.
25. Ford, *Revelation,* 22.
26. Ford, *Revelation,* 18.
27. Ford, *Revelation,* 28.
28. Ford, *Revelation,* 33 (adapted).
29. Matt. 3:2, 3:11–12 (RSV; adapted).
30. Yarbro Collins, *Crisis and Catharsis,* 34.
31. Yarbro Collins, *Crisis and Catharsis,* 47.
32. Yarbro Collins, *Crisis and Catharsis,* 47.
33. Cited but also criticized in Yarbro Collins, *Crisis and Catharsis,* 37, 47.
34. Farrer, *Rebirth of Images,* 23.
35. Miles, *Christ,* 109.
36. Rev. 17:1–2, 17:4 (KJV; adapted).
37. Rev. 17:9 (RSV).
38. Yarbro Collins, *Crisis and Catharsis,* 57.
39. Schüssler Fiorenza, *Book of Revelation,* 15.
40. Yarbro Collins, *Crisis and Catharsis,* 47.
41. Yarbro Collins, *Crisis and Catharsis,* 47.
42. Rev. 17:5 (KJV).
43. Victorinus, *Commentary on the Revelation* (10:11), quoted in Ladd, *Revelation of John,* 8 n. 1 ("... condemned to the mines ..."); Farrer, *Rebirth of Images,* 24 ("... concentration-camp ...").
44. Yarbro Collins, *Crisis and Catharsis,* 55.
45. Rev. 1:9 (NLT).
46. Adela Yarbro Collins, "Revelation, Book of," in Freedman, *Anchor Bible Dictionary,* 5:701.
47. Barclay, *Letters,* 14.
48. Barclay, *Letters,* 15 (adapted).
49. Rev. 17:4 (KJV; adapted).
50. Rev. 2:13 (RSV); Schüssler Fiorenza, *Book of Revelation,* 193.
51. Rev. 14:9 (KJV).
52. Rev. 14:9–10 (RSV; adapted).
53. Rev. 16:2 (RSV).
54. Rev. 19:20 (KJV).
55. Rev. 13:16–17 (RSV; emphasis added).
56. Ladd, *Revelation of John,* 178.

57. Ladd, *Revelation of John*, 185.
58. Ladd, *Revelation of John*, citing 3 Macc. 2:29. See also Ford, *Revelation*, 116–17.
59. Quoted in Ford, *Revelation*, 117.
60. Mark 11:15 (RSV).
61. Mark 11:17 (KJV).
62. Rev. 18:11 (RSV).
63. Rev. 18:12–13 (RSV).
64. Rev. 21:8 (KJV).
65. Rev. 18:15, 18:17–19, 18:22 (RSV; adapted).
66. Matt. 10:9–11 (RSV; adapted).
67. David Aune, quoted in Yarbro Collins, *Crisis and Catharsis*, 45.
68. Matt. 8:20 (RSV).
69. Yarbro Collins, *Crisis and Catharsis*, 102–3, describing the theories of J. N. Saunders.
70. Paraphrased in Yarbro Collins, *Crisis and Catharsis*, 35.
71. Schüssler Fiorenza, *Book of Revelation*, 144.
72. Rev. 2:2 (RSV).
73. Rev. 2:6 (KJV).
74. Rev. 2:19, 2:20 (RSV; adapted).
75. Num 22:23 ff.
76. 2 Kings 9:22 (JPS).
77. Acts 15:20 (RSV).
78. Rev. 3:16–17 (NKJ; adapted)
79. Rev. 2:14, 2:20 (KJV).
80. Adela Yarbro Collins, "Revelation, Book of," in Freedman, *Anchor Bible Dictionary*, 5:705.
81. Schüssler Fiorenza, *Book of Revelation*, 15.
82. Rev. 2:18, 2:21–23 (NKJ, KJV, RSV; adapted).
83. Rev. 2:15 (KJV), 2:24 (RSV).
84. Acts 6:5.
85. Schüssler Fiorenza, *Apocalypse*, 48–49. See also Adela Yarbro Collins, "The Book of Revelation," in Collins, *Origins of Apocalypticism*, 392.
86. Barclay, *Letters*, 66.
87. Schüssler Fiorenza, *Apocalypse*, 48–49 ("social, political and commercial life"); Schüssler Fiorenza, *Book of Revelation*, 195 ("code names").
88. Rev. 14:4 (RSV).
89. Rev. 14:4 (RSV).
90. Rev. 7:3, 14:4 (RSV).
91. Rev. 14:4 (NKJ).
92. Adela Yarbro Collins, "The Book of Revelation," in Collins, *Origins of Apocalypticism*, 407, quoting 1 Enoch 10:11 (adapted).
93. Lev. 15:18 (RSV).

94. Adela Yarbro Collins, "The Book of Revelation," in Collins, *Origins of Apocalypticism,* 405.
95. Yarbro Collins, *Crisis and Catharsis,* 159.
96. Quoted in Yarbro Collins, *Crisis and Catharsis,* 169.
97. Rev. 17:4 (RSV; adapted).
98. Rev. 13:18 (KJV).
99. Rev. 13:17, 13:18 (KJV; adapted).
100. Rev. 17:3 (KJV).
101. Rev. 17:7 (RSV).
102. Rev. 17:8 (RSV).
103. Rev. 17:8 (RSV).
104. Rowley, *Relevance of Apocalyptic,* 130 n. 2.
105. Rev. 2:10 (KJV).
106. Rev. 13:7 (RSV).
107. Rev. 13:15 (RSV).
108. Rev. 6:9 (RSV).
109. Rev. 2:13 (RSV; adapted).
110. Yarbro Collins, *Crisis and Catharsis,* 102.
111. Quoted in Schüssler Fiorenza, *Book of Revelation,* 193.
112. Quoted in Schüssler Fiorenza, *Book of Revelation,* 193.
113. Rev. 21:1 (KJV).
114. Schüssler Fiorenza, *Apocalypse,* 45.
115. Quoted in Yarbro Collins, *Crisis and Catharsis,* 69.
116. Yarbro Collins, *Crisis and Catharsis,* 71 (emphasis added).
117. Bernard McGinn, "Introduction: John's Apocalypse and the Apocalyptic Mentality," in Emmerson and McGinn, *Apocolypse,* 13.
118. Gibbon, *Decline and Fall,* 1:420–21.
119. Ladd, *Revelation of John,* 9, citing Tacitus.
120. Adela Yarbro Collins, "Revelation, Book of," in Freedman, *Anchor Bible Dictionary,* 5:706.
121. Ladd, *Revelation of John,* 104.
122. Yarbro Collins, *Crisis and Catharsis,* 94.
123. Adela Yarbro Collins, "Revelation, Book of," in Freedman, *Anchor Bible Dictionary,* 5:705.
124. John J. Collins, "From Prophecy to Apocalypticism: The Expectation of the End," in Collins, *Origins of Apocalypticism,* 144.
125. Rev. 16:14 (KJV); Rev. 18:20 (NKJ).
126. Rev. 17:14, 1:16 (KJV).
127. Rev. 18:14, 14:13 (NKJ).
128. Rev. 19:2 (RSV).
129. Rev. 13:10 (RSV; adapted).
130. Rev. 3:9 (RSV; adapted).
131. Gen. 2:2 (KJV).
132. Rev. 10:5-6 (KJV, RSV; adapted).

133. Ezek. 2:10–11 (KJV; adapted).
134. Rev. 10:9 (KJV); Rev. 10:10–11 (RSV).
135. Stendahl, quoted in Schüssler Fiorenza, *Book of Revelation,* 197.
136. Stendahl, quoted in Schüssler Fiorenza, *Book of Revelation,* 135.
137. Quoted in Schüssler Fiorenza, *Book of Revelation,* 136.
138. 2 Kings 23:5 (TNK).
139. Rev. 12:9 (KJV).
140. Rev. 12:5 (KJV).
141. Farrer, *Rebirth of Images,* 141.
142. Ford, *Revelation,* 188.
143. Adela Yarbro Collins, "The Book of Revelation," in Collins, *Origins of Apocalypticism,* 408.
144. Schüssler Fiorenza, *Apocalypse,* 30 (adapted).
145. Isa. 27:1 (TNK).
146. Adela Yarbro Collins, "The Book of Revelation," in Collins, *Origins of Apocalypticism,* 394.
147. Rev. 12:12 (KJV).
148. Dan. 2:28 (KJV).
149. Rev. 1:10–11 (KJV).
150. Rev. 1:13–14, 1:16, 1:17 (RSV).
151. Rev. 1:11, 1:19 (RSV; adapted).
152. Rev. 22:10, 22:19.
153. Richard K. Emmerson, "Introduction: The Apocalypse in Medieval Culture," in Emmerson and McGinn, *Apocalypse,* 330.
154. Quoted in Cohn-Sherbok and Cohn-Sherbok, *Jewish and Christian Mysticism,* 104 (adapted).
155. Quoted in Richard K. Emmerson, "Introduction: The Apocalypse in Medieval Culture," in Emmerson and McGinn, *Apocalypse,* 298.
156. Graves, *White Goddess,* 344–45.
157. Graves, *White Goddess,* 345.
158. Yarbro Collins, *Crisis and Catharsis,* 154.
159. Rev. 3:13 (KJV).
160. Quoted in de la Bedoyere, *Meddlesome Friar,* 204 (adapted).
161. Yarbro Collins, *Crisis and Catharsis,* 155 (adapted).
162. Rev. 1:1 (KJV).
163. Rev. 22:7 (KJV).
164. John J. Collins, Bernard McGinn, and Stephen J. Stein, "General Introduction," in Collins, *Origins of Apocalypticism,* x.

CHAPTER 4: THE APOCALYPTIC INVASION

1. Quoted in Bernard McGinn, "Revelation," in Alter and Kermode, *Literary Guide,* 523.
2. Matt. 5:44 (KJV; adapted).
3. Rev. 19:13–14 (RSV).

4. Rev. 19:15, 19:17, 19:18 (RSV). The Greek text refers to "birds," but some translations render the word as "vultures" because John clearly refers to carrion eaters.
5. Matt. 25:40 (KJV).
6. Rev. 14:4 (RSV).
7. Rev. 20:12 (RSV).
8. Rev. 21:8 (RSV).
9. Schüssler Fiorenza, *Book of Revelation*, 24.
10. Quoted in Schüssler Fiorenza, *Apocalypse*, 8.
11. Quoted in Ehrman, *Jesus*, 17.
12. Tertullian, quoted in Greenslade, *Schism*, 110.
13. Rev. 21:9, 21:10, 21:18, 21:19 (RSV).
14. Rev. 11:8 (KJV).
15. Quoted in Brian E. Daley, "Apocalypticism in Early Christian Theology," in McGinn, *Apocalypticism*, 11–12.
16. Quoted in Brian E. Daley, "Apocalypticism in Early Christian Theology," in McGinn, *Apocalypticism*, 11.
17. Malone, *Women and Christianity*, 1:113.
18. P. Hughes, quoted in Festinger, Riecken, and Schachter, *When Prophecy Fails*, 6–7 (adapted).
19. Brian E. Daley, "Apocalypticism in Early Christian Theology," in McGinn, *Apocalypticism*, 7.
20. Fox, *Jesus in America*, 253 (referring to "Protestant millennialists" such as Seventh-day Adventists and Jehovah's Witnesses).
21. Rev. 17:4 (RSV).
22. Rev. 2:24 (NKJ).
23. Matt. 22:21 (RSV).
24. Rom. 13:1 (NKJ).
25. Eusebius, "The Oration of Eusebius Pamphilus in Praise of the Emperor Constantine," in Schaff and Wace, *Eusebius*, 584.
26. Rev. 17:5 (RSV). (John refers here to "Babylon," a term that is understood to refer to Rome); Rev. 14:8 (KJV).
27. McGinn, *Visions of the End*, 25.
28. Quoted in Smith, *Constantine the Great*, 201.
29. Rev. 1:1 (KJV).
30. Paula Fredriksen, "Tyconius and Augustine on the Apocalypse," in Emmerson and McGinn, *Apocalypse*, 20–21.
31. Dan. 12:11, 12:12 (NKJ).
32. Dan. 12:10 (JPS).
33. Matt. 24:15–16 (NKJ).
34. Matt. 24:19–21 (RSV; adapted).
35. Matt. 24:7 (KJV).
36. Mark 8:38 (KJV).

37. Mark 9:1 (RSV). (See also Mark 13:30, 14:62.)
38. Matt. 24:34 (RSV).
39. 1 Thess. 4:16–17 (NKJ; adapted).
40. McGinn, *Visions of the End*, 11.
41. 2 Thess. 1–2, 3 (RSV).
42. Mark 13:7 (NKJ; adapted).
43. Mark 13:22 (RSV).
44. Mark: 13:21, 13:32 (NKJ; adapted).
45. Rowley, *Relevance of Apocalyptic*, 119.
46. Quoted in Fallon, "Gnostic Apocalypses," 143.
47. Adela Yarbro Collins, "Revelation, Book of," in Freedman, *Anchor Bible Dictionary,* 5:695.
48. Yarbro Collins, "Revelation, Book of," in Freedman, *Anchor Bible Dictionary,* 5:695.
49. Quoted in Schüssler Fiorenza, *Book of Revelation*, 87.
50. Adela Yarbro Collins, "Revelation, Book of," in Freedman, *Anchor Bible Dictionary,* 5:706, quoting Eusebius, *Hist. Eccl.* 725.
51. Adela Yarbro Collins, "Early Christian," in "Apocalypses and Apocalypticism," in Freedman, *Anchor Bible Dictionary,* 1:290.
52. Quoted in Colwell, *Study of the Bible,* 21–22.
53. Colwell, *Study of the Bible,* 34.
54. Colwell, *Study of the Bible,* 32, 35.
55. Quoted in Colwell, *Study of the Bible,* 35 (adapted).
56. Quoted in Bernard McGinn, "Revelation," in Alter and Kermode, *Literary Guide,* 529.
57. Ellul, *Apocalypse,* 1977, 9–10 (adapted).
58. Akenson, *Surpassing Wonder,* 226–27.
59. Rev. 11:2 (NKJ; "tread the holy city underfoot"); Rev. 11:3–4, 11:7 (RSV; "the beast that ascends").
60. Rev. 11:13 (RSV).
61. Rev. 11:8 (RSV).
62. Rev. 17:7 (NKJ).
63. Rev. 1:20 (NKJ).
64. Brian E. Daley, "Apocalypticism in Early Christian Theology," in McGinn, *Apocalypticism,* 6.
65. Quoted in Boyer, *When Time Shall Be,* 47.
66. Paula Fredriksen, "Tyconius and Augustine on the Apocalypse," in Emmerson and McGinn, *Apocalypse,* 21.
67. Bernard McGinn, "Revelation," in Alter and Kermode, *Literary Guide,* 528 ("moral conflict ..."); Augustine, *City of God,* XX:7, 719 ("ridiculous fancies").
68. Bernard McGinn, "Revelation," in Alter and Kermode, *Literary Guide,* 528, referring to *City of God,* XX:7 and XX:9.

69. Paula Fredriksen, "Tyconius and Augustine on the Apocalypse," in Emmerson and McGinn, *Apocalypse*, 35.

70. Quoted in Robert E. Lerner, "Millennialism," in McGinn, *Apocalypticism*, 328 (adapted).

71. Adapted from Augustine, *City of God*, XX:7, 719, and a quoted passages from *City of God* that appears in "Tyconius and Augustine on the Apocalypse," by Paula Fredriksen, in Emmerson and McGinn, *Apocalypse*, 29.

72. Augustine, *City of God*, XX:7, 719 (adapted).

73. Augustine, *City of God*, XX:17, 736.

74. Quoted in"The Medieval Return to the Thousand-Year Sabbath, in Emmerson and McGinn, *Apocalypse*, 52.

75. Augustine, *City of God*, XX:7, 720.

76. Augustine, *City of God*, XX:11, 729.

77. Paula Fredriksen, "Tyconius and Augustine on the Apocalypse," in Emmerson and McGinn, *Apocalypse*, 34 ("radical agnosticism"); Robert E. Lerner, "The Medieval Return to the Thousand-Year Sabbath," in Emmerson and McGinn, *Apocalypse*, 60 n. 29 ("eschatological uncertainty principle").

78. Augustine, *City of God*, XX:20, 742 (referring specifically to the resurrection of the dead).

79. Robert E. Lerner, "Millennialism," in McGinn, *Apocalypticism*, 356.

80. Bernard McGinn, "The Last Judgment in Christian Tradition," in McGinn, *Apocalypticism*, 378.

81. Paula Fredriksen, "Tyconius and Augustine on the Apocalypse," in Emmerson and McGinn, *Apocalypse*, 35.

82. Rev. 17:9 (KJV).

83. 1 John 2:18 (NKJ; adapted).

84. Rev. 12:9 (RSV).

85. Rev. 13:2, 13:8 (RSV; adapted).

86. Rev. 13:18 (KJV).

87. Rev. 17:8 (KJV).

88. Rev. 13:3 (RSV).

89. Quoted in Ladd, *Revelation of John*, 233 (adapted).

90. Quoted in Brian E. Daley, "Apocalypticism in Early Christian Theology," in McGinn, *Apocalypticism*, 23.

91. Quoted in Brian E. Daley, "Apocalypticism in Early Christian Theology," in McGinn, *Apocalypticism*, 23 (adapted).

92. Paula Fredriksen, "Tyconius and Augustine on the Apocalypse," in Emmerson and McGinn, *Apocalypticism*, 30.

93. Rev. 6:12 (KJV; adapted).

94. Quoted in Robert E. Lerner, "The Medieval Return to the Thousand-Year Sabbath," in Emmerson and McGinn, *Apocalypticism*, 52.

95. Dan. 12:7 (KJV).

96. Rev. 12:14, 12:6, 11:3, 13:5.

97. Ps. 90:4 (KJV).
98. 2 Pet. 3:8 (KJV).
99. Quoted in John Williams, "Purpose and Imagery in the Apocalypse Commentary of Beatus of Liébana," in Emmerson and McGinn, *Apocalypse*, 225.
100. Bernard McGinn, "The Last Judgment in Christian Tradition," in McGinn, *Apocalypticism*, 379.
101. Rev. 21:16 (KJV).
102. John 2:21 (KJV).
103. Schüssler Fiorenza, *Apocalypse*, 8. Schüssler Fiorenza specifically refers to the fact that "the author speaks of divine wrath and fierce revenge but not of God's love and grace."
104. Quoted in Robert E. Lerner, "The Medieval Return to the Thousand-Year Sabbath," in Emmerson and McGinn, *Apocalypse*, 4 ("The saints will in no wise have an earthly kingdom ..."); Jerome, *Commentary on Isaiah*, quoted in Bernard McGinn, "Introduction: John's Apocalypse and the Apocalyptic Mentality" in Emmerson and McGinn, *Apocalypse*, 18–19 ("To take John's Apocalypse according to the letter ...").
105. Rev. 2:9 (KJV; "synagogue of Satan"); Rev. 5:5 (KJV; "the Lion of the tribe of Judah").
106. Dale Kinney, "The Apocalypse in Early Christian Monumental Decoration," in Emmerson and McGinn, *Apocalypse*, 209.
107. Dale Kinney, "The Apocalypse in Early Christian Monumental Decoration," in Emmerson and McGinn, *Apocalypse*, 200, quoting Frederik van der Meer.
108. Quoted in McGinn, *Visions of the End*, 55.
109. Quoted in Brian E. Daley, "Apocalypticism in Early Christian Theology," in McGinn, *Apocalypticism*, 33.
110. Rev. 10:9 (KJV).
111. Rev. 1:16 (KJV).

CHAPTER 5: "YOUR OWN DAYS, FEW AND EVIL"
1. Thompson, *End of Time*, 36.
2. Strictly speaking, *The Seventh Seal* is set in mid-fourteenth-century Scandinavia, but the director paints a highly stylized picture of the High Middle Ages drawn from medieval church murals that he first saw in early childhood. (Commentary by Peter Cowie, *The Seventh Seal*, Criterion Collection, 1987.)
3. McGinn, *Visions of the End*, xx n. 1.
4. Abbo of Fleury, *Apologetic Work*, quoted in McGinn, *Visions of the End*, 89.
5. Thompson, *End of Time*, 38.
6. Richard K. Emmerson and Bernard McGinn, "Introduction: The Apocalypse in Medieval Culture," in Emmerson and McGinn, *Apocalypse*, xxii, 294 (adapted).

7. Malone, *Women and Christianity,* 2:30.
8. Quoted in Malone, *Women and Christianity,* 2:48.
9. Quoted in Malone, *Women and Christianity,* 1:18.
10. Quoted in Malone, *Women and Christianity,* 1:18 (adapted).
11. Quoted in Roberto Rusconi, "Antichrist and Antichrists," in *Apocalypticism,* 294.
12. Malone, *Women and Chrisitanity,* 2:96.
13. Bernard McGinn, "Apocalypticism and Church Reform: 1100–1500," in McGinn, *Apocalypticism,* 86.
14. Quoted in Bernard McGinn, "Revelation," in Alter and Kermode, *Literary Guide,* 532.
15. Quoted in McGinn, *Visions of the End,* 130.
16. Quoted in Bernard McGinn, "Revelation," in Alter and Kermode, *Literary Guide,* 528. See also Rev. 5:5.
17. Bernard McGinn, "Revelation," in Alter and Kermode, *Literary Guide,* 528.
18. Quoted in Ehrman, *Jesus,* 15.
19. Thompson, *End of Time,* 63, 65.
20. Robert E. Lerner, "The Medieval Return to the Thousand-Year Sabbath," in Emmerson and McGinn, *Apocalypse,* 64.
21. McGinn, "Revelation," in Alter and Kermode, *Literary Guide,* 528.
22. Quoted in Richard K. Emmerson, "Introduction: The Apocalypse in Medieval Culture," in Emmerson and McGinn, *Apocalypse,* 319 (adapted).
23. Bernard McGinn, "Apocalypticism and Church Reform: 1100–1500," in McGinn, *Apocalypticism,* 86.
24. John Fox, *Actes and Monuments* (1563), quoted in Marjorie Reeves, "Dragon," in Drane, *Revelation,* 32 (adapted).
25. Malone, *Women and Christianity,* 2:111, 112.
26. *Scivias,* quoted in McGinn, *Visions of the End,* 101.
27. Richard K. Emmerson, "Introduction: The Apocalypse in Medieval Culture," in Emmerson and McGinn, *Revelation,* 298.
28. Bernard McGinn, "Apocalypticism and Church Reform: 1100–1500," in McGinn, *Apocalypticism,* 83–84.
29. Bernard McGinn, "Apocalypticism and Church Reform: 1100–1500," in McGinn, *Apocalypticism,* 83.
30. Quoted in Robert E. Lerner, "Millennialism," in McGinn, *Apocalypticism,* 341.
31. Quoted in David Burr, "Mendicant Readings of the Apocalypse," in Emmerson and McGinn, *Apocalypse,* 96.
32. Robert E. Lerner, "The Medieval Return to the Thousand-Year Sabbath," in Emmerson and McGinn, *Apocalypse,* 65–66.
33. Peter John Olivi, *Commentary on Revelation,* quoted in McGinn, *Visions of the End,* 208–09.
34. Marjorie Reeves, "Dragon," in Drane, *Revelation,* 31.
35. Paraphrased and quoted in Robert E. Lerner, "Millennialism," in McGinn, *Apocalypticism,* 352.

36. Quoted in Gian Luca Potestà, "Radical Apocalyptic Movements in the Late Middle Ages," in McGinn, *Apocalypticism,* 125 (adapted; "The world will be filled with indignation ..."); and Robert E. Lerner, "Millennialism," in McGinn, *Apocalypticism,* 352 (adapted; "Many princes, nobles and mighty ones ...").

37. Roberto Rusconi, "Antichrist and Antichrists," in *Apocalypticism,* 306.

38. Robert E. Lerner, "Millennialism," in McGinn, *Apocalypticism,* 353, 354.

39. Robert E. Lerner, "Millennialism," in McGinn, *Apocalypticism,* 351–52.

40. Robert E. Lerner, "Millennialism," in McGinn, *Apocalypticism,* 332 (adapted). (Lerner is referring here specifically to the so-called Tiburtine Sibyl.)

41. Quoted in McGinn, *Visions of the End,* 218–19 (adapted).

42. Quoted in McGinn, *Visions of the End,* 220–21.

43. Quoted in Richard K. Emmerson, "Introduction: The Apocalypse in Medieval Culture," in Emmerson and McGinn, *Apocalypse,* 318–19.

44. Quoted in Malone, *Women and Christianity,* 2:131–32 (adapted).

45. Malone, *Women and Christianity,* 2:177, 178.

46. Rev. 3:8 (KJV).

47. Rev. 7:2, 10:1, 10:6 (KJV, RSV).

48. Paraphrased in Gian Luca Potestà, "Radical Apocalyptic Movements in the Late Middle Ages," in McGinn, *Apocalypticism,* 120.

49. Quoted in Malone, *Women and Christianity,* 2:211.

50. Yarbro Collins, *Crisis and Catharsis,* 159.

51. Rev. 2:19, 2:20 (RSV; adapted).

52. Quoted in McGinn, *Visions of the End,* 19. (The fragment from Heracleitus is preserved in the writings of Plutarch.)

53. McGinn, *Visions of the End,* 50.

54. McGinn, *Visions of the End,* 50.

55. Bernard McGinn, "Apocalypticism and Church Reform: 1100–1500," in McGinn, *Apocalypticism,* 92.

56. Quoted in McGinn, *Visions of the End,* 169.

57. Roberto Rusconi, "Antichrist and Antichrists," in McGinn, *Apocalypticism,* 303.

58. Quoted in McGinn, *Visions of the End,* 190 (adapted).

59. McGinn, *Visions of the End,* 188.

60. Robin Barnes, "Images of Hope and Despair: Western Apocalypticism: ca. 1500–1800," in *Apocalypticism,* 154.

61. Rev. 9:1 (KJV).

62. Quoted in McGinn, *Visions of the End,* 150.

63. Rev. 16:12 (KJV).

64. Robert E. Lerner, "Millennialism," in *Apocalypticism,* 343.

65. Richard K. Emmerson, "Apocalyptic Themes and Imagery in Medieval and Renaissance Literature," in *Apocalypticism,* 406.

66. Robin Barnes, "Images of Hope and Despair: Western Apocalypticism: ca. 1500–1800," in *Apocalypticism*, 156. (Raimarus's calculations are "reckoned from 1596").

67. Richard K. Emmerson, "Apocalyptic Themes and Imagery in Medieval and Renaissance Literature," in *Apocalypticism*, 402 (adapted).

68. Rev. 20:12 (KJV; adapted).

69. Penn Szittya, "Domesday Bokes: The Apocalypse in Medieval English Literary Culture," in Emmerson and McGinn, *Apocalpyse*, 374, 375.

70. Quoted in Roberto Rusconi, "Antichrist and Antichrists," in *Apocalypticism*, 298.

71. Geoffrey of Monmouth, *The History of the Kings of Britain*, quoted in McGinn, *Visions of the End*, 183.

72. *Henry IV, Part 2*, act 5, scene 3, lines 40–45, quoted in in Richard K. Emmerson, "Apocalyptic Themes and Imagery in Medieval and Renaissance Literature," in *Apocalypticism*, 426.

73. Quoted in Richard K. Emmerson, "Introduction: The Apocalypse in Medieval Culture," in Emmerson and McGinn, *Apocalpyse*, 324.

74. Rev. 12:4 (RSV).

75. See, e.g., Ronald B. Bond, "Whore of Babylon," in Drane, *Revelation*, 54.

76. Dante, *Inferno*, 19:106–8, quoted in Richard K. Emmerson, "Apocalyptic Themes and Imagery in Medieval and Renaissance Literature," in *Apocalypticism*, 431–32.

77. Dante, *Purgatorio*, 33:43, quoted in Ronald B. Herzman, "Dante and the Apocalypse," in Emmerson and McGinn, *Apocalpyse*, 401.

78. Quoted in Schüssler Fiorenza, *Apocalypse*, 8.

79. Bernard McGinn, "Revelation," in Alter and Kermode, *Literary Guide*, 529.

80. Quoted in McGinn, 529 (adapted).

81. Quoted in Roberto Rusconi, "Antichrist and Antichrists," in McGinn, *Apocalypticism*, 311 ("[T]he true Antichrist …"), 312 ("I do not know …").

82. "Against Hanswurst," quoted in Ronald B. Bond, "Whore of Babylon," in Drane, *Revelation*, 54.

83. Jean-Robert Armogathe, "Interpretations of the Revelation of John: 1500–1800," in *Apocalypticism*, 187–88.

84. Rev. 19:13, 15 (KJV).

85. Quoted in Boyer, *When Time Shall Be*, 50.

86. McGinn, *Visions of the End*, 89.

87. Quoted in McGinn, *Visions of the End*, 92–93 (adapted).

88. Boyer, *When Time Shall Be*, 51.

89. Quoted in Boyer, *When Time Shall Be*, 55.

90. Quoted in Cohn, 237, 239, 247 (adapted).

91. Robin Barnes, "Images of Hope and Despair: Western Apocalypticism: ca. 1500–1800," in *Apocalypticism*, 163.

92. Cohn, *Pursuit of the Millennium*, 271.

93. Cohn, *Pursuit of the Millennium,* 268 (adapted).
94. Quoted in Cohn, *Pursuit of the Millennium,* 272.
95. Cohn, *Pursuit of the Millennium,* 275.
96. Quoted in Cohn, *Pursuit of the Millennium,* 274.
97. Cohn, *Pursuit of the Millennium,* 278.
98. Gian Luca Potestà, "Radical Apocalyptic Movements in the Late Middle Ages," in *Apocalypticism,* 133.
99. Tizio, "the Sienese chronicler," quoted in Thompson, *End of Time,* 80.
100. Quoted in Van Paassen, *Crown of Fire,* 50.
101. Rev. 18:12–13 (RSV).
102. Quoted in de la Bedoyere, *Meddlesome Friar,* 28.
103. Robin Barnes, "Images of Hope and Despair: Western Apocalypticism: ca. 1500–1800," in *Apocalypticism,* 145.
104. Quoted in Van Paassen, *Crown of Fire,* 63.
105. Quoted in Van Paassen, *Crown of Fire,* 114.
106. Quoted in Van Paassen, *Crown of Fire,* 178.
107. Quoted in Van Paassen, *Crown of Fire,* 180.
108. Quoted in de la Bedoyere, *Meddlesome Friar,* 34.
109. Van Paassen, *Crown of Fire,* 230.
110. Van Paassen, *Crown of Fire,* 230.
111. Van Paassen insists that only illustrated copies of Petrarch and Boccacio, featuring "miniatures of a salacious character," were burned. Van Paassen, *Crown of Fire,* 234.
112. Quoted in de la Bedoyere, *Meddlesome Friar,* 170.
113. Quoted in de la Bedoyere, *Meddlesome Friar,* 176. Another version of the same account attributes to Savonarola a slightly different remark: "A cardinal's purple will not be bestowed on us, but of a martyr's gown drenched in blood I am absolutely certain." Quoted in van Paassen, 214.
114. Quoted in Van Paassen, *Crown of Fire,* 98.
115. Quoted in de la Bedoyere, *Meddlesome Friar,* 245–46.
116. Bernard McGinn, quoted in Thompson, *End of Time,* 80
117. Quoted in de la Bedoyere, *Meddlesome Friar,* 246.
118. Rev. 21:5 (KJV).
119. Robin Barnes, "Images of Hope and Despair: Western Apocalypticism: ca. 1500–1800," in *Apocalypticism,* 144.
120. McGinn, *Visions of the End,* 88.
121. Quoted in McGinn, "Apocalypticism and Church Reform: 1100–1500," in McGinn, 102.
122. Bernard McGinn, "The Last Judgment in Christian Tradition," in *Apocalypticism,* 378.
123. Quoted in Boyer, *When Time Shall Be,* 225 (adapted).
124. Rev. 21:1 (KJV). (The phrase is rendered in the Vulgate, a Latin translation of the Bible, in the objective case—that is, *terram novam.*)

CHAPTER 6: TO BEGIN THE WORLD OVER AGAIN

1. David L. Jeffrey and Marjorie Reeves, "Millennium," in Drane, *Revelation*, 46.
2. *The Day of Trouble Is Near*, quoted in David L. Jeffrey and Marjorie Reeves, "Millennium," in Drane, *Revelation*, 46.
3. William Blake, "Jerusalem" (1804), quoted in Boyer, *When Time Shall Be*, 184.
4. Blake, "Jerusalem" (1804), quoted in Boyer, *When Time Shall Be*, 184.
5. Not every historian is quite so convinced, however. "Whether or not English Puritans justified their removal to the New World in eschatological terms is an issue that has divided the scholarly community since the 1980s." Reiner Smolinski, "Apocalypticism in Colonial North America," in Stein, *Apocalypticism*, 36.
6. Quoted in Boyer, *When Time Shall Be*, 68.
7. Cotton Mather, quoted in Boyer, *When Time Shall Be*, 69 ("Flying from the Depravations ..."); http://www.mytholyoke.edu/acad/intrel/winthrop.htm ("a City Upon a Hill ..."); Perry Miller, quoted in Wagar, *Terminal Visions*, 59 ("the first bestseller ...").
8. Quoted in Boyer, *When Time Shall Be*, 64.
9. Quoted in Robin Barnes, "Images of Hope and Despair: Western Apocalypticism: ca. 1500–1800," in *Apocalypticism*, 163.
10. Quoted in Thompson, *End of Time*, 92 (adapted).
11. Quoted in Boyer, *When Time Shall Be*, 64.
12. *Bartholomew Fair* (1614), quoted in Boyer, *When Time Shall Be*, 64.
13. Quoted in McGinn, in Alter and Kermode, *Literary Guide*, 537.
14. Paraphrased in Boyer, *When Time Shall Be*, 65.
15. Boyer, *When Time Shall Be*, 67.
16. Perry Miller, "The End of the World" (1950), paraphrased in (and adapted from) Boyer, *When Time Shall Be*, 67.
17. Cotton Mather, *Memorable Providences, Relating to Witchcrafts and Possessions* (1689), http://www.law.umkc.edu/faculty/projects/ftrials/salem/ASA_MATH.HTM.
18. Quoted in Wendell, *Cotton Mather*, 207.
19. Thompson, *End of Time*, 96.
20. *Magnalia Christi Americana*, quoted in David L. Jeffrey and Marjorie Reeves, "Millennium," in Drane, *Revelation*, 46.
21. Quoted in Wendell, *Cotton Mather*, 82.
22. Quoted in Reiner Smolinski, "Apocalypticism in Colonial North America," in Stein, *Apocalypticism*, 52.
23. Quoted in Boyer, *When Time Shall Be*, 70.
24. Emma Lazarus, "The New Colossus," www.sonnets.org/lazarus.
25. Cotton Mather on John Mather, quoted in Wendell, *Cotton Mather*, 9.
26. *The Jefferson Bible*, http://www.angelfire.com/co/JeffersonBible/jeffintro.html.
27. *A Sermon Preached Before the Honorable Council, May 29th, 1776*, quoted in Reiner Smolinski, "Apocalypticism in Colonial North America," in Stein, *Apocalypticism*, 68.

28. Quoted in Boyer, *When Time Shall Be,* 74.
29. Reiner Smolinski, "Apocalypticism in Colonial North America," in Stein, *Apocalypticism,* 55.
30. Smolinski, "Apocalypticism in Colonial North America," in Stein, *Apocalypticism,* 55.
31. Quoted in Reiner Smolinski, "Apocalypticism in Colonial North America," in Stein, *Apocalypticism,* 56.
32. Paul Boyer, "The Growth of Fundamentalist Apocalyptic in the United States," in Stein, *Apocalypticism,* 144 (adapted).
33. Boyer, "The Growth of Fundamentalist Apocalyptic in the United States," in Stein, *Apocalypticism,* 144–45; Matt. 25:40 (KJV).
34. Richard T. Ely (1854–1943), quoted in James H. Moorhead, "Apocalypticism in Mainstream Protestantism, 1800 to the Present," in Stein, *Apocalypticism,* 95.
35. Samuel Hopkins, *Treatise of the Millennium* (1793), quoted in Reiner Smolinski, "Apocalypticism in Colonial North America," in Stein, *Apocalypticism,* 61.
36. *Ladies' Repository* (February 1850), quoted in James H. Moorhead, "Apocalypticism in Mainstream Protestantism, 1800 to the Present," in Stein, *Apocalypticism,* 76.
37. John L. O'Sullivan, "The Great Nation of Futurity" (1839), Cornell University Library, http://cdl.library.cornell.edu.
38. Dan. 8:14 (KJV).
39. Quoted in Ehrman, *Jesus,* 13.
40. Quoted in Stephen J. Stein, "Apocalypticism Outside the Mainstream in the United States," in Stein, *Apocalypticism,* 116.
41. Paul Boyer, "The Growth of Fundamentalist Apocalyptic in the United States," in Stein, *Apocalypticism,* 146.
42. Quoted in Thompson, *End of Time,* 100.
43. Weber, *Living in the Shadow,* 42.
44. Quoted in Boyer, *When Time Shall Be,* 81.
45. Quoted in Thompson, *End of Time,* 100.
46. Quoted in Stephen J. Stein, "Apocalypticism Outside the Mainstream in the United States," in Stein, *Apocalypticism,* 116.
47. Rev. 11:19 (KJV).
48. Thompson, *End of Time,* 287.
49. Fox, *Jesus in America,* 253.
50. Fox, *Jesus in America,* 255.
51. Quoted in Stephen J. Stein, "Apocalypticism Outside the Mainstream in the United States," in Stein, *Apocalypticism,* 114.
52. Fox, *Jesus in America,* 254.
53. James H. Moorhead, "Apocalypticism in Mainstream Protestantism, 1800 to the Present," in Stein, *Apocalypticism,* 73 (adapted).
54. Rev. 14:19 (KJV). See also Isa. 63:3.

55. http://www.cyberhymnal.org.
56. Quoted in James H. Moorhead, "Apocalypticism in Mainstream Protestantism, 1800 to the Present," in Stein, *Apocalypticism,* 85.
57. Weber, *Living in the Shadow,* 83.
58. Boyer, *When Time Shall Be,* 92, quoting John Charles Ryle.
59. Robin Barnes, "Images of Hope and Despair: Western Apocalypticism: ca. 1500–1800," in *Apocalypticism,* 172 ("... the triumph and rule of the true church ..."); Paul Boyer, "The Growth of Fundamentalist Apocalyptic in the United States," in Stein, *Apocalypticism,* 143 ("... human progress and moral advance ...").
60. Quoted in James H. Moorhead, "Apocalypticism in Mainstream Protestantism, 1800 to the Present," in Stein, *Apocalypticism,* 81.
61. 1 Thess. 4:16–17 (RSV).
62. Weber, *Living in the Shadow,* 22.
63. Weber, *Living in the Shadow,* 21.
64. Paul Boyer, "The Growth of Fundamentalist Apocalyptic in the United States," in Stein, *Apocalypticism,* 151, 152.
65. Martin E. Marty, "The Future of No Future," in Stein, *Apocalypticism,* 462.
66. Quoted in Paul Boyer, "The Growth of Fundamentalist Apocalyptic in the United States," in Stein, *Apocalypticism,* 154.
67. Paul Boyer, "The Growth of Fundamentalist Apocalyptic in the United States," in Stein, *Apocalypticism,* 156.
68. Quoted in Weber, *Living in the Shadow,* 174.
69. Quoted in Boyer, *When Time Shall Be,* 93.
70. Quoted in Boyer, *When Time Shall Be,* 94.
71. Scofield, *Scofield Reference Bible,* 1342 n. 2.
72. Isaac Haldeman, *The Signs of the Times* (1910), quoted in Boyer, *When Time Shall Be,* 95.
73. Weber, *Living in the Shadow,* 62.
74. Quoted in Weber, *Living in the Shadow,* 62.
75. Quoted in Cohn-Sherbok and Cohn-Sherbok, *Jewish and Christian Mysticism,* 145.
76. Quoted in Boyer, *When Time Shall Be,* 299.
77. Quoted in Boyer, *When Time Shall Be,* 95.
78. Quoted in Boyer, *When Time Shall Be,* 182.
79. Brian E. Daley, "Apocalypticism in Early Christian Theology," in *Apocalypticism,* 13.
80. Quoted in Boyer, *When Time Shall Be,* 183.
81. Boyer, *When Time Shall Be,* 89.
82. Domb, *Transformation,* vii, 133.
83. Rev. 22:20 (KJV).
84. Quoted in Klagsbrun, *Voices of Wisdom,* 442.
85. Dubnow, *History of the Jews,* 1:205.

86. Dubnow, *History of the Jews,* 1:206.
87. Weber, *Living in the Shadow,* 136.
88. Quoted in Weber, *Living in the Shadow,* 138–39.
89. Weber, *Living in the Shadow,* 140.
90. Quoted in Weber, *Living in the Shadow,* 140.
91. Weber, *Living in the Shadow,* 141.
92. Weber, *Living in the Shadow,* 144.
93. Quoted in Weber, *Living in the Shadow,* 144–45.
94. Quoted in Weber, *Living in the Shadow,* 145–46.
95. Weber, *Living in the Shadow,* 188.
96. Quoted in Weber, *Living in the Shadow,* 190.
97. Arthur W. Pink, *The Redeemer's Return,* quoted in Weber, *Living in the Shadow,* 54.
98. Deut. 32:41–42 (TNK; adapted).
99. James H. Moorhead, "Apocalypticism in Mainstream Protestantism, 1800 to the Present," in Stein, *Apocalypticism,* 88, 89, 89, quoting *Bibliotheca Sacra* (1907) ("... queer bird ...") and *Biblical World* (1910) ("... highly imaginative Jewish thought ...").
100. Paul Boyer, "The Growth of Fundamentalist Apocalyptic in the United States," in Stein, *Apocalypticism,* 154.
101. Quoted in James H. Moorhead, "Apocalypticism in Mainstream Protestantism, 1800 to the Present," in Stein, *Apocalypticism,* 95.
102. Quoted in James H. Moorhead, "Apocalypticism in Mainstream Protestantism, 1800 to the Present," in Stein, *Apocalypticism,* 99.
103. Paul Boyer, "The Growth of Fundamentalist Apocalyptic in the United States," in Stein, *Apocalypticism,* 159.
104. Quoted in Stephen J. Stein, "Apocalypticism Outside the Mainstream in the United States," in Stein, *Apocalypticism,* 123.
105. Quoted in Boyer, *When Time Shall Be,* 100–101.
106. Fussell, *Great War,* 24.
107. Dan. 11:3–4 (KJV; adapted).
108. Quoted in Weber, *Living in the Shadow,* 103.
109. Quoted in Weber, *Living in the Shadow,* 103.
110. Ezek. 39:1 (JPS; adapted).
111. E. L. Langston, *Great Britain, Palestine, Russia and the Jews* (1918), quoted in Boyer, *When Time Shall Be,* 186.
112. Langston, *Great Britain, Palestine, Russia and the Jews* (1918), quoted in Boyer, *When Time Shall Be,* 186.
113. Rev. 22:17 (KJV).
114. Colwell, *Study of the Bible,* 100–101 (adapted).
115. Quoted in Boyer, *When Time Shall Be,* 108–9.
116. Rev. 13:16 (KJV).
117. Weber, *Living in the Shadow,* 180 (adapted).

118. Rev. 17:5 (KJV).
119. Quoted in Weber, *Living in the Shadow,* 109.
120. Quoted in Boyer, *When Time Shall Be,* 110.
121. Quoted in Boyer, *When Time Shall Be,* 110.
122. Quoted in Boyer, *When Time Shall Be,* 218.
123. Quoted in Boyer, *When Time Shall Be,* 111.
124. Quoted in Shirer, *Rise and Fall,* 240.
125. Thompson, *End of Time,* 129.
126. Thompson, *End of Time,* 129–30 (adapted).
127. From a newspaper interview with Norman Cohn quoted in Thompson, *End of Time,* 130.
128. Rev. 4:6 (RSV).
129. James A. Hijiya, "The *Gita* of Robert Oppenheimer," Proceedings of the Americna Philosophical Society, 144:2 (June 2000), 123–67.

CHAPTER 7: THE GODLESS APOCALYPSE

1. *On the Beach.*
2. *On the Beach* (adapted).
3. Stephen D. O'Leary, "Apocalypticism in American Popular Culture: From the Dawn of the Nuclear Age to the End of the American Century," in Stein, *Apocalypticism,* 396.
4. Susan Sontag, "The Imagination of Disaster," in Sontag, *Against Interpretation,* 215.
5. Dick and Zelazny, *Deus Irae,* 29.
6. Dick and Zelazny, *Deus Irae,* 29.
7. *The Omega Man.*
8. Stephen D. O'Leary, "Apocalypticism in American Popular Culture: From the Dawn of the Nuclear Age to the End of the American Century," in Stein, *Apocalypticism,* 400.
9. *Dr. Strangelove.*
10. Quoted in Boyer, *When Time Shall Be,* 150. (The quote is taken from *Blessed Assurance,* a 1986 study of attitudes toward nuclear war and religion conducted by A. G. Mojtabai.)
11. Boyer, *When Time Shall Be,* x, 255.
12. Boyer, *When Time Shall Be,* x, 255.
13. Weber, *Living in the Shadow,* 234.
14. Huffey, *Hallelujah Side,* 65.
15. Rev. 1:7 (KJV).
16. Quoted in Boyer, *When Time Shall Be,* 106–7.
17. Donald Grey Barnhouse, *Eternity,* December 1945, quoted in Boyer, *When Time Shall Be,* 118.
18. Boyer, *When Time Shall Be,* 137.

19. Quoted in Paul Boyer, "The Growth of Fundamentalist Apocalyptic in the United States," in Stein, *Apocalypticism,* 164–65 (adapted).

20. M. R. DeHaan, quoted in Boyer, *When Time Shall Be,* 320 ("Every single inhabitant ..."); Reiner Smolinski, "Apocalypticism in Colonial North America," in Stein, *Apocalypticism,* 62 ("... the ratio between the eternally lost and saved ..."); S. Dwight Coder, quoted in Boyer, *When Time Shall Be,* 242 ("... the Lord is going to judge ...").

21. Quoted in Boyer, *When Time Shall Be,* 244.

22. Wilburt Smith, quoted in Boyer, *When Time Shall Be,* 235.

23. M. R. DeHaan, quoted in Boyer, *When Time Shall Be,* 233.

24. David Wilkerson, *Set the Trumpet to Thy Mouth,* quoted in Boyer, *When Time Shall Be,* 234.

25. Dave Hunt, *The New Age Movement in Prophecy,* quoted in Boyer, *When Time Shall Be,* 233–34 ("a cosmic conspiracy to install the Antichrist").

26. Rev. 2:24 (RSV).

27. Rev. 16:2, 13:17 (RSV).

28. Paul Boyer, quoted in Barkun, *Culture of Conspiracy,* 44.

29. Paul Boyer, "The Growth of Fundamentalist Apocalyptic in the United States," in Stein, *Apocalypticism,* 176.

30. Boyer, "The Growth of Fundamentalist Apocalyptic in the United States," in Stein, *Apocalypticism,* 175.

31. Weber, *Living in the Shadow,* 211.

32. Ehrman, *Jesus,* 7.

33. Lindsey, *Apocalypse Code,* 186.

34. Lindsey, *Apocalypse Code,* 131–32.

35. Boyer, *When Time Shall Be,* 126.

36. Lindsey, *Apocalypse Code,* 137.

37. Lindsey, *Apocalypse Code,* 97.

38. Rev. 16:13 (KJV).

39. Lindsey, *Apocalypse Code,* 166.

40. Zech. 14:12 (KJV), quoted in Lindsey, *Apocalypse Code,* 175.

41. Lindsey, *Apocalypse Code,* 175.

42. Lindsey, *Apocalypse Code,* 5 ("the Best Seller"), 103 ("Future Fuehrer"), 122 ("Scarlet O'Harlot"), 146 ("World War III"), 111 ("Jewish Billy Grahams"), 137 ("The ultimate trip").

43. Lindsey, *Apocalypse Code,* 144.

44. Quoted in Ehrman, *Jesus,* 10.

45. Ehrman, *Jesus,* 10.

46. Quoted in Boyer, *When Time Shall Be,* 142.

47. Quoted in Halsell, *Prophecy and Politics,* 45.

48. Ezek. 30:3, 30:5, 38:22 (KJV; adapted).

49. Quoted in Halsell, *Prophecy and Politics,* 44–45.

50. Quoted in Halsell, *Prophecy and Politics,* 47.
51. Quoted in Halsell, *Prophecy and Politics,* 48.
52. Quoted in Boyer, *When Time Shall Be,* 141.
53. O'Leary, *Arguing the Apocalypse,* 177.
54. Quoted in Boyer, *When Time Shall Be,* 142.
55. Quoted in Boyer, *When Time Shall Be,* 143 (adapted).
56. Quoted in Boyer, *When Time Shall Be,* 143.
57. Rev. 17:5 (KJV).
58. Quoted in Halsell, *Prophecy and Politics,* 48.
59. Quoted in Boyer, *When Time Shall Be,* 10.
60. *The Omen.*
61. *The Omen.*
62. Stephen D. O'Leary, "Apocalypticism in American Popular Culture: From the Dawn of the Nuclear Age to the End of the American Century," in Stein, *Apocalypticism,* 422 (adapted).
63. Quoted in Boyer, *When Time Shall Be,* 12.
64. Weber, *Living in the Shadow,* 239.
65. Wagar, *Terminal Visions,* 3.
66. Quoted in Boyer, *When Time Shall Be,* 142–43.
67. http://www.newhumanist.com.uk.
68. Quoted in Boyer, *When Time Shall Be,* 145.
69. Quoted in Boyer, *When Time Shall Be,* 138.
70. Quoted in Boyer, *When Time Shall Be,* 138.
71. Quoted in Boyer, *When Time Shall Be,* 299.
72. Quoted in Weber, *Living in the Shadow,* 232.
73. Weber, *Living in the Shadow,* 236.
74. Wikipedia (http://en.wikipedia.org/wiki/).
75. *Playboy* interview quoted in Robert Scheer, "Hullabaloo Over Lust Lasts 20 Years," *Los Angeles Times,* December 17, 1996, http://www.robertscheer.com/; Matt. 5:28 (KJV; adapted).
76. Matt. 25:35 (NKJ).
77. Graham, *Approaching Hoofbeats,* 188–89, 192, 196.
78. LaHaye, *Beginning of the End,* 1973 (adapted).
79. Quoted in Thompson, *End of Time,* 146.
80. Quoted in Thompson, *End of Time,* 146.
81. Num. 19:2 ff.
82. Quoted in Gorenberg, *End of Days,* 16.
83. Gorenberg, *End of Days,* 154.
84. Rev. 18:11 (RSV) .
85. Quoted in Boyer, *When Time Shall Be,* 208.
86. Quoted in Boyer, *When Time Shall Be,* 207.
87. Quoted in Dowd, "Rapture and Rupture."

88. Gorenberg, *End of Days,* 162.
89. Chafets, "Rabbi Who Loved Evangelicals."
90. Quoted in Goldberg, May 24, 2002.
91. Quoted in Halsell, *Prophecy and Politics,* 138.
92. Paul Boyer, "The Growth of Fundamentalist Apocalyptic in the United States," in Stein, *Apocalypticism,* 172.
93. Quoted in Barkun, *Culture of Conspiracy,* 43.
94. Quoted in Gorenberg, *End of Days,* 240.
95. Quoted in Goldberg, May 24, 2002.
96. Quoted in Dowd, "Rapture and Rupture."
97. Quoted in Goldberg, May 24, 2002.
98. 1 Kings 18:20-40.
99. Quoted in Thompson, *End of Time,* 289.
100. Thompson, *End of Time,* 289.
101. Quoted in Thompson, *End of Time,* 289.
102. Thompson, *End of Time,* 290.
103. Thompson, *End of Time,* 294.
104. Thompson, *End of Time,* 288.
105. Rev. 5:5 (RSV).
106. Thompson, *End of Time,* 294.
107. Thompson, *End of Time,* 291, quoting comments by David Koresh to FBI negotiators during the siege in 1993.
108. Rev. 6:2 (KJV).
109. Rev: 6:9–10 (KJV).
110. Rev. 6:11 (KJV; adapted).
111. Thompson, *End of Time,* 297.
112. Thompson, *End of Time,* 298.
113. LaHaye, *Beginning of the End,* 8.
114. LaHaye and Jenkins, *Left Behind,* 16.
115. Lampman, "Apocalyptic."
116. Quoted in Gorenberg, *End of Days,* 31.
117. Quoted in Lampman, "Apocalyptic."
118. Quoted in Lampman, "Apocalyptic."
119. Gorenberg, "Intolerance: The Bestseller."
120. Gorenberg, "Intolerance: The Bestseller."
121. "A Library of Quotations on Religion and Politics by George Bush," citing *Times-Picayune* (New Orleans), December 25, 1999, http://www.beliefnet.com/.
122. Suskind, "Without a Doubt."
123. *Christianity Today.*
124. *Christianity Today.*
125. Wills, *New York Times,* March 30, 2003 (New York Times Premium Service; adapted).

126. http://www.newhumanist.com.uk.

127. Quoted in Thompson, *End of Time*, 311. (Robertson is here referring to George H. W. Bush.)

128. Barkun, *Disaster and the Millennium*, 146.

129. Quoted in McGinn, "Revelation," in Alter and Kermode, *Literary Guide*, 523.

130. Schüssler Fiorenza, *Book of Revelation*, 8.

131. Quoted in Boyer, *When Time Shall Be*, 260 (adapted).

132. Fasching, *Auschwitz and Hiroshima*, 303–4.

133. Fasching, *Auschwitz and Hiroshima*, 303.

134. Barkun, *Disaster and the Millennium*, 59.

135. Quoted in Douglas Robinson, "Literature and Apocalyptic," in Stein, *Apocalypticism*, 363.

136. Thompson, *End of Time*, 129.

137. Saïd Amir Arjomand, "Islamic Apocalypticism in the Classic Period," in *Apocalypticism*, 239, quoting Q. 22:7, Q. 40:59 (61), and Q. 82:5.

138. Quoted in Gorenberg, *End of Days*, vi.

139. Quoted at Wikipedia (http://en.wikipedia.org/wiki/).

140. Eric Hoffer, *True Believer* (1951), quoted in Cottle, "Prayer Center," 24.

141. Barkun, *Disaster and the Millennium*, 15.

142. Paul D. Hanson, "Introductory Overview," in "Apocalypses and Apocalypticism," in Freedman, *Anchor Bible Dictionary*, 1:282 ("… hearten the faithful …"); Rowley, *Relevance of Apocalyptic*, 47 ("… those engulfed by suffering …").

143. Yarbro Collins, *Crisis and Catharsis*, 94.

144. Quoted in Weber, *Living in the Shadow*, 228.

145. Thompson, *End of Time*, xiv.

146. Quoted in Thompson, *End of Time*, 339.

147. Gorenberg, *End of Days*, 211.

148. Mark 14:17 (KJV).

149. K. C. Cole, personal communication with the author.

150. Rev. 1:8 (KJV).

151. Deut. 29:29 (JPS).

152. Deut. 30:19 (JPS).

153. Mic. 6:8 (TNK) ("… do justice …"); Isa. 58 (TNK) ("… share your bread …").

Glossary

Amillennialism. See *Millennialism.*

Antimillennialism. See *Millennialism.*

Apocalypse. Derived from the Greek word that literally means "unveiling" (*apo-kalypsis*), an apocalypse is the disclosure of something that has been concealed. "Revelation" is derived from the Latin word (*revelatio*) for the same concept, and both words have been used as the title of the last book of the New Testament. As used by biblical and literary scholars, an apocalypse is a text in which the author purports to reveal divine secrets. Among the features that are commonly found in the genre are a human author who writes under the name of a biblical character and a heavenly figure who conducts the human author on a "guided tour" of heaven or earth.

Apocalyptic eschatology. "Eschatology," strictly speaking, is the study of "last things"—that is, the end of the world and what comes afterward. "Apocalyptic eschatology" refers to the study of what God has supposedly revealed to human beings about "last things," generally including predictions of a final and successful battle of the forces of good against the forces of evil, the resurrection of the dead, a final judgment with rewards for the good and punishments for the evil, and the advent of a new and eternal realm of divine perfection. Jewish apocalyptic eschatology focuses on the coming of an earthly redeemer and savior (see *Messiah*) whose name and nature are the subject of speculation. According to Christian theology, Jesus of Nazareth is identified as the Messiah, and so Christian apocalyptic eschatology focuses on the return (or "Second Coming") of Jesus. (see *Parousia.*)

Apocalypticism. A belief in the notion that God has disclosed various divine secrets to human beings through visions or other forms of revelation, including "the mysteries of heaven and earth" and, generally but not invariably, the time and circumstances of the end of the world. (See *Apocalyptic eschatology.*) Some scholars regard apocalypticism purely as a theological matter, but others insist that it also applies to social and political movements and phenomena. Apocalypticism is often (but not always) alloyed with a belief in the establishment of a golden age on earth. (See *Millennialism.*)

Armageddon. The place-name used in the book of Revelation to identify the site of the final battle between the armies of God and the armies of Satan at the end of the world. The name is apparently derived from the Hebrew phrase *Har Megiddo* ("Hill of Megiddo"), a site in northern Israel that controls the approach to a strategic pass and thus figured in several historical battles, some of which are mentioned in the Hebrew Bible (e.g., 2 Kings 23:29).

Bible. The Bible as it is known and used in Jewish tradition is called the *Tanakh,* a Hebrew acronym for the Five Books of Moses (*Torah*), the Prophets (*Nevi'im*), and the various other biblical writings (*Ketuvim*). *Torah,* a Hebrew word that carries the meaning of both "law" and "teaching," refers to the first five books of the Bible, also known as the "Five Books of Moses" because they were traditionally ascribed to Moses, or the "Pentateuch" (a Greek word that means "five scrolls"). The Hebrew Bible is known in Christian usage as the "Old Testament," and the "New Testament" is the term used to describe the four Gospels, the letters (or "epistles") of Paul and other Christian authors, and the historical narrative titled the Acts of the Apostles. "The Bible," as the term is used in Christian circles, includes both the Old Testament and the New Testament.

Chiliasm. See *Millennialism.*

Dispensational premillennialism. See *Dispensationalism.*

Dispensationalism. A doctrine in Christian apocalyptic tradition that divides the history of humankind into ages (or "dispensations"), each one characterized by a distinctive theme and set of events, and all of which are believed to be stages in the divine plan for the end of the world. One variety of dispensationalism, variously known as "dispensational premillennialism" or "premillennial dispensationalism," holds that we are now living in the so-called Church Age, which began with the rejection of Jesus of Nazareth by the Jewish people in antiquity and will end only when Jesus returns to earth and establishes a millennial kingdom. (See also *Millennialism.*) Among the articles of faith in dispensational premillennialism is the doctrine of the Rapture—that is, the belief that faithful Christians will be spared the sufferings of the Tribulation by sudden removal to heaven before the end-times. (See also *Rapture* and *Tribulation.*) Dispensational premillennialism also assigns an important role to the Jewish people, whose return to sovereignty in Israel is seen as an event that must take place before the second coming of Jesus Christ and the end of the world.

Eschatology. See *Apocalyptic eschatology.*

Futurism. See *Preterism.*

Historicism. See *Preterism.*

Messiah. "Messiah" is an English word derived from the Hebrew word *moshiach,* which means "the anointed one"—that is, someone who has been anointed with oil. As used in the Hebrew Bible, *moshiach* usually refers to a priest, a king, or some other human being who is designated by God for a special and important task. By late biblical antiquity, however, the Messiah came to be seen in Jewish tradition as a savior who would be sent by God to relieve the suffering of the Jewish people and reign over an earthly realm of peace and security. In Jewish tradition, the Messiah is understood to be human rather than divine, although it is believed that he will be sent by God and endowed with remarkable power and authority. Christianity sees Jesus of Nazareth as the long-promised Messiah but also introduces the concept that the Messiah is divine—that is, the Son of God. "Messianism" is a term used to describe the belief in the coming of a savior or redeemer, whether human (as in Judaism) or divine (as in Christianity).

Messianism. See *Messiah.*

Millennialism. "Millennialism," a term derived from the Latin word for "thousand," is the belief in the coming of a future golden age on earth under a redeemer sent by God, a concept that is rooted in Jewish messianic tradition but finds its fullest expression in the book of Revelation with the prediction that Jesus Christ will reign over a divine kingdom on earth for one thousand years after his second coming. (See *Parousia.*) Used more loosely, the same term is sometimes used to identify the belief in a future age of peace and prosperity on earth without specific reference to the Christian tradition of the thousand-year reign of Jesus Christ. "Millennialism," "millenarianism," and "chiliasm," which is derived from the Greek word for "thousand," are all roughly equivalent in meaning and are sometimes used interchangeably. However, "millenarianism" is often reserved for the beliefs and practices of the most radical and violence-prone millennial movements.

Variants of the term are used in scholarly and religious writings to describe a variety of specific beliefs about the timing and nature of the millennial kingdom. "Premillennialism" is the belief that Jesus Christ will return *before* the millennial kingdom is established. "Postmillennialism" is the belief that Jesus Christ will return only after the millennial era—that is, after the world (or, according to some varieties of postmillennialism, the church) has been purged of evil. "Amillennialism" or "antimillenialism" is the belief that the thousand-year reign of Christ as described in Revelation should be understood purely as an allegory for the spiritual perfection of the human soul or human institutions and not as a prediction that Jesus Christ will actually return to earth for a thousand years prior to the end of the world and the final Day of Judgment.

Premillennialism can be subdivided into several categories. "Pretribulationists" believe that faithful Christians will be removed to heaven (or "raptured") before the Tribulation. "Midtribulationists" believe that the Rapture will take place after Antichrist has come to power but before the final Day of Judgment. "Posttribbulationists" believe that even faithful Christians must endure the Tribulation before they are removed to heaven at the end of the world. (See *Rapture* and *Tribulation*.)

Parousia. Derived from the Greek word for "presence," the term refers to the return (or "Second Coming") of Jesus Christ to earth. According to Revelation, Jesus Christ will return to earth at some point in the future to reign over a kingdom of saints for a thousand years before the end of the world, the final judgment, and the creation of a "new heaven and a new earth" that will endure forever.

Postmillennialism. See *Millennialism*.

Premillennialism. See *Dispensationalism* and *Millennialism*.

Presentism. See *Preterism*.

Preterism. The belief that the prophecies in the book of Revelation have already been fulfilled. A "preterist" (or "historicist") interpretation of Revelation focuses on what its imagery and symbolism meant to its original author and his readers and hearers. By contrast with a "preterist" (or "historicist") reading of Revelation, a "futurist" reading focuses on the meaning of the text as a prophecy of events that will take place in the future, and a "presentist" reading holds that the prophecies are being fulfilled now.

Pseudepigrapha. A term used by modern scholars to describe various ancient writings on biblical themes, many of them Jewish in origin and others apparently composed or revised by Christians, all of which were excluded from the Bible in both Jewish and Christian tradition. "Pseudepigrapha" means "false writing" in Greek, and the term refers to the fact that the texts are generally ascribed to biblical figures rather than their actual authors. Among the Pseudepigrapha are early Jewish apocalyptic writings, including the various writings that make up the book of Enoch, and apocalypses attributed to Adam, Abraham, Elijah, and Daniel.

Rapture. The belief that faithful Christians who are worthy of salvation will be suddenly and miraculously removed from earth and lifted to heaven by God at some point during the end-times. The doctrine, which is based on the text of 1 Thess. 4:15–17 rather than the book of Revelation, achieved popularity in certain Protestant circles in the nineteenth century and still figures prominently in the apocalyptic doctrine known as "dispensationalism"—that is, the belief that faithful Christians will be "raptured" to heaven before the time of suffering known as the Tribulation. (See also *Dispensationalism, Millennialism,* and *Tribulation.*)

Revelation. See *Apocalypse.*

Second Coming. See *Parousia.*

Tribulation. A period of oppression and persecution under the sovereignty of the Antichrist, described in Revelation and other apocalyptic passages of the New Testament, that will supposedly precede the second coming of Jesus Christ, the Battle of Armageddon, and the establishment of the millennial kingdom on earth. (See also *Millennialism.*)

Bibliography

Akenson, Donald Harman. *Surpassing Wonder: The Invention of the Bible and the Talmuds.* Chicago: Univ. of Chicago Press, 2001.

Alter, Robert, and Frank Kermode, eds. *The Literary Guide to the Bible.* Cambridge, MA: Belknap Press of Harvard Univ. Press, 1987.

Armstrong, Karen. *Jerusalem: One City, Three Faiths.* New York: Alfred A. Knopf, 1996.

Augustine. *The City of God.* Trans. Marcus Dods, with an introduction by Thomas Merton. New York: Modern Library, 2000.

Baker, Peter, and Peter Slevin. "Bush Remarks on 'Intelligent Design' Theory Fuel Debate." *Washington Post,* August 3, 2005, A01. http://www.washingtonpost.com/.

Barclay, William. *Letters to the Seven Churches.* New York and Nashville: Abingdon Press, 1957.

Barkun, Michael. *A Culture of Conspiracy: Apocalyptic Visions in Contemporary America.* Berkeley: Univ. of California Press, 2003.

———. *Disaster and the Millennium.* Syracuse, NY: Syracuse Univ. Press, 1974.

Barnwell, F. Aster. *Meditations on the Apocalypse: A Psychospiritual Perspective on the Book of Revelation.* Rockport, MA: Element, 1992.

Berrigan, Daniel. *The Nightmare of God.* Portland, OR: Sunburst Press, 1983.

BibleWorks 5: Software for Biblical Exegesis and Research. Norfolk, VA: Hermeneutika Bible Research, 2001.

Bloom, Harold, and David Rosenberg. *The Book of J.* New York: Grove Weidenfeld, 1990.

Blunt, Sheryl Henderson. "Bush Calls for 'Culture Change.'" *Christianity Today,* August 28, 2004. http://www.christianitytoday.com/.

Boyer, Paul. *When Time Shall Be No More: Prophecy Belief in Modern American Culture.* Cambridge, MA: Belknap Press of Harvard Univ. Press, 1992.

Chafets, Zev. "The Rabbi Who Loved Evangelicals (and Vice Versa)." *New York Times,* July 24, 2005. New York Times Premium Archive.

Cohn, Norman. *The Pursuit of the Millennium: Revolutionary Millenarians and Mystical Anarchists of the Middle Ages.* London: Paladin (Granada Publishing Limited), 1970.

Cohn-Sherbok, Dan, and Lavinia Cohn-Sherbok. *Jewish and Christian Mysticism: An Introduction.* New York: Continuum, 1994.

Collins, John J. "Introduction: Towards the Morphology of a Genre." *Semeia* 14 (1979), 1–20.

———. "The Jewish Apocalypses." *Semeia* 14 (1979), 21–59.

———, ed. The Origins of Apocalypticism in Judaism and Christianity. Vol. 1 of *The Encyclopedia of Apocalypticism.* New York: Continuum, 2000.

Colwell, Ernest Cadman. *The Study of the Bible.* Rev. ed. Chicago: Univ. of Chicago Press, 1964. First published 1937.

Cornell University Library. *Making of America.* http://cdl.library.cornell.edu/moa/.

Cottle, Michelle. "Prayer Center." *New Republic,* May 23, 2005, 21–25.

de la Bedoyere, Michael. *The Meddlesome Friar and the Wayward Pope: The Story of the Conflict Between Savonarola and Alexander VI.* Garden City, NY: Hanover House, 1958.

Dick, Philip K., and Roger Zelazny. *Deus Irae.* New York: Dell Publishing Co., 1976.

Domb, I. *The Transformation: The Case of the Neturei Karta.* Brooklyn and Jerusalem: Hachomo, 1989.

Dowd, Maureen. "Rapture and Rupture." *New York Times,* October 6, 2002. New York Times Premium Archive.

Dr. Strangelove, or How I Learned to Stop Worrying and Love the Bomb. Directed by Stanley Kubrick. Screenplay by Stanley Kubrick, Terry Southern, and Peter

George. Based on the novel *Red Alert* (a.k.a. *Two Hours to Doom*), by Peter George. Columbia Pictures Corporation, 1964.

Drane, John, ed. *Revelation: The Apocalypse of St. John.* New York: St. Martin's Griffin, 1977.

Dubnow, Simon. *History of the Jews in Russia and Poland: From the Earliest Times Until the Present Day.* Trans. I. Friedlaender. 3 vols. Philadelphia: Jewish Publication Society, 1916.

————. *A Short History of the Jewish People.* Trans. D. Mowshowitch. London: M. L. Cailingold, 1936.

Ehrman, Bart D. *Jesus: Apocalyptic Prophet of the New Millennium.* New York: Oxford Univ. Press, 1999.

Ellul, Jacques. *Apocalypse: The Book of Revelation.* Trans. George W. Schreiner. New York: Seabury Press, 1977.

Emmerson, Richard K., and Bernard McGinn, eds. *The Apocalypse in the Middle Ages.* Ithaca, NY: Cornell Univ. Press, 1992.

Encyclopaedia Britannica Premium Service. http://www.britannica.com/.

Encyclopedia Judaica. Corrected ed. 17 vols. Jerusalem: Keter, n.d.

Fallon, Francis T. "The Gnostic Apocalypses." *Semeia* 14 (1979), 123–58.

Farrer, Austin. *A Rebirth of Images: The Making of St. John's Apocalypse.* Westminster, England: Dacre Press, 1949.

————. *The Revelation of St. John the Divine: Commentary on the English Text.* Oxford: Clarendon Press, 1964.

Fasching, Darrell J. *The Ethical Challenge of Auschwitz and Hiroshima: Apocalypse or Utopia?* Albany: State Univ. of New York Press, 1993.

Festinger, Leon, Henry W. Riecken, and Stanley Schachter. *When Prophecy Fails: A Social and Psychological Study of a Modern Group That Predicted the Destruction of the World.* New York: Harper & Row, 1964. First published 1956.

Ford, J. Massyngberde, trans. *Revelation.* Introduction and commentary by J. Massyngberde Ford. Vol. 38 of *The Anchor Bible.* Garden City, NY: Doubleday & Company, 1975.

Fox, Richard Wrightman. *Jesus in America: Personal Savior, Cultural Hero, National Obsession.* San Francisco: HarperSanFrancisco, 2004.

Freedman, David Noel, ed. *The Anchor Bible Dictionary.* 6 vols. Garden City, NY: Doubleday, 1992.

Friedman, Richard Elliott. *The Hidden Book in the Bible.* San Francisco: Harper-SanFrancisco, 1998.

———. *Who Wrote the Bible?* Englewood Cliffs, NJ: Prentice Hall, 1987.

Frye, Northrop. *The Great Code: The Bible and Literature.* New York: Harcourt Brace Jovanovich, 1982.

Fukuyama, Francis. *The End of History and the Last Man.* New York: Avon Books, 1992.

Fussell, Paul. *The Great War and Modern Memory.* New York: Oxford Univ. Press, 1975.

Gibbon, Edward. *The Decline and Fall of the Roman Empire.* 3 vols. 1776. Reprint, New York: Heritage, 1946.

Goldberg, Michelle. "Antichrist Politics." *Salon,* May 24, 2002. http://www.israel-blog.org/Articles/Antichrist_Politics_Salon_com.html.

———. "Fundamentally Unsound." *Salon,* July 29, 2002. http://www.salon.com/books/feature/2002/07/29/left_behind/index.html.

Gorenberg, Gershom. *The End of Days: Fundamentalism and the Struggle for the Temple Mount.* New York: Oxford Univ. Press, 2002.

———. "Intolerance: The Bestseller." *American Prospect,* Sept. 23, 2002. Archived at http://www.prospect.org/print/V13/17/gorenberg-g.html.

Graetz, Heinrich. *Popular History of the Jews.* Trans. A. B. Rhine. 6 vols. New York: Hebrew Publishing Company, 1930. First published 1919.

Graham, Billy. *Approaching Hoofbeats: The Four Horsemen of the Apocalypse.* Minneapolis: Grason, 1983.

———. *Storm Warning.* Dallas: Word Publishing, 1992.

Graves, Robert. *The White Goddess: A Historical Grammar of Poetic Myth.* Amended and enlarged ed. New York: Farrar, Straus and Giroux, 1966.

Greenslade, S. L. *Schism in the Early Church.* New York: Harper & Brothers, n.d.

Gruen, Erich S. *Heritage and Hellenism: The Reinvention of Jewish Tradition.* Berkeley: Univ. of California Press, 1998.

Halsell, Grace. *Prophecy and Politics: Militant Evangelists on the Road to Nuclear War.* Westport, CT: Lawrence Hill & Company, 1986.

Harrison, G. B., ed. *Shakespeare: The Complete Works.* New York: Harcourt, Brace & World, 1952.

Hijiya, James A. "The *Gita* of Robert Oppenheimer." Proceedings of the American Philosophical Society. 144: 2 (June 2000).

Huffey, Rhoda. *The Hallelujah Side.* Harrison, NY, and Encino, CA: Delphinium Books, 1999.

The Jefferson Bible. http://www.angelfire.com/co/JeffersonBible/jeffintro.html.

Klagsbrun, Francine. *Voices of Wisdom.* Middle Village, NY: Jonathan David Publishers, 1980.

Ladd, George Eldon. *A Commentary on the Revelation of John.* Grand Rapids, MI: William B. Eerdmans, 1972.

LaHaye, Tim. *The Beginning of the End.* Wheaton, IL: Tyndale House Publishers, 1972.

LaHaye, Tim, and Jerry B. Jenkins. *Left Behind.* Wheaton, IL: Tyndale House Publishers, 1995.

Lampman, Jane. "Apocalyptic—and Atop the Bestseller Lists." *Christian Science Monitor,* August 29, 2002. Archived at http://www.csmonitor.com/2002/0829/p14s01-lire.html.

Lawrence, D. H. *Apocalypse.* Middlesex, England: Penguin Books, 1974. First published 1931.

Lazarus, Emma. "The New Colossus." Archived at http://www.sonnets.org/lazarus.

Lebreton, Jules, and Jacques Zeiller. *Heresy and Orthodoxy.* Book 3 of *A History of the Early Church.* New York: Collier Books, 1962. First published 1947.

"A Library of Quotations on Religion and Politics by George Bush." http://www.beliefnet.com/.

Lilla, Mark. "Extremism's Theological Roots." *New York Times,* October 7, 2001. New York Times Premium Archive.

Lindsey, Hal. *Apocalypse Code.* Palos Verdes, CA: Western Front Ltd., 1997.

Lindsey, Hal, with C. C. Carlson. *The Late Great Planet Earth.* Grand Rapids, MI: Zondervan Publishing House, 1970.

Lopez, Steve. "Fixing an Unholy Mess." *Los Angeles Times,* October 24, 2004, B-1.

Malone, Mary T. *Women and Christianity.* Vol. 1, *The First Thousand Years.* Dublin: The Columbia Press, 2000. Vol. 2, *From 1000 to the Reformation.* Maryknoll, NY: Orbis Books, 2002.

McGinn, Bernard, ed. *Apocalypticism in Western History and Culture.* Vol. 2 of *The Encyclopedia of Apocalypticism.* New York: Continuum, 1998.

———. *Visions of the End: Apocalyptic Traditions in the Middle Ages.* New York: Columbia University Press, 1998.

Miles, Jack. *Christ: A Crisis in the Life of God.* New York: Alfred A. Knopf, 2001.

Neusner, Jacob. *A Life of Yohanan Ben Zakkai, ca. 1–80 C.E.* Leiden: E. J. Brill, 1962.

Neusner, Jacob, and Bruce D. Chilton. *Revelation: The Torah and the Bible.* Valley Forge, PA: Trinity Press International, 1995.

Nims, John Frederick, ed. *The Harper Anthology of Poetry.* New York: Harper & Row, 1981.

O'Leary, Stephen D. *Arguing the Apocalypse: A Theory of Millennial Rhetoric.* New York: Oxford Univ. Press, 1994.

The Omega Man. Directed by Boris Sagal. Screenplay by John Williams and Joyce H. Corrington. Based on the novel *I Am Legion,* by Richard Matheson. Warner Bros., 1971.

The Omen. Directed by Richard Donner. Screenplay by David Seltzer. 20th Century Fox, 1976.

On the Beach. Directed by Stanley Kramer. Screenplay by John Paxton. Based on the novel by Nevil Shute. United Artists, 1959.

Peterson, Merrill D., ed. *Thomas Jefferson: A Reference Biography.* New York: Charles Scribner's Sons, 1986.

"President Discusses Schiavo, WMD Commission Report," March 31, 2005. http://www.whitehouse.gov.

Random House Webster's Unabridged Dictionary. CD-ROM, version 2.2. Random House, 1999.

The Rapture. Directed by Michael Tolkin. Screenplay by Michael Tolkin. New Line Cinema, 1991.

Revelation: Its Grand Climax at Hand! Brooklyn: Watchtower Bible and Tract Society of New York, 1988.

Robertson, Pat. *The New World Order.* Dallas: Word Publishing, 1991.

Rowley, H. H. *The Relevance of Apocalyptic: A Study of Jewish and Christian Apocalypses from Daniel to the Revelation.* New York: Harper & Brothers, n.d.

Schaff, Philip, and Henry Wace, eds. *Eusebius. A Select Library of Nicene and Post-Nicene Fathers of the Christian Church,* 2nd ser., vol. 1. 1890. Reprint, Grand Rapids, MI: William B. Eerdmans, 1997.

Scholem, Gershom. *The Messianic Idea in Judaism and Other Essays on Jewish Spirituality.* New York: Schocken Books, 1995. First published 1971.

Schüssler Fiorenza, Elisabeth. *The Apocalypse.* Chicago: Francisco Herald Press, 1976.

———. *The Book of Revelation: Justice and Judgment.* Philadelphia: Fortress Press, 1985.

Scofield, C. I., ed. *The Scofield Reference Bible.* New York: Oxford Univ. Press, 1945. First Published 1909.

The Seventh Seal. Directed by Ingmar Bergman. Screenplay by Ingmar Bergman. Commentary by Peter Cowie. Criterion Collection, 1987. Original release: Svensk Filmindustri, 1957.

Shaw, Eve. *Eve of Destruction: Prophecies, Theories, and Preparations for the End of the World.* Los Angeles: Lowell House, 1996.

Shirer, William L. *The Rise and Fall of the Third Reich.* New York: Simon & Schuster, 1960.

Smith, John Holland. *Constantine the Great.* New York: Charles Scribner's Sons, 1971.

Sontag, Susan. *Against Interpretation.* New York: Dell Publishing Co., 1966.

Stark, Freya. *Alexander's Path.* Woodstock, NY: Overlook Press, 1988. First published 1958.

Stein, Stephen J., ed. *Apocalypticism in the Modern Period and the Contemporary Age.* Vol. 3 of *The Encyclopedia of Apocalypticism.* New York: Continuum, 2000.

Steiner, Rudolf. *The Apocalypse of St. John: Lectures on the Book of Revelation.* Hudson, NY: Anthroposophic Press, 1993. First published 1945 in German.

Suskind, Ron. "Without a Doubt." *New York Times,* October 17, 2004. New York Times Premium Archive.

Thompson, Damian. *The End of Time: Faith and Fear in the Shadow of the Millennium.* Hanover, NH: Univ. Press of New England, 1996.

Van Paassen, Pierre. *The Crown of Fire: The Life and Times of Girolamo Savonarola.* New York: Charles Scribner's Sons, 1960.

Wagar, W. Warren. *Terminal Visions: The Literature of Last Things.* Bloomington: Indiana Univ. Press, 1982.

Wallstein, Peter. "Faith 'War' Rages in U.S., Judge Says." *Los Angeles Times,* April 26, 2005, A-10.

Watts, Alan. *The Nature of Consciousness.* Tapes 1 and 2 of *Out of Your Mind: Essential Listening from the Alan Watts Archive.* Boulder, CO: Sounds True, 2004.

Weber, Timothy P. *Living in the Shadow of the Second Coming: American Premillenarianism 1875–1982.* Chicago: Univ. of Chicago Press, 1987.

Wendell, Barrett. *Cotton Mather: The Puritan Priest.* New York: Harcourt, Brace & World, 1963. First published 1891.

Wills, Gary. "With God on His Side." *New York Times,* March 30, 2003. New York Times Premium Archive.

Woo, Elaine. "Betty Hill, 85; Claim of Abduction by Aliens Led to Fame." *Los Angeles Times,* October 24, 2004, B-18.

Yarbro Collins, Adela. *Crisis and Catharsis: The Power of the Apocalypse.* Philadelphia: Westminster Press, 1984.

———. "The Political Perspective of the Revelation to John." *Journal of Biblical Literature* 96/2 (1977), 241–56.

Index

Acknowledgments

As always, my first thought is for my wife and lifelong best friend, Ann Benjamin Kirsch, and my children, Jennifer Rachel Kirsch and Adam Benjamin Kirsch, whose love, encouragement and support were and are indispensable to the writing of this book and to every aspect of my life and work.

Along with my family, this book is dedicated to my brother and sister-in-law, Paul and Caroline Kirsch, my sister and brother-in-law, Marya and Ron Shiflett, and my aunt, Lillian Conrad Heller, cherished relations and, more than that, gracious and generous human beings.

I am deeply grateful to Gideon Weil, my editor at HarperSanFrancisco, and Laurie Fox, my agent and friend, who have brought their vision and wisdom to bear in the making of this book.

Among the many people at Harper San Francisco with whom I also worked, with both pleasure and admiration, were Michael Maudlin, Mark Tauber, Kris Ashley, Krista Holmstrom, Lisa Zuniga, Cynthia DiTiberio, Carl Walesa, and Joseph Rutt.

All of my work is supported and improved, literally every day of the week, by my colleague and dear friend, Judy Woo.

I owe a special debt of gratitude to Jack Miles, Karen Armstrong, and K.C. Cole, whose books have always been a source of illumination and inspiration, and whose friendships are among the greatest rewards of my life.

I am also grateful for the support of David Noel Freedman, Leonard Shlain, Don Akenson, and David Rosenberg, each of whom has offered encouragement at crucial moments and in an important ways.

I have been supported and encouraged by family, friends, and colleagues to whom I now express my heartfelt appreciation:

My beloved daughter-in-law, Remy Elizabeth Holzer, and her family, Harold, Edith and Meg Holzer.

My niece, Heather Kirsch, and my nephew and his wife, Joshua and Jennifer (Kibrick) Kirsch.

Eui Sook (Angie) Yoon, Charlie Alexiev, Jacob Gabay, and Inge-Lise DeWolfe.

Leslie A. Klinger, gifted author and attorney.

Candace Barrett Birk and Raye Birk, Maryann Rosenfeld and Shelly Kadish, Pat and Len Solomon, John Rechy and Michael Ewing, Diane Leslie and Fred Huffman.

Jane Fitch, Carolyn See, Bernadette Shih, Dora Levy Mossanen, Rhoda Huffey, and Dolores Sloan.

Linda Chester and her colleagues at the Linda Chester Agency.

Michele Goldman, who provided research assistance into Jewish apocalyptic texts and traditions.

David Ulin, Nick Owchar, Orli Low, Kristina Lindgren, Sara Lippincott, Susan Salter Reynolds and Ethel Alexander at the *Los Angeles Times Book Review*.

Doug Brown, Tom Crouch, Barbara Morrow, Maret Orliss, and Kristine Erbstoesser at the *Los Angeles Times*.

Jan Nathan and Terry Nathan at the Publishers Marketing Association.

Sarah Spitz and Ruth Seymour at KCRW-FM.

Larry Mantle, Patt Morrison, Aimee Machado, Jackie Oclaray, Linda Othenin-Girard and Polly Sveda at KPCC-FM.

Rob Eshman at *The Jewish Journal*.

Gwen Feldman and Jim Fox at Silman-James Press, and Tony Cohan at Acrobat Books.

Connie Martinson, host of *Connie Martinson Talks Books*.

Doug Dutton, Lise Friedman and Ed Conklin at Dutton's Books in Brentwood.

About the Author

JONATHAN KIRSCH is the author of eleven books, including the best-selling and critically acclaimed *The Harlot by the Side of the Road: Forbidden Tales of the Bible; King David: The Real Life of the Man Who Ruled Israel; Moses: A Life; The Woman Who Laughed at God: The Untold History of the Jewish People;* and *God Against the Gods: The History of the War Between Monotheism and Polytheism.* Kirsch is also a contributing writer for the *Los Angeles Times Book Review,* an attorney specializing in intellectual property and publishing law, and a guest host and commentator on the NPR affiliates KPCC-FM and KCRW-FM. A member of the National Book Critics Circle and a three-time past president of PEN Center USA West, Kirsch lives in Los Angeles, California.